The Advent of
STEAM

The Advent of
STEAM

The Merchant Steamship
before 1900

Editor: Robert Gardiner
Consultant Editor: Dr Basil Greenhill

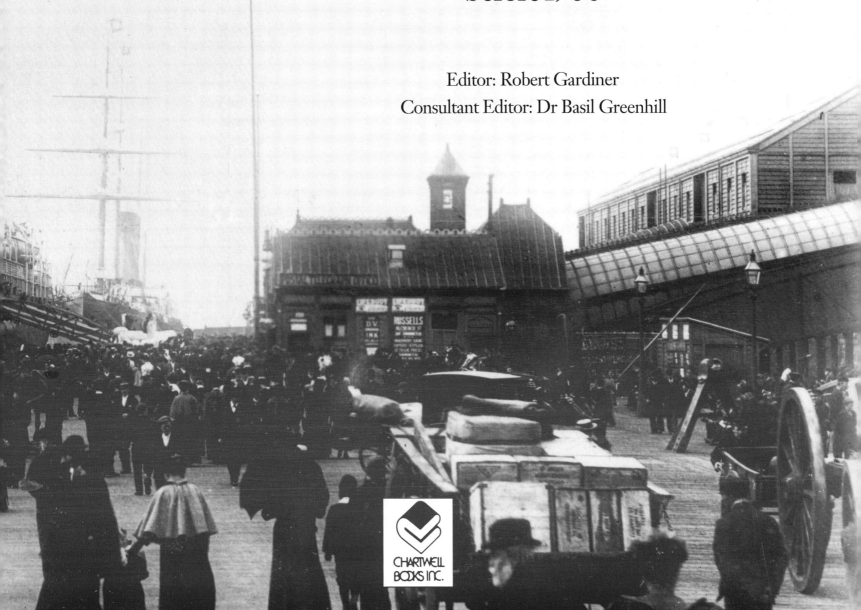

CHARTWELL BOOKS INC.

Series Consultant Dr Basil Greenhill
CB, CMG, FSA, FRHistS

Series Editor Robert Gardiner

Consultant Editor Dr Basil Greenhill

Contributors Peter Allington, Master Mariner
Rev E C B Corlett, OBE, MA, PhD, F.Eng, FRINA,
   FIMarE, FRIN, FNI
Dr Basil Greenhill
Denis Griffiths B.Eng, MSc, FIMarE, C.Eng
Adrian Jarvis
Dr Andrew Lambert MA, PhD
Bradley Rogers MA
W F Roff
Dr David J Starkey MA, PhD
Professor William N Still, JR PhD
Gordon P Watts MA

Frontispiece: The advent of steam profoundly affected the public perception of sea travel. From being a hazardous, uncomfortable and lengthy affair, to be undertaken only from dire necessity, a sea journey became relatively safe, potentially luxurious, and predictable in duration, encouraging more and more people to travel. However, ports retained the old atmosphere of adventure and the drama of arrivals and departures attracted photographers throughout the late nineteenth century. This view of the White Star's Majestic *and* Germanic *at Liverpool at some time in the 1890s is a fine illustration of that theme.* (CMP)

© Conway Maritime Press 1993

This edition published in North America in 2000 by
CHARTWELL BOOKS INC.
A Division of Book Sales Inc.
114 Northfield Avenue
Edison, New Jersey 08837

ISBN 0-7858-1270-9

First published in Great Britain 1992 by
Conway Maritime Press,
a division of Chrysalis Books Ltd
9 Blenheim Court, Brewery Road
London N7 9NT

Designed by Tony Hart
Typeset by Swift Typesetting Ltd, Dagenham, Essex
Printed and bound in Spain by Bookprint, S.L, Barcelona

Contents

Preface

THIS is the fifth title in an ambitious programme of twelve volumes intended to provide the first detailed and comprehensive account of a technology that has shaped human history. It has been conceived as a basic reference work, the essential first stop for anyone seeking information on any aspect of the subject, so it is more concerned to be complete than to be original. However, the series takes full account of all the latest research and in certain areas will be publishing entirely new material. In the matter of interpretation care has been taken to avoid the old myths and to present only the most widely accepted modern viewpoints.

To tell a coherent story, in a more readable form than is usual with encyclopaedias, each volume takes the form of independent chapters, all by recognised authorities in the field. Most chapters are devoted to ships specifically, but others deal with topics that relate to many ship types, like the industrial background, thus avoiding repetition and giving added depth to the reader's understanding of developments. Some degree of generalisation is inevitable when tackling a subject of this breadth, but wherever possible the specific details of ships and their characteristics have been included (a table of typical ships for each relevant chapter includes a convenient summary of data from which the reader can chart the evolution of the ship type concerned). With a few historically unavoidable exceptions, the series is confined to seagoing vessels; to have included boats would have increased the scope of an already massive task.

The history of the ship is not a romanticised story of epic battles and heroic voyages, but equally it is not simply a matter of technological advances. Ships were built to carry out particular tasks and their design was as much influenced by the experience of that employment – the lessons or war, or the conditions of trade, for example – as by purely technical innovation. Throughout this series an attempt has been made to keep this clearly in view, to describe the *what* and *when* of developments without losing sight of the *why*.

The series is aimed at those with some knowledge of, and interest in, ships and the sea. It would have been impossible to make a contribution of any value to the subject if it had been pitched at the level of the complete novice, so while there is an extensive glossary, for example, it assumes an understanding of the most basic nautical terms. Similarly, the bibliography avoids very general works and concentrates on those which will broaden or deepen the reader's understanding beyond the level of the *History of the Ship*. The intention is not to inform genuine experts in their particular area of expertise, but to provide them with the best available single-volume summaries of less familiar fields.

Each volume is chronological in approach, with the periods covered getting shorter as the march of technology quickens, but organised around a dominant theme – represented by the title – that sums up the period in question. In this way each book is fully self-sufficient, although when completed the twelve titles will link up to form a coherent history, chronicling the progress of ship design from its earliest recorded forms to the present day.

This volume is dedicated to explaining the introduction of steam into the merchant fleets of the world, a technical revolution which is only equalled in the history of maritime endeavour by the advent of the three-masted full rigged ship. It is a complex story that for a full understanding requires knowledge of parallel developments not only in the world's navies but also in the fleets of sailing vessels that for so much of the nineteenth century continued to operate quite successfully alongside the new technology. As a result the reader will find numerous references in the following pages to both *Steam, Steel and Shellfire* and *Sail's Last Century*, the companion titles in this series. All volumes are generally similar in their approach and organisation, but these three were designed as a particular unit and accordingly depend more on one another than the rest of the series.

The coming of steam was a complex and long drawn out affair, and we have chosen to approach the subject from the point of view of the increasing economy of this form of propulsion, which tends to emphasise machinery development. There were many other factors, political, economic and social, that exerted their influence, but in the final analysis merchant ships existed to provide a return on capital, and in this regard the economy of the new technology was paramount. Without the progressive advances of the iron hull, the screw propeller, and multi-expansion engines, steam navigation (as represented by the first wooden paddlers) would have been confined to a tiny proportion of maritime activity.

Much of the pioneering work was carried out on the rivers and inland waterways of the USA and Britain, so we have felt obliged to ignore the general series restriction on dealing with boats. Many early steamers were clearly not ships in the accepted sense, but to omit them would have been to miss important aspects of the story.

Robert Gardiner
Series Editor

Introduction

THIS is the first of two volumes dealing with the history of the merchant ship in the nineteenth and early twentieth centuries. As will become clearer from the second of these two volumes, that dealing with the history of the merchant sailing vessel of this period (*Sail's Last Century*), the division of steam and sail into two separate volumes is artificial, but probably inescapable. In recording the history of the ship we are dealing with one aspect of the history of a great industry which involved many activities, all interlocked and all affecting each other. Finance, management, shipbuilding, brokerage, the freight markets, insurance, shipowning, iron- and steel-making, steam engine technology, politics, government legislation and regulation, developments in the law, develop-

ments in communications, naval requirements, general industrial development ashore including transport and harbour and dock development and developments in cargo handling, human migrations such as that by which North America was populated, wars, like the First China War, all influenced separately and together the development of the merchant ship, steam or sail, as many of them did the development of naval vessels in the nineteenth century.

The sailing vessel and the steamship have too often been presented in popular history as rivals in an organic sense, as if there was some kind of continuous warfare between eternally separate factions of the shipowning world. One of these factions is treated as wedded to power, reality and development, and the other irrationally to

an eternal affair with doomed and beautiful sailing vessels which had some kind of abstract, undefined, moral worth which powered vessels lacked. This is very far from the truth.

The reality, as these two volume show, was, of

The relationship between sail and steam in the nineteenth century was a complex one, and not the straightforward battle between old and new so often presented in earlier histories. As this volume reveals, the wooden paddle-propelled steamer had only very limited applications and rapid progress had to await iron hulls and the screw propeller. However, the early use of paddlers in the role of tug was one of the most widely recognised advantages of steam, as demonstrated in this lithograph of Dutch merchant vessels being towed to sea from Portsmouth in 1833 (they had been embargoed following a political dispute with the Netherlands). (The Parker Gallery)

The growth of steam shipping was heavily influenced by the costs of coal provision at bunkering stations far from the sources of supply. Initially, it restricted the spread of services but also encouraged the search for more economical machinery. As an example, in the late nineteenth century P&O kept stocks of around 90,000 tons at any one time, and whereas it was only necessary to stockpile 2000 tons at Southampton, holdings at overseas bunkering stations were as follows: Malta 5000 tons; Alexandria and Suez 6000 tons; Aden 20,900 tons; Bombay 8000 tons; Point de Galle (Ceylon) 12,000 tons; Singapore 8000 tons; Hong Kong 10,000 tons; plus smaller stations. This was moved by the cheapest means possible – sailing ships, 170 of which were employed in any one year to get the coal to its locations. Coaling ship was also messy, time-consuming and labour-intensive, as this view of the Orphir *at Port Said in 1891 graphically demonstrates. (Leicester Collection)*

course, quite different and very much more complex. We are dealing with the ship as part of the merchant shipping industry as a whole. A merchant ship, it cannot be over emphasised, is built for one purpose only: to make money, to produce, like any other piece of machinery, a reasonable return on capital invested. Very broadly speaking capital did not confine its movement to one class of tonnage, but moved to where the best returns could be gained at any given time. As the complex history of the ship developed in the nineteenth century, so, subject to various qualifications of the type which applied in most industries, such as local knowledge and loyalties, access to special trades and markets, the understanding of technical developments, the existence or otherwise of specialised managerial techniques necessary to operate steam vessels profitably etc, market forces determined whether steam or sail tonnage should be employed in different sectors of the world's carrying trade. The merchant ship, however driven, must be considered as part of sea transport as a whole.

In fact, as these two volumes make very clear, the nineteenth century 'battle' between sail and steam which has been presented by so many pseudo historians simply did not exist. Quite apart from the reasons already given, there had

to be two great technical achievements before the steamship could represent a practical and commercially viable alternative investment to sail tonnage for use in the great bulk of the general overseas carrying trade. These were the development of a propelling mechanism without the crippling disadvantages of the side paddle – these are explained in detail in Chapter 1 of this volume – and the development of compact, fuel-efficient, marine steam engines.

Both these developments depended on a complex pattern of industrial innovations ashore. The technical and industrial problems of the introduction of screw propulsion, the close interplay between merchant shipping and navy over this vital leap forward in the history of the ship, are dealt with in this volume in chapters by Dr Ewan Corlett and Dr Andrew Lambert in a degree of detail and with a cohesion never before attempted. The successful use of screw propulsion depended on a complex of other developments mainly in the engineering field. Among the most important of these was the adoption of iron construction – for the problem of the application of the screw to the flexible hull of a wooden vessel built to merchant ship standards was too great to be commercially practical.

This in turn depended on the availability of iron plate of tolerable quality at reasonable cost

and the introduction of a technical system to enable the use of the magnetic compass in an iron environment. These things came together in the late 1830s and the immediate result was that Brunel, and his financial backers in Bristol and elsewhere, were able to turn the development of the steamship in a new direction with the great iron screw vessel *The Great Britain*, now partially restored and preserved in her building dock at Bristol.

In a closely linked series of parallel developments, described by Andrew Lambert in detail in the companion volume to this on the nineteenth-century navy (*Steam Steel and Shellfire*), the Admiralty moved rapidly towards the construction of a steam screw battlefleet. This fleet was ready to play the decisive role in the war with Russia, the mis-named Crimean War, of 1854–56. The initiation of screw propulsion in both the merchant shipping industry and the navy was, as the relevant chapters in this volume show, the result of entrepreneurial enterprise by financiers who had both political clout and the social standing which ensured they could operate the machinery of patronage – still all-pervading at this period.

The Great Britain introduced to the world the modern ship and showed the way all ships would go with her metal construction and screw propulsion, and she was big enough to begin to take advantage of the economies of scale. There is a close parallel with aviation, almost exactly a century later, when the Douglas DC-3, the Dakota, in all its variations, with its all-metal construction, its retractable undercarriage, its flaps and slots, showed the way all big passenger aircraft were to go. But *The Great Britain* and the Dakota had also in common that they lacked efficient engines. Until a fuel-efficient power system was available the screw steamship, like her paddling predecessor, though aided by her very sophisticated sail-assist, was confined to a very limited number of services with passengers and low-bulk high-value cargoes and she had a normal steaming time of about three weeks at the most.

Thus the wooden sailing ship had no real competition in the general carrying trade. Sailing ship tonnage statutorily registered under the British Merchant Shipping Acts in 1850 totalled around 3,400,000 tons, steamer tonnage 170,000 tons. A decade later, in 1860, sailing tonnage, despite the advent of the screw steamer, had increased by 34 per cent to 4,200,000 tons, but steam tonnage, though it had increased some 2½ times, still totalled only 450,000 tons (see Table 1). Steamers were still confined to packet routes, towing duties, short sea bulk carriers and subsidised deep sea routes. For reasons explained in the chapter on the use of sails by steamers in this volume, these vessels were for the most part fully powered steamships with what is now called sail-assist. For a number of reasons, technical and economic, which are also explained in that chapter, the steam auxiliary deep sea square rigged merchant vessel never developed in any number. She was less of a dead end than a non-starter.

The 1850s were a period of unprecedented industrial development when Britain was moving towards the summit of economic power. The boom of 1854–55, triggered off by the Crimean War, affected shipping particularly and, with its postwar bankruptcies and disasters, was succeeded by two decades of expansion, consequent upon the extension of currency and credit based on the Californian and Australian gold discoveries, the repeal of the Navigation Acts which gave to British seafarers the stimulus of much stronger foreign competition, the passing of the Companies Act of 1861 which encouraged greater risk-taking, and the general development of banking, the spread of settlement in North America and the steadily developing industrialisation of the northeast of the United States, and the development of railways on both sides of the Atlantic.

By 1865 it was clearly demonstrated that the steamship had at last developed to a point at which she was a commercially viable alternative to the sailing vessel in the world's ocean carrying trades. From this year onwards the demise of the sailing vessel could be predicted by far-sighted businessmen, though it was still some thirty years away. Chapters by Denis Griffiths and David Starkey in this volume explain how this happened.

For years it had been known that more power could theoretically be developed in a marine steam engine for the same consumption of fuel if the steam could be expanded a second time in a second, bigger, cylinder after it had passed through a first small high-pressure cylinder. Experiments on these lines in France and America in the early nineteenth century had always ended in failure, principally because of the difficulty of generating steam at sufficient pressures to enable such a system to be worked. But in 1856 the Pacific Steam Navigation Company successfully operated two vessels with compound engines. The technology of this change is explained by Denis Griffiths while Adrian Jarvis' chapter summarises the events leading to the most dramatic demonstration of the success of compounding. Alfred Holt of Liverpool, a civil engineer by training who had become a businessman and shipowner, installed and operated an improved compound engine in one of his ships. Its success led him in 1865 to build (in a yard right alongside one building tea clippers of iron frames and wooden planks) three iron steamers each fitted with compound engines so small and efficient that each vessel could carry a cargo of 3000 tons, two or three times as much as almost all contemporary sailing vessels, and at the same time sufficient coal to drive her at a steady 10mph for 8500 miles without refuelling. It is most unlikely, in fact, that she ever did so, since it would have been more profitable to carry more cargo and no more fuel than was demanded by the distance between bunkering ports on her trade routes.

The secret lay largely with the boilers. Iron was now available of such quality, and boiler building techniques had developed to such a degree, that steam pressures of 60psi (pounds per square inch) could be achieved. The steam pressures achieved in the engines of early paddle steamers had been no more than 5psi. The coal consumption of Alfred Holts' vessels was as little as 2¾lb per hour per ton, less than a quarter of that of early steamers. The new steamers were put immediately into the China trade and since they could travel to and from regularly in sixty-four days against the crack sailing ship time of an uncertain ninety days and they could, four years later when it was opened, exploit the advantages of the Suez Canal (which was effectively closed to sailing ships) and could carry three times the cargo of a sailing ship, it was in this high-freight, prestigious trade that the making of an end of the merchant sailing ship was at last begun.

But there were many trades in which an economic return on capital could still be earned by sail tonnage, so in the 1870s something of a balance was established between compound engined steam vessels and merchant sailing vessels. But in the early 1880s when the compound engined vessel seemed to have settled at the limits of its possibilities another development established the steamship as the normal method of sea transport and brought about the end of the building of new large sailing vessels within about fifteen years. This second revolution had its preliminaries. Iron plates were cheap in the 1870s, but steel for shipbuilding was expensive. There was an enormous demand for steel for other industrial purposes, and particularly for railway development throughout the world. But by the end of the 1870s steel was being used for boilers and furnace construction and this meant that steam pressures could be increased, with the further consequent improvement to the efficiency of the compound engine – and fuel consumption was reduced by more than 60 per cent.

On 7 April 1881 the steamship *Aberdeen* sailed from Plymouth towards Melbourne. As Denis Griffiths explains in more detail, she had an engine in which the steam, having done its work in the second cylinder of the compound engine was admitted to a third cylinder, even larger than the second and there completed its expansion. This process was made possible by the high steam pressures obtained from steel boilers and improved furnaces. The *Aberdeen* completed her passage to Melbourne in forty-two days with 4000 tons of cargo and only one coaling stop, working at steam pressures of 125psi. Within three years 150psi was achieved in new steamships. In 1885 the two-cylinder compound engine virtually ceased to be built and triple expansion engines working at 200psi shortly followed. By the beginning of the 1890s a tramp steamer could operate at 9kts on a fuel consumption of half an ounce of coal per ton mile steamed – to put this in vivid terms, a first class cargo steamer of the late years of Queen Victoria's reign could carry one ton of cargo one mile using the heat in her furnace equivalent to that generated by burning one sheet of high quality Victorian writing paper. By the mid 1880s the steam vessel was as economical as the newly-developed big steel sailing vessels described in *Sail's Last Century*, the companion volume in this series, bearing in mind that she could make three passages and thus carry three tons of cargo to the latter's one. It was the production and use of steel good enough and cheap enough to manufacture commercially practicable high-pressure boilers which finally established the screw steamer as the normal method of sea transport. This process was assisted by improved port facilities, water ballast, better cargo gear, the introduction of self trimming and the exploitation by steamship owners of the economies of scale.

Dr Basil Greenhill

Table 1: Net Tonnage of the Leading Mercantile Fleets of the World, Sail and Steam, from 1850 to 1910

Countries		1850	1860	1870	1880	1890	1900	1905	1907	1910
United Kingdom	Sail	3,396,659	4,204,360	4,577,855	3,851,045	2,936,021	2,096,498	1,670,766	1,461,376	1,113,944
	Steam	168,474	454,327	1,112,934	2,723,468	5,042,517	7,207,610	9,064,816	10,023,723	10,442,719
British Possessions	Sail	648,672	1,096,464	1,369,145	1,646,844	1,338,361	915,096	906,372	883,448	879,926
	Steam	19,157	45,817	89,200	225,814	371,189	532,188	696,430	814,808	926,399
British Empire	Sail	4,045,331	5,300,824	5,947,000	5,497,889	4,274,382	3,011,594	2,577,138	2,344,824	1,993,870
	Steam	187,631	500,144	1,202,134	2,949,282	5,413,706	7,739,798	9,761,266	10,838,531	11,369,118
Russia (including Finland)	Sail	–	–	–	655,771	560,267	556,614	511,518	564,721	581,316
	Steam	–	–	–	100,421	234,418	417,922	440,643	501,638	535,040
Norway	Sail	298,315	558,927	1,009,200	1,460,596	1,502,584	1,002,675	813,864	750,862	628,287
	Steam	–	–	13,715	58,062	203,115	505,443	668,230	819,282	897,440
Sweden	Sail	–	–	–	421,693	369,680	288,687	263,425	238,742	175,916
	Steam	–	–	–	81,049	141,267	325,105	459,664	532,515	596,763
Denmark	Sail	–	–	168,193	197,509	189,406	158,303	149,310	141,035	131,342
	Steam	–	–	10,453	51,957	112,788	250,137	334,124	404,946	415,496
German Empire	Sail	–	–	900,361	965,767	709,761	593,770	553,817	533,652	506,837
	Steam	–	–	81,994	215,758	723,652	1,347,875	1,915,475	2,256,783	2,396,733
Netherlands	Sail	289,870	423,790	370,159	263,887	127,200	78,493	54,417	49,640	45,936
	Steam	2,706	10,132	19,455	64,394	128,511	268,430	356,890	398,026	488,399
Belgium	Sail	33,315	28,857	20,648	10,442	4,393	741	2,844	964	3,402
	Steam	1,604	4,254	9,501	65,224	71,553	112,518	96,889	119,223	187,730
France	Sail	674,228	928,099	917,633	641,539	444,092	501,175	676,193	662,828	636,081
	Steam	13,925	68,025	154,415	277,759	499,921	527,551	711,027	739,819	815,567
Portugal	Sail	–	–	–	–	–	57,925	43,126	38,363	43,844
	Steam	–	–	–	–	–	51,506	58,077	62,675	70,193
Spain	Sail	–	–	–	326,438	210,247	95,187	58,201	45,185	44,940
	Steam	–	–	–	233,695	407,935	679,392	685,680	676,926	744,517
Italy	Sail	–	–	980,064	922,126	634,149	571,164	541,171	468,674	432,695
	Steam	–	–	32,100	77,050	106,567	376,844	484,432	526,586	674,497
Austria Hungary	Sail	–	–	279,400	258,642	138,796	52,736	39,565	37,658	32,235
	Steam	–	–	49,977	63,970	97,852	246,989	366,070	418,838	477,616
Greece	Sail	–	263,075	398,703	–	226,702	175,867	145,312	145,283	145,284
	Steam	–	–	5,360	–	44,684	143,436	225,512	257,900	301,785
United States of America– (a) Registered for foreign trade	Sail	1,540,769	2,448,941	1,325,256	1,206,206	749,065	485,352	353,333	269,021	234,848
	Steam	44,942	97,296	192,544	146,604	197,630	341,342	601,180	602,125	556,977
(b) Enrolled for river and lakes	Sail	1,418,500	1,982,297	1,795,389	1,650,270	1,816,344	2,021,690	2,361,716	2,450,405	2,372,873
	Steam	481,005	770,641	882,551	1,064,954	1,661,458	2,316,455	3,140,314	3,677,243	4,343,384
China	Sail	–	–	–	21,694	11,801	20,541	19,560	18,243	14,314
	Steam	–	–	–	–	29,766	18,215	45,617	57,604	88,888
Japan	Sail	–	–	–	41,215	48,094	320,571	334,684	366,013	412,859
	Steam	–	–	–	–	93,812	543,365	938,783	1,116,193	1,233,785
Total		9,032,191	13,295,302	16,765,205	19,991,863	22,265,598	26,205,398	30,849,067	33,132,066	34,629,742
World Total	Sail	8,300,378	11,844,810	14,111,006	14,541,684	12,016,963	9,993,075	9,559,194	9,126,113	8,435,874
	Steam	731,813	1,450,492	2,654,199	5,450,179	10,248,635	16,212,323	21,289,873	24,005,953	26,193,868

Percentage of world total

	1850	1860	1870	1880	1890	1900	1905	1907	1910
British	46.86	43.33	42.64	42.25	43.51	41.02	39.99	39.79	38.58
United Kingdom	39.47	34.80	33.94	32.88	35.83	35.50	34.80	34.66	33.37
United States of America	38.58	39.51	25.02	20.38	19.87	19.70	20.92	21.12	21.68
German	-	-	5.85	5.91	6.43	7.40	8.00	8.42	8.38
British, in terms of steamship tonnage, reckoning 1 ton steam = 4 tons sailing	42.7	40.86	43.49	47.56	48.91	45.39	43.98	43.46	41.93
United Kingdom *ditto*	36.25	33.95	36.51	40.57	43.58	41.32	40.00	39.48	37.88
United States of America include (a) and (b) *ditto*	45.09	44.55	30.00	21.19	19.46	17.55	24.24	18.86	19.61
German *ditto*	–	–	5.85	4.03	6.79	7.99	8.67	9.09	8.91

From A W Kirkaldy, *British Shipping* (London 1914).

1

Steam Before the Screw

THE history of the steamship, as this volume will show, was in three distinct stages. In each of these stages there was a process of development to a point at which a plateau was reached and it seemed that the use of steam at sea could go no further. Then there was a breakthrough, a fundamental change so profound in its effects as to produce a new vehicle of sea transport, so much more efficient than

An early engraving of steam packets by R Ackermann published in London in May 1817. Note the sail set from the tall funnel of the vessel on the right, a device sometimes employed by the first generation of steamers. With craft such as these operating on the rivers of Britain and the United States the steam vessel may been seen to have passed from the experimental stage to one which was commercially viable, albeit severely limited in application. (By courtesy of Basil Greenhill)

the ships of the previous stage as to render all predecessors obsolete.

The first of these stages was the era of the paddle steamer, which, as we shall demonstrate, was a dead end, incapable of development for either merchant shipping or naval purposes beyond a point at which only limited and somewhat specialised usage was possible. The paddle steamer was never going to play a significant part in the world's carrying trade, nor was she even in her largest and most powerful forms a substitute for the sailing ship of the line, though she became by the late 1840s an essential unit of any fleet as a tug, dispatch boat, landing craft, transport, and diplomatic presence at moments of crisis. She was also a formidable foe to the smaller units of a sailing navy.

The second stage was the era of the screw propelled vessel driven by ever more sophis-

ticated 'simple engines' which used the expansion of steam only once. These vessels, which did not suffer from some of the grave weaknesses of the paddler, which will be explained later in this chapter, nevertheless as far as merchant shipping was concerned were limited in profitable operation by the inefficiency of their engines, which meant that for a given power output they consumed prodigious quantities of coal. This coal was often expensive, particularly in foreign ports, and of very varying quality. It took up a great deal of space which had to be taken from cargo-carrying capacity; to move it required a great many firemen (called stokers in the navy) who had to be paid and fed, whose accommodation took up further space in the vessel and who had to be managed – not always an easy task. This on top of the fact that in the era of steam-and-sail, which lasted perforce until the

latter part of the nineteenth century – see Chapter 8 in this volume – merchant vessels had to carry enough men to handle something approaching a full standard sailing ship rig. Steamers on scheduled passages of twenty days or less which could steam continuously and tended to be fully powered ships with sophisticated sail-assist rigs requiring minimum deck crew were an exception. It is clear, therefore, that even at this stage, the simple engine screw steamship, though she was a considerable step up on the paddler in short sea trades and limited passages on deep water (as on the transatlantic routes) – and especially if she was built of iron – bearing in mind that the sole purpose of a merchant ship is to make a reasonable net return on invested capital, was not going to make any very significant contribution to the world's carrying trade. And indeed she did not. The tonnage of merchant steamers of all kinds registered under the Merchant Shipping Acts as of home ports in the United Kingdom in 1850, when the navy had already ceased to build new large sailing vessels and was committed to steam screw driven battle-fleet, was 168,474 and they were about 1200 in number, while the tonnage of sailing vessels was, 3,396,659. Two years later only fifty-eight screw driven merchant steamships were registered, most of them under 1000 tons.[1] Ten years later steamers still comprised only roughly one-tenth of the total tonnage registered.

For the navy, as the *Steam, Steel and Shellfire* volume in this series shows, it was a different story. The urgent necessity of constructing a fleet of vessels with power which could fire a full broadside and which were not susceptible to the weaknesses of the paddle steamer led to the construction at the very beginning of the 1850s of a battlefleet of large ships of the line fully rigged as sailing vessels and equipped with relatively compact auxiliary steam engines driving screws. These vessels could sail as well as the best of the old sailing fleet. The navy with its huge fighting crews was not inhibited as to manpower for handling the sails, manning the engine rooms and stoking the furnaces. The use of their engines gave these vessels a mobility in action in restricted waters, and safety in bad weather never before achieved at sea.

The third stage in the development of the steamship was the introduction of the marine compound engine. With steadily increasing boiler pressures these engines, expanding steam twice in two linked cylinders, dramatically cut fuel consumption, the number of furnaces and the space needed for bunkers. At last the steamship in this period – the middle 1860s – began to show that she would one day break the wooden sailing ship's monopoly of the world's carrying trade. From now on steamships became steadily more efficient and soon the marine engine expanded its steam three times over. The history of this later development of the steamer is given in Chapters 5 and 10 in this volume. The merchant sailing vessel was at long last doomed and by the end of the century new construction of sailing vessels of all sizes had virtually ceased.

The wooden paddle steamer

The story of the development of the screw and of the compound engine is told in detail later in this volume. This chapter is concerned with the paddle steamer between its inception as a sea-going vessel and its establishment as a profitable vehicle for very limited deep sea service with the building and successful operation of the *Great Western* in 1837.

Early steam engines, either the 'atmospheric' engines of Newcomen and others which derived their power from air pressure rather than directly from steam, or those early steam engines which operated on the actual expansion of steam itself, were suitable for pumping purposes and in due course, with refinement, for driving machinery ashore. Working usually on very low pressures they were with a few exceptions too big and bulky to be suitable for application to land transport; but from the late eighteenth century attempts were made to apply steam power to marine propulsion. The early history of steam propelled vessels is associated, not surprisingly, with river transport. There was a period of adaptation of crude and unreliable machinery to the driving of rotating paddles, the period of experiment when the flowering confidence of early engineers was pitted against commercial realities and the reluctance of the navy, in time of war and immediate postwar contraction of the defence budget, to bear development costs for very uncertain results. Denis Griffiths gives a brief account of these experiments in Chapter 10. The paddles themselves had to be designed and developed as an entirely new application of power for transport on water and this was done long before the steam engine was adapted to the regular propulsion of vehicles on land. But there were great advantages to be derived from applying power to river transport, the ability to move upstream, increased speed and, machinery breakdowns permitting, regularity of service, were factors big enough to push development over the gulf between invention and practical application and so encourage investment in an age which rightly thought of rivers and canals as the natural highways for bulk transport inland.

1. Figures from A W Kirkaldy, *British Shipping* (London 1914), Appendix 17, and R Murray, *Rudimentary Treatise on Marine Engines and Steam Vessels* (London 1852), Table IV and pp 172-3. 'Return of the Whole of the Registered Steam Navy', *British Parliamentary Papers* (XLVIX) (1852).

The first steam vessel to cross the English Channel was the Margery *shown here. She was built at Dumbarton in 1814 with an engine of 14nhp. After service on the Thames she was sold to French owners and on her delivery passage steamed from Newhaven to Havre on 17–18 March 1816. She subsequently served on the Seine. (From an old print)*

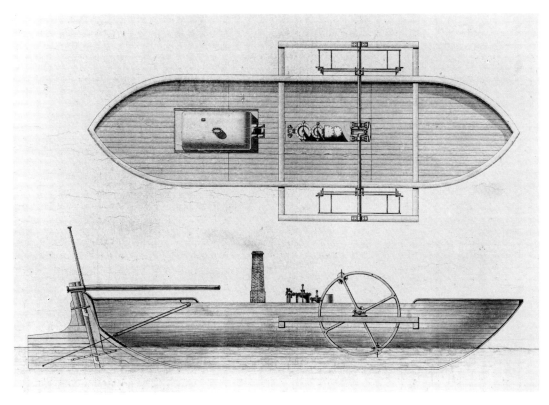

2. Charles Jordan, 'Some Historical Records and Reminiscences Relating to the British Navy and Mercantile Shipping', *Lloyd's Register of Shipping, 1924-25* (London), p23.

3. H P Spratt, *The Birth of the Steamboat* (London 1958), pp92-95.

4. G Dodd, *An Historical Explanatory Dissertation on Steam Engines and Steam Packets* (London, 1818).

5. K Y Watson, *Doubly in Crown Service* (London 1902), pp93–110.

One of the first European steamers to operate outside Britain was the Elizabeth, *which Charles Baird converted from a wooden barge at St Petersburg in 1815 for service on the Neva river. This early drawing of the vessel shows the notable innovation of feathering paddle boards, kept vertical by a bevel gear arrangement. (ScM)*

She was clearly a very well-designed and well-built vessel with excellent machinery for her time.[4]

Thereafter the development of the paddle steamer for commercial use on short river and coastal runs with passengers and light cargoes was steady, if not rapid. The various published works do not always agree with one another as to detail, but it appears that the first steamer in service on the Mersey was steamed there from Scotland in 1815.[5] By 1818 a Greenock–Belfast service was already running and is claimed by

Refuelling points could be established on the banks of rivers. A broken-down vessel could tie up and await assistance. So the paddle steamer began her commercial career on the Clyde and the Hudson, on the Thames and the Elbe, on the Neva, on the Rhine, the St Lawrence, the Swedish lakes, and the Brahamaputra. With the end of the Napoleonic Wars development was rapid. By 1815 a steamer service was established between Gravesend and London and in the same year a service to Richmond is said to have been established. In 1816 the first steamboat was built on the Thames. By 1817 the first steamers were running regularly between London and Margate and soon afterwards there were services to Southend and Ramsgate.[2] A year later a steam vessel made the first crossing of the English Channel.[3]

In the year of Waterloo, 1815, what might be regarded as the first long seagoing passage in British waters was made by the *Thames*, built on the Clyde as the *Duke of Argyle* in 1814. Having been sold to London owners she was steamed to the Thames via Dublin, Ramsey Island (making what appears to have been the first crossing of the Irish Sea under steam), Milford Haven, St

Ives, Plymouth and Portsmouth. She completed the whole passage of 758 nautical miles in 122 hours steaming at an average of 6.2kts. She subsequently served on the Thames between London, Gravesend and Margate with success.

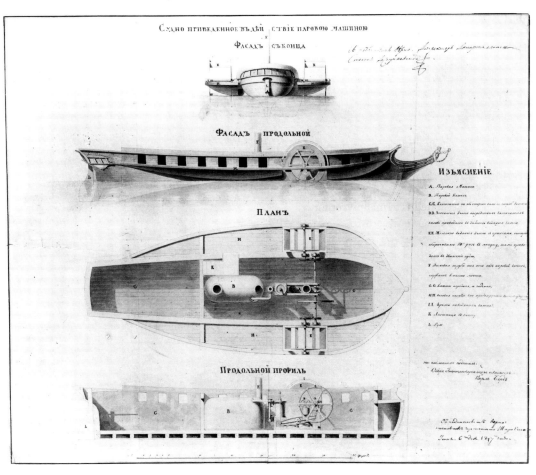

Following the converted Elizabeth, *Baird designed a new steamer for the Neva service in 1817. This original draught shows the vessel to have been 72ft long overall and measuring about 56 tons. Driven by a side lever engine with a flywheel, the paddles have abandoned the feathering gear of the earlier vessel in favour of fixed floats. (ScM)*

The first steamer built in Prussia was the Prinzessin Charlotte, *launched in September 1816 for service on the rivers Elbe, Havel and Spree. The engine was probably supplied by the famous English firm of Boulton & Watt, and drove a paddle between the divided hull amidships. Like many contemporary British and American river steamers there was a large cabin below deck for the passengers.* (ScM)

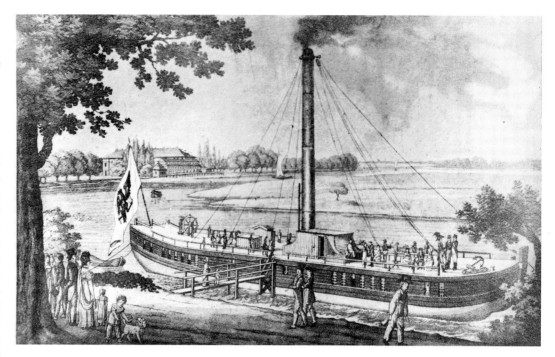

some authorities as the first regular steam service in open coastal waters.[6] A year later a Liverpool–Belfast service was established,[7] and in 1821 a Bristol–Cork service began operation,[8] as well as an open sea service across the Åland Sea between Stockholm and Turku in southwestern Finland.[9] In 1821 also there was a steamer in service on Lake Mäleren, just west of Stockholm. Sweden was, in fact, the first European country after Britain to build steam vessels. As early as 1816 Samuel Owen, a British engineer resident in Sweden, was experimenting with screw propulsion in a little vessel called the *Stockholmshäxan*. Owen went on to other successful paddle steamers.[10]

Russia had a steamboat as early as 1815 when the *Elizabeth* was fitted with a side lever engine by a British engineer resident in St Petersburg and ran in daily service between that city and Kronstadt, covering the 18 miles up and down the Neva and across the head of the Gulf of Fin-

In British waters the Anglo-Scottish London–Leith packet service was a forcing ground for steamer development. Built for this route in 1821, the famous James Watt *of 1821 was the largest steamship of the day at 448 tons and the first to be entered in Lloyd's Register. The builder, John Wood & Co of Port Glasgow, is often credited with the introduction of fine bow lines for steamers instead of the bluff convex lines inherited from sailing ships. Draught from the* Transactions of the Institution of Naval Architects II *(1861).*

land in three hours. A year later a steam service on the Elbe was established with the *Prinzessin Charlotte* with a British side lever engine built by Boulton & Watt. Early experiments in France at the same period ended in failure, but in 1818 the first steamer to serve in the Mediterranean, the *Ferdinando Primo* was launched, also with a British-built engine. Indeed, throughout the era of the paddle steamer British industrial technology was so much in the ascendant that the great majority of paddle steamers built on the mainland of Europe were either fitted with British-built engines or engines built locally from British designs.

Such were the advantages of steam propulsion on the western rivers of the United States, where supplies of wood fuel were almost limitless, that already by 1819 some one hundred steam vessels had been constructed there as op-

posed to forty-three in the whole of the British Empire.[11] As an American historian has put it, the steamboat changed 'the relations of the west

6. H P Spratt, *op cit*, pp104-5.

7. R Sinclair, *Across the Irish Sea* (London 1990). Dr Freda Harcourt in her paper, 'Ownership and Finance 1820-1850', published in *Anglo-Dutch Mercantile Marine Relations 1700-1850* (Leiden 1991), has demonstrated the prominent role of the Irish Sea trade and of Irish shipowners in the early years of the development of the merchant paddle steamer.

8. G E Farr, *West Country Passenger Steamers* (London 1956), pp16 and 22.

9. H Forsell, *Sea Finland* (Helsinki 1985), p52.

10. C O Cederlund, 'The Eric Nordevall', in Burenhult *et al, Theoretical Approaches to Artifacts, Settlement and Society* (Oxford 1987), p515, and W A Baker, *From Paddle Steamer to Nuclear Ship* (Göteborg, 1965), p26.

11. E C Smith, *A Short History of Naval and Marine Engineering* (Cambridge 1937), p16.

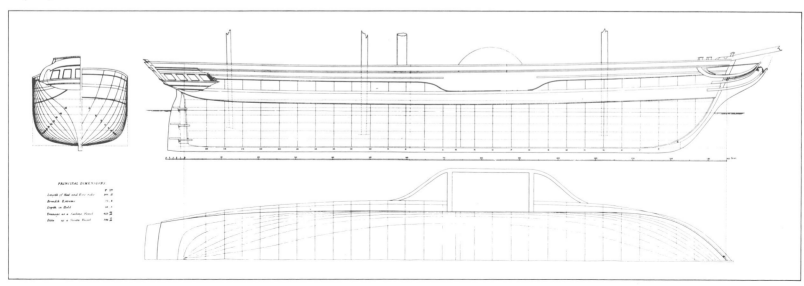

Built five years after the James Watt, *the* United Kingdom *measured 1000 tons gross and her machinery was rated at twice the nhp of the earlier ship – indicative of the rapid development of steamers during the 1820s. There was considerable public interest in the* United Kingdom *– she and her sisters were known as the 'leviathan class' – and this etching by the well-known artist E W Cooke is one reflection of their popularity.*

which may almost be said to change its destiny'.[12] The history of the application of steam power to water transport in and from the United States is dealt with by Professor William Still and his associates in Chapter 3 of this book.

So it was that by the middle 1820s there was a network of short sea, river and lake services operated by paddle steamers in British and European waters and extensive use of paddle propelled vessels on the rivers of the United States and in eastern coastal waters. By 1827 there were 225 steamships registered as of British home ports under the Merchant Shipping Acts. Many of these were tugs, but they already included some large and powerful vessels, notably those employed on the London–Leith packet service. As early as 1821 these included two vessels of over 400 tons and by 1826 the *United Kingdom* of 1000 tons and 200hp, probably the largest steamship built to that date anywhere in Europe. In 1826 the General Steam Navigation Company of London sent a vessel as far as Lisbon.[13] A year later, what appears to have been the first regular steam service beyond the home trade limits of Brest to the Elbe was established by the Dublin and London Steam Marine Company between Dublin and Bordeaux.[14] Vessels equip–ped with steam engines and paddles had made long passages using both sail and steam on delivery from Britain to countries overseas.[15] These included the *Conde de Palmella* which in 1820 sailed and steamed to Lisbon from the Mersey in four days and is believed to have been the first of the countless steam vessels to have been built in Britain for European owners. Also included was the *Rising Star* of 1821 which steamed and sailed to Valparaiso, the American *Savannah*, also of 1821, which made a double crossing of the north At-

lantic, mainly under sail, and the *Enterprise*, which in 1825 used steam for roughly two-thirds of the 113-day passage to Calcutta.

But the navy, unconstrained by commercial necessity, was more enterprising than the merchant shipping industry in the operation of its first paddle steamers on ocean voyages. Thus the *Lightning* of 1823 made a round voyage to Algiers in 1824 and another to Kronstadt, the great Russian fortress which defended the entrance to St Petersburg, in 1826. In the same year the *African*, built in 1825, made the outward passage of a round voyage to Sierra Leone, probably the longest round voyage made by a fully-powered steam vessel to that date; from it she returned to sail to Ancona on the Adriatic coast of northern Italy.[16]

But the operative expression is 'unconstrained

by commercial necessity'. Merchant steamships had to pay their way. An attempt to follow in the footsteps of the *Lightning* with a commercial service to St Petersburg by the General Steam Navigation Company of London in 1827 was a

12. J H Morrison, *History of American Steam Navigation*, (New York 1958), p191.

13. E C Smith, *op cit*, p26.

14. Oral communication from Dr Freda Harcourt, Queen Mary College, London.

15. For a comprehensive and well illustrated account of the histories of many of the earliest steam vessels written by a distinguished naval architect see W A Baker, *op cit*.

16. For detailed accounts of early naval paddle steamers see Basil Greenhill and Ann Giffard, *Steam, Politics and Patronage: A new view of the Royal Navy, 1815-1854* (London, forthcoming), and D K Brown, *Before the Ironclad* (London 1990). Also the relevant chapters by Dr Andrew Lambert in *Steam, Steel and Shellfire* in the present series.

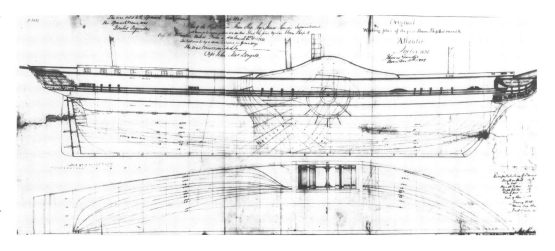

Built at Quebec for Canadian coastal service in 1831, the Royal William *was sent across the Atlantic in 1833, fourteen years after the first crossing by the* Savannah, *but like the earlier ship, in order to be sold. However, unlike* Savannah, *she carried a few fare-paying passengers and steamed for much of the crossing (three days out of four were claimed, the fourth day being necessary to clear salt scale from the boilers). This is a copy of the original draught.* (ScM)

failure. The short sea routes and inland waterways were soon saturated and in 1837, the year in which the merchant paddle steamer was to come of age with the building of the *Great Western*, there were still only 624 steamships registered under the British Merchant Shipping Acts. The development of early steam packet services around the coasts of Britain and to Continental ports was fraught with hazard, physical, financial and managerial. The paddle steamer was an unsatisfactory vehicle both for sea transport and as a warship. The latter function is dealt with in detail in *Steam, Steel and Shellfire*; here we consider the merchant paddle steamer.

From the start, merchant paddle steamers tended to be fully powered vessels, that is vessels which could proceed under steam power throughout the short passages they made around the coasts between bunkering facilities. They therefore did not have to carry so much fuel that they were unable to find adequate space for paying cargo. They carried masts, spars and sails and they used their sails from time to time as conditions varied in the ways which are examined in Chapter 8 of this volume. Early naval paddle vessels were operated in much the same way, but since they did not have to carry cargo and were relatively lightly armed and manned they could carry more fuel and their steaming range was greater. The emphasis in the navy at this early stage, the 1820s, was on an efficient and reliable towing machine capable of long passages at sea. The merchant shipping requirement was certainly for efficient tugs in numbers, but for a packet service the requirement was for a vessel so fast and reliable on short runs that, despite the fear of the unproven and the well-justified fear of boiler explosions, she attracted a sufficient number of passengers and sufficient light cargo, to pay her way despite the very considerable investment cost she represented and the high cost of operating her.

The paddle steamer was unsatisfactory for a number of reasons. What Murray wrote in 1852 when the alternative, the screw, was becoming well established, sums up the situation very well. He pointed out that 'Variable Immersion' was

This engraving, after a painting by J Walter, depicts the Great Western *departing from Bristol for her maiden voyage on 8 April 1838. Although narrowly beaten into New York by the chartered* Sirius, *and thus missing the distinction of completing the first Atlantic crossing under continuous power, the* Great Western *was a more significant ship. Designed by I K Brunel specifically for North Atlantic service, she took only 15 days 5 hours to cross (*Sirius *needed 18 days 10 hours from Cork), and began the era of regular transatlantic liner operation. (By courtesy of Basil Greenhill)*

the 'Great Objection To The Paddle Wheel'.[17] A paddle wheel propelling system was of necessity designed to work at a certain optimum depth of immersion but, as coal, stores, and water were consumed, differing weights of cargo loaded and discharged as the vessel proceeded on her voyage, so her draught varied and with it the immersion of her paddles, so that it was only at times and for relatively short periods that the paddles were working at maximum efficiency. To some extent this difficulty could be overcome by disconnecting the boards or floats from the wheel and securing them nearer the centre, but, at sea, this was a difficult, time-consuming and dangerous occupation, much easier in a naval vessel with her big crew than in a merchant ship. A very good example of this process of varying draught is demonstrated by the operation of the *Great Western*. As one of her transatlantic crossings progressed coal consumption caused a gradual reduction in draught with the result that the paddle wheels lost about 3ft of immersion during a crossing, which meant that the optimum immersion was achieved only for a limited part of the passage.[18]

Moreover, in anything of a rough sea, as the paddle vessel rolled, one paddle or the other was immersed too deep or too shallow or out of the water altogether, and the system was working at half, or less than half, efficiency. It is obvious that the vessel had to roll very little to bring about a situation in which neither paddle was working at anywhere near its optimum efficiency, even though the vessel was loaded to an ideal draught in still water. With a strong wind on the beam and the windward paddle almost out of the water the lee wheel constantly drove her up into the wind. In these circumstances a paddle steamer, carrying excessive weather helm, could become almost uncontrollable. Sail set forward

was essential to help her maintain her course, as was the shifting of movable weights to windward.

In addition to these difficulties the paddle steamer suffered from a built-in design weakness which imposed serious limitations on the cargo and fuel-carrying capacity of the merchant paddle steamer, and the fuel, armament and stores capacity of naval vessels. The difficulty can be summed up in no better terms than those used by Campbell MacMurray, Director of the Royal Naval Museum at Portsmouth.[19] MacMurray wrote:

> ... in the first place steps have to be taken at the design stage to ensure that the wave profile abreast of the paddle should be reasonably flat, or at least, not likely to form a hollow immediately in front of the floats. Should the latter take place the thrust of the float takes place in something less than the full, free, flow of water, leading to excessive slip in the action of the float and consequent loss of efficiency. The second point is related: it is vital to ensure that the bow diverging waves trail aft outside of the paddles, since when they come inside, serious vibration is encountered in the running gear, bringing attendant damage. The solution to these and associated problems is often related to the fineness of the entrance and run, combined with their length vis a vis the total immersed length of the vessel. The outcome is usually to provide such ships – ie fast, passenger-carrying paddle steamers – with much

17. R Murray, *op cit*, pp109-110.

18. D Griffiths, *Brunel's Great Western* (Wellingborough 1985), p47.

19. See C MacMurray, *Old Order, New Thing* (London 1972), pp22 and 23.

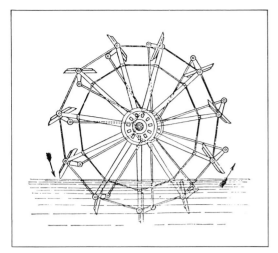

It was realised early in the history of paddle propulsion that power was lost by the action of a fixed paddle float striking the water at an oblique angle and splashing as it left it. The answer was a feathering paddle wheel in which the float was kept nearly vertical during the propulsive part of the wheel's revolution. The first half of the nineteenth century saw many versions patented, but the most common was the Morgan modification of Elijah Galloway's patent of 1829 based on the workings of an eccentric gear. From A & R Murray's Shipbuilding and Steam Ships *(Edinburgh 1861).*

lower block coefficients than would be thought acceptable for general deep sea work.

This means that the vessels had to be long, lean, and narrow. This shape limited the cargo-carrying capacity and therefore the commercial viability of a merchant vessel. She could not profitably (or even physically) carry bulk cargoes, and these were the great majority of cargoes – coal, ores, cereals, stone, and so forth. She was effectively limited to the carriage of light, preferably high-value and high-freight, materials and, above all, passengers. It was for this, among a number of other reasons, that large fleets of paddle steamers carrying, for instance, coal from the Tyne to London simply never developed. There were few, if any, paddle driven tramp coasters or deep sea paddle propelled tramp steamers.

A further problem emerged from the nature of the paddles themselves. They were inefficient, partly because the only time when the board or float acted perpendicularly to the water was when it was vertically below the centre of the wheel. Various solutions were tried. The most successful and widely adopted was the feathering system. By an arrangement of cams and levers the floats were constantly adjusted as to angle as the wheel went round so that they were constantly more or less at right angles to the surface of still water. This meant that the whole, or most, of their thrust was exerted in a sternward

direction. The mechanism by which this constant adjustment was achieved can be studied at leisure and under ideal conditions in the port paddle of the steam tug *Reliant*, preserved in the main display hall of the National Maritime Museum at Greenwich. But the installation of a feathering system meant that the floats could not be sent out to the perimeter of the paddle wheel as a vessel floated higher and higher as she consumed her various weights on a long passage. It was also unreliable and subject to frequent breakdown.[20] Therefore, the feathering system never appears to have found much favour in the navy, with its long range operations for steamers, but it was extremely useful for merchant vessels operating where there was not much variation in depth of immersion during short passages round the coasts as little fuel, stores, water, and so forth were consumed and what was used was replaced at many ports of call. The system was always invaluable in tugs, ensuring that they could exercise the maximum drawing power.

The paddle steamer had yet another problem. She had very poor handling characteristics at low speeds. The rudder of a paddler had no slipstream from the screw to render it immediately effective when the vessel got under weigh or operated at low speeds when coming alongside. In consequence, her manoeuvrability at low speeds was poor, except in the case of vessels in which the paddles could be operated separately. Gordon Jackson has referred to the managerial and financial consequences of the difficulty of handling paddle steamers in congested waters and to the simple fact that 'In close quarters steamers were difficult to stop and impossible to steer'.[21] It is perhaps no wonder that very sophisticated direct control of engines from the deck was developed for vessels operating in restricted waters at a very early date indeed. The Tay ferries were equipped with such a device as early as 1821. Basil Hall describes their advantages in vivid terms.

The object of the contrivance we are about to describe, is to regulate the motions of the steam vessel in a more easy manner than heretofore. By the simple motion of a small handle or index, placed on the table upon deck, in view and in hearing of the man at the helm, and of the master of the vessel, every movement which the engine is capable of giving to the paddle wheel may be at once commanded. The vessel may be moved forwards or backwards, – or may be retarded, or entirely stopped, at any given moment – by merely turning the handle to the places denoted by the graduations of a dial plate. No skill is required for this purpose; so that the master himself, or a sailor under his directions, can perform the office as well as the ablest engineer. Thus, the confusion which frequently arises at night in calling out to the engineer below, is avoided, and any ambiguity arising from the word of command being transmitted through several persons entirely prevented. In point of fact, it places the engine as much under the command as the rudder is – an undoubted improvement on the clumsy method of bawling out to the engineer below, who either may not hear, or may chance to be out of the way – circumstances which may lead to the most serious accidents.[22]

Although the first written evidence for the use of engine room telegraphs appears to be dated 1845,[23] an Admiralty draught dated 1833 in the collection of the National Maritime Museum at Greenwich of the *Lightning*, built in 1823, the first naval steamer to make a deep sea passage and the first to be formally commissioned into the navy, shows what appears to be a telegraph control on deck.

The paddle steamer, like all early power driven mechanical devices, was dependent for its rate of development on the general state of industry ashore. The cost, availability and quality of iron and copper were fundamental, as was the availability and improvement of lubricants – tallow was used widely in the early stages. But there was a greater problem than all these. In the 1830s and '40s marine steam engines developed and improved very rapidly, but nevertheless they continued to suffer from a fundamental defect which imposed strict limits on their use as a means of propulsion at sea – their very heavy fuel consumption.

Denis Griffiths describes the side lever engines which were the principal means of propulsion adopted for merchant steamers throughout the paddle wheel era in Chapter 10 of this volume. Again that very important vessel the *Reliant*, preserved in the National Maritime Museum, has her side lever engines intact and working, and she is probably the only vessel in the world to have such a set of machinery intact in the original hull and available on public view, though the *Eric Nordevall* at the bottom of Lake

20. C Jordan, *op cit*, p13.

21. 'Operational problems of the transfer to steam: Dundee, Perth and London Shipping Company, c1820-1845', in T C Smout (ed), *Scotland and the Sea* (Edinburgh 1992).

22. See Basil Hall, *An account of the Ferry across the Tay at Dundee* (Dundee 1825), appendix.

23. In W Gordon, *The Economy of the Marine Steam Engine* (London 1845).

A major driving force in the early development of steamers was their suitability for fast mail services. In Britain the Post Office packets were the responsibility of the Navy, who used them to test many of the advanced ideas of the time. Widgeon, represented by this model, was built at Chatham Dockyard in 1837, and was one of the fastest packets on the cross-Channel service. This wooden hulled vessel was used as the 'control' when comparing relative costs with Laird's iron-built Dover of 1839, and was raced against the pioneer screw steamer Archimedes during a series of trials in 1840. (NMM)

Vättern in Sweden is intact with her engines. These engines were reliable and relatively easy to maintain, but they consumed vast quantities of fuel. Although they steadily improved during the period covered by this chapter, the way in which the steam was utilised meant that much of its potential power was wasted. This in turn meant that the vessel had to carry many times as much coal as she would have done if her engine had worked at higher efficiency. Every ton of coal carried meant that a ton of cargo could not be carried. More than that, a bigger stokehold gang was required, which put up costs further and took up more space, however roughly the men were housed. In 1841, when the merchant paddle steamer had already reached the apogee of her development, Samuel Seaward, a member of a famous engineering firm, read a paper to the Institute of Civil Engineers which put the problem in clear and simple terms:

> Notwithstanding the numerous improvements which have been made in the form and dimensions of steam vessels, and the perfection to

which the machinery has been brought, still the weight of the latter, together with the space required for the fuel, has rendered it hitherto impractical to extend the duration of the steam voyage beyond the period of twenty days, without the necessity of taking in a fresh supply of coal. It must therefore be concluded that until some great reduction can be made in

In 1837 the British Government entered into a contract with a commercial firm for the carriage of overseas mails, to take over from the naval-run packets on the services to the Iberian peninsular (Portugal, Spain and Gibraltar). The newly formed company was the Peninsular Steam Navigation Co, the forerunner of P&O, which at that time had a fleet of seven ships, one of the largest of which was the Tagus (900 tons, 300nhp) depicted in this contemporary painting. (CMP)

the weight of the engines and the amount of fuel required to keep them in motion, the use of steam as the sole moving power must be limited to voyages of three weeks duration, a period of time wholly inadequate for the performance of an Indian or South American voyage.[24]

This simple fact of fuel consumption was to limit not only the paddle steamer but the early screw steamer likewise. Until it was overcome by the introduction of compound engines in the 1860s – see Chapters 5 and 10 in this volume – the merchant steamship, whether paddle or screw propelled, was strictly limited in its use. The navy, once again untrammelled by the necessity of showing a return on capital though still circumscribed by the limited funds available in what we should now describe as the defence budget, was able to be more experimental in the matter of engine types and hull forms. Its responsibilities were increasingly worldwide. Its requirements were for a vessel which had an almost indefinite sailing range backed up by an engine and paddles to give her higher mobility and handiness in restricted waters and in action, and to enable her to act as a tug. Thus it was that the first British steam-and-sail vessel to cross the Atlantic was the naval sloop *Rhadamanthus*, Commander George Evans, sailing in April 1833; and the first steam-and-sail vessel to circumnavigate the earth was the paddle sloop HMS *Driver* in the early 1840s.

It was the navy which initiated and ran the first regular deep sea steamer service and one which tested the reliability and operating endurance of paddle steamers to the utmost. In 1830 the decision was taken to send the mail to the Mediterranean in steam vessels and that the Royal Navy would provide this service, a decision which led to the navy acquiring unparalleled experience in the continuous operation of steam vessels under rigorous conditions. Paddle sloops steamed to the Ionian Isles, Egypt, and occasionally to Syria. A passage from Falmouth

to Alexandria was of 2800 miles and it was for seven years performed under almost continuous steaming, with help from the limited sail plan carried by the sloops when the wind was favourable to give some assistance. The steam sloops took a month to make the round voyage to Corfu. The sailing vessels which had preceded them had often taken three. The establishment of a regular merchant steamer service from Britain to the Iberian peninsula was to begin only with the formation of the Peninsula Steam Company in 1835 and this company made little money until it obtained government subsidies in the form of mail contracts in 1837 and 1840. Thus the mail service was privatised and the navy's sloops freed for service in other forms.

Indeed, the merchant paddle steamer represented a high risk investment. The difficulties were made clear in the 1839 half-yearly report of the General Steam Navigation Company of London – the company which had first sent a paddle steamer on service to Lisbon in 1826 and unsuccessfully experimented with the St Petersburg service a year later. Quoted by Dr Sara Palmer,[25] it reads as follows:

For several years after the general introduction and application of steam navigation, large and indeed extravagant expectations were formed of the profit to be acquired. The cost of the management of steamships was judged from the results of the first five years, from the returns obtained while the ships were in perfect condition and before reparations to any serious extent had been required ... The expenses required in order to maintain steamships in a proper state of efficiency and repair have been found to reach so large an annual amount that, of the numerous steam companies which have been formed, scarcely one has been found, upon review of their operations for ten years, able to maintain for the average of that period a dividend of five per cent; consistently of a proper sum to the maintenance of their capital, while, in many instances, the operations have terminated in the sacrifice of almost the whole of the property embarked. Steam boats have been found to require in a very great degree the exertion of the most indefatigable activity and rigid economy in every particular of their employment and conduct in order to obtain from them any returns ...

The limitations of the paddle steamer meant that its operation for merchant shipping purposes could be profitably carried out only in conditions for which it was specially suited. A recent paper by Gordon Jackson sums up the situation very well. He observes that 'Although

transport historians usually view steamers as a cost-effective move into modern efficiency, the early ones were costly experiments tending to ruin each other in a desperate search for superior freights.'[26]

There were some deep sea services which were within the twenty-day steaming range correctly defined by Samuel Seaward. Of these potentially the most profitable was the transatlantic route to New York. In the *Report to the Committee Formed with the View of Considering Foreign Steam Navigation, Bristol, January 1st, 1836* the progenitors of the steamship *Great Western* argued:

The principal voyages now regularly performed by steamers are the following: to Hamburg, Bordeaux, Lisbon, Cadiz, Gibraltar, Malta and the Ionian Isles; in the West Indies from Jamaica to Barbados against the trade winds; from Bombay to Suez; and from New York to Charlestown. The voyages from, to, and between these places, have been performed, winter and summer, with regularity and safety, which fact of itself furnishes data sufficient for drawing conclusions favourable to feasibility, and which will be the more decisive when it is considered that most of them have been accomplished in vessels of less than 500 tons, not built for their stations, and with steam power disproportionately weak.

It is not therefore too much to assume that vessels built expressly for their stations, modelled upon scientific principles, and propelled by efficient engines, may be capable of performing long voyages, and may encounter the heaviest gales.[27]

It was on the New York run that the merchant paddle steamer reached her maturity with the building of the *Great Western* in 1837. There had been a number of transatlantic passages by steam-and-sail vessels before then. Besides the *Rhadamanthus*, the *Curacao*, the *Cape Breton*, and the *Royal William* had crossed the Atlantic on one-way delivery passages under steam-and-sail. By the middle 1830s the development of the side lever engine and knowledge of the financial hazards of steamship operation had reached the stage at which investment in vessels constructed for transatlantic service was a matter for serious consideration. Three companies were formed, more or less simultaneously. The British & American Steam Navigation Company of London, the Transatlantic Steamship Company of Liverpool and the Great Western Steamship Company of Bristol. These companies, between 1838 and 1840, operated a total of seven paddle vessels (see Tables 1/1 and 1/2).

24. Samuel Seaward, 'Memoir On The Practicability Of Shortening The Duration Of Voyages By The Adoption Of Auxiliary Steam Power To Sailing Vessels', *Journal of the Institute of Civil Engineers* (February 1841).

25. S Palmer, 'Experience, Experiment, and Economics: Factors in the Construction of Early Steam Ships', in K Matthews and G Panting (eds), *Ships and Shipbuilding in the North Atlantic Region* (St Johns, Newfoundland 1978). Alan Pearsall noted the abortive St Petersburg service in 'British Steamships in the Baltic, 1820-1870', in *The Balticas a Trade Road*, (Poorvao, Finland 1991).

26. G Jackson, in T C Smout, *op cit.*

27. Admiral James Hosken, *Logs of the First Voyage made with the unceasing aid of Steam, between England and America by the* Great Western *of Bristol* (Bristol 1838), p55.

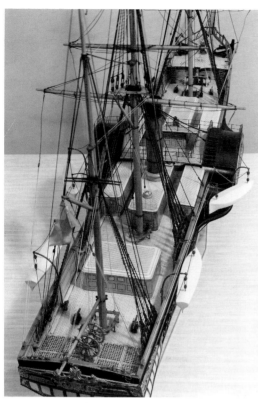

The Britannia *was the first of a quartet built for the British & North American Royal Mail Steam Packet Co, better known by its later name of the Cunard Steamship Co. In 1840 she inaugurated the new company's monthly mail service from Liverpool to Halifax and Boston, becoming the first steamer to carry the mails between Britain and America. This model shows the deck arrangement of these early steamers. The ship was still steered from aft as in sailing ship days but to allow better forward vision there was a tendency to construct a 'bridge' between the paddle boxes from which to con the ship; the wheel was later moved to this platform, a practice from which the modern bridge-wheelhouse derives.* (ScM)

It will be seen from Table 1/3 that the performance of the *Great Western* with her nine points for shutting off steam during the piston stroke and her highly sophisticated sail-assist completely outclassed those of the other vessels, all of which soon dropped out of service while the *Great Western* went on to provide the only steamer service to New York for a number of years – the early Cunarders worked to Halifax, Nova Scotia. Designed by a Bristol group under the leadership of Isambard Kingdom Brunel and built by William Patterson on a site now occupied by the Bristol Industrial Museum, with 450hp engines by Maudslay, Sons & Field, she was the most powerful steamship built to date. Here, again, there was cross-fertilisation between the merchant shipping industry and the Royal Navy. Those responsible for the design of the *Great Western* acknowledged their debt to Oliver Lang, to whom is sometimes attributed

Table 1/1: Particulars of Ships

Ship	Length (Feet)	Breadth (Feet)	Tonnage	Builder
SIRIUS	178	25½	703	Menzies
GREAT WESTERN	236	35¼	1320	Patterson
ROYAL WILLIAM	175	27	617	Wilson
LIVERPOOL	223	30⁵/₆	1150	Humble & Milcrest
BRITISH QUEEN	245	40½	1863	Curling & Young
BRITANNIA	207	34¼	1154	Duncan
PRESIDENT	?43	41	2366	Curling & Young

Table 1/2: Particulars of Engines

Ship	Diameter of cylinder (Inches)	Stroke (Feet - Ins)	Horse power (nhp)	Maker
SIRIUS	60	6-0	320	Wingate
GREAT WESTERN	73½	7-0	400–750	Maudslay
ROYAL WILLIAM	-	-	270	Fawcett & Preston
LIVERPOOL	75	7-0	468	Forrester
BRITISH QUEEN	77½	7-0	500	Napier
BRITANNIA	72½	6-10	440–740	Napier
PRESIDENT	80	7-6	540	Fawcett & Preston

Table 1/3: Transatlantic Voyages, 1838-40

Ship	Port	Date of departure	Port	Date of arrival	No of voyages, 1838-40
SIRIUS	Cork	4 Apr 1838	New York	23 Apr 1838	2
GREAT WESTERN	Bristol	8 Apr 1838	New York	23 Apr 1838	17
ROYAL WILLIAM	Liverpool	5 July 1838	New York	24 July 1838	3
LIVERPOOL	Liverpool	22 Oct 1838	New York	23 Nov 1838	7
BRITISH QUEEN	Portsmouth	12 July 1839	New York	27 July 1839	8
BRITANNIA	Liverpool	4 July 1840	Boston	18 July 1840	3
PRESIDENT	Liverpool	1 Aug 1840	New York	17 Aug 1840	2
ACADIA	Liverpool	4 Aug 1840	Boston	–	2
CALEDONIA	Liverpool	1 Sep 1840	Boston	–	2 out, 1 home

the design of the navy's pioneer deep water steamship *Lightning* and many other early naval steamers, and to Sir William Symonds, then Surveyor of the Navy. In time the navy benefited from the operational experience gained with the *Great Western*. She was bigger and more powerful than the two largest naval steam-

ers, both built in the same year (1837), the *Gorgon* and the *Cyclops* and, although designed for an entirely different sort of service than that of the naval vessels, there was much to be learned from her operation, and information was duly passed over by those responsible for running her.

The *Great Western* demonstrated that a fully

In the 1850s Cunard's hegemony on the North Atlantic was challenged by the US-flag Collins Line. Everything about this undertaking was on the grand scale, its ships being designed to be larger, faster and more luxurious than those of its rival (they featured steam heating, bathrooms and even a barber shop). One of the initial four sister-ships was the 2860-ton Baltic, *built of wood in 1850. Although fast, the ships were hard on their machinery and it was rumoured that they were only kept going by hordes of maintenance engineers working night and day on repairs when the ships were being turned round at New York. (CMP)*

powered paddle steamer with a sail-assist of advanced design could operate continuously on the North Atlantic (albeit with extensive maintenance) and be commercially profitable. With her the paddle steamer reached maturity and she pioneered the way which just over two years later was to be followed by the early Cunard vessels. But even in her maturity she had great limitations. There were still plenty of difficulties for those who had to sail and manage her and these have been vividly described by Denis Griffiths in his full and scholarly study of the ship.[28] The paddle steamer could never be a fighting ship of the line in the navy, and in merchant shipping she could pay her way without subsidy only on a relatively few ocean routes and around the coasts. It was to be more than a generation

28. D Griffiths, *op cit*. In more popular works some extraordinary claims have been made for the *Great Western*. Thus *The National Maritime Museum Guide to Maritime Britain* has it on p143 that she made seventy crossings of the North Atlantic in her first eighteen months of service, which would indeed have been an incredible feat. In fact she made twenty.

before the monopoly of the world's carrying trade by the small wooden square rigged sailing ship was to pass under even a distant threat. But great experience in marine engineering and in the management of steamships was gained with the paddlers, just as in the navy a whole generation of engineers and officers familiar with steam had grown up. The *Great Western* influenced the development of the naval paddle steamship, French and American as well as British. She did more than that. Her commercial success gave the Great Western Steamship Company the confidence to build the huge iron screw driven *The Great Britain*, the first ship that showed the direction of development for all ships, merchant and naval, down to the present day. *The Great Britain* met three of the necessary constituents for the steamship to be generally competitive in the world's carrying trade. She was built of metal, she was big enough to begin to take advantage of the economies of scale, and she was propelled by a screw. All that was needed was an efficient engine, and for that the shipping world had to wait for another generation.

The introduction of iron construction

Wooden construction and steam propulsion were not compatible. The wooden ship was built up of hundreds – in a big vessel thousands – of separate pieces of timber of different kinds, fastened together with wooden trenails or iron or yellow metal bolts. The metal fastenings of a wooden vessel made up a surprisingly high percentage of both her weight and her cost: 300 to 400 tons of metal – and incidentally some 50 miles or so of spun oakum thread for the caulking of the seams – went into the construction of a large wooden vessel. This meant inevitably that she was a flexible structure. All wooden ships leaked to greater or lesser degree, but this was perhaps less important than the lack of coherence in a structure built in this way, which meant that she was ill suited to the vibration and stress which followed the installation of powerful steam machinery, the rotation of the crankshaft and the working of paddles. And if she was ill suited to paddle propulsion she was totally unsuited to propulsion by screw. Wooden vessels had to be treated very carefully in

A powerful constraint on the adoption of iron hulls in Britain was the government mail contract. Mail steamers were subsidised and, with a view to their employment in wartime as auxiliaries, their construction was subject to Admiralty approval. After an initial flirtation with iron construction in the early 1840s the Admiralty decided that iron was too vulnerable in battle and insisted on wooden hulls. For example, on the West India and Latin America mails the Royal Mail Steam Packet Co were not free to employ iron paddlers until 1853 (and screw steamers until 1863). Following the loss of RMSP's wooden Amazon *by fire in 1852, the policy was changed, but as an interim measure this ship was replaced by the wooden paddler* La Plata *shown here. She was launched by Robert Steele of Greenock in 1851 as the* Arabia *for Cunard, who built another ship of the same name. (CMP)*

This rather stylised print of the Aaron Manby *is the only known contemporary depiction of the first seagoing iron ship. Built of ¼in plate with lapped and riveted seams over angle-iron frames, the ship was knocked down after initial construction inland in Staffordshire and reassembled at London's Surrey Docks in 1822. After crossing the Channel the ship served for twenty years on French rivers and was not broken up until 1855, a testament to its sturdy construction.* (ScM)

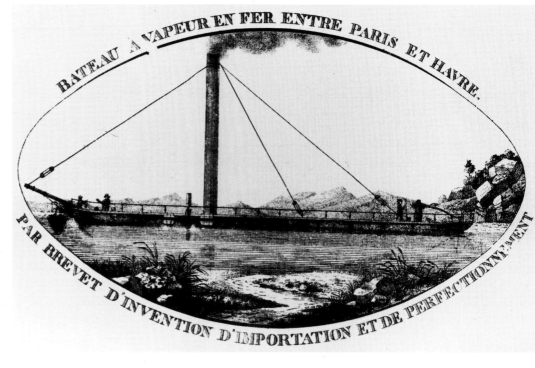

port. Before the middle of the nineteenth century floating harbours were a rarity; most vessels, in British ports at least, had to lie in tidal berths to load and discharge their cargoes. The shape of a wooden vessel changed as she took the ground or floated off. This process would have disastrous effects on the screw shaft and its bearings.

Wooden vessels had another vice, which was their tendency to hog as they aged. Their sharp ends, structurally the weakest parts of the vessel, were, of course, less buoyant than their full amidships sections. So they tended over the years to drop at the ends and a concave curve developed, to greater or lesser degree, in the keel. Combined with their general flexibility and liability to disintegrate into their constituent parts these weaknesses really ruled wooden vessels out of court as screw propelled merchant steamers. It is no coincidence that the birth of the screw propelled merchant steamer coincides not only with the registration of Francis Pettit Smith's patent for the placing of the screw between the sternpost and the rudder (see Chapters 4 and 7) but also with the development of the use of iron in shipbuilding.

Thus there were good reasons why steamship owners, rather than owners of sailing vessels, made the running in the development of iron construction. Moreover, the distribution of the necessary skills for iron shipbuilding and ship maintenance and repair was very limited. Few ports had these facilities, but they developed in the ports into which steamers, limited by the economics of their operation and limited patterns of trade, tended to operate. The merchant sailing ship had to operate worldwide and the skills of wooden shipbuilding were available worldwide also. Thus the majority of merchant sailing vessels continued to be built of wood. For a time the economic advantages of metal construction were much greater for the steamer than for the sailing vessel.

There were a number of difficulties in the way of the introduction of iron construction. For a long time iron girders and plate were of uncon-

trolled and uneven quality and they were not readily available, because of transport difficulties, in many shipbuilding districts. Moreover, they were expensive. It proved possible to build the world's first modern ship, *The Great Britain*, in iron in the very late 1830s because iron of acceptable, if uneven, quality was available at an acceptable price by way of the rivers Severn and Avon from the foundries of Coalbrookdale, now the site, approximately, of the Ironbridge Gorge Museum. Skill in iron working on the scale involved in building a large vessel was very rare and the techniques of iron shipbuilding had to be developed in the light of experience. We do not now know the basic order in which the early large iron vessels were constructed, though the evidence is that the most studied of them, *The Great Britain*, was built shell first, like a clinker-built wooden boat. The iron plates appear to have been riveted together around wooden formers to make a great shell, at least in the lower parts of the vessel, and the frames shaped to this shell and added to fit as reinforcement. This was the type of construction used to build the Viking ships and countless other small vessels and boats throughout the world and throughout history.

A very early pioneering venture was that of the *Aaron Manby*. Completed in April 1822 she was probably the first iron vessel to go to sea. She was built by the Horseley Iron Works in Staffordshire to serve on the river Seine, and anticipated many steamers built in Britain for inland waterways abroad by being fabricated in sections, which were taken to London for assembly at the Surrey Docks. She had oscil-

lating cylinders, a very early example of this type of propulsion, delivering 30hp and she steamed from London to Paris in June 1828. She appears to have been a technical success (she was still working in 1842 and reported to be in good condition as late as 1849) but she was a financial disaster for her promoters. That controversial naval officer Charles Napier, then a captain on half pay, lost his family fortune in this venture and was for some years forced to reduce his standard of living.[29] The Horseley Company was responsible for the second iron steam vessel, built for service on the river Shannon between 1823 and 1825, and she was soon followed by the early iron vessels of William Laird & Sons of Birkenhead to which reference will be made later in this chapter.

There were grave difficulties in the way of the

Iron hull construction: early practice as utilised by Laird for the pioneer iron warship Nemesis. (By courtesy of D K Brown).

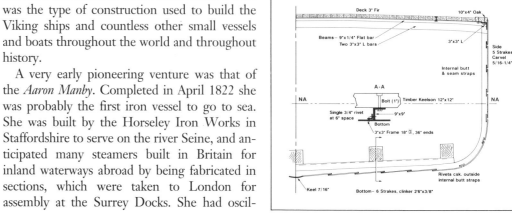

29. W A Baker, *op cit*, p30. H N Williams, *The Life and Letters of Admiral Sir Charles Napier*, (London 1917), p62.

introduction of iron construction for ships, including numerous technical problems to be solved.[30] There was the problem of corrosion which occurred most in the area of the boot-topping, between wind and water, and in the bow and stern sections, which tended to be working in heavily aerated water. This problem could be met by the liberal use of white lead paint with pitch as a top coat. But another problem proved more intractable. This was the business of fouling by marine organisms of various kinds. At first this was regarded as of little importance, and indeed the problem was negligible in the short sea trades around the coasts of Europe which were the main areas of employment of most early steamers. Those operating in British waters dried out in tidal harbours where any accretion could be relatively easily scraped off. But as vessels became larger and were more constantly employed entirely afloat the problem was to become formidable and to occupy much

time and talent, without early result. The method used in wooden vessels to discourage both marine growth and wood boring marine organisms was to sheath the vessel with a yellow metal alloy (laid over felt frequently soaked in Stockholm tar) the oxides of which were not adherent, so that as they washed off so did any nascent marine growth which had attached itself to the vessel's underbody. But 'coppering', as this process was called at first – later, more accurately, 'felting and yellow-metalling' – could not be the solution with an iron structure, since yellow metal and iron together in salt water constituted a primitive electric cell and disastrous electrolytic corrosion of the iron resulted.

This problem became more and more significant over the next generation as the use of iron tonnage developed. Dr Ewan Corlett gives a good summary of the problem, pointing out that as late as 1870 P&O was spending some £70,000 a year on cleaning the bottoms of its vessels, while ironclads of the French navy in 1866 spent an average of fifty-five days each in dry-dock being scraped down.[31] All sorts of preparations were applied in the hope that they would discourage growth, but it was to be a very

long time before effective antifouling paints were developed. The 'composite' vessel, usually wooden planked over iron frames and keel, stem and sternpost, in various combinations, was developed for a limited period in the 1860s and '70s largely because of this problem. She could be felted and yellow-metalled but had some of the advantages of iron construction – lighter and smaller frames – and she was probably cheaper to build than a wooden vessel of the same tonnage. It is an indication of the economic advan-

In every respect a forward-looking company, P&O introduced iron construction with the Pacha *in 1842 and had a screw propelled ship – Shanghai – by 1851. Nevertheless, P&O continued to find paddle steamers useful up to the mid 1860s for subsidised services like the Alexandria mails – part of the overland route to India – where economy and seakeeping were a secondary consideration to speed. One of the last was* Delta, *an iron vessel built in 1859, which could manage 14kts at deep draught, an impressive performance for the time. This engraving from* The Illustrated London News *can be compared with the internal profile draught from A&R Murray's* Shipbuilding and Steam Ships *(Edinburgh 1861), which shows both the accommodation and the mail rooms.*

30. For an excellent technical account of the difficulties and problems of early iron ship construction see E C B Corlett, *The Iron Ship* (London 1990), especially pp21-39.

31. *Ibid*, p38.

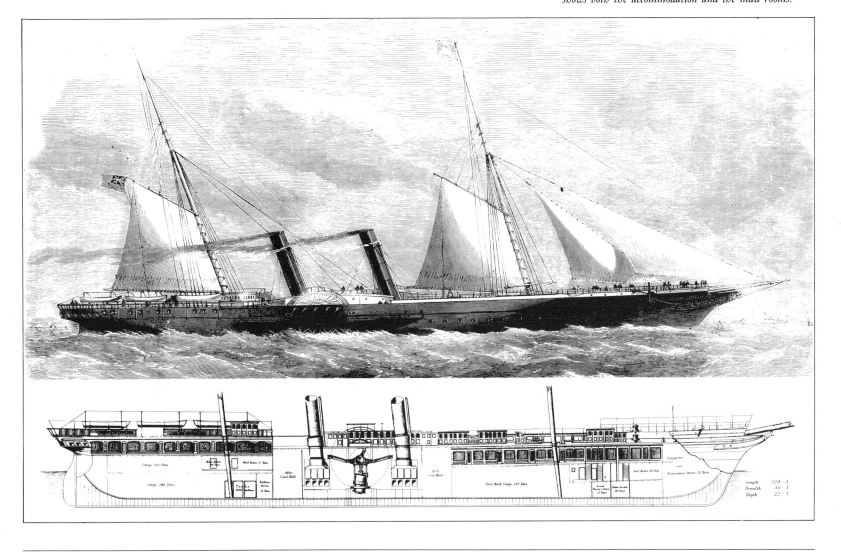

Cunard had screw ships from 1852 and built its last wooden ship the following year when the government gave up its requirement for wooden hulls in mail steamers. However, to have the fastest ships on the route still implied paddle propulsion and Cunard's last paddler, the iron-hulled Scotia *of 1862, held the Blue Riband for the fastest crossing until 1867 with average speeds of about 13.5kts, although it is claimed that she achieved 16.5kts on trials.* (CMP)

tages of employing iron tonnage that, despite these grave difficulties, the use of iron ships, particularly steamers, grew rapidly in the early decades of the second half of the nineteenth century.

Perhaps even more important was the problem of compass deviation. This great difficulty was overcome, at least to an extent which made iron vessels on deep water an acceptable insurance risk, by a series of experiments initiated by William Laird & Sons of the Birkenhead Iron Works, who were at the time engaged in a marketing drive to sell the iron ship which may well have been fundamental in the long run to the widespread adoption of iron tonnage. Trials were carried out by Commander Edward Johnson on board the Laird-built iron paddle steamer *Garry Owen* on the river Shannon as early as 1835. These experiments (which established Johnson in a successful career as an authority on the compass) led to a further series of trials in 1838 by Professor George Airy, then the As-

32. A Fanning, *Steady As She Goes* (London 1986), pp xxxii–xlii.

tronomer Royal, of a system of magnets and soft iron correctors placed within and around the binnacle. Airy's work was done on board the *Rainbow*, an iron paddle steamer built by Lairds for the General Steam Navigation Company. Modern research has shown that Airy's work had grave flaws[32] and the loss of many ships followed from the placing of undue faith in his methods. But the effect of his report, published in the *Transactions* of the Royal Society of 1839, was to lead to confidence that the problems of deviation had been solved. One of the more spectacular effects of these trials was a decision of the Great Western Steamship Company, made in late 1838 after Christopher Claxton, its Managing Director, had made passages in the *Rainbow*. This he revealed in a letter to Professor Charles Babbage, now thought of as the father of the computer, of 27 November, 1838.

We have settled to build an iron ship – and mean to construct her ourselves... I made a voyage in the *Rainbow*, took the bearings and the distance, worked the course and perfectly satisfied myself of the perfect adjustment of Professor Airy's Apparatus. Took some of my own on board and made many interesting experiments, found my compass correct in his Binnacles... The Professor explained them fully to me and so satisfied am I of his having

The General Steam Navigation's 580-ton Rainbow. *This paddler was important in the history of iron ships since she was the trials vessel for Airy's experiments into compass correction in 1838 while in the same year a voyage aboard the ship convinced the Managing Director of the Great Western Steamship Co that oceanic iron vessels were both possible and desirable: from this resolution* The Great Britain *was born.* (NMM)

conferred a vast benefit upon seamen that I would have no hesitation in crossing any sea or latitude with his corrections.[33]

Then Claxton drew attention to one of the weaknesses of Airy's system. 'The only doubt appears to be in the length of time the magnet will retain its power, or rather the exact degree of power necessary for the occasion. Should it wear off practice will detect it, it is well wrapped up in tallow, flannel & wood.'

The effect of the decision to build *The Great Britain* in iron was to prove very important. Grantham wrote in 1858, '*The Great Britain* iron steamer built in Bristol was at the time the boldest effort in iron shipbuilding, and formed a most remarkable feature in the history of this science.'[34] *The Great Britain* gave a crucial impetus both to iron construction and to the adoption of screw propulsion, and her successful survival of many winter months ashore in Dundrum Bay in 1846–47, in Dr Corlett's words, 'probably did more than anything else to convince the shipbuilding and shipping fraternities that iron was practicable material for large ships.'[35]

The Great Britain provides an admirable example of the specific advantages of iron construction. She benefited by about 24,000 cubic feet of hull space over her best capacity had she been built of wood and she weighed some 600 tons less – that much additional weight could be taken on board as fuel, cargo or passenger facilities, compared to the load capacity of a wooden vessel of similar size.

Perhaps the most enterprising of several industrial concerns which sought to promote the iron steamer in the late 1820s and '30s was that of William Laird & Sons of Birkenhead. Indeed,

this company played a large part in the establishment of the iron steamer as a viable structure for merchant shipping purposes. William Laird & Sons launched three small iron vessels in 1829-30 and then in 1831 built the first iron vessel to make an ocean voyage, the *Elburkah*, which was used with great success in the exploration of the river Niger. This vessel was followed by five more iron steamships built in 1833 and 1834 including the *Garry Owen* (236 tons, 80hp) already referred to in connection with compass experiments, which was steamed to the Shannon river in western Ireland and then operated there by the Dublin Steam Packet Company for thirty years, and two vessels which were to play an important part in the early surveying of the river Euphrates.

This survey was a necessary part of the work towards the establishment of fast communication with India. The Aleppo – Euphrates – Persian Gulf route was a possible alternative to that via the Red Sea to India.[36] These two vessels, the *Tigris* and the *Euphrates*, were respectively of 109 and 179 tons and of 20 and 50hp. Built at Birkenhead, they were dismantled, shipped out to the Middle East and re-assembled. Colonel Francis Chesney, the Commanding Officer of the Euphrates expedition of 1833, for which the vessels were built, reported on them most favourably:

It is but right to tell you that the iron vessels constructed by you far exceeded my expectations, as well as those of the naval officers employed in the late expedition, who would one and all bear testimony anywhere to their extraordinary solidity ... the *Euphrates* was as perfect when they laid her up in Bagdad as the first day when she was floated... It is my belief

Cunard suffered some short-term competition in the early 1860s from the Galway Line running from the west coast of Ireland. Four vessels were built specifically for this service, including the iron-hulled Hibernia *depicted here (Palmers, Newcastle 1863; 3008 tons), but the vessels proved to be too lightly built for Atlantic conditions and disappointingly slow. (CMP)*

that they will entirely supersede wood, on account of their comparative strength, cheapness, and durability, whenever people are satisfied that their only disadvantage – the free working of the compass – has been overcome.[37]

In the article quoted above it was asserted (perhaps under the inspiration of William Laird & Company) that 'there are boats built by Mr Laird in both north and south America – in all parts of India and on the Euphrates and the Indus – in Egypt, on the Nile – in the Mediterranean – on the Vistula, on the Shannon and on the Thames'. The claim that Laird's contacts were more or less worldwide is substantiated by his correspondence, part of which has recently become available for study.[38]

This correspondence does indeed show that the company was vigorously promoting the iron steamer at a time when iron was becoming available in quantities, qualities, and at prices, which made the building of iron ships a reasonable commercial proposition. Inherent in that prop-

33. Babbage MSS, British Library Add 37,191, f39.

34. J Grantham, *Iron Shipbuilding* (London 1858), p15.

35. E C B Corlett, *op cit*, p194.

36. J Sutton, *Lords of the East* (London 1981), pp133-4.

37. Quoted in an article by Augustin F B Creuze in the *United Services Journal* (May 1840), pp98-99.

38. Laird correspondence – in private hands.

osition, indeed, was the fact that by the late 1830s and early '40s it was possible to build in iron more cheaply than in wood – at least in some sizes of vessel. Iron ships were lighter and, as has already been shown in the case of *The Great Britain*, could offer more cargo space with the same tonnage and dimensions. From the very beginning they were built with effective watertight bulkheads and double bottoms, which made them better insurance risks. Lloyd's Register began the classification of iron vessels as early as 1837.

The marketing of the iron ship was faced, nevertheless, with difficulties. These included the fact that, for the very good reasons explained in Chapter 3 of *Steam, Steel and Shellfire*, uncertainties as to cost, as to the effectiveness of Airy's compass correction, and also as to the effect of shot on hull structures built of contemporary iron, conspired to make the naval authorities in the 1830s and early '40s still wary of this material. This meant that Admiralty contracts for iron vessels were slow in coming forward, although Lairds worked vigorously to promote them. It also meant that the paddle steamer postal packets, which ran from Falmouth to the Mediterranean and which at this time were naval vessels, and the subsidised merchant ship services which, as a condition of the mail contract, had to be vessels acceptable to the navy for possible war service, were also mostly wooden construction (although the *Dover*, a Laird-built packet of 1840, was perhaps the first British government-owned iron steamer). This limited the number of possible future orders for iron ships from government sources while the merchant shipping industry, as already explained, was slow in taking up iron construction for sailing vessels.

In this situation William Laird & Company engaged in a remarkable piece of sales promo-

tion, worthy of the most vigorous techniques of the end of the twentieth century. They built the *Nemesis* under conditions of some secrecy. She was a shallow draught iron paddle steamer which, while registered as a merchant ship and under Lairds' ownership, acted as a kind of privateer during the First China War of 1840–42. Lairds ensured vigorous publicity through instant journalism. A book hyping the *Nemesis'* role in the war was published shortly after its end in which as much attention as possible was drawn to the technical success of the *Nemesis*, particularly in river warfare. It seems likely that she played a not insignificant role in the wider adoption of iron construction.

The P&O took to iron construction for its paddle steamers as early as 1842. These early steamers were employed in service to the eastern Mediterranean. The P&O iron paddle steamer *Pottinger* of 1846 was the largest vessel ever built on the Thames to that date. Lloyd's Register classed iron vessels from the late 1830s, but with the proliferation of iron steamships in the '40s the formulation of rules for classification became a more and more complex problem and it was not until 1854, when the paddle steamer was no longer developing, that the first set of Rules was drafted. Thereafter the construction of wooden steamships rapidly ceased and by 1858 Grantham wrote,

It would not be difficult to follow the history of iron ships. The science which has been thus established was pursued most actively in the Clyde, the Thames, the Mersey and latterly in the Tyne and no port of any magnitude but can claim now a share in the work. Builders can number the vessels built by them by tens of hundreds and to attempt to list the aggregate numbers built up at this time in the United Kingdom would be a work of no mean difficulty.[39]

Despite the enthusiasm of this statement the merchant shipping industry's adoption of steam propulsion was, given the limited trades in which steam vessels could profitably be employed before the introduction of the compound engine and the considerable financial risks involved, rightly slow and cautious. Thus Lloyd's Register for 1853 shows only 187 steam vessels out of the 9934 listed, less than 2 per cent. Of these the greatest number, seventy-four, were iron screw vessels, fifty-four were wooden paddlers and fifty-three iron paddlers. Not surprisingly only six were wooden screw ships.

Dr Basil Greenhill

39. J Grantham, *op cit*, p15.

Typical European Paddle Vessels 1814–1865

Name	Flag	Built	Completed	Hull	Dimensions (length × breadth × depth in hold; tonnage) Feet–Inches Metres	Machinery (Maker, type, cyl diam × stroke in inches; power; max speed)	Remarks
THAMES, ex-DUKE OF ARGYLE	British	Alexander Martin, Port Glasgow	1814	Wood	76–6 × 14–6 × 7–0; 72 tons bm 23.3 × 4.4 × 2.1	Cook of Tradeston, side lever, 22 × 36; 14nhp; 6kts	Made first long seagoing passage in British waters (Glasgow–Thames in 1815)
MARGERY	British	Archibald MacLachlan, Dumbarton	1814	Wood	73–0 × 12–0 × 5–6; 38 tons bm 22.3 × 3.7 × 1.7	Cook of Tradeston, side lever, 22 × 24; 10nhp; 6kts	First steam packet on Thames and first across the English Channel
ELIZABETH	Russian	Charles Baird, converted at St Petersburg	1815	Wood	72–0 × 15–9 × c5–0; c38 tons disp 21.9 × 4.8 × c1.5	Baird, side lever, 18 × 21; 20nhp; 6kts service	Maintained regular St Petersburg–Kronstadt
STOCKHOLMSHÄXAN	Swedish	Samuel Owen, Stockholm	1816	Wood	31–3 × 11–6 × c3–0; tonnage unk. 9.5 × 3.5 × c0.9	Samuel Owen, oscillating; 4nhp; driving a screw	Sweden was the first European country after Britain to build steamers
PRINZESSIN CHARLOTTE	Prussian	John Rubie, Pichelsdorf, Prussia	1816	Wood	130–5 × 19–4 × c6–0; 236 tons grt 39.7 × 5.9 × c1.8	Boulton & Watt, side lever, 23.5 × 30; 14nhp;	First steamer built in Prussia; served on the Elbe
FERDINANDO PRIMO	Neapolitan	Libetta & Wolff, Naples	1818	Wood	127–4 pp × 20–2 × 9–6; 247 tons grt 38.8 × 6.2 × 2.9	Cook of Tradeston, side lever, 27 × 36; 50nhp; 6kts	First steamer to serve in the Mediterranean
ROB ROY	British	Archibald MacLachlan, Dumbarton	1818	Wood	80–10 × 15–10 × 9–0; 88 tons bm 24.7 × 4.8 × 2.7	David Napier, side lever, 30 × 36; 30nhp; 7kts	Claimed first regular steamer service in open coastal waters (Greenock–Belfast)
RISING STAR	British	Daniel Brent, Thames	1821	Wood	123–7 × 27–10 × 6–1; 428 tons grt 37.7 × 8.5 × 1.9	Maudslay, side lever, 42 × 36; 70nhp; 6kts	First steamer in the Pacific; built as a warship but served as a merchantman
AARON MANBY	British	Aaron & Charles Manby, Tipton, Staffs	1822	Iron	120–0 × 17–2 × 7–2; 116 tons bm 36.6 × 5.2 × 2.2	Manby, 2cyl oscillating, 27 × 36; 30nhp; 7kts	First iron steamer; built for service on the Seine
PALMERSTON	British	Hilhouse, Bristol	1823	Wood	105–8 × 19–10 × 11–2; 115 tons 32.2 × 6.1 × 3.4	J Dove of Liverpool, side lever	Inaugurated the Bristol–Dublin packet service
ENTERPRISE	British	Gordon, Thames	1824	Wood	133–0 × 27–0 × 16–5; 470 tons grt 40.6 × 8.2 × 5.0	Maudslay, side lever, 42 × 48; 120nhp; 7kts	First steamer to reach India (under sail and steam)
UNITED KINGDOM	British	Robert Steele, Greenock	1826	Wood	160–0 × 26–6 × 17–6; 1000 tons grt 48.8 × 8.1 × 5.3	David Napier, side lever, 51 × 60; 200nhp; 8kts	Largest packet steamer ever built (Leith–London service)
CONSTITUTIONEN	Norwegian	Unknown but possibly W E Evans, Thames	1826	Wood	99–0 × 17–0 × c10–0; 145 tons 30.2 × 5.2 × c3.0	Maudslay, side lever, 60nhp;	Inaugurated the Norwegian coast passenger service and worked it until 1866
ROYAL WILLIAM	British	Black & Campbell, Quebec	1831	Wood	176–0 × 28–0 × 17–9; 1370 tons grt 53.6 × 8.5 × 5.4	Bennet & Henderson, side lever, 51 × 60; 200nhp; 8kts	Made the first transatlantic crossing from Canada (1833)
TORRIDGE	British	William Clibbeth, Jr, Appledore, N Devon	1835	Wood	114–4 × 17–0 × 11–0; 207 tons 34.8 × 5.2 × 3.4	Cornish Copper Co, side lever; 90nhp	Established the Bristol–Bideford packet service; not broken up until 1871
GREAT WESTERN	British	Patterson, Bristol	1838	Wood	236–0 × 35–4 × 23–2; 1320 tons grt 71.9 × 10.8 × 7.1	Maudslay, 2cyl side lever, 73.5 × 84; 450nhp; 9kts	First steamer designed for transatlantic service
NEMESIS	British	Laird, Birkenhead	1840	Iron	184–0 × 29–0 × 6–0; 660 tons bm 56.1 × 8.8 × 1.8	Forrester, side lever, 44 × 48; 120nhp; 9kts	Registered in builder's name, serving as a privateer in Chinese war of 1841
PRESIDENT	British	Curling & Young, Thames	1840	Wood	268–0 × 41–0 × 32–9; 2360 tons grt 81.7 × 12.5 × 10.0	Fawcett & Preston, 2cyl side lever; 540nhp; 9kts	First transatlantic steamer lost
HIBERNIA	British	Robert Steele, Greenock	1843	Wood	248–0 × 35–10 × 24–2; 1422 tons grt; 75.6 × 10.9 × 7.4	R Napier, 2cyl side lever, 77.5 × 90; 500nhp; 12kts	One of the second batch of Cunard steamers
PERSIA	British	Robert Napier, Govan	1856	Iron	398–0 × 45–4, 29–10; 3300 tons grt 121.3 × 13.8 × 9.1	R Napier, 2cyl side lever, 100.5 × 120; 950nhp; 14kts	Cunard's first iron paddler and the first on the North Atlantic
MASSILIA	British	Samuda Bros, Thames	1860	Iron	309–11 × 36–1 × 22–4; 1640 tons grt; 94.5 × 11.0 × 6.8	Penn, 2cyl oscillating, 72 × 84; 400nhp; 14kts	One of the last group of P&O paddle steamers
WASHINGTON	French	Scott, Greenock	1864	Iron	345–7 × 43–7 × 30–2; 3408 tons grt 105.3 × 13.3 × 9.2	Greenock, 2cyl side lever, 95 × 104; 850nhp; 13kts	CGT (French Line); last transatlantic line to build paddlers

Notes Tonnage: bm = builder's measurement; disp = displacement; grt = gross registered tons.

2

Early Steamships in Eastern Waters

TRADE between Europe and the East was well established even in classical antiquity. However, it was well understood that the 'Far East' was very, very remote from western Europe, and to reach it meant making a lengthy and arduous journey, travelling ever *eastwards*, that involved crossing high mountains and inhospitable deserts. Nevertheless, towards the end of the fifteenth century it came to be recognised that the East might also be reached by travelling ever *westwards*. As this was the era of the great navigators, instead of proceeding by land in a caravan the new explorer–traders went, if possible, all the way by sea, hoping to fill a ship's capacious hold with a profitable return cargo.

The first properly documented attempt to find a way to the Indies by sailing westwards, by Columbus in 1492, ended in the Caribbean. Sailing eastwards, no all-sea route to the East was known until 1497 when the Portuguese admiral, Vasco da Gama, by sailing down the long western coast of Africa eventually rounded the stormy Cape of Good Hope and entered the Indian Ocean. Some twenty-three years later another Portuguese navigator, Ferdinand Magellan, discovered the strait (named after him) that leads round the bottom of South America to the Pacific – thereby establishing, potentially, a westwards seaway to the East. However, even by the Cape route to the East the distances and the times involved were of quite unprecedented length.[1]

Despite the drawbacks and hazards, the rewards from the disposal of an eastern cargo brought safely home could be great, and for the next four centuries (following de Gama's lead) rounding the Cape of Good Hope became the

accepted way to India and China. First to use the route were the Portuguese themselves. They were interested, particularly, in the Moluccas – the spice islands – a group situated far to the east in the East Indian Archipelago. The large island of Sumatra lay in the way to them and obliged shipping to traverse either the Strait of Malacca or that of Sunda. The Strait of Malacca was, and remains today, a 'choke point' since it comprises also the prime seaway between India and China, and for this reason the town of Malacca (though some 2000 miles from the Moluccas) attained too much importance as an *entrepôt* for the market in spices; so much so that in 1511 the Portuguese took it by force from the Malays, thereby establishing the first European settlement in the East.

Both the Portuguese and the Spaniards obtained trading concessions in the far-off Moluccas, to be joined and later ousted by the Dutch; but Britain and France, having fared less well in that region, were content for a while to trade in Malacca though at the same time both turned their eyes towards India.

However, on the last day of the year 1600 Queen Elizabeth I granted a charter to certain

merchants of London, by which they received the title of 'The Honourable East India Company' (the EIC or 'the Company') and a monopoly of English commerce with the East. At that time 'East India' meant almost anywhere east of Africa, but it soon came to imply India and especially the territory the Company acquired there – initially at Surat (1629) then at Madras (1639), Bombay (1668) and Calcutta (1690).

By the beginning of the nineteenth century other western powers had acquired their own enclaves in the East. Russia, and to a lesser extent Persia, were able to push their frontiers forward by land, but the more westerly nations still went by sea, sailing perforce round the Cape to the

---

1. The distance factor is rendered very clear when the distances from London to the following ports are compared with crossing the Atlantic from London to New York; *viz* Cape Town, nearly twice; Bombay, about three; Calcutta, three and a half; Canton, about four; while from London, via the Pacific, to Canton is nearly six times as far as from London to New York. The time factor (complicated by sailing ships being seldom able to follow a direct course) was much in evidence when, as an instance, Robert Clive first took passage to India in 1743; the vessel got aground off the Brazilian coast before it could round the Cape of Good Hope, and the voyage – including time in port for repairs etc – occupied in all fourteen months.

The Diana *of 1823 was the first steam vessel built in the East for which proper documentation survives, although like all the early vessels her machinery had to be imported from Britain. She was also the first steamer known to have seen action, since the earlier* Rising Star *arrived too late for the conflict for which she was designed and does not seem to have ever fired a gun in anger. (By courtesy of D K Brown).*

East, where the Dutch held sway in what today is Indonesia. The French were in Indo-china, the Spaniards were in the Philippines, and the Portuguese still retained a scattered variety of possessions. With Britain emerging as the premier manufacturing nation and with the Company's inheritance (following Clive's military successes) of a lion's share of India's wealth, it was therefore clear that the safety of the lines of communication between the two countries was becoming all-important.

However, with Lord North's Regulating Act (1773) and Pitt's India Act (1784) the British Government had begun to take a hand in the Company's affairs, and with Lord Grey's Act of 1834 the EIC was deprived of its unpopular monopoly; whereupon it ceased to engage in trade and turned instead – by reason of its long experience and great possessions – virtually to running India for the British Crown.

Despite these changes, the Company was still left managing all its major matters from its London headquarters (East India House, in Leadenhall Street) and, though phasing out its mercantile East Indiamen, it retained control not only of the vessels that transported the mails (also passengers, their servants, and their goods) between Britain and India, but also those that policed the eastern seas (and co-operated with the Royal Navy in times of conflict or rebellion). Those vessels based on the western side of India continued to be classed as the Bombay Marine (renamed the Indian Navy in 1830) while those based to the east, at Calcutta, comprised the Bengal Marine.

But around this time the introduction of steam navigation in India began to bring about revolutionary changes in the character of certain of the local ships, which led far-seeing persons to enquire whether steamships might also prove of benefit to the extremely lengthy voyage between Britain and India. However, before dealing with the problems associated with long distance steamer services, it is appropriate to list below some examples of the earliest steam vessels in the East.

The earliest steamers in the East

These vessels have little in common, because the early wooden steamers that are here described were built in India (or elsewhere in the East) but the iron steamers were first fabricated in Britain

then sent out in parts – by sailing ship – for assembly at an appointed destination. For both kinds of steamer, however, it would appear that the engines were made in Britain.

The Nabob's steamer (1819)

What was perhaps the first mechanically aided vessel to be seen in the East was a small steam yacht that was built around 1819, by William Trickett of Lucknow, for the Nabob of the native state of Oudh. It is reported to have been 50ft long, about 19 tons in burthen, and equipped with an 8hp engine that had been made at the Butterly Ironworks, near Ripon, in Derbyshire, England.

Unfortunately, being soon set aside as a toy and left to decay, few details relating to this vessel have survived, but it was said to be capable of a speed of 7kts or 8kts.

Diana [i] (1823), *Pluto* [i] (1822–24) and *Enterprize* [i] (1825)

These steam vessels, unlike each other in origin and structure, are grouped together because, as the only ones available on the occasion, they were the first steamers anywhere to engage in warfare. For the parts they played in the First Burma War, see the later sections on steamers in action.

Diana [i][2]

This small wooden paddle steamer, an outcome of private enterprise, was to have been built of English oak on the Pearl river in China, but the project had to be modified and she was instead built of Asian teak at Calcutta. The shipwrights were J Kyd and Company of Kidderpore, working under the supervision of John Anderson, a Scottish engineer; and the ship was launched on the Hooghly river on 12 July 1823. She had a tonnage of 132bm (Builder's Measurement; 89 as a steamer), was 100ft long pp (between perpendiculars), and was powered by two 16hp steam engines made by Maudslay, Sons & Field of Lambeth, London; the paddle wheels were only 12ft in diameter.

When she plied for hire as a tug on the lower reaches of the river, the Calcutta *John Bull*, with prophetic and lyrical insight, hailed the *Diana* as 'the harbinger of future vessels of her kind who will waft us to our native shores.' However, when in the following year the Burma War broke out, the Bengal Government purchased the little steamer, equipped her with Congreve rockets, and ordered her to the Irrawaddy river.

When the war was over *Diana* stayed on in Burma, and in the course of time was partly re-

built at Moulmein. Later she underwent a complete overhaul at Calcutta, following which she went back to Burma to be employed mostly along the Tenasserim coast (then newly annexed by Britain); but in 1835 she returned to Calcutta to be broken up – happily, however, her Maudslay engines, still in good order, were installed in the new steamer *Diana* [ii].

If the Nabob's steamer is discounted, *Diana* [i] claims to be the first steamship in India, as well as the first anywhere to engage in warfare.

Pluto [i]

This historic craft began life as a dredger, sweeping the Hooghly river for the Bengal Government, the steam engine which she had on board not being employed to propel the vessel but to drive a continuous chain of buckets. The engine was made in 1818 by T & W Gladstone of Liverpool, England, and the dredger was built, like *Diana* [i], by Kyd & Company at Kidderpore, where she was launched into the Hooghly in 1822.

However, when the war began the Bengal authorities converted the dredger into a paddle steamer, and subsequently she rendered valuable service in Burma both as a powered floating battery and as a transport vessel. After the war *Pluto* was despoiled of her engine (which was sold for use elsewhere) and suffered the indignity of being used as a coal hulk until 1829, when she sank in a gale.

Enterprize [i]

This renowned paddle steamer was built entirely in Britain; by rounding the Cape of Good Hope and proceeding to India, she became the first steamship to achieve those distinctions.

The reason for her lengthy voyage had its origin in the early 1800s, when a syndicate of London merchants, having come to the conclusion that it might be advantageous to establish a steamship service to India, decided to send Captain J H Johnston, RN, to sound out the opinion of their counterparts in Calcutta. The Calcutta merchants reacted enthusiastically to the proposal, and with assistance from the Indian Government raised a lakh of rupees (Rs100,000, about £10,000 at the time) to be awarded to the first steamship to make two round trips before the end of 1826 and averaging not more than seventy days per passage.

Perhaps the challenge was too rigorous relative to the inducement, the sole competitor

2. The same names were used repeatedly for many of the early steamers. They are distinguished by [i] or [ii] after their name to differentiate between first and second vessels of that name.

The Enterprise of 1824 was the first vessel to steam from Britain to India, endeavouring to win an Indian Government prize for a steamer service that could reach Calcutta in 70 days. In the event she took 113 days but demonstrated the potential of steam which was quickly followed up in the East. (ScM)

being provided by the London syndicate. They arranged to purchase a vessel already on the stocks (being built speculatively), named her – as a pun, it was said – *Enterprize*, and appointed Captain Johnson as her master. *Enterprize* was under construction at Deptford in the Thames-side yard of Gordon & Company (a firm about which little now seems to be known). However, considering that the date was some twelve years prior to the commencement of the Victorian era, she appears on a number of counts to have been a steamship in advance of her time.

Built of oak with fir decks, she was 141ft long pp, 27ft broad and 15ft in draught. Maudslay, Sons & Field of Lambeth fitted her with two 60hp engines, each with a cylinder 42in in diameter and a stroke of 4ft; and with paddle wheels 15ft in diameter her speed was expected to reach 9kts (though it seems not to have exceeded 6). There was bunkerage for 380 tons of coal, 10 to 12 tons of which were consumed per twenty-four hours, and she was equipped with an all-copper corrosion-resistant boiler weighing 32 tons.[3]

The ship was launched on 23 February 1825,

departed Falmouth on 16 August, called at Cape Town from 13 to 21 October (having put into a number of ports en route) and after battling with heavy storms in the Indian Ocean arrived safely on 7 December at Diamond Harbour (downstream from Calcutta). She had logged 13,522 nautical miles (15,572 statute miles) and taken just over 113 days on her historic voyage.

Enterprize had not met the rules of the competition but demonstrated that a steamer could make the long haul to India via the Cape of Good Hope (even though it might not be an economic proposition) and she was received with enthusiasm in Calcutta, and in Madras which she visited later. It is understood that Captain Johnston was given some of the prize money, but the steamer never attempted to return to Britain, because the Bengal Government shortly saw fit to purchase her for service in the Burma War.

After the war *Enterprize* was put to work as a tug on the Hooghly, with occasional trips to the Tenasserim coast and Singapore. But in 1829 she was sold to the Bombay Government to work with the paddle steamer *Hugh Lindsay* (described later) in developing the overland route to Britain via Suez. By then, however, she was ageing and it is not clear that she ever got as far as Suez. Therefore, later in the same year the Bengal Government bought her back and had her reconditioned while still at Bombay; she then returned to Calcutta (a voyage of some 2000 miles) to resume, for several years, her employment as a Hooghly tug. She paid a further visit to Singapore in 1834, having aboard the Bishop of Calcutta on a tour of his extensive dio-

cese. But in 1838 this romantic old steamer was condemned as unseaworthy and was broken up, though her Maudslay engines, being still in good order, were transferred to the replacement vessel, *Enterprize* [ii] under construction for the EIC at Kidderpore.

Willem de Eerste (1825)

This Dutch-owned steamship, fitted with British-made Maudslay engines, that saw service in the East Indies, was launched at Amsterdam on 4 August 1823, and thus pre-dates *Enterprize* [i] by eighteen months. However, she was first employed to run between Amsterdam and Hamburg, and did not follow *Enterprize* round the Cape until several years later. Unfortunately, in 1837 she was totally wrecked on one of the Lucipari Islands, off Amboina (Ambon) in the Moluccas.

Comet and *Firefly* (1825)

These were small sister-ships built in 1825 for John Anderson, the engineer of *Diana* [i], by Alexander & Company at Kidderpore docks, Calcutta. Each was 89ft long pp and 76 tons bm in burthen (55 as a steamer), and each was equipped with two 10hp London-made Maudslay engines which drove paddle wheels only 9ft in diameter. Although intended to be hired as tugboats on the Hooghly, they could also take passengers. However, the project seems to have been unprofitable, and after the death of Anderson followed by the winding up of Alexander & Company in 1831, the two little steamers were broken up.

---

3. Before it became possible to use freshwater in boilers, the deposit and corrosion occasioned by employment of seawater in iron boilers was such as to necessitate frequent cleaning and de-scaling, rendering them short-lived.

Vander Capellen (1825)

This Dutch-owned paddle steamer (236 gross tonnage) was built under British supervision at Kerr's yard in Surabaya, Java, and was the first steamer to be seen in that region. Her building arose out of a British proposal to establish a steamer service between the chief ports along the north coast of the island. Constructed of oak and fitted with two 25hp engines supplied by Fawcett & Company of Liverpool, England, she was launched on 23 November 1825; she was armed (principally against pirates) with eight carronades and four swivel guns; and according to the natives (impressed with the emissions from her smoke-stack) she owed her motion to 'the agency of the Devil'.

The steamer was soon chartered to carry troops and stores when the Dutch Government had a rebellion on its hands. She then sailed for Batavia (Djakarta) whence she was sent to Anjer, in the Sunda Strait, and then to Pontianak on the west coast of Dutch Borneo; and in April of 1827, being sent to Singapore to take in military supplies, she became the first steamer to be seen there. With the rebellion suppressed, the *Vander Capellen* reverted to her intended role and provided a regular service between Surabaya and Batavia. In 1840, however, she was replaced by a larger steamer and then undertook a variety of work, including a second visit to Singapore, until setting off northwards – having been purchased by the King of Cochin-China – after which her history is obscure.

Irrawaddy and three sister-ships (1827-28)

Diana [i] provided the first demonstration in the East of the advantages of a steamship, namely an ability to proceed under her own power, independently of the wind and/or current, and to *tow* other vessels (an item hitherto confined to a horse on a towpath); also by an ability to manoeuvre, particularly in shallow water by reason of a light draught. Protagonists of steam navigation in the East, like Captain Johnston and the Governor-General of India, Lord William Bentinck, saw the advantages clearly and were instrumental in following them up, one way in which they did so being to introduce a steamer service on the river Ganges.

With this purpose in mind, two steamers were built for the Indian Government by J Kyd & Company at Kidderpore, Calcutta, each constructed of teak and fitted with two 40hp Maudslay engines shipped out from London. Named *Irrawaddy* and *Ganges*, the vessels were launched respectively on 1 January and 14 February 1827,

and though essentially river craft they occasionally put to sea, for example running down the Burmese coast and to Rangoon, while in 1829 *Ganges* was for a time based at Bombay.

Two smaller steamers, *Burhampootur* and *Hooghly*, were added in 1828; the first, built at Kyd's yard, was launched on 19 January, while the second was constructed by the Howrah Dock Company (across the river from Calcutta) and launched on 20 March. After tests on the Hooghly the second was judged the better steamer, and *Burhampootur* was relegated to local work. *Hooghly*, under Captain Johnston, became a kind of research vessel and undertook a series of experimental voyages up the Ganges.

Setting out on the Hooghly from Calcutta on 8 September, she reached the Ganges after five days, upstream of which she continued (steaming against the current and anchoring at night) until arriving at Allahabad on 1 October – an 800-mile voyage on which she spent in all twenty-three days, though the return voyage downstream took only fourteen days. The experiment was repeated in 1829 and again in 1830 (this time with Lord Bentinck also aboard) and the information gathered paved the way for regular steamer services on the great river.

However, by the 1830s all four steamers were becoming dated and showing their age, a circumstance that gave rise to Captain Johnston's mission to England, described later. Summarised data for the four wooden steamers are given in Table 2/1.

Forbes (1829) and *Hugh Lindsay* (1829)

By this time steamships, becoming more reliable, were being increased in size and power. The *Forbes*, planned as a steam tug by Captain W N Forbes, was built at the New Howrah Dock Company on the Hooghly; she was 302 bm in tonnage, 127ft in length, and 120hp, the last catered for by a pair of engines supplied by Boulton & Watt from England.

She was launched on 21 January 1829, and duly took her place as a tugboat on the Hooghly river. But her claim to fame derives from the fact that in 1830 she was chartered to tow a sailing barque, *Jamesina*, down to Singapore then up – against the monsoon – to the Pearl river estuary off Canton, the purpose being to outstrip other sailing vessels and capture the annual market with the 840 chests of Bengal opium that the *Jamesina* had aboard. By re-coaling at Singapore, with additional fuel loaded on the barque, the tug and her client made the journey in thirty-six days, and *Forbes* became the first steamship to be seen in China.

In later years she was chartered to run in the EIC's service between Calcutta and Suez but, proving too old and slow, by 1837 she returned to work for many years as a tug on the Hooghly river.

It is chronologically correct that the *Hugh Lindsay*, a once well-known vessel belonging to the EIC's Bombay Marine, should appear in the present mixed collection of early steamships. She

Table 2/1: Early Steamers in Eastern Service

Name	Launched	Length (feet)	Tonnage (bm)	Horsepower (nhp)
Wooden steamships built at Calcutta				
IRRAWADDY & GANGES	1827	110	305	80
BURHAMPOOTUR	1828	99	152	50
HOOGHLY	1828	105	158	50
British-built iron steamers assembled at Bombay				
COMET	1839	132	205	40
METEOR	1839	102	150	25
PLANET	1840	129	397	60
SATELLITE	1840	129	335	60
ARIADNE & MEDUSA	1839-40	134	132	70
British-built iron steamers assembled in Mesopotamia				
EUPHRATES	1835*	105	179	50-55
TIGRIS	1836*	87	109	20
NIMROD, NITOCRIS & ASSYRIA	1840+	103	153	40

Notes: *Launched at Bir. +Launched at Busorrah (Basra).

A model of the Lord William Bentinck *and her sister-ships* Thames, Megna *and* Jumna. *Built to the order of the Hon East India Co by Maudslay, Sons & Field in 1832, they were the first iron vessels built on the Thames and were shipped to India in sections. These vessels were known as 'Peacock's iron chicks' after their promoter Thomas Love Peacock the novelist, who was also an East India Co official; they were used to tow trains of 'flats', or barges, on the Ganges. (ScM)*

was constructed of teak in the Company's dock-yard, as the first steamer to be built in Bombay. Her tonnage was rated at 411 bm, her length was 140ft pp, and she was powered by two 60hp engines supplied by Maudslay of Lambeth, London. Launched in 1829, *Hugh Lindsay* was intended to provide a mail and passenger service between Bombay and the Red Sea, and further details will be found on page 36.

Lord William Bentinck **and three others (1832-35)**

Because the *Irrawaddy* and her sister-ships, though doing good work on the Hooghly and Ganges, were becoming dated and slow the Governor-General of India (Lord William Bentinck) sent Captain Johnston on a mission to seek out the latest developments in steamship design. In London, Johnston met Thomas Love Peacock, who not only held a high-ranking post as Assistant Examiner at East India House but also – and in addition to his eminence as a novelist and poet – had become an expert in the principles and practice of steam navigation. The outcome was that the two men co-operated in planning four new river steamers that were to be built of iron in Britain and sent out to Calcutta.

But since river steamers could hardly be expected to tackle a very long ocean voyage, the manner of getting them to their destination called for the application of a novel feature that

had been introduced a few years earlier.[4] The steamers were to be prefabricated in Britain then crated up in parts and sent round the Cape, in a sailing vessel, to be re-assembled in Calcutta. These early iron steamers came to be nicknamed 'Peacock's iron chicks'; planned at the same time were four 'accommodation boats' to be towed behind a steamer.

The four steamers were alike in their main features; 275 tons bm, 120ft (or 125ft) long, and with oscillating cylinder engines developing 60hp to drive paddle wheels that were only 15ft in diameter and 20in in width. The contract for their construction was awarded to Maudslay, Sons & Field, a London firm that usually made engines rather than complete ships.

These ships were the first iron steamers built on the River Thames, and were the first to be sent to India. The first, *Lord William Bentinck*, was launched at Pedlar's Acre, near Westminster Bridge, in July 1832, and after satisfactory tests was dismantled for trans-shipment to Calcutta where she was re-launched in April 1834 (the voyage out lasting from March until August 1833). *Thames* followed in 1832, with *Jumna* and *Megna* in 1833, to be reassembled and operational at Calcutta in October 1834, and March and June 1835, respectively.

Indus [i] (1833) and *Indus* [ii] (1837)

Though not a prefabricated vessel, it is convenient on chronological grounds here to mention the *Indus* [i], a small wooden paddle steamer that was built by Ardaseer Cursetje (a member of a famous family of shipwrights) at Bombay's Mazagon dockyard in 1833. He fitted her with an engine of about 12hp that he imported from Britain, and for a while in 1834 he ran her daily as a mail and passenger ferry across Bombay harbour. But in 1835 the vessel was acquired by a

Bombay merchant for a trading venture in the province of Sind (then newly opened to commerce). He secured the temporary service of Lieutenant John Wood RN as her commander, in which office – as he records in his books – on taking the little steamer up the river Indus, to visit Hyderabad, he had 'the proud satisfaction of unfurling our country's flag on the Indus from the first steamer that ever floated on its celebrated waters.'[5]

Builders of iron ships soon saw the advantages of prefabrication, and in particular the firm of William Laird & Son was quick to develop the technique at its Birkenhead Ironworks, on the river Mersey. One vessel so produced was the armed paddle steamer *Indus* [ii] (308 tons, 115ft long, 60hp) which, on completion at the Birkenhead yard (as vessel No 10) in May of 1837, was shipped in sections to Bombay – following those of *Lord William Bentinck* and the 'iron chicks' round the Cape of Good Hope, to be assembled in the East India Company's dockyard, whence she was eventually launched in 1839.

The subsequent movements of *Indus* [ii] are somewhat obscure, but she seems to have run between Bombay and the river Indus, transporting troops and stores, though spending much of her time on the Indus itself or on its major tributaries.

---

4. In 1821 the *Aaron Manby*, an iron steamer (116 tons, 30hp) was built at the Horseley Company's works at Tipton, near Birmingham. Since Tipton was virtually in the centre of England, the vessel was built in sections which were then taken by canal transport to be put together at Rotherhithe, on the Thames. It seems to have been the first instance of the prefabrication of an iron ship (made at one place and reassembled at another) and it was entirely successful, even to the extent that the *Aaron Manby* safely crossed the English Channel to France and worked for several years on the river Seine.

5. *Journey to the Source of the River Oxus* (London 1841 & 1872).

Comet and Meteor (1839), Planet and Satellite (1840), Ariadne and Medusa (1839–40)

In January 1839 Lairds of Birkenhead completed two small river steamers, *Comet* and *Meteor* as ships numbered 18 and 19, which were duly launched at Bombay dockyard later in the same year. Likewise, the somewhat larger *Planet* and *Satellite*, probably built by Forrester & Co at Liverpool, were eventually launched at Bombay in 1840. These vessels were armed with both heavy and light guns, being destined to serve principally in the Indus flotilla – that is, on the great river and its tributaries, and sometimes they operated several hundreds of miles from the sea. *Satellite* is listed as stationed in Sind up until 1873.

The four astronomically-named iron steamers were soon followed by the classically-designated sister-ships *Ariadne* and *Medusa* which, as the largest prefabricated steamers to date, were completed at Birkenhead (as Nos 25 and 26) in December 1839 and duly launched at Bombay in 1840. Like their predecessors these two vessels served in the Indus flotilla, but in September 1841 they were ordered to join the British task force in China, a venue they reached in May 1842, after first calling at Calcutta then having to put back to Singapore for repairs following an encounter with a violent hurricane in the South China Sea. However, soon after her arrival *Ariadne* struck an uncharted rock off an entrance to Chusan harbour and, despite great efforts to save her, was so badly holed that she sank in deep water.

Medusa carried on and earned a name for herself, since her shallow draught allowed her to lead the way (often with other vessels in tow) into harbours or fortified rivers. After the war *Medusa* was employed in mapping the Chusan archipelago, until she returned to Bombay at the end of 1845. She next saw active service in 1852, taking part in the Second Anglo-Burmese War, but afterwards, in 1853, while still on the Irrawaddy, she struck a submerged rock and suffered the same fate as befell her sister-ship (though no lives were lost and her five guns were later salvaged).

Data on the six prefabricated iron paddle steamers are sparse, but their principal dimensions and so on are summarised in Table 2/1.

Early steamers of the Royal Navy serving in the East.

Some early steamships were neither built in, nor imported, to the East, but on occasion were directed there by the Admiralty in support of diplomatic or more forceful missions. As explained in the companion volume *Steam, Steel and Shellfire*, paddle steamers had limited appeal to a navy wedded to a battlefleet strategy; consequently, it was the East India Company that first gained experience with steamers and was the first ever to use them in warfare (in Burma).

Even so, their value in warfare was not fully appreciated until the First China War when it was clearly demonstrated that steamers could

A sophisticated development of the line of towed flats was this 'steamer train' on the Ganges. The barges were shallow draught and articulated, towed by paddlers built by Vernon & Co of Liverpool with engines by Rennie. The scheme was an ultimately unsuccessful attempt to cope with the gradual shoaling of the upper river and the competition of the railways. (By courtesy of Jean Sutton)

Table 2/2: Early Steamers of the Royal Navy that saw Service in the East

Name	Type	Built	Launched	Tonnage (bm)	Horsepower (nhp)	Guns	Service in the East
MEDEA	Wooden, paddle	Woolwich	1833	835	220	4	Mediterranean 1834-40; China 1844
HERMES	Wooden, paddle	Portsmouth	1835	716	220	6	Mediterranean 1836; Burma 1852-53
DRIVER	Wooden, paddle	Portsmouth	1840	1056	280	6	China 1842; Borneo 1845
VIXEN	Wooden, paddle	Pembroke	1841	1054	280ihp	6	China 1842-44; Borneo 1845
SPITEFUL	Wooden, paddle	Pembroke	1842	1054	280	6	Borneo 1846
FURY	Wooden, paddle	Sheerness	1845	1124	515	8	China 1849, 1856-57
INFLEXIBLE	Wooden, paddle	Pembroke	1845	2122	350	6	China 1849, 1957
SPHINX	Wooden, paddle	Woolwich	1846	1056	500	–	Borneo/Thailand 1850; Burma 1851; China 1860
REYNARD	Iron, screw	Deptford	1848	516	60	8	Borneo 1849; China 1851 (wrecked)
VULCAN	Iron, screw	Blackwall	1849	1747	350	–	China 1860

Notes: The *Vulcan* was built as an iron screw frigate by Ditchburn & Mare and converted to a troopship in 1851.

prove of great value, not only because of their mobility and shallow draught, and their ability to tow other vessels (be they small boats or battleships), but also because they could serve as warships in their own right. However, at the commencement of the China War the only steamers mingling with the British warships were those of the Company, and it was not until near the end of hostilities that steamers of the Royal Navy rounded the Cape and reached the

6. In M Levien (ed), *The Cree Journals* (Exeter 1981), p116.

distant theatre of operations. Brief details of these and other early steamships of the Royal Navy that saw service in the East are listed in Table 2/2.

The two Admiralty steamers that reached China towards the end of the war were HMS *Vixen* (which arrived in the spring of 1842, in time to be present at the attack on Chin-keang-foo and the siege of Nanking) and HMS *Driver* (which, as noted by Surgeon E H Cree,[6] arrived on 25 August 1842, bringing the mail, including a letter from his sister dated nearly six months previously. Later, Cree mentions that in Sep-

tember 1845, when at Hong Kong, *Vixen* temporarily took aboard 500 boxes containing $2 million in silver and weighing about 50 tons, as part of China's reparation money. The other ship, *Driver*, on leaving China returned to England by way of Borneo, New Zealand and Rio de

Typical of the numerous small assignments carried out by British naval steamers in the East was Medea's *attack on a nest of piratical Chinese junks in Mirs Bay in March 1850. The 835-ton paddle sloop was armed with two 10in shell guns and two 32pdr smooth bores, to which the Chinese vessels had no answer. Engraving of the action from* The Illustrated London News.

Janeiro, becoming the first steamer to circum-navigate the world.

HMS *Fury* and HMS *Inflexible* served in the Second Anglo-Chinese War (1856-57) and were present at the Battle of Fatshan (Foshan) Creek, near Canton. *Spiteful* took part (with the Company's steamer *Phlegethon*) in the attack on Brunei in 1846 and in other operations in Borneo. *Sphinx*[7] (accompanied by *Nemesis*) in 1850 took Sir James Brooke on his abortive diplomatic mission to Siam, a task carried out successfully in 1855 by Sir John Bowring when he went there in HMS *Rattler*.

After the war with China it fell to the lot of the Royal Navy to protect British shipping from depredation by the many native pirates, whose lairs lay along the much-indented south coast. Steamers played a significant role in these activities. Thus, in September 1849 HMS *Medea* destroyed a number of piratical junks at Tienpak, 130 miles west of Hong Kong; and in March 1850, in co-operation with the Chinese authorities, accounted for thirteen junks and 250 pirates in Mirs bay northeast of Hong Kong. Also in September 1849, HMS *Fury*, with the sailing sloop HMS *Columbine*, inflicted a resounding defeat in Bias Bay (beyond Mirs Bay) on the pirate chief Chui-apoo; while in the next month *Fury*, *Columbine* and the Company's steamer *Phlegethon* utterly defeated the notorious Shapng-tsai, blowing up his 12-gun flagship and destroying twenty-seven junks in the Tonquin estuary. These efforts brought piracy in the south of China temporarily to a halt.

The routes to India

Before the Suez Canal an eastbound voyager would find no outlet at the end of the Mediterranean Sea, but there existed an option of disembarking from one ship, then travelling overland to a port from which, in another ship, the voyage might be resumed. A journey of that kind, though still largely made by water, came to be known as an 'overland route'; and for overland routes to India there were at least two possibilities:
1. To disembark at, say, Alexandria, then travel through the inhospitable isthmus of Suez to the Red Sea, whence to continue onwards in another ship (thus avoiding a long haul down to, and up from, the southern cape of Africa).

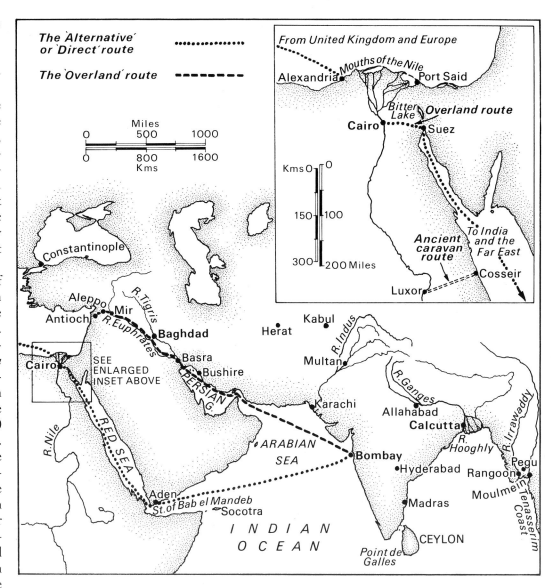

The Overland Routes to India. (Map drawn by Denys Baker)

2. To disembark at, say, Antioch, then travel through what again was very inhospitable terrain to the upper reaches of the river Euphrates, down which to continue in another ship to the Persian Gulf and the Indian Ocean (thus avoiding a voyage round not only Africa but also Arabia).

However, in the mid-nineteenth century not much was known about the overland sections – nor, for that matter, about the Red Sea, the Euphrates or the Persian Gulf – save that they were by no means pleasant or safe places in which to be.

The Euphrates route

The prime instigator of this option was Colonel F R Chesney, who, to begin with, worked largely alone, braving the hostility of local tribesmen, secretly to survey the great river while travelling down it on a cabined raft. Impressed by his results, the British Government appointed him

leader of The Euphrates Expedition, which was to utilise the technique of prefabrication to put two small iron steamers on the upper waters of the river.

Accordingly, Laird & Co constructed at Birkenhead Ironworks two small steamers (numbered initially as ships 4 and 5) which, duly named *Euphrates* and *Tigris*, were in January 1835 shipped out in sections, in the sailing vessel HMS *Columbine*, to Antioch whence teams of camels carried them over some 100 miles of difficult country to be assembled on the riverside at Mir.

Euphrates, launched on her eponymous river on 26 September 1835, made a safe if lengthy descent and arrived at Bussorah (Basra) on 19 June 1836. *Tigris*, however, though keeping in

7. In 1865 HMS *Sphinx*, returned from the East, was assigned as escort to the *Great Eastern* when she had been specially converted to lay a submarine telegraph cable across the Atlantic.

The small iron paddler Fire Queen *was originally built at Liverpool in 1843 and went out to the East via the Cape, but in 1847 she was purchased by the Royal Navy for use as a yacht. She enjoyed a long career and was not sold out of the service until 1883. (CMP)*

close touch with her colleague, was suddenly and fatally wrecked by a violent storm on 2 May 1836, with a tragic loss of some twenty lives.

Euphrates continued her valuable survey work into the Gulf, and the East India Company – having in mind both an overland route and the security of western India – ordered from Lairds three prefabricated iron war steamers (Nos 22, 23 and 24) which, named *Nimrod*, *Nitocris* and *Assyria*, were shipped out in June of 1839 and assembled in the spring of 1840, this time at Busorrah, on the Shatt-al-Arab waterway (formed by the confluence of the Euphrates and the Tigris).

The three steamers were first employed on the lower Tigris, but during 1841–42 *Nimrod* (Lieutenant C D Campbell) and *Nitocris* (Lieutenant J F Jones) made an epic *ascent* of the Euphrates, steaming upstream for 1130 miles before their return. Meanwhile, *Assyria* carried out a survey of the river Karun (flowing into the Shatt-al-Arab from Persia).

In September 1842 *Euphrates*, *Nimrod* and *Assyria* were sent to Bombay, supplementing the Indus flotilla during the Sind campaign (though *Assyria* and probably *Nimrod* returned to the Gulf in 1856 during the war with Persia); but *Nitrocris* continued to conduct an extensive survey of the Gulf region.[8] In 1844 *Euphrates* was listed as an engineless 'iron flat' and reduced in complement; *Nitocris* followed the same path in 1855, but *Assyria* seems to have continued in good shape, being used in surveying the Punjab rivers in 1860.

Some details of these prefabricated iron steamships are listed in Table 2/1.

The Suez route

Though Captain Johnston had taken *Enterprize* [i] round the Cape of Good Hope, his lengthy voyage had shown that the all-sea route would not provide a commercially viable steamer service to India, and even he himself had long been an advocate of a shorter overland route. But an overland service did not become possible until February 1835, when it was arranged that the Admiralty's packet boat service to Malta would be extended to call monthly at Alexandria, while

the East India Company would run a corresponding steamer service between Suez and Bombay. However, the joint service experienced many teething troubles: the first steamer the Company sent to Suez was the *Hugh Lindsay* and her bunkerage proved hardly adequate for a long run against the monsoon, and there were difficulties over establishing suitable coaling stations. Thus the timekeeping of the Company's ships could seldom be relied on, and there was poor co-ordination with the Admiralty's ships.

Moreover, the overland section, though short in length compared with the two voyages, introduced problems of its own, since it proved no easy task to disembark the passengers, unload the mails and the often considerable passengers' baggage, and transport the lot across some 50

miles of hot dusty desert – on a bewildering assortment of native carts, camels, horses and donkeys – only to trans-ship the whole into a second vessel, while ensuring that nothing was left behind or lost.

Despite the drawbacks, it was the Suez route that was favoured for development, and eleven years after the debut of *Enterprize* [i] (and after she was found too lacking in efficiency for the Suez run), the *Hugh Lindsay* was joined by *Atalanta*, as the first of a series of ocean-going steamships built in Britain which, of necessity (being inappropriate for prefabrication), reached India under their own sail and steam around the Cape.

Table 2/3 shows that after the initial gap such steamships were launched in fairly rapid suc-

Table 2/3: Early Steamers Built in Britain that went to the East via the Cape of Good Hope

Name	Built	Launched	Hull	Tonnage	Horsepower (nhp)	Destination
ENTERPRIZE [i]	Deptford	1825	Oak	450	120	Calcutta
ATALANTA	Blackwall	1836	Oak	616	210	Bombay
BERENICE	Glasgow	1837	Oak	664	230	Bombay
SEMIRAMIS [i]	Liverpool	1837	Oak	733	300	Bombay
MADAGASCAR	Blackwall	1838	Oak	350	110	Calcutta*
ZENOBIA [i]	Glasgow	1839	Oak	684	280	Bombay
QUEEN	Limehouse	1839	Oak	760	220	Calcutta
CLEOPATRA	Gravesend	1839	Oak	769	220	Bombay
SESOSTRIS	Gravesend	1840	Oak	876	220	Bombay
NEMESIS	Birkenhead	1840	Iron	660	120	Calcutta*
PHLEGETHON	Birkenhead	1840	Iron	510	90	Calcutta
INDIA	Greenock	1840	Oak†	1200	350	Calcutta
PROSERPINE	(Thames)‡	1841	Iron	400	90	Calcutta
PLUTO [ii]	Deptford	1841	Iron	450	90	Calcutta
FIRE QUEEN	Liverpool	1843	Iron	313**	200	Calcutta

8. See J F Jones, *Narrative of a Journey ... in the Steamer Nitocris* (Baghdad 1847).

Notes: *Directed first to China. **Also listed as 500 tons. †With iron bulkheads. ‡Probably Blackwall or Deptford (Ditchburn & Mare).

The newly delivered HEIC's Phlegethon *(far right) in action alongside Royal Navy warships at Chusan in 1841 during the First Anglo-Chinese War. This paddle sloop was an early product of the Lairds' iron shipbuilding expertise, being launched from their Birkenhead shipyard in 1840.* (NMM)

cession. Some were commercial ventures (like the *India* and *Fire Queen*) but most were built for the EIC and went either to Bombay – to join the Company's Indian Navy,[9] to be assigned to patrolling the seas of western India or to the Suez run – or to Calcutta, to join the Bengal Marine to maintain order and communications in the eastern seas.

The paddle sloop *Atalanta* was built in Blackwall, on the Thames, by Wigram & Green, and engined by Maudslays of Lambeth. She was the second steamer to round the Cape, and the first to use steam all the way, leaving Falmouth on 29 December 1836, and arriving at Bombay after 106 days (36 of them spent in ports), having logged 11,806 nautical miles and consumed 989 tons of coal. *Berenice*, built and engined by Robert Napier of Glasgow, covered the same course in 89 days (25 in ports) but logged 12,929 nautical miles and burnt 1,076 tons of coal. Both steamers were assigned to the Bombay-Suez run, but *Atalanta* served in the First China War, and *Berenice* later featured in the Second Burma War, the Persian War and the Second China War.

Semiramis [i], assigned to the Indus flotilla, carried troops to the Indus and the Persian Gulf during the First Afghan War, but in 1839, after suffering severe damage in Bombay harbour, she was replaced by *Zenobia* [i] (purchased as an Irish cargo steamer built by Napier). *Madagascar*, first in Portuguese ownership, was purchased for the First China War but was lost by fire in 1841, her

officers and men suffering grievously in the hands of their Chinese captors before their release could be negotiated.

The Thames-built wooden steamers *Queen*, *Cleopatra* and *Sesostris*, and the iron steamers *Nemesis*, *Phlegethon*, *Proserpine* and *Pluto* [ii] all featured prominently in the First China War. In 1847, when en route from Bombay to Singapore, *Cleopatra* was lost with all aboard without trace, somewhere off the Malabar coast. *Sesostris* and *Proserpine* served in the Second Burma War, while *Nemesis*, *Phlegethon* and *Pluto* [ii] were involved in various actions in Borneo.

The Clyde-built wooden merchant vessel *India* was the first steamer to carry a cargo round the Cape of Good Hope. In 1845 she was acquired by the P&O Company but, developing dry rot, was within four years reduced to a hulk. The iron *Fire Queen* (not to be confused with a wooden steamer with the same name, owned by the EIC) was a commercial vessel built for Mackay & Company, of Calcutta, on behalf of a projected steamer service between that city and Singapore. However, following an unpromising beginning, the venture seems to have been outclassed in 1845, when a branch service of the P&O was inaugurated over the same route.

When early steamships were being imported to India from Britain, others were being constructed nearer to hand. Usually these were built of teak, a wood resistant to rot and marine boring worms, and it was claimed that they lasted longer and sailed faster than equivalent vessels built of oak. However, all of the engines, and also the prefabricated parts of the iron ships, were made in Britain.

Table 2/4 details some steamers acquired by the EIC during this period (see also *Diana* [i] and *Pluto* [i] detailed earlier).

Diana [ii], built to the orders of the Straits Settlements Government by J A Currie & Company of Salkia, Calcutta, was fitted with the London-made Maudslay engines recovered (still in good condition) when *Diana* [i] was dismantled. As an armed steamer, *Diana* [ii] patrolled the seas from the Strait of Malacca to Borneo, employed in maintaining communications and the suppression of piracy. Similarly, *Enterprize* [ii] was fitted with Maudslay engines taken out of *Enterprize* [i] but was also given a newly-available corrosion-resistant boiler system. She saw service in the First China War.

Snake, a small steamer of the Indian Navy, had only one gun and a complement of but six men, but she was one of the first warships to navigate the river Indus; she survived as a harbour boat and later as a hulk until at least 1863. *Tenasserim*, half-sister to the British-built *Queen*, ran regularly between Calcutta and Burmese ports and also served in the First China War. *Victoria* was employed on the Bombay–Suez run but in 1843 inaugurated the first steamer service between India and the Straits Settlements. In 1860 she and *Zenobia* [ii], with their engines removed, helped to lay the first Indo-European telegraph cable.

---

9. Prior to 1830 the Indian Navy was known as the Bombay Marine.

Table 2/4: Early Steamers Built in the East

Name	Built	Launched	Hull	Tonnage	Horsepower (nhp)	Main base
DIANA [ii]	Calcutta	1836	Teak	133 bm*	50	Singapore
ENTERPRIZE [ii]	Calcutta	1838	Teak	300 bm	120	Calcutta
SNAKE	Bombay	1838	Iron	40 bm	10	Bombay
TENASSERIM	Moulmein	1839	Teak	513	220	Calcutta
VICTORIA	Bombay	1839	Teak	705	230	Bombay
AUCKLAND	Bombay	1840	Teak	945	220	Bombay
SEMIRAMIS [ii]	Bombay	1842	Teak	960**	330	Bombay
NAPIER				445	90	
CONQUEROR	Bombay	1844	Iron	259	50	Bombay
MEANEE				208	-	
FEROOZ	Bombay	1848	Teak	1147 bm	500	Bombay
ZENOBIA [ii]	Bombay	1851	Teak	1003 bm	280	Bombay

Notes: The iron steamers were probably first prefabricated in Britain. *Also listed as 168 tons. **Also listed as 1031 and 1143 tons.

The warship *Auckland*, assigned to 'general services', had a varied career. After the First Afghan War she evacuated troops from the Persian Gulf, following which she saw action in the First China War and was chosen to convey the peace treaty 'with all expedition' from Nanking to India; in 1846 she visited Singapore, Borneo, and the new colony of Labuan; by 1854 she was again in the Gulf, while in 1855 she took Sir John Bowring on his diplomatic mission to Siam. In the second conflict with China *Auckland* destroyed war junks in the Pearl river, and in 1865 when the Indian Navy was disbanded the teak-built ship was converted to a floating battery for the defence of Bombay.

Semiramis [ii], incorporating engines adapted from *Semiramis* [i], nominally ran between Bombay and Suez but in 1850 was transferred to China, then to Singapore, and next to Borneo. Returning for a time to the Suez run, she was next deployed in the Gulf for the Persian War, and in 1863 after completing missions to Zanzibar and Maculla she was sold.

Napier, *Conqueror* and *Meanee* were armed steamers of the Indian Navy employed for 'general duties on the river Indus'. They are sparingly documented but probably took part in the

The HEIC's early iron ships were built in Britain, but wooden steamers were also constructed in India, continuing the tradition of excellent teak shipbuilding for the Company that stretched back to the eighteenth century. One of the largest of these was the Ferooz *(Bombay 1848), which played a major role in the Second Burmese War. Engraving from* The Illustrated London News.

First Sikh War and were certainly in the Second Sikh War; they were probably included in the large fleet sent to the Gulf during the Persian War in 1856.

The large, armed, teak-built steamers *Ferooz* and *Zenobia* [ii], each with a complement of 200 men, nominally ran between Bombay and Suez until playing more distinctive roles in the Second Burma War (the first vessel serving also in the Second China War); they took troops to Calcutta during the Mutiny of 1857, and when the Indian Navy was disbanded both vessels were retained for 'general government services'.

'The P&O'

In the early 1820s neither Brodie Wilcox nor Arthur Anderson, newly engaged as his assistant but soon made his partner, could have foreseen the future expansion of their London-based shipping business that dealt with passengers and freight for the Iberian Peninsula (Portugal and Spain). At first, progress was scant and irregular, though by 1835 the partners were able to buy their first steamship (*William Fawcett*). A greater advance was realised in 1837 when Richard Bourne, an influential shipowner, helped the partners to secure an Admiralty contract for 'a steamer of not less than 140 horsepower' regularly to carry Post Office mails as far as Gibraltar. The first ship to do so (*Iberia*)[10] was the first steamer built specifically for what was then named The Peninsular Steam Navigation Company.

By 1840 the contract was extended to carrying mails and passengers into the Mediterranean (to Malta, Alexandria and even Constantinople) with 'a steamer of not less than 400 horsepower', the first to do so being the *Oriental*. A greater advance came two years later when the company entered the 'overland' market and arranged to run a regular service between Suez and Calcutta, via Ceylon and Madras. The new service was inaugurated in 1843 by the *Hindostan*, at which time the firm extended its name to The Peninsular and Oriental Steam Navigation Company, known to history as The P&O.

10. The first voyage was, in fact, made by the *Don Juan*, but when returning from Gibraltar she was wrecked on the Spanish coast, though all the mails were saved.

Thus, by the time when the East India Company was about to undergo its metamorphosis, to emerge as a major part of a British Empire, the P&O (founded by two shipbrokers in a London office) had become not only – through its efficient mail service – a lifeline for that Empire, but also – through the extensive network of its fleet of ships – in its own right virtually an empire afloat.

In 1842 the Peninsular Steam Navigation Co was awarded the contract to carry the mails between Suez, Madras, Ceylon and Calcutta. The service was opened in 1843 by the specially-built 2017-ton Hindostan, *launched in 1842 by Thomas Wilson of Liverpool and powered by twin-cylinder direct acting engines. Her sister, the* Bentinck, *also joined the service shortly afterwards.* (Painting of the Hindostan *by courtesy of P&O*)

11. On her initial outward voyage, after rounding the Cape of Good Hope *Chusan* went directly to Sydney, via Perth, Adelaide and Melbourne. After a great welcome in Sydney she returned along the same southern coast then headed for Singapore.

In 1845 a branch service between Ceylon and Hong Kong, via Singapore, was inaugurated by the *Lady Mary Wood*, with another branch following between Calcutta and Singapore, via Penang. Next, in 1852, the P&O's *Chusan*[11] inaugurated the first regular mail service between Singapore and Australia; while ultimately, in 1854, the P&O managed to take over the service that the EIC had so long cherished as a monopoly, the ailing Bombay–Suez run.

The extension of the P&O network from Point de Galles (Ceylon) to Singapore and Hong Kong in 1845 was served initially by the Lady Mary Wood, *a small wooden paddler launched in 1841. By 1850 P&O's eastern fleet consisted of five wooden and seven iron paddlers, but because of poor repair facilities for iron hulls east of Suez, wooden ships served the company longer in those waters than elsewhere; indeed, as iron ships were introduced on the Southampton–Alexandria services, the wooden paddlers were transferred to the East.* (P&O)

In 1852 P&O inaugurated a service from Singapore to Australia, providing a ship every two months to King George's Sound, Adelaide, Melbourne and Sydney. It was operated by the new iron screw steamer Chusan, which went direct from the Cape to Australia on her maiden voyage before beginning the Singapore–Australia shuttle. (P&O)

Table 2/5: Steamships that Inaugurated the Eastwards Expansion of the P&O

Name*	Built	Launched	Tonnage (nhp)	Horsepower	Main service, date inaugurated
IBERIA	Limehouse, London	1836	516	190	Falmouth–Gibraltar via Iberian ports, 1837
ORIENTAL	Liverpool	1839	1650	420	Falmouth–Alexandria via Gibraltar and Malta, 1840
HINDOSTAN	Liverpool	1842	2017	520	Suez–Calcutta via Ceylon and Madras, 1843
LADY MARY WOOD	Liverpool	1841	553*	260ihp	Ceylon–Hong Kong via Singapore, 1845
CHUSAN	Newcastle-on-Tyne	1852	669	80†	Singapore–Sydney via Perth and Melbourne, 1852

Notes: These were wooden paddlers except for *Chusan*, which was an iron screw steamer.
*Also listed as 650 tons. †Also listed as 100hp.

Early steamers in action in Eastern waters

The contribution of the East to the early history of steamers includes much of the first experience of warfare under steam. These little-known but historically important actions are outlined below, and since few of the vessels involved were designed as warships it is more appropriate to include them in this volume – to make complete the story of steam in the East – than to cover them in *Steam, Steel and Shellfire*.

The First Anglo-Burmese War (1824–26)

Early in 1824 Burma overran her northern frontiers to invade Assam, Manipur, British-protected Cachar, and also India in the region of Chittagong. The Burmese saw it as a land war, but the British (alarmed for the safety of Ben-gal), while despatching troops to deal with the invaders, chose to assemble off the Irrawaddy delta a large fleet, with which to draw off the pressure in the north by attacking Burma, by water, in the south.

The first objective was the capital city, Rangoon, 20 miles up the Rangoon river, which was bombarded and fell to the fleet on 10 March 1824; and subsequently other towns, like Danubyu and Prome up the rivers, and Moulmein and Martaban along the coast, were captured. In these operations valuable assistance was rendered by the solitary small steamer *Diana* [i], though at the same time the other early steamer, *Pluto* [ii], was doing good work along the Arakan coast, and *Enterprize* [i] joined in at a late stage of the conflict.[12]

Diana [i], the first steamship ever to engage in warfare, became feared by the enemy as 'the fire ship' and her rockets were 'the Devil's sticks'. By her mobility and exploits up the Irrawaddy she undoubtedly contributed to Britain's eventual success in the grim jungle war (where far more casualties resulted from disease than from the fighting). After the war *Diana* navigated the Irrawaddy for over 500 miles upstream. *Pluto* became a tug on the Hooghly river and *Enterprize* was tried out, not very successfully, on the Bombay–Suez run.

The First Anglo-Afghan War (1838–42)

In 1838, alarmed that Persia, egged on by Russia, had besieged Herat (a strategic fortress-city on the route eastwards), the Governor-General of India, Lord Auckland, sought an alliance with the Amir of Afghanistan, Dost Mohammed. But the price asked by the Dost for going to the assistance of Herat was that the British, in turn, would help him to recover the fortress-city of Peshawar from the Sikh leader Rangit Singh, of the Punjab. To avoid a clash with the Sikhs this request was refused, whereupon the Dost sought help from Russia. This was too much for Lord Auckland, and, ill-advisedly, he decided to capture Kabul, the Afghan capital, and replace the Dost by Shah Shuja, a former amir living on a British pension.

Accordingly, the army, although starting from the northwest frontier of India, avoided the direct route to Kabul (through Sikh territory and the Khyber Pass) and marched down the Indus valley into Sind. Then, joined by additional troops brought up the river from Bombay, the 'Army of the Indus', after crossing the river to Sukkur, entered Afghanistan by the Bolan Pass, and eventually took Kabul where they installed Shah Shuja as a puppet-amir – though thereafter things began to go radically wrong.

The military, over-complacent with their successes, gave insufficient heed to the hostility of the natives and were slowly led into a drastic situation where a British army, and its many followers, was forced into a retreat (down the Khyber Pass route) from which but one man survived. A punitive force was sent to Kabul soon afterwards but soon left again.

Shah Shuja had been assassinated but by then

12. Additionally, because of the speed with which *Enterprize* [i] was able to carry the news of peace to Calcutta, she arrived in time to stop the despatch to Burma of vast quantities of stores etc, whereby it was claimed that she saved the Bengal Government much money.

there was no need for him, since, in the meantime, adopting the tactic they used in Burma, the British had sent a fleet into the Gulf – the 'underbelly' of Persia – whereupon, sooner than fight on two fronts, the Shah called off the siege of Herat. And in the end the wily Dost was joyfully restored as amir among his own people in Kabul.

The steamers from Bombay probably included *Berenice* and *Semiramis* [i], with *Snake* and *Indus* [ii] on the river Indus where they contravened the treaty made with Sind in 1832, by which Britain had agreed not to put warships on the river. Among the fleet sent to the Gulf were the steamers *Hugh Lindsay* and *Semiramis* [i].

The Conquest of Sind (1843)

The mirs (minor rulers) of Sind and their Baluch neighbours resented the violation of their territory by the British army, and the warships on

One of the most active of the HEIC steamers was the paddle sloop Berenice *of 664 tons, built of wood by Robert Napier on the Clyde in 1837. She was armed with one 68pdr pivot gun and two 32pdr smooth bores and saw action in the Second Burma War, the Persian War and the Second Chinese War. (India Office Library)*

their river, and in February 1843 an angry mob attacked the British Residency in Hyderabad. The guard steamer *Planet* opened fire and continued until her ammunition was exhausted; after which, joined by *Satellite*, she managed to evacuate the Resident and his staff to safety down the river.

In a crushing reprisal for the riot, the newly-appointed Commander-in-Chief, Sir Charles James Napier, by making an epic forced march with only 2000 men, managed utterly to defeat a much larger Baluch army at Meanee (or Miani); following which the next steamers of the Indus flotilla were named, pretentiously, *Napier*, *Conqueror* and *Meanee*.

The Anglo-Sikh Wars (1845–49)

The death of the veteran ruler, Rangit Singh, left the Punjab restless, and in 1845 the Sikh army crossed the river Sutlej into India, where fierce land battles resulted; until, following a decisive victory at Sobraon, the British pushed the invaders back, and on 11 March 1846, an uneasy peace was negotiated in Lahore. Steamers were probably used in this First Sikh War, but their involvement is poorly documented.

By 1848 the Sikhs had rallied to a new leader,

Mulraj, residing in a huge city-fortress at Multan, near the river Chenab; and when Mulraj became implicated in the murder of two British officers the Second Sikh War began. To besiege Multan the British transported great numbers of troops and supplies by water – using such steamers as *Indus* [ii], *Comet*, *Meteor*, *Planet*, *Satellite*, *Assyria*, *Nimrod*, *Napier*, *Conqueror* and *Meanee* – and also employed a volunteer Naval Brigade that operated its gun batteries at a distance of 700 miles from the sea. Ultimately, the fall of the citadel yielded much treasure (about 1.7 million Rupees) and after a further defeat at Gujrat the Punjab was annexed as a province of India.

The First Anglo-Chinese War (the Opium War, 1840–42)

In the 1830s, because many Chinese had become addicted to opium[13] and it was being paid for in Chinese silver, the authorities discouraged all forms of foreign commerce and closed the 'factories' (warehouses) that British merchants had previously been allowed to build at Canton.

Britain saw this as interference with legitimate

---

13. Obtained from the poppy *Papaver somniferum*, cultivated at that time principally in Bengal.

The 1140-ton Memnon, *built by Fletcher of Limehouse on the Thames in 1841, was one of the largest of the Company's armed steamers but had a tragically short life, being wrecked on a reef approaching Aden in August 1843.* (India Office Library)

trade, and mobilised a fleet that blockaded the Pearl river and attacked the forts defending the approaches to Canton. Then, when numerous talks with the Chinese had come to nothing (though in 1838, before the war began, Britain – caught in a corner – agreed to the destruction of 20,000 chests of opium; and in 1841 China – cornered in turn – agreed to cede to Britain the island of Hong Kong), a change was made in the British Administration and, leaving Canton still under blockade, the main fleet moved eastwards along the coast to attack in succession such ports as Amoy, Chusan, Ningpo, Woosung and Shanghai; until eventually the ships sailed 235 miles up the Yangtze river and began to prepare for the bombardment and assault of Nanking.

This forbidding situation at length forced the Emperor to acknowledge the unmatchable superiority of the British fleet and, rather than suffer the undoubted destruction of Nanking, China sued for peace by the terms of which she agreed to pay an enormous indemnity, to ratify the transfer of Hong Kong island to Britain 'in perpetuity', and to open up the ports of Canton, Amoy, Foochow, Ningpo and Shanghai to international commerce.

Thus did Britain, tiny and remote, win her first encounter with the vast empire of China. That she did so was due to the competence of the Royal Navy coupled with the then 'new weapon' – the versatile steamship. As indicated earlier, the merit of a steamship was its mobility, independent of wind or current, allowing it to act in its own right as a warship or to tow other vessels (from ships' boats to battleships). First tried out in Burma, there were by now several EIC steamers available, which were shortly joined by steamers of the Royal Navy.

Space will not here permit descriptions of the services rendered by each steamer, but those of the celebrated *Nemesis* deserve mention. The *Nemesis*, under her irrepressible commander, W H Hall, had survived a perilous outward voyage as the first iron steamer to round the Cape of Good Hope. She not only found much employment up and down the Pearl river and in a number of actions with the rest of the fleet, but also undertook exploits of her own, such as the navigation of a previously uncharted channel leading to Canton, or when – being forced by a storm to seek shelter at Sheipoo – she 'poured in shot, shell and canister' until its harbour defences were silenced.

When the war was over *Nemesis* visited Calcutta then underwent a refit at Bombay, and by 1845 she was assigned to service in the Straits Settlements and Borneo.

Steamer assignments in Borneo

The two incidents that follow are typical of the range of duties undertaken.

When news reached Singapore that the Sultan of Brunei, acting under the evil influence of one Hashim Jelal, had – on the (false) grounds that the security of the throne required it – consented to the assassination of Rajah Muda Hassim along with thirteen of his relatives, Admiral Sir Thomas Cochrane at once made preparations to pay him a cautionary visit.

On arrival at the mouth of the Brunei river the Sultan ordered Sir Thomas's squadron out of it, and opened fire as the ships continued to advance. Whereupon they had to attack and silence the forts before proceeding upstream. The EIC steamer *Phlegethon* followed by HMS *Spiteful* advanced under fire to an almost deserted Brunei Town, the Sultan having fled into the jungle where he could not be traced. The Admiral left a notice telling the people what the Sultan had done, then took the ships away to destroy two pirate bases that Jelal had set up at Pandassan and Tampassuk.

Later, it was thought prudent to let the Sultan return to his capital and to gloss over his part in the sorry affair; and though in no way a subject of Queen Victoria, he wrote a letter to her expressing his sincere contrition. It was rumoured

---

14. A letter addressed to Captain Wallage, relating to this action, is in the possession of the present contributor (a great-grandson); it reads as follows.

Sir,   Labuan, 2 June 1847
I have great satisfaction in expressing to you my sense of the judicious and gallant manner you fought the Honorable Company's Steamer *Nemesis* under your command in the late action with the Balanini Pirate Fleet. You must allow me at the same time to express my sense of the gallantry and good conduct of the officers and crew of the steamer under your command.
    I have the honor to be, Sir,
        Your obedient servant,
          J Brooke
Commissioner to Her Majesty.
Captain Wallage,
HCS *Nemesis*.

15. For an illustration and an account of the battle, see *Illustrated London News* 15 (1849) pp312-314, also p298.

---

that Captain Mundy (HMS *Iris*) persuaded him that the Queen might forgive him if he presented her with the island of Labuan for a naval base (which he did, James Brooke – see below – becoming the first governor). The power of Hashim Jelal had been broken, and he made no further public appearance until 1885 when he became Sultan of Brunei through the normal process of succession.

On several occasions James Brooke, the Englishman who became the first white Rajah of Sarawak, used a fleet of native boats augmented by the presence of HMS *Dido* (Captain Keppel) or the *Nemesis* steamer (Captain Wallage) to seek out and punish local tribes that practised piracy; and on a different occasion, when aboard the *Nemesis* off Brunei and she unexpectedly came upon a fleet of Balanini pirates, Brooke was particularly gratified when the steamer proceeded to destroy them in an engagement that lasted for most of the day.[14]

But the most memorable occasion was provided by the battle that ensued at Batang Maru when a combined fleet of the Sakarran and Sarebas tribes, while returning at night from a piratical expedition, fell into a trap carefully set for them by boats of Brooke's native force, joined by

boats from the sailing ships HMS *Albatross* and HMS *Royalist*, along with boats of the *Nemesis* and the steamer herself.[15]

Much fighting took place, with the *Nemesis* at one time getting between some of the pirates' boats and the shore to run them down one by one; and by the morning light it was seen that, in the engagement with an estimated 1200 pirates, 87 prahus (long multi-oared war-boats) had been destroyed.

The large sum (over £20,000) claimed for 'head-money' was disputed in London, but the law upheld it and the awards were duly paid out. The present writer discovered records of them in the *Woodhead Prize Account Ledger*, which shows that Captain Wallage received £735 3s 9d, while the five lowest-rated participants each received £18 7s 7d.

W J Roff

Laird's pioneer iron warship the Nemesis *in action against Chinese junks during the so-called Opium War of 1840-42. It was originally thought that* Nemesis *was built to the order of the HEIC but new research has revealed that the ship was sent to the East 'on spec' by the builders to gain publicity for the advantages of iron hulls; it was only later that the ship was acquired by the Company.* (NMM)

3

Steam Navigation and the United States

THE physical environment of the United States provided both the incentive and the means to develop new industry, transportation facilities, and the accompanying technology. The United States achieved extraordinary expansion during the nineteenth century, adding nearly 1.8 million square miles during the first half-century, yet its population remained small and scattered. Transportation facilities to link the far-flung territory were essential, providing avenues for inventiveness and exploitation. The transportation revolution cheapened and facilitated the movement of goods and provided an impetus for industrial growth.

The mechanisation of industry was an integral part of the economic revolution in the United States in the nineteenth century. Blowing engines for blast furnaces, as well as machinery for rolling mills, saw mills, sugar mills, and other industries developed. The most important products, however, were stationary steam engines, and railway engines or locomotives, steamships, and steamboats.

The early experimentation with steamboats in North America occurred along the waterways of the Atlantic seaboard where the great majority of the population was located. Here, during the latter years of the eighteenth century and the first decade of the nineteenth, a number of individuals tried out various steam propulsion mechanisms associated with water transportation.

In the late eighteenth century, two innovators in the United States constructed successful steam powered vessels. John Fitch, a native of Philadelphia, experimented with a variety of steam powered craft. In August 1778 Fitch successfully piloted a small boat driven by paddle wheels on the Delaware river. Although this boat made a number of trips some 20 miles upstream to Burlington, he could never attract enough business to make it commercially successful. A Virginian, James Rumsey, experimented with steam powered vessels until his death in 1792.[1]

Soon afterwards, several men picked up where Fitch and Rumsey had left off. Between 1790

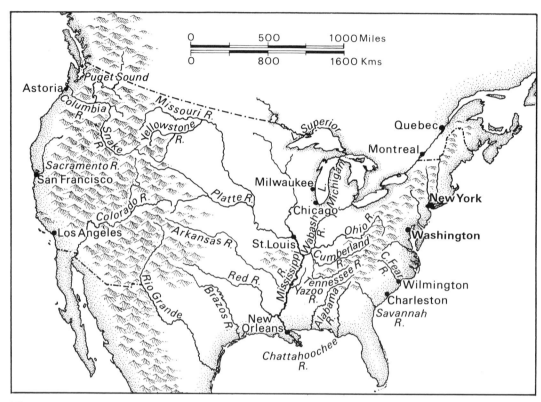

The principal navigable waterways of the USA. (Map drawn by Denys Baker)

and 1797 Samuel Morey operated a small number of experimental steam powered vessels on the Connecticut, Hudson, and Delaware rivers.[2] Early in the nineteenth century both John Stevens and Oliver Evans built and successfully tried out the commercial acceptability of steam powered water transportation.

In 1803 Robert Fulton, who had gone to Great Britain originally to study painting, became extremely interested in mechanical and engineering innovations, including steamboats. Although Fulton was not an inventor and certainly should not be put in the same category as Fitch, Rumsey and other experimenters, he nevertheless deserves recognition for convincing various individuals that they could assemble a successful steam vessel. This was especially true in the case of Robert R Livingston, who became his partner and who already had an exclusive right of steam navigation on the Hudson river.[3]

Fulton did considerable research in Europe on steam propulsion, some experimentation himself, and finally returned to the United States to build a steamboat. In New York he hired workmen to construct the hull and install the English-built machinery. On 17–21 September 1807 his *Steam Boat* made her famous trip to Albany. (Fulton's first vessel was named *Steam Boat* until 1809 when she became the *North River Steam Boat*. She was never named the *Clermont*.) Although later rebuilt, Fulton's *Steam Boat* would run on the Hudson for more than eight years.

1. James Thomas Flexner, *Steamboats Come True* (New York 1944).

2. K Jack Bauer, *A Maritime History of the United States*, (Columbia 1988), p68.

3. James Thomas Flexner, *op cit*, pp280-293; Louis C Hunter, *Steamboats on the Western Rivers* (Cambridge, Mass 1949), pp5-6.

During these years Fulton designed twenty-one successful steamboats. On the Hudson, *The North River*, the *Car of Neptune*, the *Paragon*, the *Richmond*, and the *Chancellor Livingston* monopolised mechanised water transportation. On the Mississippi river system, the *New Orleans*, the *Etna*, the *Natchez*, and the *Buffalo*; on Long Island Sound, the *Fulton* and the *Connecticut*; on the New Brunswick run, the *Raritan*, and the *Olive Branch*; on the Potomac, the *Washington*; and four Manhattan ferries, the *Firefly*, the *Jersey*, the *York*, the *Nassau*, and the *Camden*.[4]

Despite a monopoly awarded by the New York State Legislature awarding Fulton and his powerful partner Livingston all rights to steam navigation in the state, other builders challenged Fulton. In the spring of 1808 the *Phoenix*, built by John Stevens, was launched. In 1811, a company in New York City contracted to build two steamboats, named *Hope* and *Perseverance*. On Lake Champlain, in upper state New York, the *Vermont*, a small (25ft) flush deck steamer was launched in 1808.[5] Others, however, were not as successful. The monopoly along with the outbreak of the War of 1812 were contributing factors to the paucity of challengers. The two partners tried to extend their monopoly to other states but with no success except Louisiana. Fulton died on 23 February 1815, less than a month after the news of the signing of the Treaty of Ghent ending the War of 1812 reached the United States. The Fulton-Livingston monopoly was finally broken in 1820 by the United States Supreme Court. By that date there were already more than a hundred steam vessels operating in American waters, the majority of them in the West.

---

4. *Ibid*, p352.

5. H Philip Spratt, *The Birth of the Steamboat* (London 1958), pp77-78.

The Eastern rivers and sounds

Robert Fulton's *North River Steam Boat* was the product of decades of experimentation. Its success confirmed what many nineteenth-century Americans felt was the inevitable advancement of nascent technology, and marked the beginning of a revolution in transportation that had been long anticipated. The United States provided a somewhat undeveloped but fertile environment for that revolution and the application of steam propulsion to vessels spread rapidly throughout the country. Within little more than a decade of the *North River Steam Boat*'s successful voyage, early steam vessels appeared on virtually every major waterway on the Atlantic coast. Two years later a New Jersey-built vessel was operating on the Delaware river. By 1813 a Baltimore-built steamboat was operating on the upper Chesapeake Bay and in 1815 a Fulton-designed vessel entered Long Island South and reached New Haven without difficulty. Southern coastal cities such as Wilmington, Charleston and Savannah were all home ports for steamboats before the *Savannah* crossed the Atlantic in 1819.

As steam technology rapidly improved, the focus of its maritime application expanded. In that early stage of development steam propulsion systems were relatively simple and required only limited industrial capability to produce or maintain. That factor contributed significantly to the rapid dissemination of steam technology. It also contributed to the preliminary and localised focus of its application to vessels. Thus most of the early vessel development concentrated on navigating on rivers and protected sounds. As the technology improved and became more reliable, vessel operations were expanded to include

coastal routes and limited oceanic voyages. The final stage of expansion, transoceanic navigation, required a much higher level of sophistication and dependability.

In the United States these phases of development were not entirely the consequence of technology. It was also a factor of both environment and philosophy. The United States was a young nation when Robert Fulton brought the essential elements of marine steam propulsion together successfully for the first time. Without a system of well developed roads, the rivers of the Atlantic coastal plain provided the most convenient arteries of communication, transportation and trade. As anticipated for decades the power of steam freed riverine navigation from the influence of wind and tide and unlocked the fullest potential of that natural system. Americans were also more internally focused during the early nineteenth century. Their sense of manifest destiny led them into the interior of the continent exploiting an untapped and seemingly inexhaustible supply of natural resources. The river steamboat provided an important mechanism for developing that environment.

Once the steamboat's power and reliability had been developed it was possible to employ them on a broader environmental scale. Limited oceanic voyages were practical and coastal trading patterns developed between the major centres of population. Intrastate commerce and transportation was also a major preoccupation for Americans during the first quarter of the

An illustration from Robert Fulton's original patent drawings captioned 'View of the Steam Boat passing the Highlands'. Although dated 1 January 1809, the drawing must depict Fulton's first boat, usually referred to as the Clermont. *The drawing was part of the documentation associated with the order for the machinery Fulton placed with Boulton & Watt in England.* (Birmingham Public Libraries)

nineteenth century and the steamboat helped re-alise that objective. While Americans actively pursued the development of riverine and coastal steamboats in the early nineteenth century, it would be five decades after the *North River Steam Boat*'s first Hudson river voyage before transoceanic vessels would become a priority. Although the technology existed to develop routes across the Atlantic much earlier, it would take government support to make that a priority. In the nineteenth century Americans focused on Atlantic steamship routes only sporadically.

The New York area

News of the voyage of the *North River Steam Boat*'s successful voyage clearly demonstrated the practical application of steam propulsion for in-land navigation. Passengers could ride in comfort and relative safety from New York to Albany in approximately 36 hours for a charge of $7. The service that the *North River Steam Boat* provided was an immediate success and con-firmed that steam navigation was also profitable. Fulton and his partner Chancellor Livingston moved quickly to secure the advantage of an ex-clusive monopoly granted by the State of New

A slightly simplified model of the first steamer capable of open water operation, the Fulton *of 1813. The hull is more seaworthy than those of the pioneer river craft and covered accommodation for the passengers is provided for the first time. Once the war with Britain was over in 1815 the boat made a number of voyages through Long Island Sound to New Haven.* (CMP)

York. That provided protection from compe-tition that permitted Fulton and Livingston to control exclusively steam navigation in the State of New York. For Fulton and Livingston the Hudson river became one of the most important routes in the United States.[6]

In response to the success of *North River Steam Boat*, Fulton and Livingston quickly built a number of additional vessels to provide servic-es between New York and towns along the Hudson. Until the construction of the *Fulton* in 1813 and the *Chancellor Livingston* in 1815, Ful-ton's steamboats reflected a rather spartan and utilitarian concept that combined the flat bot-tom, bluff bow hull design of a canal barge with a flush deck fitted around the exposed engine and boiler. They carried masts and sails but no deck or pilothouses, and passengers who trav-elled on deck were protected from the elements by awnings at the bow and stern. Those who went below shared the shallow hull with the ma-chinery, boilers and fuel.[7] Unlike previous steamers designed and built by Robert Fulton, the *Fulton*'s 134ft long, 30ft 9in broad hull was designed with a draught of 6ft 3in to better op-erate in open water. To provide additional strength the *Fulton*'s scantlings were also heavier than those of previous vessels. To power the ves-sel Fulton ordered an engine with a 36in diameter cylinder and a 48in stroke. In spite of the weak powerplant the vessel made reasonably good time on the *Fulton*'s Hudson river excur-sions in 1814 and voyages through Long Island Sound to New Haven in 1815.[8] The lines of *Ful-*

ton's hull also reflected a somewhat sharper bow and deadrise in the floors that would improve handling and comfort in heavy weather. These improvements were included in a second vessel, named the *Connecticut*, which was also built for service on Long Island Sound. *Connecticut* was larger, more seaworthy and more powerful than the *Fulton*.[9]

In the design and construction of the steamer *Chancellor Livingston* many of the characteristics of the second generation Hudson river steam-boat were present. The hull was constructed at the New York yard of Henry Eckford and meas-ured 157ft in length pp (between perpen-diculars) with a moulded beam of 33ft 6in; it was designed with a virtually flat bottom amidships. The *Chancellor Livingston* was equipped with a ladies' cabin on deck aft of the machinery that contained twenty-four berths. This was a depar-ture from the previous steamboats which had no deck cabins, only accommodation within the hull, like the *Chancellor Livingston*'s 54ft long male passenger cabin. That early deck cabin configuration ultimately evolved into the multi-deck design associated with most American river steamers. The *Chancellor Livingston*'s ornamental

6. John H Morrison, *History of American Steam Navigation* (New York 1958), pp22-27.

7. *Ibid*, p41.

8. Cedric Ridgely-Nevitt, *American Steamships on the Atlantic* (Newark, Delaware 1981), pp36-37.

9. Fred Erving Dayton, *Steamboat Days* (New York 1939), pp176-177.

bow and galleried stern also prefigured the ornate decorations that would epitomise later American steamers. Furthermore, by employing steering tackle, the *Chancellor Livingston* could be commanded from a bridge between the machinery and boiler, a major step in the development of the enclosed pilothouse.[10]

Compared with previous Fulton steamboats, the *Chancellor Livingston*'s machinery configuration was reversed. The boiler was placed within the hull forward of the crosshead steam engine and the paddle wheels were approximately amidships. The machinery was constructed by James P Allaire and consisted of a 75hp engine with a 45in diameter cylinder and a 7ft stroke. Steam was supplied by a copper boiler 25ft 3in in length, 12ft 3in wide and 10ft 6in high. Perhaps more significantly, the boiler was fitted with grate bars that permitted coal to be burned more effectively. Paddle wheels 17ft in diameter were covered by boxes and guards to protect the wheels extended well fore and aft before fairing into the hull. The machinery was considered reliable enough to dispense with masts and sails and was capable of driving the *Chancellor Livingston* at a speed of 12mph. When running with the tide the vessel made the trip from New York to Albany in 18 hours on 5 December 1817. That cut by nearly a half the time registered by the *North River Steam Boat* almost a decade earlier and demonstrated that the vessel had speed, one of the most essential elements in measuring success as competition developed.[11]

The speed and comfort of the early Hudson river steamers offered passengers an appealing alternative to stage coaches and other means of terrestrial travel. Virtually free of the influence of wind and tide, they provided increasingly dependable passenger services on the Hudson. The impact of this revolution in transportation was not lost on others, and after the Fulton-Livingston monopoly was ruled unconstitutional by the Supreme Court, competition blossomed. Without the monopoly to ensure customers, vessels were increasingly required to depend upon speed and comfort to attract passengers. In a period when speed could mean success or failure, many captains were induced to race their vessels. This led to several disastrous boiler ex-

plosions and wrecks. Until the situation was brought under control because of public outrage, passengers were even killed jumping from a moving vessel to the dock. The exercise was called making a 'fly landing' and was designed to save time when racing.

Within two years of the Gibbons *versus* Ogden ruling the number of vessels in service on the Hudson had increased to approximately sixteen.[12] The search for speed, reliability and comfort produced rapid changes in design and construction that improved service and attracted passengers. One example of those changes was the 389-ton steamer *Albany*. Although built on the Delaware in 1826 by J Vaughn of Philadelphia, the *Albany* exhibited most of the attributes that were embodied in the classic Hudson river steamboat. First, the vessel was large, with a length to beam ratio slightly in excess of eight to one and virtually no deadrise. The hull measured 212ft in length as completed but was increased to 289ft and 2ft added to the beam when the steamboat was rebuilt in 1839. Hogging trusses, developed by Robert L Stevens and employed to add longitudinal strength to the shallow hull, rose above the deck. *Albany*'s accommodation was also more fully developed and the saloon was embellished with contemporary paintings.[13]

Although not the first, the vessel was powered by an early beam engine. *Albany*'s diamond-shaped skeleton beam was connected to a 65in diameter cylinder and operated on a stroke of 10ft. Between the hogging trusses the massive beam of the engine was visible above two paddle wheels located slightly forward of amidships. Following the Fulton design, adopted by most

of the Hudson river steamboats, *Albany*'s paddle wheels were enclosed in boxes or wheelhouses that were built upon guards that extended fore and aft before fairing into the hull. After being rebuilt, steam for the *Albany* was produced by two boilers located on the paddle-wheel guards aft of the paddles. This configuration provided a measure of protection from all too frequent explosions and freed additional space within the vessel's hull for fuel and accommodation. The first vessel to carry boilers on the guards was apparently the *New Philadelphia*, also built in Philadelphia in 1828 for service on the Delaware. While the *Albany* contained most of the features of the classic Hudson river steamer, the deck structures more closely resembled the early style vessels. The pilothouse was built forward of the machinery and accommodation was provided on deck aft of the machinery, but canopies still provided protection at the bow and stern.[14]

By mid century passengers on the New York to Albany route had a choice of more than twenty fast and well appointed steamers. When the Isaac Newton-designed and the John English-built steamer *Hendrick Hudson* was launched for the People's Line in 1845, the basic Hudson river design reflected in the *Albany* remained essentially the same, although the size had in-

10. C Ridgely-Nevitt, *op cit*, pp36-37; F E Dayton, *op cit*, pp36-37.

11. C Ridgely-Nevitt, *op cit*, pp39-43.

12. F E Dayton, *op cit*, p40.

13. *Ibid*, p42; J H Morrison, *op cit*, pp46, 50; Donald C Ringwald, *Hudson River Day Line* (Berkeley, Cal 1965), p109.

14. F E Dayton, *op cit*, p42; J H Morrison, *op cit*, pp46, 50.

A model of the Empire, *built by William H Brown of New York in 1843 for the New York–Troy service on the Hudson river. The hull measured 307ft 6in by 30ft 6in (62ft 6in over guards), but drew only 4ft 6in; grt was 936 tons. The boat was sunk in collision in 1849, raised and returned to service, but then broken up in 1853 following a further collision.* (ScM)

creased dramatically and superior accommodation had become an integral part of the contest for patronage. Newton's vessel was 330ft in length, and at 1179 tons the *Hendrick Hudson* was the first Hudson river steamer over 1000 tons. Power also increased along with size and the vessel's Allaire-built beam engine was 72in in diameter and had a stroke of 11ft. The 1332-ton steamer *Isaac Newton*, built by William Brown for the same line the following year, was 338ft in length, 40ft in the beam, and had a 10.6ft depth of hold. Steam was supplied by two massive iron boilers 38ft in length and 12.6ft in diameter. The Allaire Works engine was based on a cylinder 81½in in diameter and accommodating a 12ft piston stroke. Power was applied to the water by 39ft diameter paddle wheels equipped with double buckets.[15]

In 1848 the People's Line also added the 1418-ton William H Brown-built steamer *New*

15. F E Dayton, *op cit*, p56; George W Hilton, *The Night Boat* (Berkeley, Cal 1954), p119.

16. F E Dayton, *op cit*, p58; J H Morrison, *op cit*, pp120-122; D C Ringwald, *op cit*, pp8-11; G W Hilton, *op cit*, p119.

17. D C Ringwald, *op cit*, p8; F E Dayton, *op cit*, pp56-58; G W Hilton, p119.

18. F E Dayton, *op cit*, p58.

World to their fleet in an effort to attract passengers. The *New World* was originally 353ft in length with a beam of 36ft and a depth of hold of 10ft 4in. In 1855 the hull was lengthened to 371ft and the beam increased to 47ft. Power for the *New World* was supplied by a T F Secor & Company engine of 76in cylinder diameter and 15ft stroke. Boilers for the *New World* were placed on the guards aft of the 46ft diameter paddle wheels.[16]

The quest for size and power evident in the *Hendrick Hudson*, *Isaac Newton* and *New World* did not eclipse the contest for ostentatious accommodation that continued when the vessels were rebuilt by the New Jersey Steamboat Company in the 1850s. Advertised as 'new steam palaces' the vessels were the largest of their type afloat and were uncompromisingly furnished. On the main deck panelled cabins equipped with plush furnishings extended from the stern to a point half way between the paddle boxes and the bow. Additional first class accommodation and a 'grand saloon' were located on the hurricane deck and extended from below the pilothouse to a point half way to the stern. Aft of the hurricane deck structure the traditional canopy extended to the stern for protection of the passengers. When the *New World* was rebuilt a third deck was added to extend the grand saloon and include additional galleries. The interior was additionally enhanced with carved and gilded woodwork, oil paintings, Belgian carpets, mirrors, plushly upholstered furniture and private dining areas that were as pleasant as a 'Parisian café'.[17] Each of the vessels was equipped with a

generating plant to provide gas for illuminating chandeliers in the grand saloon and later the entire vessel. The concept of the 'floating palace' worked and the *New World* set a record for carrying more than a thousand passengers on a single trip in 1857.[18] Perhaps the most elegant of

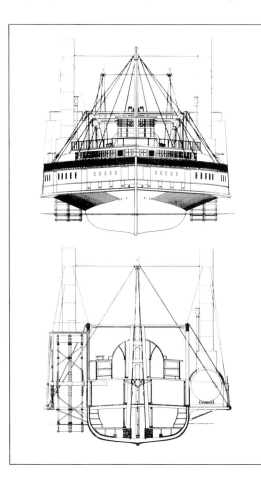

Above: A lithograph published in 1874 by the famous Currier & Ives partnership of two of the largest Hudson steamers, the Daniel Drew *and the huge St John of 1864. In complete contrast, a humble river tug,* Excelsior, *manoeuvres her barges out of the way of the speeding passenger packets (*Drew *was capable of 25mph). (CMP)*

Below: American river steamers were unique in their appearance and construction and were a source of amazement to the marine engineers of other nations – especially the British, who were otherwise undisputed leaders in shipbuilding. These exquisite drawings were prepared to illustrate a paper by Norman Russell, the son of the builder of the Great Eastern, *and depict the* Commonwealth, *built at New York in 1854. After commenting on the bizarre first impressions of 'a large white moving house, two black chimneys, a network of iron rods and stays, and a queer looking wobbling lever',' he concludes that the American river steamboat is 'the result of years of experience, and a striking example of the best possible application of means to an end.' From the* Transactions of the Institution of Naval Architects, *Vol II (1861).*

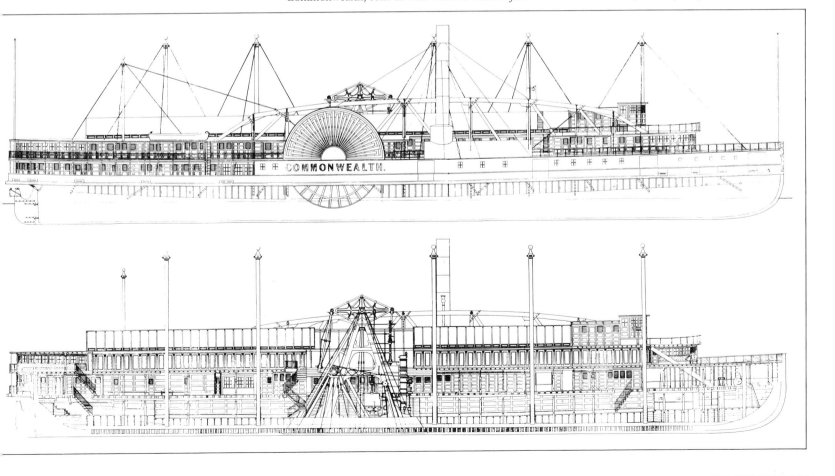

the People's Line vessels was the *St John* built by John Englis of Brooklyn in 1864. The 420ft *St John* was 51ft in the beam and had a depth of hold of 10.2ft and set a record for size and luxurious appointments.

Like most of the fast new steamers of the late antebellum period the *Hendrick Hudson, Isaac Newton, New World* and *St John* had been designed and built for rapid transit. All four were capable of achieving a speed of approximately 20mph. The trip from New York to Albany that took the *North River Steam Boat* 36 hours in 1807 took the 1480-ton George B Collyer-designed steamer *Francis Skiddy* only 7½ hours in 1853. The 260ft *Mary Powell*, one of the last steamers built prior to the American Civil War, achieved sustained speeds of over 25mph. Although moderate in size compared with the People's Line steamers, the *Mary Powell* proved to be one of the most popular vessels to run on the Hudson river. During a career that last until the vessel was broken up in 1923, the *Mary Powell* carried several hundred thousand passengers and competed successfully with other post-Civil War steamers like the 1158-ton *Chauncey Vibbard*, which was fast enough to break the New York to Albany record with a time of only 6 hours and 45 minutes.

19. J H Morrison, *op cit*, pp82-83, 134; F E Dayton, *op cit*, p56.

20. J H Morrison, *op cit*, p134.

21. *Ibid*, p140; F E Dayton, *op cit*, p82.

Although speed, elegance, and comfort remained a trademark of the Hudson steamboats the design and size of the vessels began to change during the fourth quarter of the nineteenth century. A major factor in that change was the shift to iron and ultimately steel construction. In 1880 the Hudson River Day Line contracted with Harlan & Hollingsworth of Wilmington, Delaware, to construct the iron hull steamer *Albany*. That vessel was the first iron hull built for the Hudson river passenger service since the unsuccessful *Iron Witch* designed by John Ericsson ran in 1846.[19] W & A Fletcher Company provided an engine with 12ft of stroke and a 73in cylinder. Power was provided by three boilers mounted side by side within the hull aft of the paddle wheel shaft and machinery.[20] This arrangement was a departure from the well established tradition of mounting the boilers on the paddle guards. In 1887, the Hudson River Day Line again contracted with Harland & Hollingsworth to construct a steel hull steamer to carry the name *New York*. W & A Fletcher Company also provided an engine with 12ft of stroke and a 75in cylinder. Power was provided by three boilers mounted side-by-side within the hull forward of the paddle wheel shaft and machinery.[21] With the exception of the relocated boilers there was little in their outward appearance to distinguish them from their wooden contemporaries. Perhaps the most readily apparent difference was the absence of the hogging truss, a necessity in wood construction but

not essential in a steel hull. These vessels were periodically redesigned and refitted and both were operated successfully into the twentieth century in spite of dramatic changes in Hudson river vessels that took place in the 1890s.

During the final decade of the century the New Jersey Steamboat Company had John Englis & Son build the *Adirondack* in 1896. The *Adirondack* was a massive 3644 tons and measured 440ft in length. W & A Fletcher Company built the traditional vertical beam machinery with an 81in diameter cylinder and 12ft stroke. Like the *Albany* and *New York*, the *Adirondack*'s boilers were within the hull. Accommodation for passengers was arranged on four decks that extended out over the hull to the extremity of the paddle-wheel guards. In the new style, the *Adirondack*'s massive wheels and hogging truss were almost completely encased in superstructure. Smaller but equally impressive and perhaps more elegantly appointed, the *Hendrick Hudson* was built in 1906 by Marvel & Company. The 2847-ton *Hendrick Hudson* was 379ft in length and 45ft in the beam and had a 13ft depth of hold. Unlike the *Adirondack*, the *Hendrick Hudson* was powered by a modern compound engine driving feathering paddle wheels. A steam pow-

As late as 1896, when the huge Adirondack *was built, the Hudson steamer still sported a hogging truss, paddle wheel propulsion, and a vertical beam engine. She was a night boat with extensive cabin accommodation and less of the open deck area of the day boats.* (The Mariners' Museum, Newport News)

A serious rival to Fulton was the Stevens family, but owing to the former's commercial monopoly John Stevens' Phoenix of 1807 was forced to stay off the Hudson. The vessel was sent down to the Delaware from New Jersey in 1809, thus making the first open-ocean passage by any steamboat. This illustration shows the Phoenix after extensive modifications and a change of machinery – the crosshead for the vertical engine can be seen forward of the smoke stack. (The Mariners' Museum, Newport News)

ered generator provided electricity for lights. While the machinery reflected the technology of the twentieth century, *Hendrick Hudson* was elegantly appointed in the nineteenth-century tradition. The *Adirondack* and *Hendrick Hudson* perhaps best represent the final stage in the evolution of the Hudson river steamer.[22]

The Delaware

While the Hudson river provided a unique and highly favourable environment for the development of steam navigation, virtually every waterway in the United States provided an equally enticing, if perhaps not equally realistic, opportunity to employ that new technology. While most emulated or adapted the developments that occurred on the Hudson, shipbuilders and mechanics on the Delaware proved to be adept at innovation and made many improvements that were adopted on the Hudson. Like the Hudson, the Delaware connected several of the major commercial and industrial centres of the eastern United States. Large populations along the river were capable of supporting steam navigation.

Nineteenth-century navigation on the Delaware was geographically divided into service on the upper and lower river with Philadelphia as the centre of virtually all traffic. Service on the upper river was between Philadelphia and the New Jersey towns of Trenton and Bordentown. This service was the objective of the earliest craft on the Delaware. Steamers on that route made connections with the stage lines that provided transportation across New Jersey from New York City. That same route later connected with the Bordentown to Heightstown, Camden & Amboy Railroad that quickly replaced the stages upon its completion in 1832. Completion of the Delaware and Raritan canal connecting the Delaware and Staten Island Sound in 1838 provided another option for travellers but mostly served freight transporters. The lower Delaware routes were developed to provide connections to Wilmington, Cape May and other southern New Jersey towns as their populations and demands for transportation increased late in the nineteenth century. One of the major routes on the Dela-

ware was the connection with stages, railroads, and canal vessels near New Castle and Delaware City. This proved to be the most popular route for travellers going between Philadelphia and Baltimore until the railroad connected the two cities.

Although the Hudson river remained the primary artery of steam navigation in nineteenth-century America, commercial steam navigation had actually begun on the Delaware river even earlier. It was there that John Fitch and subsequently Henry Voight operated their vessels as early as 1787. In spite of Fitch's early successes, it was not until 1809 that another vessel steamed on the Delaware. That vessel was the *Phoenix* built in 1807 by John Stevens of New Jersey. Because Stevens' design infringed upon the Fulton–Livingston monopoly, he was forced to run his ship between Hoboken and New Brunswick until the vessel was shifted to the Delaware. The voyage of the *Phoenix* from Sandy Hook to Cape May was the first open-ocean voyage by a steam powered vessel and contributed to an expanded interest in developing steam propulsion. Although technology rapidly made *Phoenix* obsolete, the vessel ran between Philadelphia and Bordentown, New Jersey, for several years before being laid up on the Kensington Flats below Philadelphia.[23]

The demand for steamboat services on the Delaware led the Stevenses to incorporate as the Union Line. In 1815 they brought the *Philadelphia*, which had been built in 1813 at Hoboken

by Robert L Stevens, to Philadelphia to replace the *Phoenix*. Like the *Phoenix*, the *Philadelphia* was relatively small, approximately 140ft in length, 20ft in beam and drew approximately 4ft of water. Spartan passenger accommodation was no match for that available on the best Hudson river vessels. The crosshead engine had a cylinder of 33in diameter and the paddle wheels were 18ft across. The fact that the *Philadelphia* operated successfully on the Delaware for a decade was perhaps more a function of the lack of competition than the vessel's speed or level of passenger comfort. Later, many vessels without sufficient speed or luxury to compete on the Hudson were sent to the Delaware.

Perhaps not surprisingly, in 1826 the first large steamer built on the Delaware was sent to New York by Robert L Stevens to run on the potentially more profitable Hudson. That vessel was the *New Philadelphia* which had been built for service on the upper Delaware. The vessel was 170ft in length and had a beam of 24ft. A New York newspaper advertisement on 26 August 1826 described the *New Philadelphia*'s accommodation as 'light, airy, and spacious' and noted that the cabins were finished in mahogany, maple, and marble. What made the *New Philadelphia* unusual was her steam machinery. The low pressure beam engine had a cylinder 55in in di-

22. F E Dayton, *op cit*, pp82-92; D C Ringwald, *op cit*, pp92-110.

23. J H Morrison, *op cit*, pp184-185.

ameter with a 10ft stroke. It was the first to be
fitted with double poppet valves to control the
steam intake and exhaust. The *New Philadelphia*
was also the first vessel to carry the boilers on
the paddle guards in response to passengers' jus-
tifiable concern about boiler explosions. The
Philadelphia-built and similarly-equipped steamer *Albany* was also transferred to the Hudson in
1826 confirming the early and rapid transfer of
nascent steam technology.

Although rarely significant enough to capture
attention, a variety of small vessels were produced on the Delaware. An excellent example
was the 153-ton *Lehigh* built in Philadelphia in
1849. The *Lehigh* was a side-wheel freight towboat and consisted of little more than a shallow
draught low freeboard hull equipped amidships
with paddle wheels powered by a small steeple
engine. Amid the machinery *Lehigh* had a small
pilothouse. The vessel's exposed boiler was
mounted on the deck forward of the machinery.
Perhaps more unusually, Philadelphia shipbuilders also employed steam vessels to clear ice from
the Delaware. In 1837 the 325-ton *City Ice Boat
No 1* was launched. Van Dusen & Birely built
the hull and the engine was produced by Matthi-
as W Baldwin. *City Ice Boat No 1* was the first
steam propelled icebreaker. That side-wheel
steamer was followed by a second similar vessel
in 1868 and a third in 1873. After high-volume
steam powered water pumps were developed in
the 1840s, small steam tugs were also constructed for use as fireboats. The *Edwin S Stuart*,
Philadelphia's first fireboat was built in 1892 in
New York.[24]

While steam navigation on the Hudson river
overshadowed that on the Delaware early in the
nineteenth century, the development of iron and
later steel shipbuilding technology on the Delaware began to have a significant impact on
steamboat construction in the 1840s. By 1840
iron hull barges were not an uncommon sight in
Pennsylvania and more than a hundred had been
built, primarily for use on canals.[25] Experiments
had also been made with iron hull steamboats.
In 1841 the United States Navy ordered parts
for its first iron warship *Michigan* in Pittsburgh
and transported them to Lake Erie for assembly.
The following year John Ericsson built four iron
hull screw steamboats at the Phoenix Foundry in
New York, and in 1846 the *Iron Witch* which
was unsuccessfully tried on the Hudson. In Philadelphia the Starr shipbuilding family built the
tug *Camden*, the barge *Mars* and the small
steamboats *Independence* and *Appoqinimink*. After
forming the Penn Steam Engine & Boiler
Works, Thomas Reaney and Jacob Neafie began
a long iron steamboat building career with the
vessels *Conestoga* and *Barclay*.[26]

The Eastern Seaboard of the USA. (Map drawn by Denys Baker)

The leading iron shipbuilding firm on the
Delaware river became Harlan & Hollingsworth
of Wilmington, Delaware. In 1844 that firm ful-
filled an order from George Aspinwall for two
iron freight boats to operate on the Delaware
and Raritan canal. The vessels were 98ft in
length and were propelled by gear-driven twin
screws operated by a single engine. Both the
191-ton *Ocean* and the 182-ton *Ashland* successfully made the open ocean trip to New York
during the summer of 1844.[27] Impressed with
the freight boats, Aspinwall placed a second order in 1848 for a 370-ton steamer to be used in
fulfilling his mail contract on the Pacific Coast.
The *Willamette* was only 150ft in length, yet she
operated on the Columbia and Sacramento rivers after a voyage around Cape Horn and was
sailed across the Pacific in 1861 to provide service on the Yangtze between Hong Kong and
Canton.[28] The company also filled orders for
small shallow draught stern-wheel steamboats to
support Cornelius Vanderbilt's Nicaraguan San
Juan River navigation company and supplied
two steamers for the New Granada Steam Navigation Company's operations on rivers in South
America.[29]

While Harlan & Hollingsworth were building
a reputation for the construction of small vessels
it was Robert L Stevens who built the first large
iron steamboats in the United States at Hoboken, New Jersey, in 1844. Named for John
Stevens, the vessel was 245ft in length, measured
31ft in the beam and had an 11ft depth of hold.
The vibrating crosshead steeple engine had a
75in diameter cylinder and an 8ft stroke. Two
boilers were located within the hull fore and aft
of the machinery. The *John Stevens* was also one
of the first vessels to have been equipped with an
iron collision bulkhead. Under the Camden &
Amboy Railroad Company the steamer operated
between Philadelphia and Bordentown, New
Jersey, until burning in 1855. The *John Stevens*
was light and strong compared to a similar

24. Phillip C F Smith, *Philadelphia on the River* (Philadelphia 1986), pp22, 28, 30.

25. David B Tyler, *The American Clyde* (Newark, Delaware
1958), p5.

26. *Ibid*, pp5-7.

27. *Ibid*, pp7-8; J H Morrison, *op cit*, p188.

28. D B Tyler, *op cit*, p12.

29. *Ibid*, p12.

wooden vessel and was capable of making a respectable 19mph.[30]

In 1845 Harlan & Hollingsworth built a second iron passenger vessel for operation on the Delaware. Named the *W Whilden*, the steamer was built on an iron hull 192ft in length, 19ft 7in in the beam, and 8ft 9in in depth of hold. Thomas Holloway built the *W Whilden's* beam engine with a 40in cylinder and a 9ft stroke. The *W Whilden* ran successfully on the Delaware until 1857 when the vessel was rebuilt and converted to a propeller. The conversion was made to permit the vessel to navigate the Chesapeake and Delaware canal and shift operations to the Philadelphia and Baltimore route.

The success of the *John Stevens* and *W Whilden* confirmed that iron vessels were both safe and practical. That no doubt contributed to orders the firm of Harlan & Hollingsworth received for four additional iron steamboats in the 1850s. They were the 651-ton *Richard Stockton*, the 461-ton *Major Reybold*, the 481-ton *Thomas A Morgan*, and the 527-ton *John A Warner*. The *Richard Stockton* was launched in 1851 and operated by the Camden & Amboy Railroad's Union Line until 1895. That vessel was 270ft in length. The 48in cylinder had a stroke of 12ft and drove 22ft diameter Morgan patent feathering paddle wheels. Steam was originally provided by two boilers which were mounted on the paddle-wheel guards in the Hudson river fashion but were later replaced by a single boiler mounted within the hull. Demon-

<hr>

30. J H Morrison, *op cit*, p186; F E Dayton, *op cit*, p294.

31. J H Morrison, *op cit*, p172; F E Dayton, *op cit*, pp295-296; D B Tyler, *op cit*, p13.

32. F E Dayton, *op cit*, p297.

33. D B Tyler, *op cit*, p75; F E Dayton, *op cit*, p300.

strating the utility of iron hulls, the equally swift 204ft long *Major Reybold* remained in use on the Delaware route between Philadelphia and Camden, New Jersey, until 1903, and the *Thomas A Morgan* ran on the upper Delaware until 1908. The *John A Warner* was built for the upper Delaware Transportation Company in 1857. In order to navigate the Chesapeake and Delaware canal the *John A Warner* was converted from a paddle-wheel steamer to steam screw propulsion in 1905. As the *Burlington*, the vessel continued to run on the upper Delaware until sinking in 1916.[31]

Following the disruption of commerce and shipbuilding caused by the Civil War the economy recovered sluggishly. Yards like the Delaware River Iron Shipbuilding & Machine Works run by the Roach family of Philadelphia was fortunate to secure contracts in 1874 for the construction of two new vessels for the Pacific Mail Line. With many vessels returning from military service the local market for new construction was limited. Antebellum iron steamers like the *Richard Stockton, Major Reybold, Thomas A Morgan*, and *John A Warner* were still in service on the Delaware in the 1870s.[32] All proved to be profitable until new vessels dramatically increased competition in the 1880s.

That competition came with a revival of business activity in the form of the new screw propeller steamers *Brandywine* and *City of Chester*. Both the *Brandywine* and *City of Chester* were built by Harlan & Hollingworth; the *Brandywine* in 1885 and the *City of Chester* in 1887. *Brandywine* was 177ft in length, 25ft in beam, and 8ft 6in in depth of hold. The hull was constructed of steel and contained a compound engine with 24in and 42in cylinders and 24in stroke. Two locomotive boilers provided steam. Renamed *Pil-*

grim Belle in 1937, the vessel continued to run until 1954. The *City of Chester* was 185ft in length, 28ft in beam, and 9ft in depth of hold and was powered by a triple expansion engine with 18½in, 27in and 42in cylinders and 24in stroke.[33] With the exception of their boilers, which must have represented an effort to cut costs, the *Brandywine* and *City of Chester* were harbingers of the new technology that would dramatically change steamboats at the end of the nineteenth century. While the quintessential nineteenth-century vessel was the wooden hull, paddle wheel vessel equipped with return tube boilers and a walking beam engine, the shift to screw propelled iron and steel hulls, equipped with Scotch boilers and compound engines, was well under way in the last decade of the nineteenth century. At the height of the age of steam the varied products of Delaware shipbuilders were in demand on the Hudson, Long Island Sound, the Chesapeake Bay, and on southern rivers.

Chesapeake Bay and its tributaries

The steamboat technology developed on the Hudson and Delaware rivers rapidly spread throughout the Atlantic seaboard. Vessels built along the Hudson and Delaware appeared on eastern waterways almost overnight and were copied and adapted for local or regional service. One of the largest and most complex arteries of trade and transportation on the East Coast was the Chesapeake Bay and its tributaries. Steamboats were ideally suited for exploiting the Chesapeake and they rapidly replaced sailing vessels on the passenger and fast freight routes.

In the Chesapeake Bay, navigation was determined by transportation priorities well established by the nineteenth century. Although Washington was the nation's capital, centres of population at Baltimore, and to a lesser degree Norfolk, dictated the transportation needs on the Bay. As steam technology improved and population increased, transportation routes traditionally maintained by sailing vessels were taken over by steamers. Although not always financially successful the steamers provided reliable services to virtually every major tributary before the end of the century. During the earliest period of steam navigation on the Chesapeake, vessels

One of America's foremost iron and steel shipbuilders was William Cramp & Sons, Philadelphia. In one form or another the company operated from 1830 to 1927 and again during the Second World War, and was instrumental in making the Delaware the 'American Clyde'. This engraving shows the yard in 1872. (CMP)

provided important links in the transportation system that connected Philadelphia and Baltimore. Vessels from Philadelphia brought passengers down the Delaware to New Castle where they were transported overland to Frenchtown on the Elk river first by stage and later by railroad. From Frenchtown steamers provided transportation down the Elk river and upper Chesapeake Bay to Baltimore. Completion of the Chesapeake and Delaware canal in 1829 provided an alternative to the stages and railroads.[34] The first steam vessel to operate on the Chesapeake Bay was the Baltimore-built steamer *Chesapeake*. That first steamer was built in the yard of William Flannigan and was completed in 1813. *Chesapeake* was 130ft in length, with a hull resembling the Chesapeake Bay sailing packets that had traditionally provided passenger services. The steam engine was a crosshead design built to turn a paddle wheel shaft by a cogwheel arrangement similar to those used in the early Fulton steamers. In the event that the engine failed, *Chesapeake* was also equipped with sails. After several excursions to Annapolis and Rock Hall on the Eastern Shore the *Chesapeake* began to offer passenger services between Philadelphia and Frenchtown.[35]

The appearance of *Chesapeake* proved disastrous for the sailing packets operated by the firm of Briscoe & Partridge. Two years after the *Chesapeake*'s initial run they formed the Elkton Line and chartered the steamer *Eagle* which had been built on the Delaware and run down from Philadelphia under the command of Captain Moses Rogers. The 110ft *Eagle* had been built by J & F Brice of Kensington, Pennsylvania, in 1813 and operated on the Delaware before coming to the Chesapeake. Like the steamer *Chesapeake*, *Eagle* resembled the Chesapeake sailing packets with a crosshead engine built by Daniel Large that drove paddle wheels mounted forward of amidships. *Eagle* was also equipped with a mast forward of the engineering space to provide assistance in favourable winds and emergency propulsion in the event of steam breakdown. In addition to competing with *Chesapeake*, *Eagle* also made voyages down the Bay to Norfolk and up the James river to Richmond.[36]

The success of steamers on the upper Bay and the limited visits to Norfolk by steamers serving Baltimore, Washington and Richmond stimulated interest in establishing services on the lower Chesapeake. In 1817 the steamer *Virginia* was built to provides services between Baltimore and Norfolk. A contemporary description referred to the *Virginia* as a 'very large and staunch boat, elegantly fitted'. As originally built by William Flannigan, the vessel measured 136ft in length with a beam of 24ft 6in and a draught of 5ft. The vessel's low-pressure steeple engine machinery was provided by Watchman & Bratt and had a 35in cylinder with a 4ft stroke. The same demand that ensured the *Virginia*'s success no doubt contributed to the construction of the steamer *Norfolk* in Norfolk, Virginia, in 1817. While the hull was very similar to that of the *Virginia*, *Norfolk*'s machinery was more powerful. *Norfolk* was also fitted with double boilers. The increased size and improved engineering plant permitted the *Norfolk* to cut several hours off the trip from Norfolk to Baltimore. Unusual among the early Bay steam vessels was the *Surprise*. That vessel was built in Baltimore in 1815 by George Stiles, then mayor of that city. *Surprise*, although small, was equipped with an unusual rotary engine that provided considerable power for its size and weight. Stiles placed *Surprise* in service on routes that connected Baltimore with Annapolis and several Eastern Shore towns.[37]

By the 1820s more than a dozen vessels were operating on Chesapeake Bay and its tributaries. As in other areas, the early steamers changed the nature of public transportation and cultivated interest in scheduled passenger services. While that was difficult to provide with the small and frequently unreliable steam craft that were first employed on the Chesapeake, the second generation of vessels were a marked improvement. The steamer *Pautuxent* built for George Weems at Baltimore in 1827 proved to be one of the first. *Pautuxent* was built along the schooner lines similar to the earlier vessels but was slightly larger at 123ft in length. Perhaps the most obvious difference in the design of the vessel was the lack of standing and running rigging. *Pautuxent* was designed to rely on a crosshead engine and boiler provided by the firm of Watchman & Bratt. After several years of testing various routes, Weems focused *Pautuxent*'s schedule on service between Baltimore and the Wicomico river ports.[38]

In spite of difficult times for establishing profitable routes, Weems persisted in successfully operating the *Pautuxent* until, in 1845, a new vessel was ordered to serve on the Pautuxent river. Named *Planter*, the new vessel was small but represented an example of the advances in architecture and technology that had occurred since the *Pautuxent* had been launched in 1827. *Planter*'s hull measured 162ft in length, 24ft in beam, and 8ft 6in in depth of hold and was designed with a plumb bow, straight sides that swept out into sponsons above the waterline, and a flat bottom that swept up under the counter above the vessel's rudder. Above the hull forward, *Planter* had an enclosed house on the main deck. Aft of the paddle wheels the main deckhouse that provided cabins and a dining area was surrounded by an open deck or gallery over the sponsons and sweeping around the stern. Above the main deck works *Planter* was fitted with a promenade deck. Within the promenade and aft of a small pilothouse were cabins, staterooms, a saloon surrounded by another promenade aft of the paddle boxes. Forward of the paddle wheels a tall iron smoke-stack protruded from the boiler. The exposed walking beam that would become one of the trademarks of Chesapeake Bay steamers was exposed between the paddle boxes.[39]

The same year that Weems placed the *Pautuxent* in service the Maryland & Virginia Steam Boat Company was formed to provide service at 'regular stated periods' between Baltimore, Norfolk and Richmond. Although the company initiated its service using the ageing *Virginia* and *Norfolk* which had been built in 1817, they contracted with the Baltimore firm of James Beecham & George Gardiner to construct two new and much improved vessels the following year. Both vessels were 428 tons, 138ft in length, 30ft in beam and had an 11ft depth of hold. They were placed in service in 1829 as the *Pocahontas* and the *Columbus*. Both were equipped with a Charles Reeder conventional vertical

This fairly crude sketch of the Eagle *of 1813 shows the main features of the boat: the mast with its auxiliary sail forward, the engine crosshead abaft the stack, and the awning covering the after deck. The boat was operated on the Delaware before being chartered for service on Chesapeake Bay. (CMP)*

34. Alexander C Brown, *Baltimore Steam Packet Company* (New York 1959), p9.

35. F E Dayton, *op cit*, pp302-303; David C Holly, *Tidewater by Steamboat* (Baltimore 1974), p7; A C Brown, *op cit*, p11.

36. F E Dayton, *op cit*, p303; D C Holly, *op cit*, p8; A C Brown, *op cit*, pp11-12.

37. F E Dayton, *op cit*, p303; Robert H Burgess and H Graham Wood, *Steamboats Out of Baltimore* (Cambridge, Maryland 1968), p11; D C Holly, *op cit*, pp9-12; A C Brown, *op cit*, pp12-15.

38. D C Holly, *op cit*, pp35-38; R H Burgess and H G Wood, *op cit*, p 20.

39. R H Burgess and H G Wood, *op cit*, p20; D C Holly, *op cit*, pp9-12; A C Brown, *op cit*, pp12-15.

The Weems Line Planter *of 1845, seen during the Civil war when she was employed by the Federal side. The exposed walking beam is clearly visible between the paddle boxes, and the additional superstructure of the vessels of this generation can also be seen.* (The Mariners' Museum, Newport News)

beam engine.[40] The steam plant developed 100hp from a 50in cylinder and a 6ft 6in stroke. Contemporary newspapers reported that *Pocahontas* was:

in all respects a boat of the first class, and being intended exclusively for the transportation of passengers, combines the most improved arrangements, as well on the score of elegance as comfort ... The principal cabin or dining room is below deck, it is a spacious, light and airy apartment, handsomely finished and furnished, and contains thirty-two commodious berths. One hundred persons may here be accommodated at table. The centre of the boat below is occupied by boilers and machinery, the former (of copper) having been placed below in order to ensure perfect safety in navigating the Chesapeake in rough weather. The front cabin contains twenty sleeping berths, a bar-room, dressing room, etc. The cabin appropriated for the use of ladies exclusively, is an elegant apartment on the main deck. It is richly furnished and decorated, and

contains twenty sleeping berths and two state rooms. An upper deck, the loftiness of which affords abundance of light and a free circulation of air to the main deck and lower cabins, extends the extreme length and width of the boat, and presents a safe and delightful promenade of the most ample dimensions.[41]

During the decades preceding the American Civil War a variety of small steamers worked to develop profitable routes among the tributaries of the Chesapeake Bay. Many were successful and many others failed to find the support necessary to continue operations. In spite of a deteriorating economic atmosphere the Maryland & Virginia Steam Boat Company assumed an aggressive posture and invested in two new steamers in 1838. The first of those was the 676-ton *Alabama*. Initially designed to join the *Pulaski* on the run to Charleston, the *Alabama* was constructed to be ocean-going. The wooden hull was built by Levin H Dunkin and was 210ft in length, 24ft 7in in beam and had a 13ft 5in depth of hold. The ship was also fitted with three masts and rigged for auxiliary sail. Charles Reeder & Sons constructed the *Alabama*'s engine with a 48in diameter cylinder and a 126in stroke. The second vessel, named *Jewess*, was smaller and the 173ft 5in hull had a beam of 22ft 8in and a 9ft 1in depth of hold. W & G Gardin-

er constructed the hull and Wells, Miller & Clark built a lever beam engine with a 40in cylinder and a 132in stroke for *Jewess*. Both vessels were well appointed and capable of respectable speed. *Alabama* was described by the Baltimore *American* as being 'without exception the most splendid steam boat that ever floated on the waters of the Chesapeake'. That was no doubt in part a consequence of *Alabama*'s accommodation which included a total of 126 berths associated with a main saloon, ladies' cabin and forward cabin and four staterooms on deck. As for speed, *Jewess* could make 14mph and *Alabama* could develop 15.[42]

In the midst of the uncertain economic times that contributed to the collapse of the Maryland & Virginia Steam Boat Company, a group of Maryland businessmen formed what would perhaps become the most powerful line on the Chesapeake. That company was formally registered as the Baltimore Steam Packet Company, but it became popularly known as the Old Bay Line. The company was well aware of the technology developing on the Delaware and before the Civil War purchased their first iron steamers. The first of those was the *Mount Vernon*

40. A C Brown, *op cit*, p21.

41. *Ibid*, p17.

42. *Ibid*, pp24-30.

which had been built for the Washington & Fredericksburg Steam Boat Company in 1846. Old Bay purchased the *Mount Vernon* in 1847 and placed the vessel in service on the Appomattox river. The steamer *North Carolina* was built for the company in 1852. It was the largest vessel to date and was built by the Baltimore firm of Cooper & Butler. The vessel's engine was designed and built by Murray & Hazlehurst. The *North Carolina* was very fast and capable of making 18mph. In the first year of operation the *North Carolina* made a record passage to Norfolk in 10 hours and 5 minutes. In 1860, the iron steamers *Georgeanna* of 738 tons and the *Philadelphia*, 504 tons, were purchased. The *Georgeanna* had been built for G R H Leffler by Harlan & Hollingsworth in 1859, and the *Philadelphia* had been built in 1860 by Reanie, Neafie & Company in Philadelphia.[43] These and several other steamers of the Old Bay Line were employed under contract and/or ultimately sold to the United States Government when the Civil War disrupted virtually all commerce on the Chesapeake.

The Westmoreland *was the smaller of two vessels built in the early 1880s for the Weems Line's Pautuxent and Rappahannock river services. Despite being fitted with a secondhand engine, the* Westmoreland *enjoyed a long life: when scheduled service was over, she was converted to an excursion steamer and was not broken up until 1925. (The Mariners' Museum, Newport News)*

Following the war, steam navigation recovered slowly at first. The first vessels returned to routes on the Chesapeake and its tributaries were antebellum steamers that were discharged from military service. It was not until the 1870s that Chesapeake Bay companies were willing to risk new construction. However, economic recovery initiated the most progressive period of steam navigation on the Bay. That progress was not only a factor of local technological development centred in Baltimore but also one of access to the developments in yards on the Delaware. The Weems Steamboat Company provides insight into the capabilities of Baltimore builders and the Old Bay Line provides a similar example of the technology imported from the Delaware.

The Weems Steamboat Company's operations on the Rappahannock and Pautuxent provided sufficient returns after the Civil War to warrant construction of the *Mason L Weems* in 1881 and the *Westmoreland* in 1883. Both vessels were constructed by the Baltimore firm of William Skinner & Sons. The *Mason L Weems* was 221ft in length, had a beam of 55ft overall, and a depth in hold of 12ft. The walking beam engine was constructed by James Clark & Company with a 56in cylinder and a 138in stroke. Nearly twice as big as any previous Weems vessel, the *Mason L Weems* was built for speed and fitted with hand-crafted panelling, stained glass skylights, and lavish staterooms to ensure passenger comfort. The *Westmoreland* was smaller, with an

overall length of 210ft, a beam of 52ft overall, and a depth in hold of 12ft 6in. The vessel's vertical beam steam plant was removed from the ageing *Matilda* in an effort to minimise the requirements for investment capital. Although perhaps not as well appointed as the *Mason L Weems*, the *Westmoreland* was comfortable and fitted with both gas light and running water in the first class staterooms.[44]

In 1885 the Weems Line purchased its first propeller steamer. Again the Baltimore firm of William Skinner & Sons was contracted to build the vessel and the firm of James Clark & Company was selected to provide a direct acting compound engine. At 146ft overall, 27ft 6in in beam, and 12ft depth of hold, the *Essex* was considerably smaller than the Weems' most recent vessels, although reasonably well outfitted with passenger accommodation. Although the *Essex* was successful, public demand supported a trend toward larger and more luxurious vessels at the end of the century. In response, the Weems Steamboat Company ordered the *Richmond* from William Skinner & Sons in 1890.[45]

Although the *Richmond* was the Weems Line's last wooden steamer, the vessel was large, powerful, and epitomised the demand for improved

43. R H Burgess and H G Wood, *op cit*, p160.

44. D C Holly, *op cit*, pp97-104.

45. *Ibid*, pp101-102.

accommodation. The overall length was 213ft with an overall beam of 56ft and a depth of hold of 11ft. The vessel's vertical beam engine was built by James Clark & Company and the 48in cylinder operated on a stroke of 132in. Steam for the plant was provided by two modern Scotch boilers. Appointments were nothing short of luxurious: the saloon was designed by Charles Morris and finished in a mosaic of oak, sycamore, and cherry; the vessel was lit by electricity, and cabins were furnished with steam heat, running water, and toilets. The *Richmond* represented a combination of tradition and technology dictated by public demand and economics.[46]

In 1891 the Weems Line departed from their tradition of wooden steamers and contracted with the Maryland Steel Company to provide their first steel hull vessel. Named the *Lancaster* the ship was 205ft in length with a beam of 32ft and a depth of hold of 12ft. The *Lancaster* reflected the changing technology of the late nineteenth century. The hull was constructed of steel frames on 22in centres. The frames were covered with ³⁄₈in mild steel plate and longitudinal strength was provided by seven keelsons. The sternpost and rudder frames were cast along with various elements of the ship's machinery. The engine was based on a 48in cylinder with a stroke of 11ft and a walking beam drove 30ft diameter paddle wheels. Like the *Richmond*, the accommodation was elegant. The saloon was finished in brass and sycamore with ornamental alcoves and panelled doorways to forty staterooms on each side, which were furnished with brass bedsteads, oak and leather furniture, and Brussels carpet. In addition to electric lights the

Lancaster was fitted for hot and cold running water and given marble fixtures.[47] The Old Bay Line was also quick to resume normal commercial services on the Chesapeake Bay after the Civil War. Because freight services developed more quickly than passenger services the Old Bay Line also shifted considerable attention to transporting cargo. The line's first screw steamer was purchased in 1867 for the purpose of hauling freight. That vessel was the 305-ton *New Jersey* which had been built in Baltimore in 1862. The *New Jersey* was very profitable but the vessel caught fire in 1870 and was totally destroyed.[48]

That same year the Old Bay Line contracted with Harlan & Hollingsworth of Wilmington, Delaware, for the construction of the *Roanoke*. The screw steamer *Roanoke* was acquired to replace the *New Jersey* and was 167ft 7in in length with a 27ft beam and a 9ft 3in depth of hold.

The hull was fitted with a simple cylinder reciprocating engine that developed 713hp. The *Roanoke* was economical and highly profitable and the company ordered the iron freighters *Westover*, *Shirley* and *Seaboard* in 1873 and 1874. In 1881 Harlan & Hollingsworth built the Old Bay Line's freighter *Gaston*. *Gaston* was a screw steamer of 212ft equipped with the Old Bay Line's first two-cylinder compound engine.[49] Although the vessel was well designed and economical, competition from the railroads almost entirely eliminated the freight business before the end of the century and freight boats gradually disappeared from the Bay.

Because the demand for passenger service on the Chesapeake did not recover quickly after the Civil War the Old Bay Line did not build a new passenger steamer until 1875. That year William Skinner & Son of Philadelphia constructed a 259ft wooden steamer for the company. The *Florida*, as the vessel was named, was powered by a beam engine salvaged from the *State of Virginia*. What the Old Bay Line refused to invest in

46. *Ibid*, pp104-107.
47. *Ibid*, pp106-107.
48. A C Brown, *op cit*, p56.
49. *Ibid*, p61.

One of the premier iron shipbuilders in America was Harlan & Hollingsworth of Wilmington, which in 1871 built the first of a series of economical iron propeller steamers for the Old Bay Line. This is the Roanoke's *original plan, with its attractive pictorial elevation, produced by the company's drawing office. (The Mariners' Museum, Newport News)*

The iron-hulled *Virginia of 1879, the last paddler built for the Old Bay Line. By this time there were many propeller steamers on the Bay and this vessel followed them in general layout and appearance, although the paddle boxes and walking beam would always give away the propulsion system. More austerely fitted than her predecessors, she was nevertheless made popular by her speed.* (The Mariners' Museum, Newport News)

The *Georgia*'s decks were covered with deep pile red carpets that complimented armchairs and ottomans covered with crimson mohair. Gleaming brass, polished marble and gilt enhanced rich wood panelling. An Old Bay Line advertisement assured passengers that their steamers were fitted with 'every appointment assuring Luxury, Comfort, and Reliability'.[50] Speed, often a passenger's consideration, was over 19mph for the *Alabama*. The *Georgia* and *Alabama* were excellent examples of why the Old Bay Line was able to provide swift and comfortable service until the company ceased passenger service in 1961.[51] The fact that the *Alabama* was constructed in Baltimore was indicative of a late nineteenth-century revival in Chesapeake Bay shipbuilding that was based on the most modern technology.

the *Florida*'s machinery they spent on the accommodation, and at a time when other lines were employing older vessels the *Florida*'s magnificent furnishings proved to be a valuable attraction. The *Florida* was the last wooden vessel built for the Old Bay Line.

As the economy of the Chesapeake recovered the Old Bay Line ordered the iron hull steamer *Carolina* from Harlan & Hollingsworth. Although quite different in design and construction, this steamer shared something in common with the *Florida*. The engine had been salvaged from the freighter *Louisiana* which had been sunk in a collision in November 1874. Finally, in 1879, the Old Bay Line ordered the first all new passenger vessel since the Civil War. Harlan & Hollingsworth again received the contract to build the 251ft *Virginia*. Unlike the *Florida* and *Carolina*, the *Virginia* was fitted with a new vertical beam engine with a 50in cylinder and a 132in stroke. While the *Virginia* was not so lavishly fitted as the *Carolina*, the vessel was equally fast. Both the *Virginia* and the *Carolina* were capable of making 18mph. In September 1882 both

ships were equipped with electric lights thus becoming the first steamers on the Bay to benefit from this new method of illumination.

In the midst of the prosperity that returned in the 1880s the Old Bay Line ordered construction of their largest vessels to date. Those vessels were the 280ft steamer *Georgia*, built in 1887, and the 294ft *Alabama*, built in 1893. Although the *Georgia* was constructed by Harlan & Hollingsworth and the *Alabama* by Maryland Steel Company, both vessels were designed for screw propulsion. *Georgia* was powered by a Harlan & Hollingsworth compound reciprocating engine and the *Alabama* was fitted with a four-cylinder triple expansion engine. The *Georgia* was also equipped with steam steering, steam heated cabins, and electric lights. In keeping with the lavishness of the 1880s the *Georgia* and *Alabama* were also exceptionally well appointed.

Long Island Sound and the northeastern States

While the Hudson and Delaware rivers and the Chesapeake Bay and its tributaries provided the principal avenues of inland steam navigation on the Atlantic seaboard, the proliferation of steamboats extended rapidly into Long Island Sound and the rivers of the northeastern states. As the Hudson river developed as one of the major routes for early steam navigation, it was perhaps natural that Long Island Sound became one of the first markets for expansion. Due to the amount of communication, travel and commerce between New York and the coastal communities of the northeast small lines devel-

50. *Ibid*, pp86-89.

51. *Ibid*, p173.

The Old Bay Line finally adopted screw propulsion for its passenger boats with the Georgia in 1887. She had two-cylinder compound machinery, manufactured by the builders; these may not have been the most advanced marine engines afloat, but they were a big step forward in economy compared with the beam engines of the paddlers. (The Mariners' Museum, Newport News)

oped quickly. Although competition with other steamers was keen and the development of rail service cut deeply into the freight and passenger service several companies survived into the twentieth century.

The first steamboats to operate in Long Island Sound were the vessels constructed by Robert Fulton and run under his monopoly agreement with the State of New York. The first of those was the *Fulton* designed by Robert Fulton and built by Adam & Noah Brown for Cadwallader Colden under the terms of the Fulton–Livingston monopoly. As pointed out earlier, the *Fulton* was designed with a deeper hull to provide better seaworthiness in open water.[52] The *Fulton* made its first voyage into Long Island Sound on 25 March 1815 under the command of Captain E S Bunker. To the great surprise of most of her detractors the *Fulton* passed safely through Hell Gate and made the trip to New Haven in 11 hours.[53] Although minor machinery problems slowed the trip to New Haven and fog frustrated the return to New York, the *Fulton* clearly demonstrated that steamers could improve travel and communication with the coastal northeast. The success of the *Fulton* prompted Captain Bunker and his associates to purchase a second vessel to expand their operation. That second vessel was named the *Connecticut.* Launched in 1816, the *Connecticut* was larger, more seaworthy, and more powerful than the *Fulton.* With this new steamer Captain Bunker extended the route to include scheduled runs to New London by the *Fulton.* Unfortunately for Captain Bunker and his backers, resistance from the New York monopoly forced them to withdraw both steamers from Long Island Sound in 1818.[54]

The connection between New York, New Haven, Hartford and the Narragansett Bay cities of Providence and Fall River developed into

some of the strongest in the northeast, and steamers that reflected designs developed on the Hudson and later the Delaware and the Chesapeake Bay provided passenger services well into the twentieth century. By 1822 the New Haven Steamboat Company was formally organised to exploit the New Haven traffic that Robert Fulton had envisaged. Within a decade vessels of over 500 tons were being built for the New Haven service. The steamers *Newhaven* and *Newyork*, built by Lawrence & Sneden in 1836, were 524 tons. The 250ft vessels were slightly longer than vessels being built for the Hudson at the time and the depth of hold was greater, no doubt due to an increased draught. James P Allaire built beam engines with a 52in diameter cylinder and a 10ft stroke for both vessels. The engine turned paddle wheels 24ft 6in in diameter. Charles Dickens described the *Newyork* as 'less like a steamboat than a huge floating bath'. Dickens candid and revealing observation provides a rare insight into the second generation Long Island Sound steamers. Somewhat tongue-in-cheek he continued:

I could hardly persuade myself, indeed, but that the bathing establishment off Westminster Bridge, which I had left a baby, had not suddenly grown up to enormous size; run away from home; and set up in foreign parts as a steamer. Being in America, too, which our vagabonds do so particularly favour, it seemed the more probable.

The great difference in appearance between these packets and ours is that there is so much of them out of the water, the main-deck being enclosed on all sides, and filled with casks and goods, like any second or third floor in a stack of warehouses, and the promenade or hurricane deck being a-top of that again. A part of the machinery is always above this

The early Long Island steamer Newyork *is perhaps best known from literary sources, having been the subject of a somewhat satirical description by Charles Dickens. Judging by this contemporary depiction Dickens was generalising about American steamboats rather than confining himself to the particular attributes of the* Newyork, *although the cabin may indeed have seemed as long as the Burlington Arcade.* (The Mariners' Museum, Newport News)

deck; where the connecting-rod, in a strong and lofty frame, is seen working away like an iron top-sawyer.

There is seldom any mast or tackle; nothing aloft but two black chimneys. The man at the helm is shut up in a little house in the fore part of the boat (the wheel being connected with the rudder by chains, working the whole length of the deck); and the passengers, unless the weather be very fine indeed, usually congregate below ...

There is a clerk's office on the lower deck, where you pay your fare; a ladies' cabin; baggage and storage rooms; engineer's room; and in short a variety of perplexities which render the gentlemen's cabin a matter of some difficulty. It often occupies the whole length of the boat (as it did in this case) and has three or four tiers of berths on each side. When I first descended into the cabin of *Newyork* it looked, in my unaccustomed eyes, as about as long as the Burlington Arcade.[55]

Although the New Haven Steamboat Company failed when the *Newyork* was destroyed by

52. C Ridgely-Nevitt, *op cit*, pp36-37; F E Dayton, *op cit*, pp106-108.

53. F E Dayton, *op cit*, pp106-107.

54. C Ridgely-Nevitt, *op cit*, pp37-38; F E Dayton, *op cit*, p108.

55. F E Dayton, *op cit*, pp109-110.

A contemporary engraving of the Metropolis *of 1847. This vessel marked a departure in steamboat design for the waters of Long Island Sound. Heavily built and deeper hulled than earlier craft, she could dispense with the hogging truss that derived from riverine practice.* (CMP)

fire in 1839, the remaining assets of the line were sold to the Connecticut Steamboat Company of Hartford, and under the direction of Commodore Cornelius Vanderbilt continued to provide services.[56]

Steamboats also arrived in Hartford, Connecticut, following the United States Supreme Court decision on the Fulton–Livingston monopoly. The Connecticut River Steamboat Company ordered the *Oliver Ellsworth* from the New York firm of Isaac Webb & Company in 1824. The 230-ton vessel was 127ft in length, 24ft in beam and had an 8ft depth of hold. A newspaper description of the *Oliver Ellsworth* confirmed that while the vessel was equipped with sails, it was also one of the early steamers to be equipped with above-deck cabin arrangements and a covered promenade. Highly unusual was the fact that steam was supplied by a cast iron boiler. That very few vessels were so equipped can perhaps be attributed in part to the fact that the boiler exploded in 1827.[57]

The Connecticut River Company also ordered a small vessel that, unlike the lower river steamers which were also required to successfully navigate on Long Island Sound, was designed to navigate the shallow upper Connecticut river. The 75ft vessel was built by Brown & Bell of New York in 1826. Only 14ft 6in in beam the steamer was designed for a extremely shallow draught of 22in. To accommodate the shallow draught and restricted channel the *Barnet* was powered by a stern paddle wheel similar to the type that had been developed for use on the western and southern rivers. The maiden voyage was a success in spite of the extraordinary efforts required to navigate the falls and rapids. With the construction of a series of canals that improved navigation, shallow water steamers proved to be not only practical but reasonably profitable prior to the development of competition by railroads before the Civil War.[58]

Providence, Rhode Island, on Narragansett Bay, was also among the northeastern coastal cities that Robert Fulton's steamboats visited during the first quarter of the nineteenth century. The first was the small and ill-equipped *Firefly* which reached Providence in 1817 but could not compete successfully against the fast sailing sloops that provided passenger services on Narragansett Bay. The *Fulton* arrived in Providence on an excursion in 1821 and the *Connecticut* and *Fulton* offered services to New York the following year. Although still somewhat spartan by the standards of a decade later, *Fulton* and *Connecticut* provided sufficient amenities to attract passengers away from the sloops. In 1835 the railroad was completed between Boston and Providence, and Commodore Vanderbilt was invited to provide fast steamer services to New York for rail passengers arriving in Providence. Vanderbilt's *Lexington* initiated that service in June 1835. When the railroad connection with Stonington on the southeast coast of Connecticut was completed in 1837 some of the vessels operating out of Providence were shifted to that city. Within a decade more of Providence's commerce was attracted to Fall River, Massachusetts, by another railroad. It was from Fall River that one of the most significant and aggressive steamboat lines in the northeast would develop.

In 1846 a group of Fall River businessmen joined a group in Boston in establishing the Bay State Steamboat Company. While the company's first vessels proved to be fast and comfortable, they were lightly built in the Hudson river tradition. In 1847 the 2108-ton *Metropolis* was designed larger and more heavily built for operations on Long Island Sound. The *Metropolis*'s hull measured 342ft on deck, with a design draught under average load of 10ft 6in. The hull was heavily built using a white oak keel, and seven keelsons were of white oak and locust; white and live oak was used in the frames. At the keelson the floors measured 20in moulded and 20in sided and were doubled to the deck cap. Due to the increased depth of hold, the size of the frame timbers and the use of diagonal iron straps to re-inforce longitudinal strength, the traditional hogging truss was considered unnecessary. To make heavy weather passages safer and more comfortable the main deck was enclosed to the stem. *Metropolis*'s machinery was built by Novelty Iron Works and consisted of a 105in diameter beam engine with a stroke of 12ft. The sidewheels measured 41ft in diameter with thirty-two paddle boards or buckets. Although constructed for operation on Long Island Sound, steam was produced by four vertical tube boilers that, in the Hudson river tradition, were placed on the paddle-box guards forward of the wheels.[59]

Although the company was reorganised on occasion and absorbed by the Narragansett Steamship Company in 1869, it continued to offer first class service adding new vessels such as the *Bristol* and *Providence* which were uncompromisingly built in 1866 by William H Webb of New York. Both hulls were 360ft in length, and although heavily built each of the 3000-ton vessels was equipped with a hogging truss. Erastus W Smith designed massive 110in diameter, 12ft stroke engines for the vessels that were built by John Roach at the Etna Iron Works. Power was applied to the water by 38ft 8in diameter paddle wheels equipped with stepped boards to dampen vibration. Steam for the machinery was provided by E W Smith's patent tubular boilers mounted within the hull forward of the machinery.[60]

In 1881 the Fall River Line, which had been taken over by the Old Colony Steamboat Company in 1879, contracted with the Delaware River Iron Shipbuilding and Engine Works in Chester, Pennsylvania, for their first iron hull steamer. *Pilgrim*, as the ship was named, was one of the first iron steamers on Long Island Sound and was uniquely equipped with a double bottom, sectioned by floors and stringers into ninety-six watertight compartments. The engineering space was also isolated by watertight bulkheads making the vessel one of the safest in American coastal waters at the time. The 3500-

56. *Ibid*, p111.

57. *Ibid*, pp120-121.

58. *Ibid*, p123.

59. J H Morrison, *op cit*, pp314-316.

60. F E Dayton, *op cit*, p120; J H Morrison, *op cit*, p319.

Largest and last of the Fall River Line was the Priscilla of 1894. She is seen here in June 1937, only a month before the end of her long career, passing through the Cape Cod Canal on her way to Boston for dry-docking. (The Mariners' Museum, Newport News)

ton vessel measured 390ft in length, and power was provided by a single beam engine with a 100in diameter cylinder and a 14ft stroke. To add to the luxury of the *Pilgrim*, steam-generated electric lighting was installed. Again, *Pilgrim* registered first among American steam vessels.

The tradition established by *Pilgrim* was followed by the 4600-ton *Puritan* in 1899 which included feathering paddles; *Plymouth*, built in 1890 and fitted with a double inclined triple expansion engine and Scotch boilers; and ultimately *Priscilla*, last and largest of the fleet, in 1894. Each of those vessels was constructed by the Delaware River Iron Shipbuilding & Engine Works in Chester, Pennsylvania, and they were indicative of the shift from the traditional design developed on the Hudson to the more modern, safe and efficient iron and steel designs produced late in the nineteenth century by engineering works.

American river and coastal steamers developed a tradition of highly ornate interiors, in some cases little inferior to those of the great ocean liners. The Fall River Line's Priscilla of 1894 is a late but excellent example: the North Italian Renaissance style decoration was the work of one of Boston's leading architects. (The Mariners' Museum, Newport News)

Atlantic Coast river vessels

Boston did not develop as a particularly important centre of early steam navigation. There the first steamer to operate was the *Massachusetts*, a small vessel 83ft in length, 17ft 10in in beam and with a draught of 4ft, that had been built in Philadelphia. The *Massachusetts* was put into service between Boston and Salem in 1817 but was withdrawn from the route and sold several months later due to lack of patronage. From 1821 until 1829, a time when steam navigation was developing rapidly on the Hudson, Long Island Sound, the Delaware and Chesapeake Bay, Boston was without one steam powered vessel.[61]

While inland steam navigation developed slowly in the Boston area, navigation on the Merrimack river north of Gloucester provided the impetus for constructing a variety of small vessels. The first was an unusual small steamboat with side paddle wheels operated by a chain drive. The Merrimack Steam Navigation Company was formed in 1847 and launched the *Lawrence*, a small steamer designed with a 15in draught, for operation on the upper river. After a year in service the *Lawrence* was sold, broken down and transported to California. There the vessel was used on the Yuba during the Gold Rush.[62] Among the various steamers that ran on the Merrimack in the nineteenth century many were designed with a stern wheel. Although stern wheel steamers are generally considered to be a western phenomenon, several operated on the Penobscot river. The *Governor Dana* ran on the Penobscot to Oldtown until, like the *Lawrence*, it was sold and taken to California. The stern wheel steamer *Phoenix* also ran for several years after.[63] Small, shallow draught river steamers were also popular in the southeast during the nineteenth century. While river steamboat activity was concentrated in the vicinity of ports like Savannah, Charleston and Wilmington it was by no means limited to those areas. In Savannah Samuel Howard organised the Steamboat Company of Georgia and in 1816 launched the 152-ton *Enterprise* at the shipyard of John Watts.[64] Within four years there were three Charleston-built vessels on the Savannah river carrying cargo, passengers, and serving as towboats. Most were reminiscent of the early Fulton-designed vessels with limited accommodation, a crosshead engine and side-wheels. Small steamers proved to be popular due to their ability to navigate in the currents and restricted channels of the Savannah river.[65]

In 1834 the iron steamer *John Randolph* was launched in Savannah for Mr G B Lamar. The vessel was one of several shipped, unassembled, to the United States by John Laird & Company of Birkenhead.[66] Machinery for the *John Randolph* was produced by Fawcett, Preston & Company and shipped across the Atlantic with the hull. The immediate success of the *John Randolph* prompted Lamar to order two similar vessels from Laird in 1836.[67] On 6 November 1847 the Hamburg *Republican* reported that:

> there has been no time when boating business on the Savannah River was more prosperous. The Iron Steamboat Company has the *Lamar*, *John Randolph*, *Amory Sibley* ... and 16 towboats. The Steamboat Company of Georgia has the *Chatham*, *Cherokee*, and the *Thomas A Metcalf* ... 16 towboats, and several lighters. There is also a number of private boats, such as the Steamer *Ivanhoe* and the *H L Cook*. These boats appear to be all kept very busy, and it should seem from the additions recently made that they are doing well.

By 1853 there were twenty-seven steamers on the river and many were steam tugs engaged in towing barges, flats and ships. The 127-ton tug *Tybee*, built in Philadelphia in 1850, was 92ft 9in in length, 18ft 6in in beam and had a depth of hold of 8ft. The wooden hull was fitted with one deck, a single mast, and no galleries or figurehead.[68] Although many of the early tugs were propelled by side wheels, a shift to screw propulsion began in the early 1840s and by mid century most were being equipped with propellers. When the disruption of navigation on the Savannah, caused by the Civil War, ended in 1865 there were almost no steam vessels left on the river. When the economy recovered sufficiently to support steam navigation, vessels were secured from military surplus and then from yards such as those on the Delaware.

Although Charleston shipyards built a number of the first vessels used on the Savannah river, the number of steam vessels produced in that important southern port was limited. Prior to 1825, Charleston shipbuilders sent several vessels to Savannah and before the Civil War built several paddle steamers to carry on the local plantation trade. The 289-ton steamer *Darlington* was built in Charleston in 1849 for Jacob Brock. Until captured during the Civil War the *Darlington* was engaged hauling agricultural products and supplies on the Pee Dee river. While the *Darlington* was probably built much like the Philadelphia towboat *Lehigh*, the 133ft long Charleston steamer was also equipped with passenger cabins located above the freight deck.[69]

The port at Wilmington, North Carolina, also developed as a consequence of inland navigation, and steam promised to improve connections with the agricultural interior. The first steam vessel on the Cape Fear river was the side wheel *Henrietta* which was launched at Fayetteville in 1818. In spite of the hazards of operating in the shallow upper Cape Fear, that 152-ton vessel remained in service until 1858.[70] By 1837 there were five steamers operating on the Cape Fear.[71] While many were locally built, the iron hull *DeRosset* was one of those shipped unassembled to the United States by John Laird & Company of Birkenhead.[72] Machinery for the *DeRosset*, like that of the Savannah Laird steamer *John Randolph*, was produced by Fawcett, Preston & Company and shipped across the Atlantic with the hull. Like Savannah, Wilmington was located almost 20 miles up the Cape Fear river and steam tugs were employed for towing. By 1855 Wilmington, like Charleston, was also employing steam powered dredgers to maintain the navigation channel.[73] The 185-ton side wheel steamer *Sam Beery* was built in Wilmington in 1853 for use as a salvage tug. As the American economy revived in the 1870s and '80s steam was also adapted to small shallow draught fishing vessels with side wheels located in the extreme stern, and steam powered winches on the deck forward to help handle nets.[74]

Most of the small steamers built for the Cape Fear prior to the Civil War were side wheel vessels but navigation on the Cape Fear river presented many of the same problems that were present on the western rivers. Responding to similar problems the Cape Fear Steamboat Company ordered the iron hull stern wheel steamer *A P Hurt* from the Wilmington, Delaware firm of Pusey & Jones. The 81-ton *A P Hurt* was

61. J H Morrison, *op cit*, pp399-401; F E Dayton, *op cit*, p247.

62. F E Dayton, *op cit*, pp251-252.

63. *Ibid*, p266.

64. Ruby A Rahn, *River Highway for Trade*, US Army District of Savannah Corps of Engineers (Savannah, Ga 1968), pp19-20; R Fleetwood, pp90-91 and J H Goff, 'The Steamboat Period in Georgia', *Georgia Historical Society Journal* 12, pp236-237.

65. R Fleetwood, *Tidecraft*, pp90-91 and R A Rahn, *op cit*, pp19-20.

66. D B Tyler, *op cit*, p5; R Fleetwood, *op cit*, p93; J H Goff, *op cit*, pp236-237.

67. R Fleetwood, pp93-94; and R A Rahn, *op cit*, pp37-38.

68. Spence, p582.

69. P C Coker, III, *Charleston's Maritime Heritage, 1670-1865* (Charleston 1987), p193.

70. Thomas H Sloan, 'Inland Steam Navigation in North Carolina, 1818-1900', Unpublished Thesis presented to the Faculty of the Department of History, East Carolina University, Greenville, North Carolina (1971), p18.

71. *Ibid*, p32.

72. D B Tyler, *op cit*, p5; T H Sloan, *op cit*, p33.

73. T H Sloan, *op cit*, p36.

74. *Ibid*, p72.

100ft in length and had a draught of only 4ft. The steamer's two non-condensing engines were 13in in diameter and operated on a stroke of 60in and a 15ft long boiler was mounted near the bow. Passenger accommodation on the *A P Hurt* consisted of six staterooms and thirty-four berths located above the cargo deck. A small pilothouse was built above the superstructure amidships. The *A P Hurt* survived and operated profitably in the period after the Civil War when many small Cape Fear steamboat operations failed.[75] Although the vessel burned out and sank on more than one occasion, the iron hull was rebuilt and the vessel survived in service until 1923.

The West

It was in the years immediately following the War of 1812 that the area beyond the Appalachian mountain chain, the West, began to emerge as an important area for growth. Between 1810 and 1820 the population of this part of the United States increased from 14 to nearly 25 per cent of the total population. Until the opening of the Erie Canal in the mid 1820s, the mountain chain acted as a barrier to the transportation of goods between the West and East. The Mississippi river and its tributaries flowing into the Gulf of Mexico became the principal artery of transportation. Because of the vast distance involved, steam driven vessels proved the most important factor in the great economic development of the West from 1815 to the eve of the American Civil War. No section of the United States was so completely dependent upon steam for effective transportation, and in no other part of the world were so many steamboats built and operated.[76]

Even before the War of 1812 efforts had been made to introduce steam navigation in the West.

In 1802–3 a steamboat was built in New Orleans, but destroyed by a spring flood before being launched. In 1811 the Fulton–Livingston interests built the steamboat *New Orleans* at Pittsburgh, and successfully steamed down the Ohio and Mississippi rivers to New Orleans. The *New Orleans* operated effectively on the Mississippi below Natchez, but made no attempt to return to the Ohio. The *Enterprise*, built some 50 miles above Pittsburgh in 1815, was the first steamboat to steam successfully to New Orleans and return to the upper Ohio.

The *Enterprise*, built by Daniel French and captained by Henry Shreve, demonstrated the practicality and economic potential of steamboats on the western rivers. Two years later, in 1817, seventeen steamboats operated on these rivers carrying passengers and cargoes from the Gulf of Mexico up to the headwaters of the Ohio river. By 1820 the number navigating the western rivers had risen to sixty-nine, but during the next half-century the number would increase dramatically. In 1855, 727 steamboats were operating on the Mississippi/Ohio system and its tributaries.[77]

Henry Shreve has often been credited as the originator of the western river steamboat with its unique architecture and high-pressure engine.

The study of Louis Hunter has clearly proved that this is an oversimplification, and that the western river steamboat was a gradual development in which many builders made contributions. Shreve and his partner French were instrumental in building and operating a number of early steam vessels including the small *Comet* (25 tons) in 1813, the *Enterprise* (75 tons) in 1814, and the *Washington* (403 tons) in 1816. The French–Shreve steamboats, like many of the other early western steamboats, were modified eastern vessels. They were heavily built deep water boats, but the French–Shreve vessels were the first in the West to use high-pressure engines.[78]

In 1801 Oliver Evans in Philadelphia, de-

75. William N Lytle and Forrest R Holdcamper, *Merchant Steam Vessels of the United States* (Staten Island, New York 1975), p2; Gordon P Watts 'Archaeological Reconnaissance of the Wilmington Harbor/Northeast Cape Fear River, North Carolina', unpublished report on file with United States Army Engineer District, Wilmington, North Carolina (1988), pp24-27.

76. George R Taylor, *The Transportation Revolution 1815-1860* (New York 1958), p63.

77. *Ibid*, p64.

78. For Shreve, see Edith McCall, *Conquering the Rivers* (Baton Rouge, 1984).

signed and built a small stationary high-pressure engine. Although the evidence is not conclusive, it seems probable that the engines installed on the French-built boats were of Evans' design. High-pressure engines quickly became universally popular in the West because they were compact, generally weighing considerably less than the low-pressure engines found on Eastern river steamboats. They were also non-condensing, saving the weight of a condenser. These engines have a much smaller cylinder and shorter stroke than the low-pressure engines. The piston was moved entirely by the expansion of steam without the partial vacuum caused by condensation. Steam, instead of being fed into a

condenser, was exhausted into the atmosphere, which necessitated a steady supply of feed water. Cleaning the boilers of mud was a daily occurrence as were stops along the river to load wood for fuel. With no condenser these engines traded fuel efficiency for power per pound of weight. Various types of high-pressure engines were employed on the western river boats. The *Comet*, for example, had an oscillating engine while the *Washington* had an inclined cylinder connected directly to the crank. By the middle 1830s, however, the horizontal or slightly inclined engine had become standard.[79]

Steam was generated by long cylindrical return flue boilers. These were mounted horizontally, in fore and aft position, singly or in batteries of two, and on the larger vessels up to eight or more. They were connected by a steam drum overhead and underneath by sediment catching 'mud' drums. By mid century western river steamboat boilers were able to create from

150 to 170 pounds of steam per square inch. These high-pressure boilers were located in the forward third of the boat with the fireboxes at the bow end. On the early boats the firebox end faced forward in order to utilise the air's natural flow. By mid century, when steam pumps were used to force steam into chimneys, the fire doors were relocated to face aft. Western river steamers were noted for their tall (up to 90ft) stacks or chimneys connected to the forward end of the boilers. Virtually all carried two chimneys.[80] Cylinder dimensions along with the number and size of the boilers were the normal criteria for determining a steamboat's power. Horsepower (hp) ratings were only occasionally given, prob-

79. William D Sawyer, 'The Western River Engine', *Steamboat Bill* (Summer 1978), p71.

80. For a detailed discussion of the mechanical development of the western steamboat see Louis Hunter, *op cit*, pp121-180.

Taken from a British naval architectural paper, these drawings of the Memphis *do not represent a particular western river boat but incorporate all the principal features as seen by an intelligent and knowledgeable observer. From the* Transactions of the Institution of Naval Architects, *Vol II (1861).*

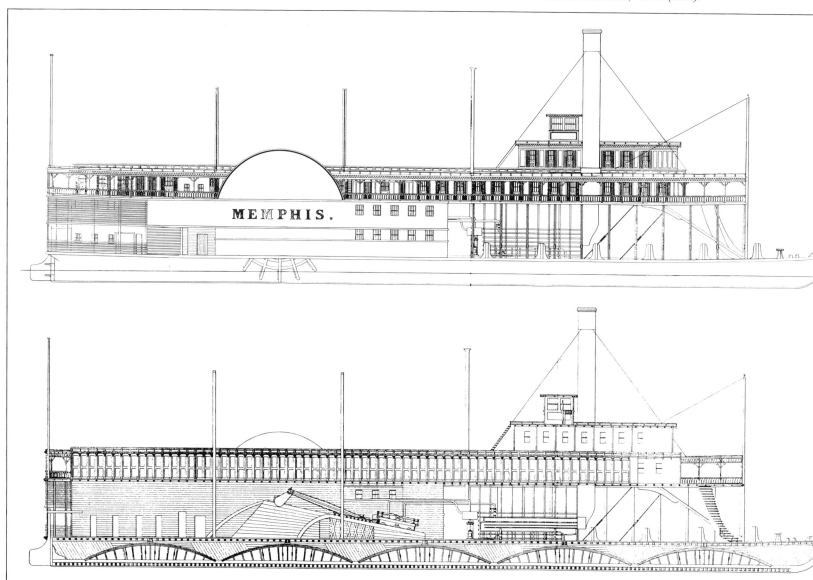

ably because of a lack of familiarity with methods of calculation.[81]

The Mississippi/Ohio system and its tributaries are shallow much of the year. This was the principle factor in the design of the western river steamboat. The hulls became longer, flatter and wider, in order to distribute weight over a larger area and reduce the draught. The bow was steeply raked to facilitate docking at river landings and for pushing through sandbars. Hulls, superstructure and cabins were made as light as possible. The engines and boilers necessarily were repositioned out of the hold onto the main deck. In order to compensate for the lost hold space, the superstructure became multi-decked. By the 1830s western river steamers commonly had three decks, and the four-decker would appear within a few years. The main deck was the largest, its width being determined by the combined width of the two side wheels and the hull. The extension beyond the hull was known as the guards and served the structural purpose of supporting the side wheels. Guards were also a structural feature on stern-wheelers. By mid century the main deck was, in extreme cases, more than twice the width of the hull. The hull of the *Crystal Palace*, for example, was 33½ft wide, while the main deck measured 69ft across at the paddle wheels.[82] By 1860 the average smaller steamboat of 100-125 tons was 132ft in length, 24ft in beam. Its average draught had decreased from 6.3ft to 3.7ft. By that date many of the boats on the Mississippi/Ohio system were more than 200ft long, 35ft in beam, but still drawing less than 7ft. As hulls grew longer and lighter, hog chains were introduced to prevent

One of the enduring images of western river steamboating was the race, here depicted by Currier & Ives in a print of Eagle *and* Diana *published in 1870. Cut-throat commercial rivalry manifested itself in attempts to become the fastest boat on a particular service, and although it was a dangerous practice – and accidents were frequent – it was popular with the travelling public and became part of the romance and legend of the Mississippi.* (CMP)

the ends of the hull drooping. These chains were iron rods made fast at their ends to hull timbers at bow and stern and running longitudinally over a series of struts and masts. A few iron hulled western river boats were built but the great majority were constructed of wood.[83]

Western river steamboats were generally paddle wheelers, although a few propellers were built during the latter years of the nineteenth century. Initially, side-wheelers were predominant. To supply the power and speed regarded as essential, paddle wheels were increased in dimensions until on 350- to 400-ton side-wheelers at mid century, each wheel was some 30ft in diameter by 12ft in width. The early side-wheelers had one engine placed in the centre of the vessel which drove both wheels. By the 1830s two engines, acting independently of each other, were found on most of the western river boats. This resulted in improved stability and manoeuvrability.

81. *Ibid*, p143.

82. *Ibid*, p93.

83. *Ibid*, pp99, 114; W Stuart Harris, 'Floating Coffins: A History of Steamboating on the Alabama-Tombigbee-Mobile Bay Water Systems', unpublished manuscript, p51.

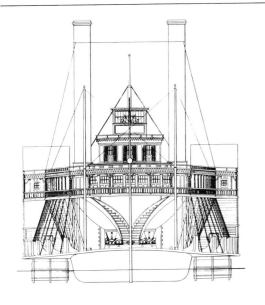

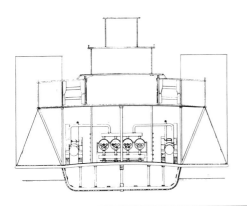

All river navigation was vulnerable to underwater obstacles or 'snags', mostly trees carried away by flood water and buried like stakes in the bed of the river. To keep channels clear special snagboats were developed, with derricks and windlass (eventually steam driven) capable of hauling out trunks that averaged 17 tons. This engraving from Hall's Report *shows the iron snagboat* Horatio G Wright *(187ft by 62ft – 90ft across the guards). In one season of eight months' work on the Mississippi in 1881 she is recorded as having removed 1909 snags, and cut down 5005 trees liable to fall into the river.*

The western river steamboats were often called the 'Brides of Babylon', because of the elaborate wooden scrollwork which was used so freely in trimming the vessels. The boats also possessed a number of large gothic arches, and even the crowns of the high chimneys or smoke-stacks were ornamented with artistic ironwork, consisting of flared-out plums, acanthus leaves, and thick rings. The western steamboat looked like a cheaply constructed, ornate, white wooden castle floating on a raft. The boats of the western rivers never attained the mechanical and structural perfection of the steamboats built in the northeastern part of the United States. Longevity was rare, the average life of a pre-Civil War boat being only four or five years. They were not only frequently made from poorly seasoned timber, but were quite vulnerable to destruction from river obstructions, fire or boiler explosions. Of approximately 584 steamboats that served at one time or another on Alabama rivers, at least 207 were destroyed by river disasters.[84] Of that number the largest number (88) was lost to snags and other river obstructions. Between 1811 and 1851 on the Mississippi/Ohio system, 985 vessels were destroyed, river obstructions accounting for 576.[85] Boiler explosions accounted for another 209. Between 1825 and 1848 almost 3000 people were killed or injured by steamboat boiler failures.[86] Thousands more were lost to fire.

Despite their poor safety record, mechanical and structural imperfections, and short life span, they were inexpensive, profitable, and most importantly, contributed significantly to the economic development of the United States. Probably no single type of vessel contributed more to the economic prosperity of the United States than did the western river steamboat.

Between 1820 and 1880 more than 6000 western river type steamboats, totalling over a million tons, had been built. Although steam vessels were built throughout the West, the majority were constructed on the upper Ohio river between Pittsburgh, Pennsylvania, and Louisville, Kentucky. More than four-fifths of the western

river steamboats were built here to ply the Mississippi/Ohio river trade and its tributaries. Many ships built on the Pittsburgh to Louisville stretch served the smaller streams flowing into the Gulf of Mexico. Of the 584 steamboats on the Alabama rivers between 1818 and 1932 all but forty-five were built on the Ohio river.[87] Two-thirds of the steam vessels that navigated the Chattahoochee river were built on the Ohio.[88] Even on the Brazos river in western Texas most of the pre-Civil War boats came from the shipyards scattered along the Ohio.[89] Unlike the Mississippi/Ohio and its tributaries, however, eastern-built steamboats would continue to be used on the Georgia and Alabama rivers throughout the nineteenth century. The western river steamboats on these rivers, however, were similar in structure and machinery to those on the Mississippi/Ohio system only. They were usually smaller and the majority had fewer decks with less ornamentation.

The large number of tributaries that flowed into the Mississippi/Ohio had steam transportation early in the nineteenth century. In the Ohio valley by 1830 a dozen of the larger streams were linked to the Ohio river by steam navigation. In 1818 the first steamboat arrived in Nashville, Tennessee, on the Cumberland river. In that same year a steamer ventured up the Wabash in Ohio. Within a decade more than fifty steamboats were operating on these rivers.

Steam navigation on the upper Mississippi above St Louis developed slowly because of shallow water and rapids. It was not until 1823 that a small steamer ascended the river above the rapids. By the 1840s steamboats had reached St Paul, Minnesota. The forties witnessed steamboats operating in all the major streams in the

middle and trans-Mississippi West. Within a decade steam powered vessels had reached the foothills of the Rockies. By mid century steamboats were ascending the Missouri river some 600 miles to reach the trading posts and forts. Steam transportation in the trans-Mississippi West was directly related to advancing settlement. Throughout much of the century steamboats followed, and contributed to, the migration of people into the West.

The rivers that joined the Mississippi below the Missouri also employed shallow-river boats. Steamboats ascended the Arkansas and Red rivers shortly after the War of 1812 ended, but it was not until a decade later that steam navigation was regularly established on these rivers. The Yazoo river, flowing through the heartland of Mississippi, also witnessed its initial steamboat operations in the 1820s. Approximately 250 navigated the Yazoo in the years before the outbreak of the Civil War.[90]

The steamboats built to operate on these rivers were basically the same as the other western

84. W S Harris, *op cit*, p78.

85. L Hunter, *op cit*, p272.

86. John K Brown, *Limbs on the Levee: Steamboat Explosions and the Origins of Federal Public Welfare Regulation, 1817-1852* (Charlottesville 1989).

87. W S Harris, *op cit*, p10; William N Still, Jr, 'Steamboating on the Alabama River', *Steamboat Bill* (Fall 1971), pp131-134.

88. Edward A Mueller, *Perilous Journeys: A History of Steamboating on the Chattahoochee, Apalachicola, and Flint Rivers, 1828-1928* (Eufaula, Alabama 1990).

89. Pamela A Puryear and Nath Winfield, Jr, *Sandbars and Sternwheelers* (College Station 1976), pp41-42.

90. Harry P Owens, *Steamboats and the Cotton Economy* (Jackson, Miss 1990).

river types, and their evolution was generally similar. However, because of the shallowness of these streams, they were smaller and usually considerably lighter, with as little draught as possible. Mark Twain, who served as a pilot on a western river boat, supposedly said that a good Missouri riverboat could sail on a heavy dew. The boats that operated on these tributaries as well as those further south were frequently referred to as 'low-water boats' or the 'mosquito fleet'. In the 1870s single-deck steamboats called 'spoonbill mountain boats', because of their extremely light draught and the shape of their bow, were built to navigate the upper reaches of the trans-Mississippi tributaries.[91] The Missouri river boat *Bertrand*, which has been archaeologically excavated, is a good example of this type of boat.

Steam navigation was first introduced to the Gulf rivers east of the Mississippi in 1818 when a steamboat was built on the Alabama river. Although this vessel was a failure, others followed. In 1830 seventeen steamboats were operating on Alabama rivers.[92] On the Chattahoochee river, which divides Georgia and Alabama before flowing through west Florida into the Gulf, the first steamboat was employed in 1827. More than a hundred steamboats operated on the Chattahoochee between 1827 and 1869.[93]

The steamboat first reached Texas before statehood. In 1829 a New York-built boat was employed briefly on the Rio Grande river. The following year a steamer ascended the Brazos. Nearly fifty steamboats, the majority of them side-wheelers, operated on the Brazos before the Civil War.[94]

In the 1850s stern-wheelers began to replace side-wheelers on the western river steamboats. Within a decade a majority of the Mississippi/ Ohio-built vessels were stern-wheelers. Stern wheel steamboats had operated on the western rivers from the launching of the *Washington* 1816. However, for technological reasons they were considered inferior to side-wheelers. Early stern-wheelers had their wheels placed within the hull between the two halves of the stern, a 'recess wheel' as it was known. This structural feature limited the wheel size and made stern-powered boats much slower than side-wheelers. In the 1850s, however, builders began to extend the wheel beyond the hull. The hog chains were

extended to support the heavy stern wheel. Placing the wheels beyond the stern led to much larger wheels and the utilisation of twin wheels. Stern-wheelers were not as manoeuvrable as side-wheelers until the single rudder gave way to the multiple balance rudder. Stern-wheelers had from the beginning certain advantages over side-wheelers. The position of the paddle wheel at the stern gave it substantial protection from driftwood, logs and ice. Stern-wheelers were generally faster and also had the ability to 'grass-hopper' over shallow bars since the rear-mounted paddles would raise the level of water under the hull when operated in reverse. Stern-wheelers were beamier, which reduced the draught and allowed the vessels to carry more cargo.[95]

The last major structural change occurred in the 1880s when the fore main deck was redesigned so that the steamboats could push barges ahead of them. Although steamboats would continue to navigate the western rivers well into the twentieth century, their importance ended long before that century began. Towboats and the railroad ended their rule as queens of the western rivers.

91. Jerome E Petsche, *The Steamboat Bertrand* (Washington, DC 1974), pp90, 98.
92. Harris, *op cit*, p1.
93. Edward A Mueller, *op cit*, C-1 – C-14.
94. P A Puryear & N Winfield, *op cit*, pp41-42.
95. W D Sawyer, 'The Western River Engine', *Steamboat Bill* (Summer 1978), pp143-145.

The last working stern-wheeler on the Mississippi, Standard Oil's Sprague *is seen working a push-tow of oil barges in 1946. The main features of these boats – low freeboard, twin stacks with pilothouse between, full length superstructure, and hogging truss – had remained essentially unchanged for nearly a century. (CMP)*

The introduction of steam navigation to the Great Lakes

The introduction and development of steam navigation on the Great Lakes is inextricably linked to the United States' westward expansion during the nineteenth century. History reveals that despite Hollywood's repeated and often illusory image of the white migration westward, which conjures pictures of endless plains dotted with trains of conestoga wagons, there lies a far more accurate, largely maritime depiction of this event. Long before the advent of roads, railroads, or prairie-bound wagon trains, industrious sea-going side wheel and propeller driven steamships, loaded to the gunwales with settlers and supplies, steamed west to the heartland of America via the inland seas. At ports such as Chicago or Milwaukee, nearly 1000 miles (1500 kilometres) inland, people and cargo were offloaded to river vessels to continue the journey.

To a large extent westward growth created the financial impetus that allowed lakes maritime steam to become economically feasible. Conversely, maritime passenger and cargo trade via steamships served as a logistical lifeline to the West. It seems a testament to steam's early and efficient development that the import and significant use of this technology on the Great Lakes, and the vital role it played in nineteenth-century westward migration and commerce, is now all but ignored.

The Great Lakes were explored early in the seventeenth century by the colonial powers which were to vie for their control. The fresh water seas comprise nearly 100,000 square miles (nearly 250,000 square kilometres) of open water and extend well over 1000 miles inland from the east coast. Early on the Lakes' potential strategic and economic value were fully appraised by France and Britain, causing them to be the centrepiece of several colonial conflicts. Greatly valued, the lakes were, nonetheless, still largely undeveloped and surrounded by primeval fores-

ted wilderness by the time the United States came into control of the southern shores.

White settlement on the Lakes proceeded from east to west with Lake Ontario the first to garner a large population along its shores. The great cataract of the Niagara Falls for a time impeded easy access to the upper lakes of Erie, Huron, and Michigan, while the rapids of the St Mary's river precluded navigation into Lake Superior until completion of locks at Sault Ste Marie in 1855.

Regional development of waterborne trade on the lakes was fostered in the seventeenth century by fishing, and fur trapping commerce. For the next century the lakes were the sole domain of shoal draught brigs and fore and aft rigged sailing vessels. However, expanding migration in the early nineteenth century created a market for fast, punctual, well appointed side wheel, and later propeller-driven, steamships. These ships carried settlers and manufactured supplies West and agricultural produce to the East. Lake Ontario, being the first settled, was the first of the Great Lakes to float a steamship.

Marine steam technology arrived on the Great Lakes in a relatively advanced state of development. East coast experiments with steam powered vessels conducted by Rumsey, Fitch, Stevens and others were shown to be economically feasible by Fulton's *North River Steam Boat (Clermont)*, launched in 1807. The diffusion of steam technology to the remoteness of the Great Lakes, therefore, awaited only the demonstrable need and projected profitability of

steamboat services for the region known as the 'Old Northwest'.

Though Canadian steam vessels plied the St Lawrence river between Montreal and Quebec as early as 1809, and may have ventured a short distance into the open lake, purpose-built lake steamers did not arrive until 1816 with the launching of the American-built *Ontario* and the Canadian *Frontenac*.[96]

Placed in service in 1817 the *Ontario* and *Frontenac* typified early Great Lakes steamers. They were schooner rigged, bluff bowed with pronounced eighteenth-century style fiddlehead and cutwater. They had a straight sheer line and a square raked transom. Obviously these vessels borrowed the typical hull structure of Great Lakes sailing vessels, not a difficult engineering feat as side-wheelers did not need the specially fine underwater run aft that later propellers required to ensure running efficiency. Though impossible to see in profile drawings of these vessels, a deck extending beyond the sheer line formed a partial sponson or guard for the paddle wheels. A semi-circular paddle box gave the side wheel final protection. Like their sailing prede-

96. J B Mansfield, *History of the Great Lakes*, Vol 1 (Chicago 1899), pp587-589; Harry Albert Musham, 'Early Great Lakes Steamboats: the *Ontario* and the *Frontenac*', *The American Neptune* III (1943), pp333-344. Mansfield's study is an extensive work on the Great Lakes, highly accurate for the time it was written and the enormity of the project. Musham's work is based on the 'Reminiscences of Early Sailing Vessels and Steam Boats on Lake Ontario', by Capt James Van Cleve, a pioneer in lake navigation. This work is located in the Chicago Historical Society's Manuscripts.

cessors, lake steamers were steered from the aft section of the quarterdeck.

Laid down later than *Frontenac, Ontario* was, nonetheless, finished sooner by builder Asahil S Roberts for the Lake Ontario Steamboat Company. *Ontario* was built at Sacketts Harbor and went into service under the shadow of the two powerful American ships of the line left on the stocks from the War of 1812.[97] Shipbuilding competition engendered during the war continued to flavour US-Canadian economic rivalry in steamship construction and, not surprisingly, timber for *Ontario* was supplied from cheap and readily available surplus US Navy stocks.

Ontario was modelled after New York's East river packet *Sea Horse*. Driven by a single cylinder low-pressure walking beam engine, *Ontario* was 140ft on deck with a 24ft beam and a Monson's Rule tonnage of 237. Her engine was designed and built by James P Allaire of New York. Steam was supplied by a large copper kidney flue boiler, the precursor of many later constructed on the Lakes. She had a shoal draught of 6ft, which was essential for the unimproved harbours and river mouths at which the vessel called.[98]

Frontenac, on the other hand, was a much larger ship at 700 tons and with a 10ft draught. Both vessels were influenced in their design by US East Coast builders. Two of the partners in *Frontenac* were formerly employed by the firm of Henry Eckford of New York. *Frontenac*'s engine, built by Boulton & Watt of Soho, Birmingham, England, operated on high pressure (60 to 80psi) and functioned without a condenser. Though larger and faster, *Frontenac*'s deeper draught made it difficult for her to compete with her shallower rival.[99]

In 1818, one year after steam navigation became a reality on Lake Ontario, the 338-ton steamship *Walk-in-the-Water* opened the upper lakes to steam navigation. Assembled at Black Rock near Buffalo and launched on Lake Erie, this ship was designed and built by Adam & Noah Brown, a shipbuilding firm located in the East River, New York area. Shipped in pieces to Black Rock, the *Walk-in-the-Water* used a low-pressure square or crosshead engine constructed by Robert McQueen also of New York. She was captained and operated by experienced steam engineers from the Hudson river area. Intended to operate as a packet between Buffalo and Detroit, the *Walk-in-the-Water* became the first steamer to visit Lakes Huron and Michigan on excursion runs.[100]

Originally envisioned as part-freighter/part-passenger ships, side-wheelers on the Great Lakes quickly evolved into pure passenger ships. Their large capital outlay and the cost of opera-

Lake Erie's pioneer steamboat, the picturesquely named Walk-in-the-Water *of 1819. This contemporary likeness is crude but shows the main features of the boat, including the low-pressure engine's crosshead.* (CMP)

tion were too high to allow them to compete economically with sailing ships in cargo hauling. Also the large inefficient low-pressure engines and boilers used in the side-wheelers took up much of the valuable midships section of the vessels. Bulk commodities such as wheat, corn and oats, along with rolling freight such as flour, beef and pork demanded a maximum hold space or deadweight tonnage for a minimum price. Fuel bunkers further reduced cargo capacity in the side-wheelers. Although wood was plentiful and used exclusively as fuel for these ships until the 1840s, a ready boiler supply took up considerable space averaging 10 to 40 cords.

Passenger services, on the other hand, placed a much higher premium on speed and reliability of service. Steamship profits were not dependent on deadweight tonnage but rather on regular schedules with large passenger registers. Profitability was guaranteed by the great number of passengers travelling from East to West during most of the first half of the nineteenth century. Passenger profits were supplemented by the transport of higher priced manufactured goods, whose speedy delivery ensured a premium price.[101]

Early on, steamship competition on the American side of the Lakes was regulated by the New York legislature which declared a monopoly for the Fulton–Livingston Company and their subsidiaries such as the Lake Ontario and Lake Erie Steamboat Companies. However, on 2 March 1824 the Supreme Court of the United States overturned this monopoly.[102]

This court ruling brought immediate competition to the Lakes. *Enterprise*, built by Levi Johnson & Turnhooven Bros, was constructed at Cleveland on Lake Erie to compete with the *Superior*, a replacement for *Walk-in-the-Water*.

The engine of the *Enterprise* was constructed in Pittsburgh, an early indication of that city's expertise in iron machining. By 1825 there were five steamers operating on Lake Erie and eleven on Lake Ontario.[103]

Two occurrences in 1825 ensured the continuation of the steamship boom on the Lakes. The first was the momentous opening of the Erie canal. This canal connected the Atlantic port of New York with both Lakes Erie and Ontario. The St Lawrence at that time was not considered navigable because of its shallowness, and Britain was reluctant to improve it for the sake of foreign commerce. The opening of the Erie canal, therefore, allowed American trade for the first time to proceed via water transport from the Atlantic coast to Fort Dearborn (later Chicago). Additionally, in 1824, the Federal Government for the first time appropriated money for harbour improvement on the Lakes. This money greatly augmented the meagre funds available to towns wishing to improve their harbours and thus their chances of attracting shipbuilders and steamship lines.[104]

Some unique experiments in ship construction were attempted at this time. Lake merchants recognised the need to lower the hull weight of wooden steamers in order to increase their deadweight capacity on the same draught, and two small steamers were constructed without frames out of ½in cross planking. The hulls were described as symmetrical or musk mellon shaped. Though light, the hulls lacked strength and were failures.[105] It would be another thirty-seven years before the lightness and efficacy of iron hulls in merchant vessels would be demonstrated on the lakes with the construction of the iron hulled *Merchant* in 1861.

The commercial success of the Erie canal was not lost on the Canadians. In 1829 the Welland canal opened on the Canadian side, securing a

97. These ships were the *Chippewa*, 74 guns, and the *New Orleans*, 106 guns.

98. H A Musham, *op cit*, p338.

99. *Ibid*, p340. Later vessels produced in Canada list their engines as being built in Montreal.

100. H A Musham, 'Early Great Lakes Steamboats: The *Walk-in-the-Water*', *The American Neptune*, V (1945), pp29-31.

101. Donald Ray Dohrman, *Screw Propulsion in American Lake and Coastal Steam Navigation, 1840-1860* (Ann Arbor, Mich 1977) Yale Dissertation (1976), pp55-58. This study is an extensive economic and technological analysis of early Great Lakes navigation.

102. H A Musham 'Early Great Lakes Steamboats: 1816-1830', *The American Neptune* VI (July 1946), p198.

103. *Ibid*.

104. Norman Beasley, *Freighters of Fortune* (New York 1930), p52.

105. H A Musham, *op cit* (1816-1830), p201.

The introduction of the Great Britain *in 1830 represented a major step forward in Great Lakes steamboat design. As represented in another of the invaluable paintings of James Van Cleve, the hull can be seen to continue the sailing ship tradition of knee bow and square transom, but the long full-width deckhouse and twin stacks more closely resemble riverboat development.*

water route between Lakes Ontario and Erie past Niagara Falls. Begun in 1824, the canal was limited in size with locks of 110ft in length by 22ft width and an 8ft depth over the sills.[106] They, therefore, could not accommodate the beamy side-wheelers. Passenger traffic continued to portage between Lakes Ontario and Erie.

Lake steamer basic design did not change for a decade after the launching of *Ontario*. Though well appointed they seldom carried over two hundred cabin passengers. The faster steamers reported doing about 12mph. These ships averaged about 220 tons, were generally underpowered, and not very manoeuvrable. Numerous incidents of collision and near collisions were reported while ships manoeuvred in the small harbours. Docking without independent power to each wheel was difficult in any sort of breeze. In an attempt to increase effective horsepower some experiments were made with high-pressure engines. These engines were lighter, not needing condensers, air pumps, or large cylinders, yet they produced only a negligible speed increase while using considerably more fuel. Their safety also came into question: in one instance, on 16 September 1830, a steam pipe on the high-pressure *William Peacock* burst, killing fifteen people.[107]

In 1830 the revolutionary 700-ton Canadian steamer *Great Britain* was launched for service on Lake Ontario. The *Great Britain* emphasised

By the time of the Great Western, *built for the Chicago–Buffalo service in 1838, Lake steamers more closely resembled river vessels in all but hull form. This boat was the first on the Lakes with a complete upper superstructure deck.*

design innovations which, though not unique in themselves, nonetheless combined to create for the first time a steamship specifically suited to the inland seas. Designed and built for John Hamilton of Queenston by Brown & Bell of New York, she became the prototype for all Lake steamers produced for at least the next decade. Outwardly the ship retained a bluff bow with fiddlehead and square raked transom. However, she had a full main deck cabin with a canopied promenade deck. She sported two side-by-side smoke-stacks followed by two walking beams athwartships. A wheel house forward of the smoke-stacks completed her modern appearance. Unlike her predecessors she had no sailing rigging, an obvious testament to the new reliability of steam power.

The *Great Britain*, as mentioned, had two low-pressure walking beam engines operated from two boilers which independently control-

led each side wheel. The independent engines added manoeuvrability and dependability. Sponsons ran the full length of the vessel at main deck level considerably enlarging this deck and fully protecting the paddle wheels. Freight was loaded through a fore deck hatch.[108]

The *United States*, a smaller version of the *Great Britain*, was reportedly capable of carrying a thousand passengers per voyage. By 1834 there were thirty-four steamers on the upper lakes, three Canadian and thirty-one US registry having transported 50,000 settlers from Buffalo to Chicago the previous year. This 1800-mile round trip cruise took the average steamer twenty days.[109]

In succeeding years paddle-wheelers on the Lakes grew larger, acquired a plumb bow, a full promenade deck, and a rounded or fantail stern. The steamers *Illinois* (1837) and *Great Western* (1838) exemplified this evolution. By the mid to late 1840s paddle-wheeler designers began to borrow the hogging truss from Hudson river craft. These large bowed arches extended over the superstructure giving lake craft their traditional mid to late nineteenth-century bowed or

106. J B Mansfield, *op cit*, Vol I, pp229-231; H A Musham, *op cit* (1816-1830), p209.

107. *Ibid*, p208. Steamers seem to have ranged in size from the 75-ton *Caroline* to the 700-ton *Frontenac*.

108. *Ibid*, p211.

109. H A Musham, 'Early Great Lakes Steamboats: Westward Ho! and Flush Times', *The American Neptune* VII (1947), p55; N Beasley, *op cit*, p55.

bridge support upperworks. The hogging truss or 'Bishop Arch' was a successful innovation used in shallow draught vessels which helped reduce the pronounced sagging of ships at the bow and stern.[110] Deeper draught, or ocean-going ships not so much concerned with draught, could afford the luxury of applying more structural support inside the hull to reduce hogging or sagging. The hogging truss was particularly effective in early wooden hulled, shallow draught propeller driven ships as all of the weight of the engines and boilers resided in the stern. This weight created a fulcrum aft of centre producing a bowed effect on the length of an empty hull.

Propellers appeared on the American side of the Great Lakes with the completion of the *Vandalia* in November 1841. *Vandalia* was made possible through a collaboration of Oswego merchants, Captain James Van Cleve, and John Ericsson. Ericsson, interested in promoting ship-borne propellers, offered a half share of his US propeller patent to Van Cleve if he would build a propeller steamer on the Lakes within a year of their December 1840 meeting. Van Cleve in turn contacted Oswego merchants as he knew they had the most to gain by the introduction of the propeller.

Oswego was important in the development of the first propeller craft because of its location. The Erie canal terminated at both Oswego on Lake Ontario and Buffalo on Lake Erie. However, because traffic up the lakes from Oswego had to pass through the limited Welland canal, Oswego merchants had a difficult time competing with Buffalo merchants in the burgeoning upper lake passenger and agra-industry trade. Propeller driven ships offered a solution to the problem, for unlike paddle-wheelers they were not restricted by narrow locks and canals.[111]

The *Vandalia* became a complete economic success and the prototype for propeller steamers designed for the Lakes. Built on the same full lines as a Welland canal schooner, with a bluff bow and transom stern, she was 91ft long by 20.17ft in beam with an 8.25ft depth. These dimensions allowed her to pass the expanded Welland canal with a maximum cargo capacity. Her Monson Rule tonnage was slightly over 138. *Vandalia* was powered by two high-pressure, vertical inverted cylinder, direct acting engines. The high-pressure engines produced 40rpm on a small stroke and turned two contra-rotating Ericsson Wheel propellers. These early propeller engines traded speed and 30 to 40 per cent reduction in fuel efficiency for size. The average Great Lakes paddle steamer engines weighed 60 to 90 tons. A propeller engine could weigh as little as 15 tons and took up far less space. The *Vandalia* could also carry fifty passengers at less cost than could the large paddle-wheelers because her main stock was package freight moving to the West and rolling and bulk freight to the East.[112]

By 1860 propeller steamers made up a far greater proportion of the entire merchant fleet on the Lakes than on the coast. Buffalo and Cleveland ranked first and second in the country in tonnage of screwships produced. Propellers on the Great Lakes were not intended to compete with the faster, more luxurious paddle wheel steamers for passenger service but rather supplemented sailing vessels in cargo shipment. Though more expensive to build and operate than sailing ships, propeller steamers offered high quality freight transport in terms of speed and reliability of service. In addition, they offered access through canals and locks, diminishing the need for cargo handling and transfer. Their role as freighters ensured their close association with railroads and canal companies at a much earlier date than on the coast.[113]

Due to the preponderance of propeller driven craft and their association with canal and railroad companies, propeller technology advanced at a faster pace on the Great Lakes than on the coast.[114] Single-shaft vessels were heralded with the conversion of the 400-ton *Porter* in 1843. By the mid 1840s additional improvements in casting techniques evolved a hybrid of the archimedean screw and the windmill type propellers. Ericsson's bladed wheel quickly fell out of use in favour of the more efficient four-bladed Loper design also known as the 'Philadelphia Wheel'. Though less efficient than contemporary British two- and three-bladed designs, the Loper Wheel created far less vibration, a very important factor for wooden hulls whose seams tended to open under intense and prolonged vibration.

Increased propeller usage in the industrialised nations is often cited as one factor in the shift from wood to iron hulls. Originally more expensive, iron hulls were simply able to stand up to continued vibration better than wooden hulls. Use of Richard Loper's design along with the relative costs and ready availability of wood on the Great Lakes ensured a late and sporadic arrival for iron hull technology on the inland seas.[115]

By 1852 the railroad reached Chicago from the East Coast. Unable to compete in speed and cost with the railways, the large paddle steamers fell on hard times. The severe economic panic of 1857 slowed migration and all but ended the reign of the paddle passenger ship as queen of the Lakes.[116] Several suffered an ignoble fate, being cut down and converted to lumber barges in the next decade. Propeller steamers, on the other hand, continued to be competitive with sail in the freight hauling industry, relegating many of the sailing vessels to towed barges or 'consorts' by 1870.[117]

Iron hulled screw ships built in Britain for Canadian owners operated in the St Lawrence and on Lake Ontario in the 1850s and 1860s. However, the first iron hulled propeller driven commercial vessel built entirely on the Lakes was the *Merchant*, built at Buffalo in 1861. This vessel was followed by a few other successful

Vandalia, the first screw-driven vessel on the Lakes, played an important part in the wider history of the propeller, being one of the first commercial successes for John Ericsson and his patent. Van Cleve was part-owner of the vessel and his painting shows that the ship was in other ways unremarkable – ignoring the unobtrusive stovepipe aft, and the cutdown rig, she was otherwise very similar to contemporary Welland Canal schooners.

110. C Patrick Labadie *et al*, *Submerged Cultural Resource Study Isle Royal National Park*, Submerged Cultural Resources Unit, National Park Service (Santa Fe 1987), p55.

111. H A Musham, 'Early Great Lakes Steamboats: The First Propellers, 1841-1845', *The American Neptune* XVII (1957), pp93-95.

112. *Ibid*, p95; D R Dohrman, *op cit*.

113. D R Dohrman, *op cit*. This paragraph contains a synopsis of many of Dr Dohrman's observations concerning the introduction of propeller driven vessels to the Great Lakes.

114. *Ibid*.

115. H A Musham, *op cit* (The First Propellers), p103; D R Dohrman, *op cit*; Robert Target, 'The Early Development of the Screw Propeller', *American Society of Naval Engineering Journal*, LXXI (May 1959), p267. In the early 1840s the federal government promoted iron hull technology with the construction of the USS *Michigan* and three other revenue cutters and survey vessels for the lakes. Despite this endorsement iron was not used to construct a merchant vessel until 1861.

116. D R Dohrman, *op cit*. Oddly enough on the Great Lakes, large luxuriously appointed passenger carrying paddle wheel steamers persisted in small numbers well into the twentieth century.

117. C P Labadie, *op cit*, pp55-56.

iron hulled propellers in the 1870s.[118] Lake ship-builders persisted in wooden hull construction due to the availability of timber, expertise in wooden ship construction, and the fact that wooden hulls operating exclusively in the fresh water of the Great Lakes demonstrated great durability.

In the final analysis, the small size of the vessels, and therefore the profit margin, finally turned Lake shippers away from wood to steel. The larger the deadweight capacity the more profitable was the ship, particularly in bulk cargo operations such as wheat, coal and iron ore. Steel ships, being stronger, could be built much larger. By 1880 advanced steel hulls and compound high-pressure machinery were available from British yards and were shipped to the Lakes in sections. Thereafter, steel, a stronger more flexible material than wrought iron, supplanted iron in most new construction. The first American steel hulls produced on the Lakes were built in 1886, with the propeller steamer *Spokane* taking the lead.[119]

In essence, therefore, steam technology arrived on the Great Lakes from the East Coast ready made. Early Great Lakes steamers were basically large versions of East and Hudson River type craft. These paddle-wheelers became an immediate economic success due to expanding westward migration and the premium paid for speed, dependability, and quality of service. Although steam technology arrived from the East Coast it was adapted to the peculiarities of the Great Lakes region. Some marine improvements, particularly propellers, went full circle passing back to the coast in a more advanced form.

Ironically, though the unique setting of the Great Lakes contributed to the early acceptance of the latest innovations in steam propulsion, it also fostered the persistent use of retrograde marine technology. Iron hulls, promoted early in the 1840s by the government, were not cost effective for commercial use until much later. This is understandable in a land blessed with seemingly endless supplies of timber. Wooden hulls on the inland seas successfully made the transition from paddles to propellers, persisting until after the turn of the twentieth century.

Surprisingly, paddle wheels forged a partial comeback during the last part of the nineteenth

The steamers of the Far West were very similar to other Western river steamboats, except that water conditions kept them smaller. This was true on both sides of the 47th Parallel, Canadian river and lake steamers being of the same overall pattern. This is Canadian Pacific's Slocan *of 1897, a stern-wheeler for service on the lakes of British Columbia. (CMP)*

and first part of the twentieth centuries. Steel hulled palatial side-wheelers, up to 600ft in length, were constructed for the railroads. Two, the *Wolverine* and *Sable*, underwent a unique conversion during the Second World War to become the only paddle wheel aircraft carriers and were used for deck landing training.

Today Lakes craft range from 1000ft ore carriers to 400ft car ferries. Wheat, coal and iron ore are still moved as bulk freight though no pure passenger ships are left to pass on the legacy of the *Ontario*.

The Far West

As a result of the war with Mexico in 1847, the United States acquired a vast area that included the present states of Arizona, New Mexico, and California. Within two years gold was discovered in California. The gold strike attracted thousands of people from throughout the United States and abroad. The strike was also responsible for the introduction of steam navigation to the California coast, and to the rivers in the Far West. In 1852 a small 40-ton single-deck side-wheeler, *Uncle Sam*, was launched on the Colorado river, then only a stream flowing from the Gulf of California to Wyoming. Approximately 600 miles of this river are considered navigable. Thousands of people crossed the

Colorado on their way to California and the gold fields. Many never made it to California but settled along the Colorado and in other parts of Arizona. The *Uncle Sam* and some fifteen other steamers became the lifeline for the ranchers, merchants, soldiers and miners in Arizona.[120] The Colorado river steamboats were primarily stern-wheelers, powered by a variety of engine types. These vessels averaged under 100 tons, although the *Mohave II* was approximately 188 tons. They had little draught, averaging under 1ft. The majority were built either in San Francisco or along the river itself.

The first steamboat in California was Russian, the 37ft long *Sitka*, used in Alaska before being dismantled and brought to the Sacramento river in 1847. Two years later four steamboats were operating on the Sacramento carrying supplies and prospectors from San Francisco to the gold fields. Three of these boats were built along the Atlantic seaboard and transported by ship around Cape Horn to California.[121] Although many of the Sacramento river and San Francisco Bay steamboats were built in the East, others,

118. *Ibid*, p58; Alexander Crosby Brown, 'Notes on the Origins of Iron Shipbuilding in the United States, 1825-1861', MA Thesis, William and Mary, Williamsburg 1951), p205.

119. *Ibid*, pp58-59.

120. Richard R Lingenfelter, *Steamboats on the Colorado River 1852-1916* (Tuscon, Arizona 1978), *passim*.

121. Frank Donovan, *River Boats of America* (New York 1966), pp166-167.

such as the *Chrysopolis*, were built in San Francisco. The *Chrysopolis* was a large side-wheeler, 245ft in length, 40ft in beam, 884 gross register tons, and powered by a low-pressure engine. The vessels that were built to operate on the Bay and lower river were generally similar to those on eastern United States rivers and sounds, having low-pressure engines and deep-water hulls with deep draughts. The steamboats built to operate on the upper Sacramento river and its tributaries were a fusion of eastern and western river boats. They were relatively flat-bottomed with draughts that were as little as 12-14in, and powered by high-pressure engines. They were also stern-wheelers. The *Latona*, built in San Francisco in 1857, was 107 tons, while *The James Blair* was 108 tons. More than sixty steamers were built on the Bay or river between 1859 and 1867.

A gold strike also influenced the development of steam transportation on the Columbia river. The *Beaver*, a British-built vessel, was the first steamer on that river. She had a brief career on the Columbia followed by a long one on Puget Sound. Other steamboats followed, most of them from the San Francisco area. In 1850 the *Columbia* was built at Astoria, the first steamboat constructed on the Columbia. The Columbia river is divided by rapids into three distinct sections. The lower river was navigable for deep draught vessels for approximately 150 miles. The two upper sections, however, were navigable only for shallow draught steamboats. The majority of the upper river boats were built on the river and were small stern-wheelers.

Steamships on the Atlantic coast

Unlike the proliferation of steamboats on the rivers and sounds of the eastern United States, oceanic steam navigation developed more slowly on the Atlantic Coast. Although numerous early vessels made successful voyages among the major ports at New York, Boston, Philadelphia, Norfolk, Washington, Charleston and Savannah, efforts to establish and maintain a regular service required larger and stronger vessels with more dependable and efficient machinery. Vessels developed to operate on Long Island Sound and the Chesapeake Bay provided the first heavy weather experiments and set the stage for the first coastal steamers of the 1830s.

The first steamship built expressly for coastal navigation was the 702-ton *Robert Fulton* constructed by Henry Eckford in New York. The vessel was built for David Dunham & Company to compete with sailing packets connecting New York, Charleston, South Carolina and Havana, Cuba. *Robert Fulton*'s hull was 159ft in length and the vessel's crosshead engine was a more powerful version of that which had been installed in the *Chancellor Livingston*, measuring 44in in diameter of cylinder. The stroke was 5ft and the engine turned the paddle wheel shaft by means of a flywheel 12ft in diameter. *Robert Fulton*'s copper boiler measured 30ft 10in in length and was designed to burn coal exclusively. To provide protection for the machinery the engineering space was isolated by watertight bulkheads. In the event of a fire the engineering space could also be flooded without sinking the ship. While the vessel was designed to employ steam as a principal means of motive power, it was also equipped with masts and sails. The original rig was to be a light one consisting only of lugsails but, the vessel was ship rigged in Charleston, South Carolina, following storm damage in 1820. The *Robert Fulton* proved to be highly successful and by 1825 had made eighteen voyages along the Atlantic coast and into the Gulf of Mexico.[122]

Equally successful was the 281-ton steam brig *New York* which was built in 1822. The *New York* was built at Norfolk, Virginia, by William F Hunter and measured 105ft in length, 27ft 6in in beam and 11ft in depth of hold. The hull was traditional in design with one deck, a square stern and billethead. Paddle wheels amidship were powered by a beam engine. The vessel proved to be effective carrying both passengers and freight between New York and Norfolk for over a year before being lost in a storm off Cape Henry.[123]

The success of early steamships such as the *Robert Fulton* and *New York* provided the initiative for a second generation of coastal vessels. Curiously the second generation of steamers were designed and constructed more along the lines of those developed for riverine service than for the Atlantic. One of the first was the 190-ton *David Brown* built by Brown & Bell in 1832. Small, *David Brown* measured 130ft 11in in length. James P Allaire produced the vessel's engine which was a crosshead design that powered paddle wheels approximately amidships. *David Brown* was originally built to transport ironware from Red Bank, New Jersey, to New York but was placed on the Charleston route before the end of the year. Allaire and his partners added the similarly designed but larger 294-ton *William Gibbons*, also built by Brown & Bell, in 1834. Like the *David Brown* the *William Gibbons* was equipped with a crosshead engine. Before

The early coastal steamer Home *was lost as a result of heavy weather off Cape Hatteras in 1837, proving that Atlantic conditions required something larger and more robust for safe passenger services.* (The Mariners' Museum, Newport News)

the *William Gibbons* was lost off the North Carolina coast the Southern Steam Packet Company put in service the 423-ton Brown & Bell-built steamer *Columbia*. *Columbia* was 164ft 6in long, 22ft 6in in beam, and had an increased depth of hold that measured 11ft 10in. The Allaire crosshead engine measured 56in in diameter and operated on a stroke of 6ft. To accommodate passengers the *Columbia* was equipped with staterooms.[124]

Increased coastal passenger service was dealt a major setback in 1837 when the Southern Steam Packet Company's vessel *Home* was lost in a storm near Cape Hatteras. Although the 537-ton *Home* was the largest vessel operated by the company, it proved to be no match for the Atlantic, and approximately one hundred lives were lost when the ship, sinking, was put ashore on the North Carolina Outer Banks.[125] The *Home* disaster was followed a year later by the loss of the 687-ton steamship *Pulaski*. The *Pulaski* was operated between Savannah, Charleston and Baltimore by the Savannah & Charleston Steam Packet Company and was the largest steamship in operation on the Atlantic seaboard at the time of loss.[126] Public reaction to these disasters combined with the economic decline associated with the Panic of 1837 caused the Southern Steam Packet Company to collapse and this significantly undermined the operations of other coastal steamships.

In 1844 a consortium of Charleston and New York merchants formed the New York & Charleston Steamship Company to resurrect sched-

122. C Ridgely-Nevitt, *op cit*, pp52-57; J H Morrison, *op cit*, pp436-437; P C Coker, *op cit*, p176.

123. C Ridgely-Nevitt, *op cit*, pp67-72; J H Morrison, *op cit*, pp435-436.

124. C Ridgely-Nevitt, *op cit*, pp73-75; J H Morrison, *op cit*, pp437-438.

125. C Ridgely-Nevitt, *op cit*, pp76-77; J H Morrison, *op cit*, pp437-438.

126. J H Morrison, *op cit*, p442.

*At 191ft by 30ft and 785 tons the New York &
Charleston's* Southerner *of 1846 was the first
American coastal steamer to exceed the early* Robert
Fulton *in size. This portrait exaggerates her size by
reducing the scale of the passengers, but the height of
the pilothouse and deckhouse give a better idea of
proportion.* (The Mariners' Museum, Newport
News)

uled steamship services between the two cities.
Their first vessel, *Southerner,* was launched by
William H Brown of New York in 1846. *Southerner* was a radical departure from those steamers previously running in the Atlantic coastal
trade. At 785 tons *Southerner* was the first steamships built for the coastal trade that eclipsed the
Robert Fulton in size. Like the *Robert Fulton,*
Southerner's hull was designed for the ocean and
heavily built. The hull resembled the successful
sailing packets of the period and incorporated a
transom stern and decorated head. The forecastle and poop were connected by a continuous
bulwark that produced an uninterrupted sheer
from bow to stern. Unlike the fragile paddle
boxes, guards and sponsons of the previous generation of steamers, *Southerner's* paddle boxes
were protected by extensions of the hull planking that swept out around the wheel. Aft of a
pilothouse on the fore deck and between the
paddle wheels amidships was a galley. Well appointed first class passenger accommodation was
located in the stern and arranged around a grand
saloon. The sail plan consisted of square sails on
the fore mast and fore and aft sails on the main
and mizzen.[127] Machinery for the *Southerner* was
also quite different from that previously employed by coastal steamships. It consisted of a
massive side lever engine, with 67in diameter
cylinder and 8ft stroke, produced by Novelty
Iron Works. The engines were located low in
the hull and, combined with a bed-plate that
weighed 15 tons, provided increased stability.
Steam was provided by a return tube boiler located forward of the machinery but also low in
the hull. Power was transferred to the water by
paddle wheels 31ft in diameter and capable of
pushing the vessel at more than 12kts.[128] *Southerner* cut the time between New York and Charleston to an average of only 60 hours.[129]

Southerner proved to be an immediate success and the New York & Charleston Steamship
Company ordered a second and larger vessel in
1847. Named *Northerner,* the vessel was 203ft
6in in length, 32ft 4in in beam and had a 21ft
8in depth of hold. Although the steamer measured 1012 tons it was designed and constructed
in the same manner as the *Southerner.* These
vessels and the 1200-ton *Union,* 900-ton *Marion,*
1150-ton *James Adger* and 1220-ton *Nashville*

represented the state of the art in antebellum
steamships and made reliable and safe coastal
operations possible. The vessels of the New
York & Charleston Steamship Company provided the model that the New York & Savannah
Steam Navigation Company emulated when
they ordered the *Cherokee* and *Tennessee* to initiate steam packet services between Savannah and
New York. Both the *Cherokee* and *Tennessee* were
built by William H Webb and Novelty Iron
Works supplied the side lever engines.[130]

Just as the New York & Charleston Steamship Company's vessels *Southerner* and *Northerner*
provided the model for antebellum paddle
steamers, their screw propeller vessels were
among the first constructed following the Civil
War. *City of Atlanta* and *City of Columbia* served
until the company ceased operations in 1885.
The Clyde Line, that continued operations between New York and Charleston into the
twentieth century, in 1886 initiated construction
of a series of iron and later steel steamers with
Delaware shipyards. Those vessels were equipped with triple-expansion engines. The first of
them, *Seminole* and *Cherokee,* were ordered from
Cramp in Philadelphia and reflected the new
technology in hull and engine construction being developed on the Delaware.[131] *Comanche,*
built for the line by Cramp & Sons in 1895, was
300ft in length, 46ft in beam and had a 26ft 3in
depth of hold. The vessel was powered by a
quadruple-expansion engine with 36in stroke
and cylinders measuring 24½in, 43½in, 49½in,
and 70in in diameter.[132]

In New England steam replaced fast sailing
packets slowly. Most of the vessels operating on
routes that connected the New England coast
and provided intercourse with Boston were a
combination of paddle and screw steamers built
in the yards of New York and on the Delaware.
With few exceptions most of those vessels were
constructed of wood until the third quarter of

the nineteenth century when iron vessel construction increased rapidly in the 1880s. One of
those exceptions was the 231-ton *Bangor,* the
first iron screw propeller steamer built by the
Wilmington, Delaware, firm of Harlan & Hollingsworth. The Bangor Steam Navigation Company ordered the *Bangor* in 1845 for service on
the Boston to Bangor route. The hull was
formed of forged iron bar frames, and plates
were attached clinker fashion by wrought iron
clips that fitted over the frames. The *Bangor's*
two engines turned independently-operated
screw propellers.

The iron hull steamer *Bangor* was considered
extraordinary in 1845 but, as in the southeast,
many New England steamboat companies turned to iron and later to steel vessels during the
last quarter of the nineteenth century. While
most of those were built by yards on the Delaware, the New England Shipbuilding Company
of Bath, Maine, began to turn out fine steamers
like the paddle steamer *Portland* built in 1890.
Portland measured 2283 tons and was 291ft in
length. Machinery for the vessel was provided by
two other important New England firms: the
1200hp engine was built by The Portland Company with a 62in diameter cylinder and a stroke
of 12ft; the venerable Bath Iron Works provided
the vessel's return flue boilers. Although certainly not impressive, *Portland* could make 12mph.

127. C Ridgely-Nevitt, *op cit,* pp99-101; P C Coker, *op cit,*
p190; J H Morrison, *op cit,* p444.

128. C Ridgely-Nevitt, *op cit,* p101; P C Coker, *op cit,* p190;
J H Morrison, *op cit,* p444.

129. C Ridgely-Nevitt, *op cit,* p101.

130. C Ridgely-Nevitt, *op cit,* pp111-112; James P Delgado,
'Steamers to Savannah: The Origins and Establishment of
the New York and Savannah Steamship Company', *The
American Neptune* XLVII (1987), pp36-37; J H Morrison,
op cit, pp445-446.

131. J H Morrison, *op cit,* pp447-448.

132. *Ibid,* p490.

Transoceanic steam navigation

Although the Fulton–Livingston monopoly forced the first open ocean steam navigation only two years after the successful operation of the *North River Steam Boat*, it was a decade before a steamship crossed the Atlantic. That first vessel was the *Savannah*, the product of the initiative of the Savannah Steam Ship Company which had been formed by prominent Savannah entrepreneurs shortly after the steamer *Charleston* arrived in that Georgia city in 1817. The purpose of the company was to 'attract either as auxiliary or as principal, the propulsion of steam to sea vessels, for the purposes of navigating the Atlantic and other oceans, and that they have provided a ship for that purpose, which is now in a sufficient state of forwardness to afford sanguine expectations of the experiment being tested...'[133] To that end the company purchased the sailing packet under construction at the New York shipyard of Samuel Crockett and William Fickett. Designed for the New York–Le Havre route, the 319-ton *Savannah* was ship rigged and measured 98ft 6in in length. In order to facilitate installation of steam machinery the vessel's second deck forward of the main mast was eliminated.

Machinery for the *Savannah* was supplied by an assortment of experienced engineering firms. Daniel Dodd of Elizabeth, New Jersey, provided two coal-fired copper boilers and a design for the inclined crosshead engine. James Allaire's New York foundry supplied the 40³/₈in steam cylinder castings and air pump while Stephen Vail's Speedwell Iron Works of Morristown, New Jersey, constructed the engine and supplied parts for the 16ft diameter collapsible paddle wheels. In spite of the unusual arrangements made for the engineering plant the *Savannah* was successfully tested in March 1819. The New York *Gazette* reported that, 'she works to advantage, and her velocity is such to give entire satisfaction'.[134]

On 27 March 1819, *Savannah* departed New York under the command of Captain Moses Rogers. Rogers was a highly experienced captain

The Atlantic was first crossed by a steamer in 1819, although the Savannah *used her engines for only about 85 hours during a voyage lasting 27½ days. As this model reveals, the vessel was a full rigged sailing ship fitted for auxiliary steam propulsion, the paddle wheels being collapsible. The ship was sent to Europe for sale, the owners having no thought of establishing a regular transatlantic service: indeed, it was eight years before another steamer made the crossing. (ScM)*

from New London, Connecticut, and had been in command of the *Phoenix* on the 1809 voyage from Sandy Hook to Cape May, and had commanded the *Eagle* during the 1815 voyage from Cape Henlopen to Cape Charles. Captain Rogers brought the *Savannah* safely from New York to Savannah in nine days. Although the engine was successfully operated during the voyage, the *Savannah* was under sail for almost the entire trip. After a celebrated arrival in Savannah, the vessel was sent to Charleston with an invitation to visiting President James Monroe to travel aboard the ship to Savannah. The President refused the invitation to avoid offending Charlestonians and the *Savannah*'s return to Georgia was eclipsed by President Monroe's visit. When a proposed voyage to Liverpool failed to attract either passengers or freight the Savannah Steam Ship Company decided to send the vessel to Russia. There they hoped to find a market for the ship.[135]

Although the *Savannah* cleared for St Petersburg at the Savannah Customs House on 20 May 1819, the ship did not sail until 22 May. Early on 20 May a member of the crew, John Weston, fell overboard and drowned while attempting to come aboard. After steaming down river on 22 May, the ship anchored to await a favourable wind. Early in the morning of 24 May the ship got underway and crossed the bar. After dropping the pilot, the paddle wheels were shipped and the *Savannah* continued into the Atlantic under sail. During the voyage steam was employed sporadically when winds were not favourable. When the British revenue cutter *Kite* spotted the *Savannah* off the coast of Ireland on 17 June the supply of coal was virtually exhausted; twenty-nine days out of Savannah, on 20

133. C Ridgely-Nevitt, *op cit*, p59.

134. *Ibid*, p59.

135. *Ibid*, pp58-60; J H Morrison, *op cit*, pp406-408.

June 1819, the *Savannah* steamed up the Mersey and into Liverpool. When news of the crossing was carried in the *Niles New York Register* on 21 August 1819, it was reported that the vessel was under steam for eighteen of the twenty-nine days at sea.[136]

The lack of financial success registered by the bold plans of the Savannah Steam Ship Company demonstrated the practical and technological limitations of transoceanic steam navigation. The voyage demonstrated that transatlantic steam navigation was certainly possible but it was clearly not yet necessarily a potentially profitable venture. In America the technological problems associated with long range steam navigation were being resolved in vessels designed for the coastal trades. Critical to the success of transoceanic steam navigation were the inseparable issues of steam plant power, reliability and economy. In addition to the technological barriers there was also the necessity for available investment capital. With few exceptions, in early nineteenth-century America that was channelled within the country. The United States was a new country with what appeared to be unlimited opportunities for profitable internal investment.

While Americans must have agreed with the New York *Courier and Enquirer*'s 24 April 1838 opinion that 'the feasibility of the passage of the Atlantic by steam, as far as regards safety, comfort, and dispatch, even in the roughest and most boisterous weather, the most skeptical must now cease to doubt', they must also have harboured similar reservations about 'whether or not the expenses of equipment and fuel will admit of the employment of these vessels in the ordinary packet service'.[137] Those doubts and the preoccupation with developing coastal and riverine steam routes funnelled American capital away from the Atlantic for almost a decade after the *Sirius* and *The Great Western* steamed into New York city.

In fact it was not until the United States decided to subsidise the development of transatlantic mail service that American steamship companies were induced and/or established to compete with well entrenched British lines. Supported by a yearly $200,000 contract to carry the United States Mail to Bremen via Cowes, the Ocean Steam Navigation Co ordered the construction of two steamers in 1846. Contracts for both vessels were signed with Westervelt & Mackay in New York. The first, named the *Washington*, was to be 230ft in length. The second, named the *Herman*, was to be 235ft in length, 40ft in the beam and have a 31ft depth of hold. Both ships were powered by side lever engines of 72in diameter and 10ft stroke designed and built by Novelty Iron Works. Both ships

were operated successfully until Congress refused to subsidise any further foreign mail contracts in 1857. When the mail contract expired that year the *Washington* and *Herman* were withdrawn from service.[138]

By building only two instead of four steamers the Ocean Steam Navigation Company failed to fulfil its contract with the United States Government, providing an opportunity for the formation of a mail service by another company. The New York & Havre Steam Navigation Company was organised by Mortimer Livingston, one of the partners in a sailing packet company that had served New York and Havre since 1830. The government contract allowed alternative sailings to Bremen and Le Havre and for the latter the new firm ordered two ships from Westervelt & Mackay. They were named *Franklin* and *Humbolt* in honour of American scientists. The 2184-ton *Franklin* was 264ft in length. Novelty Iron Works supplied the vessel's twin side lever engines of 93in bore and 8ft stroke. The 2181-ton *Humbolt* was 283ft in length, 40ft in beam and had a depth of hold of 27ft 2in. Novelty Iron Works supplied the vessel's twin side lever engines of 95in bore and 9ft stroke.[139] The hulls of both vessels were reinforced by diagonal iron straps to provide the longitudinal strength required by large wooden hull steamers.

On 5 October 1850 the *Franklin*, under the command of Captain James A Wotton, departed New York for France and the hull of the *Humbolt* was launched. While the *Humbolt*'s machinery was being installed the *Franklin*'s return trip was completed in 13 days and 22 hours at a profit. In addition to a payment of $6250 for delivering mail, the voyage produced $18,000 in freight and $6000 in passenger fares. On 6 May 1851 the *Humbolt*, under the command of Captain David Lines, joined *Franklin* and a monthly schedule that was rarely altered was established. Although the vessels were run conservatively the *Humbolt* was lost in December 1853. To replace *Humbolt* the New York & Havre Steam Navigation Company first leased the 1220-ton coastal steamer *Nashville* and then signed a long term contract for the services of the 1200-ton steamer *Union*.[140]

On 17 July 1854 the *Franklin* suffered a fate similar to that of the *Humbolt*. On a return voyage from Cowes, the steamer grounded in a fog off Moriches Inlet, approximately 50 miles west of Montauk Point on Long Island. To replace the *Franklin* the company chartered the new 1621-ton side wheel steamer *St Louis* from the Pacific Mail Steamship Company. With the *Union* and *St Louis* keeping up a satisfactory schedule, the New York & Havre Steam Navi-

gation Company placed orders for vessels to replace their losses. The first of those was the 2240-ton steamer *Arago*. Like the Pacific Mail Steamship Company's vessels *Illinois* and *Golden Gate*, *Arago* was fitted with twin oscillating cylinder engines of 65in bore and 10ft stroke and constructed by Novelty Iron Works to develop 1450hp. *Arago*'s boilers were positioned fore and aft of the machinery making the engineering space more functional. That space was also isolated from the remainder of the hull by wooden watertight bulkheads designed to improve safety.[141]

To improve safety further in heavy weather almost all of the *Arago*'s accommodation had been placed below the spar deck. The main deck contained the first and second class cabins and dining saloon, and the berth deck contained quarters for the crew, additional cabins for passengers and space amidships designated for the vessel's machinery.[142] Although not readily apparent, the hull was sharp fore and aft to facilitate easy passage through the water and was reinforced with diagonal iron straps for longitudinal rigidity.[143]

Before the *Arago* was completed the loss of the *Franklin* made a second vessel necessary. Instead of ordering a sister-ship, the New York & Havre Steam Navigation Company found that Smith & Dimon's yard had an uncompleted vessel ordered by the Pacific Mail Steamship Company. Coincidentally, the hull, nominally altered to satisfy the Havre Line, had almost the same dimensions as the *Arago*. At 287ft in length, 40ft 10in in beam and with a depth of hold of 32ft the vessel, named *Fulton*, measured 2307 tons. Machinery was supplied by the Morgan Iron Works and consisted of two 65in diameter oscillating cylinders mounted fore and aft of the paddle wheel shaft at 45 degrees and having a stroke of 10ft. Martin-type boilers with brass tubes were installed to provide adequate steam with suitable fuel economy. Although the exterior of the two ships differed substantially, the interior arrangements were almost identical.[144]

136. C Ridgely-Nevitt, *op cit*, pp58-60; J H Morrison, *op cit*, pp406-408.

137. Henry Fry, *The History of North Atlantic Steam Navigation* (London 1986), p41.

138. C Ridgely-Nevitt, *op cit*, pp128-139; J H Morrison, *op cit*, pp408-409.

139. C Ridgely-Nevitt, *op cit*, pp172, 173, 358.

140. *Ibid*, pp172-175; J H Morrison, *op cit*, p409.

141. C Ridgely-Nevitt, *op cit*, pp176-178; J H Morrison, *op cit*, pp409-411.

142. C Ridgely-Nevitt, *op cit*, pp178-179.

143. *Ibid*, p179.

144. *Ibid*, pp181-182.

The New York and Havre SN Co's Fulton, a big wooden paddler of 2061 tons, built by Smith & Dimon of New York in 1855. The ship was fast and comfortable, but not a record-breaker. She was taken up for military duties during the Civil War but returned to Atlantic service in 1865 and ran between New York, Falmouth and Le Havre until 1867; she was broken up in 1870. (By courtesy of John Bowen)

In June 1855 the *Arago* steamed out of New York under the command of Captain David Lines. The *Fulton* followed under Captain James A Wotton in February 1856. Both vessels registered excellent, although not record-breaking crossings and proved comfortable in the heavy Atlantic weather. Their popularity with passengers and shippers made it possible for the Havre Line to compete with both the Cunard steamers returning to service after the Crimean War and the French Compagnie Franco-Americaine, which put four iron screw steamers in service. Even competition from Cornelius Vanderbilt's new steamer *Vanderbilt* did not undermine the Havre Line. While the service provided by *Arago* and *Fulton* withstood both foreign and domestic competition, a drastic reduction in the mail service contract in 1857 and the death of Mr Livingston presented serious problems. However, because the line was managed by excellent businessmen the damage was contained and regular sailings continued well into the period when Atlantic navigation had been disrupted by the Civil War.[145]

Both the *Fulton* and *Arago* continued their scheduled routes until the former was taken into the Quartermaster Corps service in February 1862 and the *Arago* was taken by the Navy Department the following month. While the war disrupted American maritime commerce and transportation between New York and Havre, military charters for the *Arago* and *Fulton* brought the company excellent returns. When the conflict ended in 1865 the Havre Line was able to put both vessels into yards for extensive rebuilding. Before the end of 1865 both vessels

had resumed their commercial routes and sailed for France. Unfortunately during the war the French Compagnie Generale Transatlantique had put new plush vessels into service between Havre and New York. Both passengers and freight had been attracted and the older *Arago* and *Fulton* could not break back into the business. In 1866 both vessels were withdrawn and advertised for sale.[146]

The same year that the Ocean Steam Navigation Company was incorporated the New York & Liverpool United Mail Steamship Company was formed. Popularly identified as the Collins Line, the company also received a contract from the United States Government to carry mail and provide steamers in the event the United States Navy might find itself in need of war steamers.[147] The company ordered four vessels to support the mail contract and provide passenger services. The first was the 2845-ton *Atlantic* built at the New York yard of William H Brown in 1849. Novelty Iron Works provided the *Atlantic*'s side lever engines. That same year the *Pacific* was built by Jacob Bell of New York and James Allaire provided the side lever engines. The following year two additional vessels were constructed: the *Arctic* by William H Brown and the *Baltic* by Jacob Bell. Again Novelty Iron Works provided machinery for the *Arctic* and James Allaire supplied the powerplant for the *Baltic*. Instructions from the bridge were communicated through a telegraph produced by Charles Howland of New York, and steam from the Martin Patent water-tube boilers was piped to a signalling whistle on the smoke-stack.[148]

In accordance with the bill passed by Con-

gress, five steamers were ultimately to be built, four constructed immediately and a fifth to follow. Each of the steamers was to measure at least 2000 tons and have engines of at least 1000hp. The vessels were to be constructed under US Navy supervision and be readily adapted to support military operations.[149] The original design for the vessels proposed by the New York & Liverpool United Mail Steamship Company were found unacceptable by naval constructors John Lenthall and Samuel Hartt. As a consequence the final products were very much the result of the vessels' builders' experience and reflected some variations. The 2845-ton *Atlantic* was 284ft in length; the 2707-ton *Pacific* was 281ft in length, 45ft in beam and had a 32ft 3in depth of hold; the 2856-ton *Arctic* was 285ft in length, 45ft 11in in beam and had a 22ft 11in depth of hold; the 2723-ton *Baltic* was 282ft 6in in length, 45ft in beam and had a 22ft 6in depth of hold.[150]

Although there were differences in design the outward appearance of the vessels was almost identical.[151] The stems were raked slightly forward and were without a bowsprit. The sterns were round and without a horizontal knuckle associated with the wales. Each vessel originally contained three continuous decks but orlop decks were ultimately added fore and aft of the engineering space amidships. A large dining saloon was located forward on the main deck and the galley was on the spar deck above. Ice houses provided refrigeration and steam provided heat. Like the *Washington* and *Herman* built by the Ocean Steam Navigation Company, the Collins Line vessels were well equipped to carry about two hundred first class passengers in comfort. However, because of the potential necessity to operate as a ship of war, the vessels' specifications called for heavy scantlings. The keel and

145. *Ibid*, pp182-184.

146. *Ibid*, pp298-299.

147. F E Dayton, *op cit*, p366.

148. J H Morrison, *op cit*, pp416-417; C Ridgely-Nevitt, *op cit*, pp150-153.

149. C Ridgely-Nevitt, *op cit*, p149.

150. H Fry, *op cit*, pp66-69; J H Morrison, *op cit*, pp411-420; C Ridgely-Nevitt, *op cit*, p150.

151. C Ridgely-Nevitt, *op cit*, p150.

The operations of the Collins Line were dogged by ill luck. Two of the initial quartet of steamers were lost, including the Arctic, *depicted in this Currier & Ives print. The wooden paddler collided with the French iron steamer* Vesta *in fog off Cape Race, and although the American ship did not sink immediately 322 lives were lost, whereas the watertight bulkheads kept the French ship afloat. For E K Collins, the owner of the line, it was a double tragedy since his wife and children were among the passengers who drowned. (CMP)*

keelson of each ship were to be of white oak; heavy double frames of white oak and chestnut were to be strengthened by diagonal iron straps; and planking and ceiling both called for yellow pine. Below the waterline the vessels were to be closely fastened with copper and galvanised iron was to be employed above the waterline.[152]

Atlantic, first of the Collins steamers to be completed, departed New York on 27 April 1850. The maiden voyage proved to be a trying thirteen-day passage marred by mechanical failures but before the end of the year each of the steamers had registered a transatlantic passage in acceptable time. In spite of persistent mechanical problems, the vessels accomplished the requirements of the New York & Liverpool United Mail Steamship Company's contract. In addition, the ships attracted both cargo and passengers, the latter in numbers commensurate with those of the Cunard liners serving New York. Because of their size and design each of the new steamers proved to be a sound vessel in

bad weather. This also contributed to their popularity with the public.

Unfortunately for the Collins Line the advantage was a fleeting one. On 27 September 1854, the *Arctic* struck the French steamer *Vesta* about 40 miles off Cape Race, Newfoundland. Although the iron-hulled *Vesta*, equipped with watertight bulkheads, survived the collision, the *Arctic* sank with considerable loss of life. In 1856 the Cunard Line resumed the service with New York that had been interrupted by the Crimean War with two new vessels, *Arabia* and *Persia*. In addition, the *Pacific* disappeared on a voyage from Liverpool with 288 passengers. While the loss of the *Arctic* had not materially damaged Collins' operations, the disappearance of the *Pacific* was disastrous. Steamers, such as the *Ericsson*, that had been leased to maintain the US mail contract were found to be inadequate for the task, and the government cut payments when Collins did not remedy the situation. The

Persia, put on the New York route by Cunard, attracted passengers who refused to patronise the Collins Line's vessels. By 1857 there were only half the number of passengers that had booked passage the previous year. Completion of the 4145-ton 345ft *Adriatic*, largest and last of the five vessels required by the government contract, failed to turn the deteriorating financial situation around. When Congress failed to renew the mail subsidy at the current rate of $858,000 and cut funding to $385,000 for the contract, the operation became completely untenable. On 1 April 1858 the remaining three vessels were sold at auction for $50,000 in an unsuccessful effort to pay off the company debt.[153]

United States Mail contracts also attracted the venerable Commodore Cornelius Vanderbilt in 1855. When his inquiries failed to attract the attention of the United States Postal Service he attempted unsuccessfully to compete with the Collins and Havre lines' routes to Europe in 1855. Two years later in the spring of 1857, Vanderbilt again attempted to break into the New York–Havre route with the newly completed steamer *Vanderbilt* and initiated a service between New York and Bremen via Cowes and Havre. On that route he placed the 1867-ton *North Star* and the 1295-ton *Ariel*. While the *Vanderbilt* attempted to set records for speed the

152. *Ibid*, p151; H Fry, *op cit*, p69.

153. C Ridgely-Nevitt, *op cit*, p170.

One of the largest wooden paddle steamers ever built, the 3360-ton Vanderbilt *of 1857 was the flagship of the flamboyant Commodore Vanderbilt's short-lived attempt to become a major player in the Atlantic passenger and mail business. A notable feature of the ship was the pair of beam engines, with exposed 'walking beam' – like a scaled-up Hudson river boat – driven by two 90in vertical cylinders with a stroke of 144in, totalling 2800ihp. The ship made a number of fast crossings at about 13.8kts but was not quite the equal of the Cunarder* Persia. *The hull proved remarkably long-lived: after service in the Civil War as a merchant cruiser, the ship became a sailing vessel in 1873, and then a coal hulk at Gibraltar from 1885 until broken up in 1930. (CMP)*

North Star and *Ariel* inherited the US Mail route to Bremen from the collapsed Ocean Steam Navigation Company. Both vessels proved to be too small for year-round operations in the North Atlantic and the *Ariel* was almost lost in January 1858.[154] The following December *Ariel* was again severely damaged by gale-force winds and seas, and the captain was killed. Grounding of the *North Star* generated considerable adverse publicity for Vanderbilt in 1859 but securing a provisional contract to carry the United States Mail from New York and New Orleans to California more than compensated for the *North Star* difficulty.[155]

During the American Civil War the United States merchant marine virtually ceased to exist. It was not until 1866 that the Ruger Brothers & Associates of New York attempted unsuccessfully to re-establish a transatlantic route.

Drawings of the American Line's Pennsylvania *of 1872 from Henry Hall's* Report on the Ship-building Industry of the United States (*Washington 1884*). *The difference between the accommodation for the cabin (or first) class and the steerage (or third) class on the deck below is quite clear. Intermediate (or second) class were carried later but the drawings show the ship in her original configuration, with two-stage compound engines, triple expansion being fitted in 1891.*

Their operation was based on leased steamers which could not compete in either speed or comfort with the British opposition and the company ceased operations in 1870. The following year the Pennsylvania Railroad Company formed the American Line and ordered four first class steamers from Cramp Shipbuilding Company in Philadelphia. The *Pennsylvania*, first of the four, was launched in 1872. Each of the vessels was 360ft in length, 42ft in beam, had a 33ft depth of hold, and measured 3000 tons.[156] The ships were fitted with compound engines and capable of a respectable but unimpressive 13kts.[157] After a decade on the route from Philadelphia to Liverpool, the American Line was absorbed by the International Navigation Company.[158]

Before the turn of the century two Atlantic liners of 11,000 tons were built at the Philadelphia shipyard of William Cramp & Sons. As had been the case prior to the American Civil War, contracts to carry the United States Mail were responsible for construction. The first launched was the *St Louis* and the second was named *St Paul*. The vessels were 554ft in length. Steel was used in construction of the hulls and each was divided into seventeen watertight compartments. Power was provided by two quadruple-expansion engines that together delivered

20,000hp.[159] The engines and boilers were located in separate watertight compartments and each drove a separate screw propeller. Sufficient coal could be carried to make the complete round-trip across the Atlantic at maximum speed. Forty-nine auxiliary engines served pumps, ventilation blowers, cargo handling equipment, and steam powered generators provided electricity for the entire vessels.[160]

The hulls contained five decks with accommodation for 320 first class passengers, 200 second class passengers, and another 800 could travel in steerage. The first and second class accommodation rivalled anything available, and the steerage facilities were perhaps more impressive. They contained heat and electric lights and the rooms were fitted with berths, tables and chairs. Lavatories and water closets were also available. First and second class accommodation

154. *Ibid*, pp232-233.
155. J H Morrison, *op cit*, pp429-431.
156. *Ibid*, p432.
157. *Ibid*, p432; W Mack Angas, *Rivalry on the Atlantic* (New York 1939), p157.
158. J H Morrison, *op cit*, p433.
159. W M Angas, *op cit*, p170; H Fry, *op cit*, p132.
160. H Fry, *op cit*, p135.

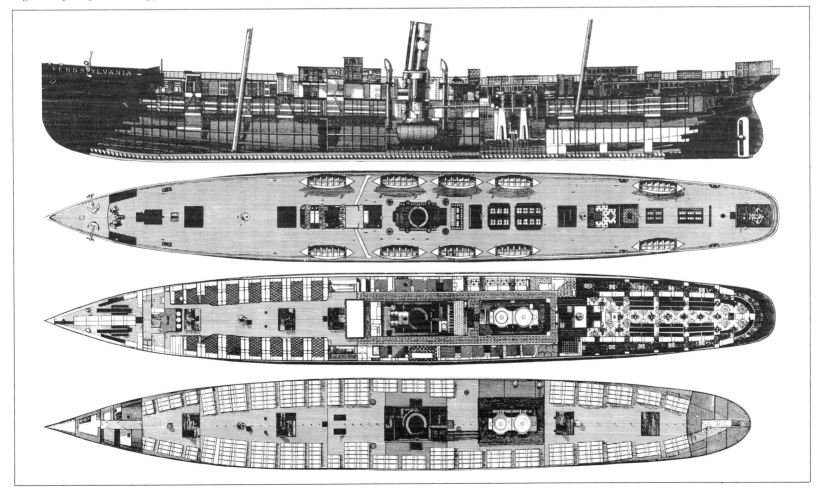

was electrically lit and ventilated with fresh air that could be heated in winter. The main dining saloon was elegantly outfitted and smaller lounges were piano and organ equipped. Each end of the ship contained hospital facilities.[161] Although designed to compete with anything afloat, the US Mail contract provided a subsidy that proved to be essential to operation of the vessels. At the end of the nineteenth century competition from government-subsidised British, French and German steamers proved to be too strong to conquer.

Professor William N Still, Gordon P Watts, Bradley Rogers

The first high-speed screw steamers built in the USA for the Atlantic trade were the St Louis *and the* St Paul *(seen here), built by Cramp of Philadelphia in 1895. They were extremely well appointed, but at first their performance was disappointing and in 1896 both ships had modifications made to their machinery which brought about considerable increases in speed. As a pointer to the future, Marconi carried out experiments in ship-to-shore radio from the* St Paul *in 1899.* (CMP)

161. *Ibid*, p133.

Typical American Steam Vessels 1807–1900

Name	Built	Completed	Hull	Dimensions (length × breadth × depth in hold; tonnage) Feet–Inches Metres	Machinery (Maker, type, cyl diam × stroke in inches; propulsion)	Remarks
NORTH RIVER STEAM BOAT	Charles Browne, Hudson river, New York	1807	Wood	133–0 × 13–0 × 7; 100 tons 40.5 × 4.0 × 2.1	Boulton & Watt 1 cyl, 24 × 48, 20nhp; side wheels	Never named *Clermont* although usually so called
The New York area						
FULTON	North River Steam Boat Co, Hudson river	1813	Wood	134–0 × 30–9 × 8–9 40.8 × 9.4 × 2.7	Crosshead, 36 × 48; side-wheels	Designed for use on Long Island Sound
CHANCELLOR LIVINGSTON	North River Steam Boat Co, Hudson river	1815	Wood	157–0 × 33–6 × 10–0; 496 tons grt 47.9 × 10.2 × 3.2	Allaire, crosshead, 45 × 84, 75nhp; side-wheels	Hull built by Henry Eckford, New York
ALBANY	J Vaughn, Philadelphia	1826	Wood	212–0 × 26–0 × 9–0; 389 tons 64.6 × 7.9 × 2.7	Beam, 65 × 120; side-wheels	Rebuilt to 289–0 × 28–0 in 1839
HENDRICK HUDSON	John Englis, New York	1845	Wood	330–0 × 40–0 × 10–0; 1179 tons 100.6 × 12.2 × 3.2	Allaire, beam, 72 × 132; side-wheels	People's Line
ALBANY	Harlan & Hollingsworth, Wilmington	1892/3	Iron	284–0 × 40–0 × 10–1; 1380 tons 86.5 × 12.2 × 3.0	Fletcher, beam, 75 × 144; side-wheels	Hudson River Day Line; first iron Hudson boat since 1846
ADIRONDACK	John Englis, New York	1896	Wood	440–0 × 50–0 × 12–0; 3644 tons 134.1 × 15.2 × 3.7	Fletcher, beam, 81 × 144; side-wheels	New Jersey Steamboat Co

Name	Built	Completed	Hull	Dimensions (length × breadth × depth in hold; tonnage) Feet–Inches Metres	Machinery (Maker, type, cyl diam × stroke in inches; propulsion)	Remarks
The Delaware						
NEW PHILADELPHIA	Robert L Stevens, Delwaware	1826	Wood	133–0 × 23–5 × 7–6; 220 tons 40.5 × 7.2 × 2.3	Low-pressure beam, 55 × 120; side-wheels	Union Line
JOHN STEVENS	Robert L Stevens, Hoboken	1844	Iron	245–0 × 31–0 × 11–0 74.7 × 9.4 × 3.4	Vibrating crosshead, 75 × 96; side-wheels	First large iron steamer built in the USA
RICHARD STOCKTON	Harlan & Hollingsworth, Wilmington	1851	Iron	270–0 × 20–8 × 8–7; 651 tons 82.3 × 6.3 × 2.6	Beam, 48 × 144; feathering side-wheels	Camden and Amboy Railroad Co
BRANDYWINE	Harlan & Hollingsworth Wilmington	1885	Steel	185–0 × 27–0 × 9–0 56.4 × 8.2 × 2.7	Compound, 24/42 × 24; screw propeller	Two locomotive boilers
Chesapeake Bay and its tributaries						
CHESAPEAKE	William Flannigan, Baltimore	1813	Wood	130–0 × 22–0 × 7–0 39.6 × 6.7 × 2.1	Crosshead, 4? × 54; side-wheels	First steamer on the Chesapeake
POCAHONTAS	Beecham and Gardiner, Baltimore	1829	Wood	138–0 × 30–0 × 11–0; 428 tons 42.1 × 9.1 × 3.4	Reeder, beam, 50 × 78, 100nhp; side-wheels	Maryland and Virginia Steamboat Co
PLANTER	Flanigan, Baltimore	1845	Wood	162–0 × 25–0 × 8–5 49.4 × 7.6 × 2.6	Beam, ? × ? side-wheels	For George Weems' Pautuxent service
GEORGEANNA	Harlan & Hollingsworth, Wilmington	1859	Iron	199–1 × 30–0 × 9–6; 738 tons 60.6 × 9.1 × 2.9	Beam, 50 × 132	Purchased by the Old Bay Line 1860
VIRGINIA	Harlan & Hollingsworth, Wilmington	1879	Iron	251–0 × ? × ?; 990 tons 76.5	Beam, 50 × 132; side-wheels	First new passenger vessel on the Bay since Civil War
MASON L WEEMS	William Skinner & Sons, Baltimore	1881	Wood	221–0 × 55–0 × 12–0 67.4 × 16.8 × 3.7	Clark, beam, 56 × 138; side-wheels	Weems Steamboat Co
Long Island Sound and the north-eastern states						
BARNET	Brown and Bell, New York	1826	Wood	75–0 × 14–6 × 1–10 22.9 × 4.4 × 0.58	? stern-wheel	For the shallow upper reaches of the Connecticut
NEW YORK	Lawrence and Sneeden, New York	1836	Wood	212–0 × 22–10 × 10–0; 524 tons 64.6 × 7.0 × 3.0	Allaire, beam, 50 × 120; side-wheels	New Haven Steamboat Co
METROPOLIS	?	1847	Wood	342–0 × 45–0 × 16–0; 2108 tons 104.2 × 13.7 × 4.9	Novelty IW, beam, 105 × 144; side-wheels	Bay State Steamboat Co
BRISTOL	William H Webb, New York	1866	Wood	360–0 × 48–6 × 16–0; 3000 tons 109.7 × 14.8 × 4,9	Etna Iron works beam, 110 × 144; side-wheels	Bay State Steamboat Co
PILGRIM	Delaware River Iron SB, Chester	1881	Iron	390–0 × 50–0 × 18–6; 3500 tons 118.9 × 15.2 × 5.6	Beam, 110 × 168; side-wheels	Fall River Line
Atlantic Coast river vessels						
A P HURT	Pusey and Jones, Wilmington	1860	Iron	100–0 × 17–0 × 4–0; 81 tons 30.5 × 5.2 × 1.2	Horizontal non-condensing 2cyl, 13 × 60; stern-wheel	Cape Fear Steamboat Co
DARLINGTON	Eason Brothers Shipyard, Charleston	1849	Wood	133–0 × 30–0 × ? 40.5 × 9.1 × ?	Horizontal direct acting, side-wheel	Built for Jacob Brock for service on the Pee Dee
The West						
NEW ORLEANS	N J Roosevelt/R Fulton, Pittsburg	1811	Wood	138–0 × 20–0 × 7–0; 210 tons 42.1 × 6.1 × 2.1	Horizontal, 34 × 48, 40nhp; side-wheels	First steamboat on western rivers
WASHINGTON	?, Wheeling	1816	Wood	148–0 × c25–0 × ?; 403 tons 45.1 × c7.6 x ?	High-pressure non-condensing 100nhp; side-wheels	First to use high-pressure machinery
LITTLE RED	?, Pittsburg	1836	Wood	169–0 × 23–0 × 6–0; 201 tons 51.5 × 7.0 × 1.8	Two high-pressure non-condensing, ? × 72; side-wheels	
ORLINE ST JOHN	?, New Albany	1847	Wood	215–0 × 33–0 × 7–0; 349 tons 65.5 × 10.1 × 2.1	Two high-pressure non-condensing, ? × 108; side-wheels	

Name	Built	Completed	Hull	Dimensions (length × breadth × depth in hold; tonnage) Feet–Inches Metres	Machinery (Maker, type, cyl diam × stroke in inches; propulsion)	Remarks
COCOPAH	?, San Francisco	1859	Wood	140–0 × 29–0 × 1–7 42.7 × 8.8 × 0.5	Two high-pressure non-condensing; two stern-wheels	For Colorado river
BERTRAND	?, Wheeling	1864	Wood	161–0 × 32–9 × 5–2; 521 tons 49.1 × 10.0 × 1.6	Two horizontal, ? × ?; two stern-wheels	For Missouri river
ROBERT E LEE	?, New Albany	1866	Wood	285–6 × 46–0 × 9–0; 1456 tons 87.0 × 14.0 × 2.7	Two high-pressure non-condensing, 46 × 120; side-wheels	

Great Lakes

ONTARIO	Asahil S Roberts, Sacketts Harbor	1817	Wood	125–0 × 24–0 × 8–6; 237 tons 38.1 × 7.3 × 2.6	Allaire beam, 34 × 48; side-wheels	For Lake Ontario
WALK-IN-THE-WATER	A&N Brown, East River (reassembled Black Rock)	1818	Wood	145–0 × 32–0 (over guards) × 8–8; 338 tons 44.2 × 9.8 × 2.6	McQueen, crosshead, 40 × 48; side-wheels	For Lake Erie; also first steamer on Huron & Michigan
WILLIAM PENN		1825	Wood	95–0 × 25–0 × 8–0; 217 tons 29.0 × 7.6 × 2.4		For Lake Erie
WILLIAM PEACOCK	?, Lake Erie	1829	Wood	102–0 × 34–0 × 7–6; 120 tons 31.1 × 10.4 × 2.3	Stackhouse, high-pressure, ? × ?, side-wheels	Boiler explosion in 1830 cast doubts on safety of high-pressure engines
UNITED STATES	?, Lake Ontario	1832	Wood	150–0 × 26–0 (hull) × 10–0; 450 tons 45.7 × 7.9 × 3.0	2cyl Avery beam, 40 × 96; side-wheels	For Lake Ontario
VANDALIA	?, Lake Ontario	1841	Wood	91–0 × 20–2 × 8–3; 138 tons 27.7 × 6.2 × 2.5	2 cyl high-pressure inverted, 14 × 28; two contra-rotating Ericsson propellers	First screw steamer on Lakes
MERCHANT	?, Buffalo	1861	Iron	200–0 × 29–0 × 18.5; 861 tons 61.0 × 8.8 × 5.6	? screw propeller	First iron-built screw steamer on Lakes

Atlantic Coast seagoing vessels

ROBERT FULTON	Henry Eckford, New York	1819	Wood	159–0 × 33–5 × 17–3; 702 tons 48.5 × 10.2 × 5.3	Allaire, crosshead, 44 × 60; side-wheels	New York – Charleston – Havana service
DAVID BROWN	Brown and Bell, New York	1832	Wood	130–11 × 18–1 × 8–4; 190 tons 39.9 × 5.5 × 2.5	Allaire, crosshead, ? × ?; side-wheels	New York – Charleston service
BANGOR	Harlan & Hollingsworth, Wilmington	1844	Iron	118–6 × 24–2 × 8–1; 231 tons 36.1 × 7.4 × 2.5	Two inverted direct acting, 22 × 24; twin screws	Boston – Bangor service
SOUTHERNER	William H Brown, New York	1846	Wood	191–3 × 30–8 × 14–1; 785 tons 58.3 × 9.3 × 4.3	Novelty IW, side lever, 67 × 96; side-wheels	New York – Charleston 67 × 96; side-wheels service
PORTLAND	New England Ship-building, Bath	1890	Steel	241–0 × 42–0 × 15–6; 2283 tons 73.5 × 12.8 × 4.7	Portland beam, 62 × 144; side-wheels	Boston – Bangor service
COMANCHE	Cramp and Sons, Philadelphia	1895	Steel	300–0 × 46–0 × 26–3 91.4 × 14.0 × 8.0	Quadruple-expansion, 24.5–70 × 36; screw propeller	New York – Charleston service

Transoceanic vessels

SAVANNAH	Crockett and Fickett, New York	1819	Wood	98–6 × 25–10 × 14–2; 319 grt 30.0 × 7.9 × 4.3	Inclined direct acting, 40 × 60, 90ihp; side-wheels	First steamer to cross the Atlantic
WASHINGTON	Westervelt & Mackay, New York	1847	Wood	230–0 × 39–0 × 31–0; 1750 grt 70.1 × 11.9 × 9.4	2cyl side lever, 72 × 120, 1100ihp; side-wheels; 9kts	Ocean Steam Navigation Co mail steamer
FRANKLIN	Westervelt & Mackay, New York	1850	Wood	264–0 × 41–8 × 25–9; 2184 grt 80.5 × 12.7 × 7.0	2cyl side lever, 93 × 96, 1250ihp; side-wheels; 10kts	First Havre Line steamer
ATLANTIC	William H Brown, New York	1850	Wood	284–0 × 45–11 × 22–11; 2845 grt 86.6 × 14.0 × 7.0	2cyl side lever, 95 × 108, 2000ihp; side-wheels; 13kts	First Collins Line steamer
PENNSYLVANIA	Cramp and Sons, Philadelphia	1872	Iron	360–0 × 42–0 × 33–0; 3000 grt 109.7 × 12.8 × 10.1	2cyl compound, 48/99 × 48, 2800ihp; single screw; 13kts	First American Line steamer
ST LOUIS	Cramp and Sons, Philadelphia	1895	Steel	554–0 × 63–0 × 42–0; 11,629 grt 168.9 × 19.2 × 12.8	Quadruple-expansion, 20,000ihp; twin screws; 19kts	American Line

4

The Screw Propeller and Merchant Shipping 1840-1865

As THE end of the twentieth century nears much of the world's goods – bulk and break bulk – are still carried by sea. At any moment a vast fleet is carrying hundreds of millions of tons of cargo, approximately ten times more cheaply per ton per mile than is possible by any other method. The world's trade depends utterly upon this galaxy of ships and they are all driven by screw propellers. The first deep sea voyage by a screw propelled ship, the *Archimedes*, was in 1840 but the story does not start there. To understand the twenty-five years of development after that voyage, one must look at its long background.

Early history

The concept of screw propulsion is very old indeed. The screw pump, attributed to Archimedes, dates back two centuries before the Christian era. Basically, a tube contains a helix on a shaft, which when turned drives water up the tube, from a lower to a higher level. Similarly, windmills for grinding grain etc have existed for ages; in Britain from the twelfth century. From fairly early times these were often in the

Archimedean screw pump: 'A' is the opening for the entry of the water.

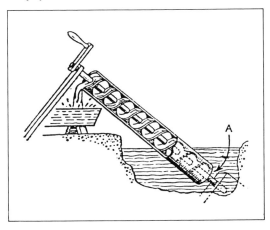

form of four blades, each twisted to form a helix. Perhaps the earliest example of using such a helix to produce thrust is shown in one of the celebrated drawings by Leonardo da Vinci from approximately five hundred years ago. In this, Leonardo showed a proposed helicopter, to be lifted by an Archimedian type screw of one complete turn and a single thread rotating on a vertical axis.[1]

Two hundred years later, in 1681, the celebrated English mathematician and inventor Robert Hooke addressed the Royal Society on 'horizontal windmills'. Hooke also considered what he called 'vertical windmills' – where the axis was still horizontal but in the direction of the fluid flow, in other words, as in a screw propeller. In his opinion the vertical type was superior to the horizontal. In 1683 Hooke demonstrated to the Royal Society an actual instrument he had built some twenty years earlier, based on a water screw, with which he could measure the speed of a ship through water. This was the forerunner of the screwlog. He went on to demonstrate a method for varying the angularity of the blades by adjusting the shaft. This was essentially a controllable pitch screw impeller, driven by the water.[2] Both Hooke and before him Leonardo da Vinci were aware that action and reaction were equal and opposite and thus a screw driven by water, producing torque in the shaft could drive water by providing torque to the shaft, as in the screw pump.

Early understanding of the application of the Archimedean screw was well illustrated by the work of Leupold in 1724.[3] His patent showed such a screw of two threads together with a segment of the screw. An Archimedean screw as understood to be made up of a large number of such segments. If it had two threads the result was that a segment looked very like a two-bladed screw propeller, as in an illustration from Leupold showing Hooke's water vane.[4]

Perhaps the first actual use of a screw propel-

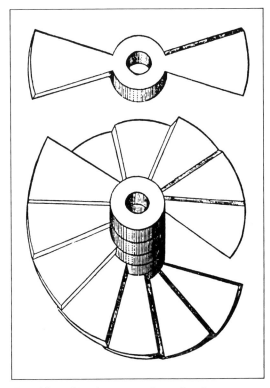

Leupold's archimedean screw of two threads.

ler in some sort of vessel was by Bushnell in his submersible, the *Turtle* of 1776. This device was intended to sink British warships and was tried during the American Revolution.[5] Hand driven screws of two complete threads were used for fore and aft and vertical movement. These, as might be expected, looking at the drawing, were quite ineffective.

What did prove reasonably effective, however,

---

1. *Notebooks of Leonardo da Vinci*, Reprint Society (London 1954), Plate 30.

2. J Bourne, *A Treatise on the Screw Propeller* (London 1857 & 1867), p5.

3. *Ibid*, p7.

4. *Ibid*, p8.

5. *Submarine Navigation* (London 1904), p11.

Cummerow's propeller: the first definite proposal to place a screw in the deadwood.

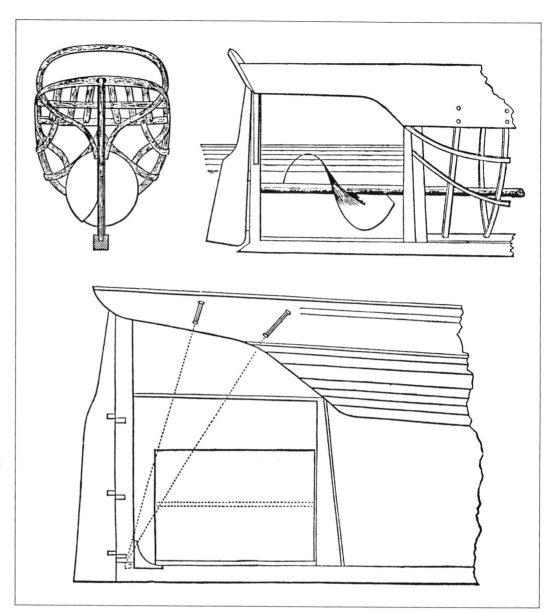

was the screw propulsion of Robert Fulton's submarine boat *Nautilus*, built in 1800 and offered to the French Government.[6] This boat had a large diameter two-bladed screw propeller driven through gears by the crew itself. Obviously power was very limited as a strong man can exert only about one horsepower for fifteen minutes or so. Nevertheless, Fulton carried out trials in the Seine in 1801 and after the boat had been overpressured with air, remained submerged for five hours at 25ft depth and managed to propel the boat an appreciable distance, probably of the order of a mile. This was probably the first successful application of the screw propeller to any vessel and in a very *avant garde* context.

The development of screw propulsion interested many inventors but progress was hampered by two main factors: lack of an adequate power source and also of any real understanding as to how propulsion was achieved. Many patents were taken out from the middle of the eighteenth century until late in the nineteenth, the bulk of them showing a complete lack of understanding of the basic principles of screw propulsion. Nevertheless, some were seminal and of primary importance. For instance, Bramah, in 1785, anticipated Fulton in proposing the proper location of the screw.[7] In 1802, a Mr Edward Shorter of London fitted a screw propeller to the *Doncaster* transport ship. This was worked by a manual capstan which propelled the ship at about 1½kts.

Shorter's propellers were of various forms: one, two, three and four threads with narrow blades, *ie* a short segment of a complete turn. It is not known where the *Doncaster*'s propeller was located, but in his patent Shorter did contemplate fixing screws in the deadwood, *ie* forward of the rudder, in an aperture. This appears to be the first time that this now standard position for single screw ships was proposed. Then in 1804

Bramah's arrangement for propulsion by a screw at the stern.

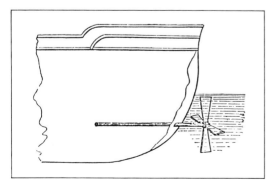

Colonel John Stevens in America built a screw propelled launch using manual power (although one source claims by steam) and demonstrated it fairly successfully on the Hudson river, also achieving a speed of 1–2kts.

Patents now came thick and fast. Experiments were conducted by many pioneers, including Sir Marc Brunel in 1820. For those interested, Bourne's early *Treatise on the Screw Propeller* makes fascinating reading. Many different screw applications were envisaged, not only fully submerged but also with their shafts above water. The so-called vane propeller was undoubtedly invented by Jacob Perkins in 1825,[8] with an arrangement of contra-rotating vane propellers aft of the rudder of a vessel. This idea was exploited by Messrs William Denny in the latter part of the nineteenth and early twentieth centuries, by others in the 1960s and in racing motor boats from 1950 onwards.

A crucial aspect in development was to decide where to place the screw. The cul de sac of placing it aft of the rudder was proposed by several inventors, but the standard single screw practice was anticipated in detail by Charles Cummerow in 1829. Cummerow proposed fitting it in a deadwood aperture forward of the rudder and in doing so anticipated Smith's master patent of 1836.[9] Interest in the whole subject was growing, particularly as practical marine engines for paddle vessels were now emerging, and inventors could see the likelihood that suitable power sources would become available; so much so that in 1825 a premium was offered for the best plan of propelling vessels without paddles.[10]

6. *Ibid*, p19.
7. J Bourne, *op cit*, p11.
8. *Ibid*, p19.
9. *Ibid*, p21.
10. J Fincham, *A History of Naval Architecture* (London 1851), p342.

By 1836 a situation had been reached where many reasonably practicable forms of screw had been proposed, patented, tried – sometimes on model scale and sometimes at full size but nearly always worked by hand. All the same, in 1836 no lasting or physically practical progress had been made with screw propulsion and no ship was in existence propelled by a screw. Paddle propulsion had developed to the point where the first regular steam transatlantic voyages were about to be made and steam was near to taking over passenger transport across the Atlantic and around the coasts of the developed countries.

As discussed in Chapter 1, paddle propulsion had many disadvantages. For merchant ships paddle immersion was crucial and obviously difficult to keep near to optimum for vessels which worked at appreciably variable draughts, *ie* with varying cargo and fuel loadings. Furthermore, when rolling in a seaway, one paddle could be immersed too far at a given moment and the other out of the water, causing loss of power and yawing. Again, with a beam wind one paddle

11. J Bourne, *op cit*, p28.
12. *Ibid*, p30.

would be too deeply immersed and the other too lightly.

Ships were limited in range under power, due to the inefficiency of contemporary engines, so sail propulsion had to be relied upon to a considerable extent on long voyages. For warships the same disadvantages applied but in addition the paddle structures amidships took up a great deal of the useful deck and side area, displacing armament while the drive and the paddles themselves were highly vulnerable in action.

The *annus mirabilis*, 1836

The time was right for the introduction of screw propulsion in a practical and seamanlike form, and 1836 proved to be the *annus mirabilis*. In May, Francis Pettit Smith took out a British patent for placing Archimedean screw propellers in the deadwood of ships,[11] followed in July by Captain Ericsson who took out a patent for a quite different type of propeller.[12]

Smith was a farmer near Hendon who, in 1835, became interested in screw propulsion. He built a 2ft long model boat with a 2in diameter wooden screw (presumably clockwork drive) which he tested on his farm pond. He obviously

had considerable engineering insight as this model proved to be very satisfactory. Smith must have been persuasive, too, as he gained the support of a Mr Wright, an enterprising and wealthy banker. Wright was sufficiently convinced by Smith to finance, first an experimental launch, and then the *Archimedes*, a ship of some size and which cost over £10,000.

After his patent was granted on 31 May 1836 Smith and his backers constructed a 34ft long launch as a pilot experiment. Of 6ft 5in breadth and 4ft draught, it was fitted with a 2ft diameter screw of 2ft 5in pitch, driven by a single-cylinder engine of 6in bore and 15in stroke. Initially, the screw consisted of two complete turns of a single blade upon a longitudinal axis.

Ericsson's equivalent to Pettit Smith's Archimedes *as a demonstration ship was the* Robert F Stockton, *a 70ft long iron vessel built by Lairds of Birkenhead in 1838. Named after a US Navy officer who was Ericsson's chief supporter, the ship was sailed across the Atlantic under canvas alone in 1839 after Ericsson failed to gain Admiralty support for his propeller. She was sold as a canal tug in 1840 but Ericsson's lobbying was successful to the point where there were forty-one screw merchant ships in America by 1843, and the US Navy had invited him to design the screw sloop* Princeton. (ScM)

Ericssons's double screws as probably first fitted to the
Robert F Stockton.

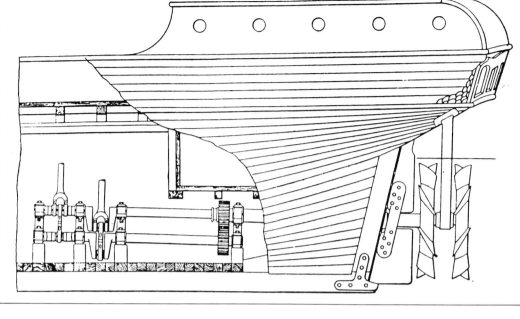

During initial trials on the City and Padding-
ton Canal half of this blade broke off, resulting,
to Smith's surprise, in distinctly improved performance. Sea trials using the shortened screw
were made in September 1837, starting from
Blackwall, out into the North Sea – destination
Margate. The voyage continued after a day or
two to Ramsgate, on through the Downs to
Dover and finally to Folkestone. After further
demonstrations and trials the launch returned to
Margate against a strong headwind and heavy
seas. She then returned to Blackwall after a voyage of over 200 miles at an average speed of 7kts.
Later, in the Thames, she towed the *Great Western* into the West India Docks at 2.5kts –
possibly Isambard Brunel's first contact with
screw propulsion. All this was a remarkable performance and inspired the building of *Archimedes*,
completed in 1838.[13]

The name was a suitable tribute and the ship
of appreciable size: 125ft overall length, 21ft
10in breadth, with a design draught of 9ft 6in.
The engines were of 80nhp driving a single
threaded screw of one complete turn upon its
axis. This screw was 5ft 9in in diameter and 8ft
pitch, but was removed after a short time and in
its place a double threaded screw fitted, each
thread forming a half turn upon the axis. The
illustration below shows both these screws located in the stern aperture of *Archimedes*.[14]

Slightly later than Smith, but also practical,
was the alternative approach of Ericsson. A
Swedish army officer, he had lived in England
for some years before 1836, and was a profes-
sional engineer with an interest in screw propulsion. His primary patent was taken out in

July 1836 and developed in London by numerous experiments, like Smith, with a model
boat 2ft long. The experimental layout was ingenious. The boat was driven round a central
axis, the tether being a steam pipe supplying the
engine with steam from the upright pipe axis.
The experiments were satisfactory, so a year later he built a vessel 45ft long, 8ft broad and 3ft
draught as his next stage in development. This
vessel, rather larger than Pettit Smith's launch,
was called *Francis B Ogden*, after the American
Consul in Liverpool who had an interest in the
venture, and was tried on the Thames at the end
of April 1837. The Ericsson screw was completely different from that of Smith and fitted
abaft the rudder.[15] It was contra-rotating, using
concentric shafts and consisted of helical segments about one-sixth of a full thread in length
attached to the screw boss by a three-bladed helical spider.

The *Francis B Ogden* proved remarkably successful, achieving a speed of nearly 8kts and able
to tow a 140-ton schooner at 6kts. Later that
year a canal boat – the *Novelty* – was built with
Ericsson screw propellers 2ft 6in in diameter
and driven by a 10hp engine. On the canal between Manchester and London this boat proved
capable of a speed of between 7kts and 8kts and
was probably the first screw propelled craft to
enter commercial service.

Ericsson constructed his equivalent of *Archimedes* in 1838 after his work had interested an
officer of the United States Navy, Captain Robert F Stockton, clearly a man of imagination and

13. *Ibid*, p29.

14. Captain E Chappell, RN, *Reports Relevant to Smith's
Screw Propeller* (London 1840).

15. A Seaton, *The Screw Propeller*, RN College (Greenwich
1909), p19.

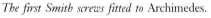

The first Smith screws fitted to Archimedes.

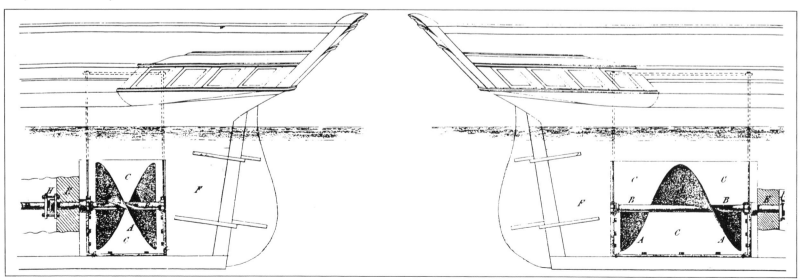

One of the most important ships of all time, Brunel's masterpiece, The Great Britain *of 1843, combined the new technology of iron hull construction and the screw propeller in an ocean-going ship of unprecedented size. She was not a commercial success on her designed route, the North Atlantic, where a government subsidy seemed to be a* sine qua non; *but the fundamental soundness of the concept was proven in thirty years of service on the Australia run. An even more striking testament to the quality of the hull construction was the survival of the ship to the present day, and appropriately the ship is now undergoing restoration in her original building dock in Bristol. This photograph, taken of* The Great Britain *by Fox Talbot in 1844, is the earliest known photograph of a ship. (By courtesy of Basil Greenhill).*

drive. *Robert F Stockton* was 70ft in length, 10ft breadth and 50hp. What was really remarkable was that the engines were direct acting, connected straight to the propeller. *Archimedes* was fitted with slow paddle-type machinery geared up 5.33 to 1 to the propeller, whereas Ericsson, a brilliant engineer, devised his own type of machinery; these were the first direct drive screw propeller engines.

Launched in Liverpool in July 1838, *Stockton* had a screw 6ft 4in diameter and 2ft length. The forward section ran at 44rpm and the aft at 49. In January 1839 the boat towed four 100-ton coal barges, lashed alongside, up the Thames at 5kts. Smith was present at these trials. It will be remembered that Smith, as the result of an accident to his first boat, found that shorter screws gave better results. Possibly as a result of this fortuitous occurrence he advised Ericsson to try deleting one of the two propellers in his contra-rotating device. Ericsson agreed to try this and Smith's surmise was correct. The performance of *Robert F Stockton* improved and thereafter Ericsson usually fitted one wheel only.

The parallels between Smith and Ericsson are remarkable. Smith narrowly anticipated Ericsson in devising a satisfactory form of screw propulsion. Both obtained the backing of men of drive and enterprise: Wright, a banker, for Smith, and Stockton, an American naval officer, for Ericsson. The time was right, the need great – both commercially and militarily. The fact that screw propulsion took off from this point onward was due to the combination of inventors of drive and imagination with backers of substance, together forming technical / entrepreneurial teams. This type of combination had not been seen before in the history of screw propeller development. This theme is developed in greater detail in Chapter 7.

Ericsson tried to interest the British Admiralty in his work but in spite of its obvious success they displayed little interest. It is thought

that this arose from their belief that a vessel with a thruster at the stern would not steer in a head wind. In the case of *Archimedes* disbelief was of course impossible because she and her 34ft predecessor had displayed quite unusually good controllability in head winds mainly because the screw race impinged directly on the rudder. To be fair to the Surveyor of the Navy, the original Ericsson arrangement with the screw aft of the rudder would have been distinctly inferior in such steering capability.

Archimedes was very successful. She made a most convincing demonstration trip, circumnavigating England and Scotland and, incidentally, giving the Great Western Steamship Company an early opportunity to hire her and experiment with different types of screw propeller.[16] The whole trip of 2000 nautical miles was carried out at an average of about 7kts. Thereafter, *Archimedes* steamed from Plymouth to Oporto in 69 hours at 9.5kts, the first authenticated seagoing voyage ever made by any screw propelled vessel.

For Smith the outcome of the Bristol visit was, of course, the adoption of screw propulsion for the great new ship building there, *The Great Britain*. Ericsson, however, was so disenchanted with his reception by the British Admiralty and in particular by the Government Surveyor that he emigrated to America, where his propeller was adopted enthusiastically by the United States Navy. The *Robert F Stockton* followed him, under sail. The first screw ship the US Navy built, fitted with Ericsson's propeller, was the steam sloop *Princeton*. This ship was appreciably larger than *Archimedes*; 164ft long, 30ft breadth, 17ft 6in draught with a 14ft diameter contra-rotating

six-bladed propeller working at 36rpm. With 400hp engines *Princeton* could attain a speed of approximately 12kts.

From there on the development of the screw propeller generally followed Smith in Britain and Ericsson in America and France. Wright, Smith and a number of other enterprising entrepreneurs formed what the Register called The Patent Screw Propeller Company. Eventually the type of propeller produced by this company was adopted almost universally. So, after many years of proposals and discussions, it had been shown beyond question that the screw propeller was the propulsion system of the future and that the paddle steamer was obsolescent.

Commercial development

The way appeared to be open for commercial and naval exploitation of the screw propeller. In Britain, in May 1840, *Archimedes* made her highly significant visit to Bristol. There were the usual demonstration runs and an excursion down the estuary to the Holms. Thereafter, the ship went round to Liverpool, encountering quite heavy weather en route. Contrary to what some Jonahs had said to the Building Committee, it was clear that the screw propeller was practicable. The Committee recommended to the Directors that construction of *The Great Britain* engines be halted together with those parts of the hull which would be affected by any possible change in engines and to screw propulsion. Brunel was asked to investigate the whole

16. E Corlett, *The Iron Ship* (London 1990), p208.

question of adoption of the screw and to report to them.

First, experiments were to be carried out, so the Great Western Steamship Company hired *Archimedes* for some months. A series of eight experimental screws were tested, including examples by Smith, Steinman and Woodcroft. The last had patented a screw with pitch increasing from the leading to the aft edge. Smith's screw, of two half-threads, made of wrought iron, gave the best results.

Brunel's Report on 10 October 1840 was the birth of a scientific approach to propeller design.[17] He pointed out that 'the resistance whether to the surface of the screw or to the paddle board offered by the fluid against which it acts is of course not perfect and there is a certain amount of yielding commonly called the slip'. At that time naval architects considered that the resistance of a vessel through the water was directly proportional to its midships sectional area. This was not correct. Comparing *Archimedes* and *Great Western* on the basis of midship section area, Brunel found that although the screw

The Sarah Sands, *an auxiliary screw steamer built of iron by Hodgson of Liverpool in 1845. The second oceanic screw ship, after* The Great Britain, *she was destined for the Australia run but was employed by the Red Cross Line on the North Atlantic from 1847. Her 17-20 day averages were longer than the equivalent paddler mail steamers could manage, but easily beat the passage times of the sailing packets with which she was intended to compete, thus allowing steerage class passengers (often emigrants) an alternative to the rigours of crossing wholly under sail. (ScM)*

had a much smaller surface than the paddle with which to act, it had no less effect. He remarked that 'the mass of water pushed back by the action of the screw appears to be very large spreading from the screw, but there is little or no appearance of any rotatory motion in the sense that the water is not put into rapid motion as in the case of the paddle ...'

Most naval architects at that time believed that a screw was really a skewed paddle: in other words, part of a paddle which if, say at 45 degrees to its axis, rotated would strike the water at 45 degrees as it went round. Of course, if the water was totally motionless relative to the screw this would be so but with inflow (*ie* water sucked into the propeller and also with the vessel in forward motion), the angle is much reduced and is in fact generally only 5 or 6 degrees, thus operating at an 'angle of incidence' rather like an aircraft wing. Brunel would have none of this current misconception:

> as regards the oblique action also a great mistake seems to be made generally and very naturally by most persons when first considering the working of the screw. It is generally assumed that the inclined plane formed by the thread of the screw strikes the particles of water at that angle ... but it is forgotten that the screw is moving forward with the ship and therefore that angle at which the water is struck by the plane is diminished by all that much as the ship with the screw advances ... the angle at which any given part of the screw does in fact strike the water is only equal to the

difference between the angle to which that part of the screw is formed and the angle or direction in which it moves by the compound motion of the revolutions of the screw and the forward motion of the ship and the screw.

Brunel went on to show that in the case of *Archimedes* the angle at which the leading edge of her screw struck the water was only 6.5 degrees – a very reasonable angle of attack.

With other naval architects of the time he considered a screw to be acting rather as a wood screw in timber. They believed that the driving face of the blade simply moved water (or wood!) aft, pushing it away. Hence it was the flat driving face that mattered. They did not appreciate the effect of camber and cross section shape upon blade efficiency.

Yet in the discussion on a paper read before the Institute of Civil Engineers in 1844 on the steamer *Liverpool Screw*, fitted with a Smith screw propeller, a Mr Cowper described model air fans that he had made with three or more blades rather like a screw propeller.[18] He made two types – one a helicoidal surface as in an Archimedean screw and the other with a cambered blade, *ie* a helical surface with the chords of the blades bowed. He tested them with a string winder, rather like the toys that are availa-

17. I K Brunel, 'Report to the Directors, of the Great Western Steamship Co on Screw Propellers', (1840) Wills Memorial Library, p1.

18. J Grantham, 'Accounts of Experiments on the *Liverpool Screw*', *Minutes of the Proceedings of the Institution of Civil Engineers* III (1841), pp71-73.

ble today. The Archimedean screw when tested in this way rose on average about 50ft and no matter which way the fan was put on the apparatus, it rose to the same height. However, with the cambered fan 'when the axis was placed vertically and a rapid rotary action imparted to it the fan rose in the air 150ft. On reversing the fan – it would not rise at all'.

The experiment was of great potential interest, not that it aroused much. It gave a clue to improving the efficiency of propellers; namely to design them as lifting surfaces like the aircraft wings of later days. Until after the end of the century, it was considered that the flat driving face of the propeller was what really mattered. This was quite wrong.

Brunel went on to analyse the losses that would arise in a screw propeller: friction as it went through the water and the resistance of the water to penetration of the 'cutting edge'. It must be remembered that at that time nothing of the modern sciences of hydro- and aerodynamics existed. Brunel was not aware of the lifting capabilities of aerofoil shaped surfaces and had to reason from a mechanistic basis. Nevertheless, his conclusion was sound:

> I think the conclusion can be drawn from the result of the experiments quoted and that is that as compared with the ordinary paddle wheel of seagoing steamers the screw is both, as regards the effect produced and the proportion of power required to obtain that effect, an efficient propeller.

He went on thereafter to cover installation and operational questions, such as how to accommodate the propeller in the stern frame of *The Great Britain*; whether the screw would be pitched out of the water in a heavy sea, and the vulnerability of the screw compared with paddles. His peers feared that the screw propeller would be inaccessible and that its bearings could not be examined. Remarkably, Brunel said 'if necessary men could be sent down with common diving jackets or hoods to replace or attach tackles to remove the screw or clear away any obstacles entangled in it'.[19]

Ever practical, he sent an engineer on a number of voyages aboard *Great Western* to make many measurements of pitching and rolling angles as well as observing, through a port cut in the stern of the ship, the rise and fall of the sea at the rudder post. He wrote,

> from this it was evident that the vessel never pitches to so great an angle as that to which she rises. Such a result may have been anticipated by considering the form of the vessel

forward and aft, and the circumstances that the steamer is always invariably meeting or passing the seas or if overtaking them still going at a good rate which reduces the relative speed of the sea. Although the vessel may be frequently throw up very violently forward yet the stern settles down heavily on the surface.

Brunel drew attention to a disadvantage of screw propulsion in the contemporary scene. Where main machinery was designed for paddles it operated typically in the 15–20rpm range. Screw propellers required at least three times that speed to develop the necessary power. *Archimedes* had a very crude gearing system to produce the necessary increase in revolutions. *The Great Britain* obtained her 3:1 revolutions increase, engine to screw, by four 'silent type' chains. Brunel considered this problem a mere mechanical difficulty but the fact remains that explosive development of screw propulsion only followed the introduction of suitable direct drive engines working at screw propeller speed.

Brunel pointed out that a screw was unaffected by the trim or rolling of the vessel and allowed the free use of sails. It gave greatly increased steering if fitted forward of the rudder, and it much reduced the overall breadth of the vessel and assisted in the structural design. In December 1840 the Great Western Steam Ship Company adopted screw propulsion and the result was the world's first large ocean-going screw propelled ship.

The first modern ship

The original propeller and stern frame arrangement of *The Great Britain* was a strikingly effective and even modern design, with a balanced rudder operating abaft a six-bladed propeller, 15ft 6in in diameter and of 25ft pitch. This is the first screw propeller of which we have full technical details.

The boss was made in several parts, the main one being 17in long, 2ft in diameter, to which were fire welded six wrought iron arms, each 6in thick, twisted into a helix of the correct pitch. This basic boss and the arms were then milled off flat at right angles to the propeller axis. To the arms were riveted 'palms', 4ft 3in wide, 2ft 7in at their inner circumference and 2ft 10in long radially. These were also helical, ⅞in thick and constituted the main driving portion of the screw. The boss was then completed with fore and aft closing portions, the whole held together by long iron bolts and rivets. The screw was buffed up, polished, painted and varnished to give a good surface. The finished weight was 3.85 tons.

Arrangement of The Great Britain *stern.*

When this propeller was tested scientifically in 1970 it was found that to obtain sufficient thrust to propel the ship at 12kts each blade would bear a steady load of about 2.5 tons giving a stress at the root of the arm of about 4.5 tons per square inch. This was very high for a live load on a wrought iron propeller blade, fire welded to its boss. The screw or tail shaft was 18in in diameter decreasing to 16in at the stern post and 15in at the bearing and propeller boss. Between the stern post and the boss, a distance of 1ft, a rope guard and bearing was fitted supported from a post below the shaft. This arrangement was not uncommon at the time but of questionable effectiveness. Water was kept out by a leather and copper stuffing gland just inside the stern post which could be reached from inboard. The aftermost inboard shaft bearing was on the 18in portion just forward of the stern post.

The propeller aperture, the afterbody lines and the mechanical details of these early propellers are described and criticised later, but there is no record that this Brunel arrangement gave any trouble during its admittedly short time in service.

A spare propeller was provided for *The Great Britain*, but of totally different type, being four-bladed, of cast iron and altogether more robust construction. The original screw failed early in service due to a combination of stranding damage and structural overloading. The second

19. J Weale, *The Great Britain Atlantic Steamship* (London 1847).

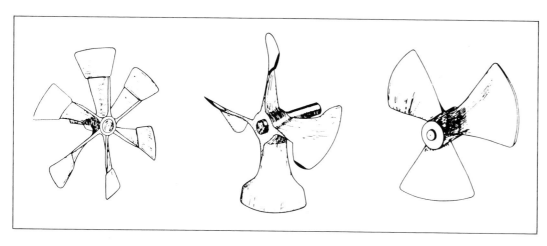

The first, second and third screws fitted to The Great Britain.

200hp *Rattler*, generally of the *Alecto* class of paddle sloops, but adapted by an additional length aft to provide space for the screw propeller and to give a clear run into it. Both Brunel and Smith were involved in the development of the screw propulsion and stern arrangements. Brunel was well aware of the need for care over the afterbody lines: 'A clean run is the most essential condition ...', he wrote in his Screw Propeller Report.

Extensive trials were made with this ship. These undoubtedly had a direct influence upon merchant ship development. First, a screw similar to the second one fitted to *Archimedes* was tried, consisting of two half-turns of the blade upon its axis (9ft in diameter, 11ft pitch and 5ft 6in in length). This was at the end of October 1843 but it does not seem to have been very successful because further experiments were made with a screw of the same diameter and pitch but reduced in length, first to 4ft 3in and then to 3ft.

screw was fitted and proved equally efficient. It is possible Brunel had doubts as to the robustness of the first screw and covered his bets with the second one. It must be said that the first screw owed little to Smith and much to Ericsson, resembling in some respects one of the two contra-rotating discs of the original Ericsson invention.

The Great Britain was model tested in 1970 at the Vickers experimental tank at St Albans with surprising results.[20] In round terms hull resistance was quite good – only about 30 per cent worse than the best modern hull of the same length, fullness and general proportions. To some extent this was not due to design deficiency but the peculiar and definitely disadvantageous midship section which Brunel was forced to adopt to get the ship out of Bristol docks. The propulsive efficiency was affected by

the rather unfavourable 'snubbed off' shape of the waterlines at the top of the propeller aperture forced upon Brunel by the conversion of a paddle ship to screw propulsion.

The screw propeller itself was remarkably efficient for the service intended; it compares well with modern ones. A plot of propeller efficiency against a non-dimensional coefficient involving thrust and speed of advance shows that at the higher loadings the Brunel propeller was quite as efficient as modern ones. At the design point it was some 5 decimal points less efficient. It is a tribute to Brunel's insight and experimental work that the operational point for *The Great Britain* came right at the peak of the efficiency curve – a remarkable achievement.

Naval practice of the early 1840s saw experiments with screw propulsion and then its introduction into service. *Princeton* in the United States was designed from scratch as a warship, but the British Admiralty was more cautious. They conducted experiments with the 888-ton,

20. 'Report on Open Water Tests on SS *Great Britain*', Vickers St Albans Testing Tank (1970).

The City of Glasgow, *built in 1850 by Tod & McGregor for their own Glasgow–New York service, may be said to have revolutionised Atlantic transport. Not receiving the substantial subsidies that went with mail contracts, the company had to compete on the economy of the ship alone, and the* City of Glasgow *was fitted for the carriage of four hundred steerage passengers (as well as fifty-two first and eighty-five second class). She was soon acquired to become the first ship of the new Inman Line and following Tod & McGregor's lead went on to prove the viability of the iron screw steamer on unsubsidised services. (NMM)*

With these the vessel gained rather over a half a knot in speed.[21]

Obviously the 3ft long screw impressed and in 1844 was tried again. Trials continued through February and into March. The screw was further reduced to 2ft in length, *ie* 18 per cent of the pitch. The result was reduced slip (13.4 per cent) and improved speed. The bit was now between their teeth and the screw was further reduced to 18in in length, *ie* just under 14 per cent of the pitch. Finally, the pure two-bladed Archimedean screw was reduced to 1ft 3in, only 11 per cent of pitch, and this gave a slip of only 10.42 per cent at 103.6rpm.

The next screw to be tried was another of Pettit Smith's, with three blades, diameter 9ft, pitch 11ft and length 2ft 3in, *ie* 22 per cent pitch. As might be expected, this gave lower rpm (94.3) but high slip. The final three-bladed attempt was with a length of 1ft, 8½in, 15 per cent of pitch. This was good, with 92rpm and 18.8 per cent slip.

Woodcroft, Steinman and Sunderland type screws were tested as well. Woodcroft, it will be remembered, had patented a screw with the pitch increasing from the leading to trailing edges. The Woodcroft screws tried were two- and four-threaded, 9ft in diameter, 1ft 7in in length, *ie* just about 14 per cent of the pitch, which increased from 11ft forward to 11½ft aft. They gave lower ship speeds and higher slip than Smith's best screws.

The next propellers tried were Steinman's of diameter 10ft and pitch 11ft 6in and a Sunderland two-threaded one, the latter 8ft 2in diameter and, grotesquely, with 26ft pitch. Steinman's was of indifferent performance and Sunderland's too small and overpitched, giving poor results.

Finally, a Hodgson's screw was tried. This device became very popular in France and Continental countries. As tested in *Rattler* in January 1845 it was 10ft in length and gave very poor performance. The speed achieved was 6.8kts contrasting with the 9.4kts of the best Smith two-bladed screw.

It was concluded that the short Smith propeller, formed of two threads or sections of the screw, was better than any other tried. It produced the greatest speed in the ship, the least slip and had the great advantage that being two-

bladed it could be hauled up into a stern recess, out of the water, when sail only was required.

The next stage was to compare screw propulsion with paddle in the famous *Rattler/Alecto* trials. Free running in head seas, in a full gale, with dynamometer and indicator diagrams taken regularly, after a run of 60 miles *Rattler* passed the Spurn light 40 minutes before her competitor. In towing trials, first *Rattler* towed *Alecto* with her paddle floats removed and then *Alecto* towed *Rattler*. *Rattler* was able to tow *Alecto* at just over 1kt faster than vice versa. The much publicised stern to stern towing test was then carried out and *Rattler* towed *Alecto* backwards at 2.5kts. From this point on naval application of the screw propeller in Britain was unstoppable. Quite as important, the *Rattler* results had a major effect upon merchant ship development. The Smith-type two-bladed screw was used widely by them.

In 1844 the Admiralty ordered the steam frigate *Dauntless*; at 218ft length between perpendiculars, 39ft 9in breadth, with a load draught of 17ft 3in and a displacement of 2343 tons, this was a considerable warship.[22]

One major consideration was the shape of the stern waterlines or 'tuck'. The Admiralty conducted a number of trials to determine how fine a stern should be to provide good flow to the screw. They were particularly interested in the possible conversion of sailing line of battle ships to screw propulsion. It was found that at the slow speeds attained by such ships with the low power machinery that could be fitted, a fine 'tuck' was not of great importance.[23] However, in faster ships it did matter; indeed, the above dimensions for *Dauntless* were after lengthening the stern sections by 10ft, so that the propeller could be accommodated in a smooth streamline flow. Initially, *Dauntless* made 7.3kts, but after the alterations just over 10kts.[24]

When *The Great Britain* was converted on the building blocks to screw propulsion the run above the propeller shaft had of necessity to be rather blunt. The model tests carried out at Vickers in 1970 showed clearly that this had a deleterious effect, causing some restriction to flow into the top of the propeller and a high thrust deduction (see later).

Inventions continued to proliferate, but only a few of the many can be considered here. Controllable pitch propellers continued to interest. In 1849 Robert Griffiths took out a patent in which each blade of a two-bladed propeller could be turned on its axis in a socket by the water pressure on the leading edge but acting against a spring. Griffiths expected that the pitch would increase as the ship speed increased and vice versa. This would be a valuable feature – if

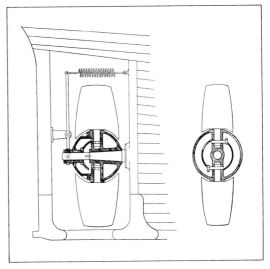

Griffiths' early patent screw (self-adjusting).

it worked. In those days of auxiliary steamers the engines could sometimes be used advantageously when the ship was under sail. If a squall arose and the ship started to accelerate the engines were liable to race to a dangerous extent (this was in the days before really efficient governors). It was hoped that this device would increase the pitch of the screw and prevent racing.[25]

Many of the screw propeller 'inventions' were useless and have not survived in any form, but some were ingenious and innovative, leading directly to today's practice. One of these was Woodcroft's controllable pitch propeller.[26] This was a workable device, even in the context of the technology of the day. A hollow propeller shaft carried a rod which worked spur gears which turned worm screws acting on worm wheels at the roots of the blades.

Most propeller designers of the day mis-

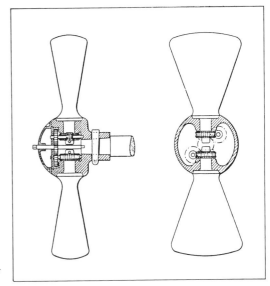

Woodcroft's adjustable blades: a practicable controllable pitch propeller.

21. J Bourne, *op cit*, p284ff.

22. J Fincham, *op cit*, p361.

23. *Ibid*, pp359, 360.

24. A Seaton, *op cit*, p21.

25. *Ibid*, p25.

26. *Ibid*, p26.

takenly took little notice of the shape of the boss. Flat faced bosses, or spherical ones such as those of Griffiths, disturb the flow at the roots of the blades and also cause a good deal of parasitic drag. In 1851 Roberts took out a patent for an improvement 'making the boss much larger than· usual in order that the vanes may act more effectively on the water and extending the boss backwards far enough to admit it being tapered or otherwise formed so as to allow the water to close upon it without a counter current being produced'. The boss/diameter ratio was to be about one-third and the boss was to have a curved conical point at its after end. Forward the boss was to be 'softened off with the body of the vessel'. This was a really valuable improvement and is obviously the basis of modern boss design.[27]

High aspect ratio screws

The aspect ratio – the ratio of length to chord – of the blades is an important consideration. The original high aspect ratio screw design was that of Lowe. Basically, a propeller is a number of wings working in cascade – producing thrust in the same manner that aeroplane wings produce lift. Long, narrow wings are more efficient than short broad ones, provided the loading is not too high, so a screw using a very short segment of its

27. *Ibid*, p27.
28. *Mechanics Magazine* XXXVII (1842), p462.
29. A Seaton, *op cit*, p30.
30. J Bourne, *op cit*, p324.

total pitch produces better thrust than an axially long one of the same diameter. James Lowe patented just this in 1839 and wrote in 1842:

> Any success that the *Archimedes* gained was when my patent segments were applied instead of Mr Smith's whole screw. The voyage from Plymouth to Oporto was performed with a propeller of my segments ... *Archimedes* left port with Mr Smith's patent which was afterwards unshipped and my patent segments fitted ...

Certainly Lowe's type of propeller became common because it was more efficient, but to be fair to Smith he never claimed a patent screw, only a method of applying the screw. Lowe's original 1838 patent diagram does rather support this allegation.[28]

Trawling through these inventions, one lights upon Herman Hirsch's avant garde patent of 1860 accompanied by a rather turgid specification. What Hirsch did was to put 'skew' on high aspect ratio propeller blades and to use deliberately cambered sections, the first time this was shown.[29] The advantage of skew is that the blade slices through the water progressively and there can be a considerable reduction of vibration. The advantage of camber is that it increases the lift and therefore efficiency of propeller blades, although it is doubtful whether Hirsch knew why his propellers were rather more efficient than those of other designers.

A later form of Hirsch's screw, patented in

1866, had increased skew so that it approached the shape of a modern highly skewed propeller – the total skew being of the order of 60 degrees. Associated with this were quite heavily cambered round back sections giving appreciably higher lift while the aspect ratio of the blades was very high, again approximating to that of modern skewed propellers.

This was an advanced screw and probably not paralleled for at least eighty years thereafter. The White Star liner *Adriatic* was retrofitted with this type of screw and cut her best voyage time across the Atlantic from 18 days 9 hours and 18 minutes to 17 days 5 hours and 1 minute. Hirsch's screws were well known to be very free from vibration, as might be expected.

Another high aspect ratio screw introduced right at the end of the period was designed by Mangin, in France, introduced into the Royal Navy in 1865 in HMS *Favorite*. As there was a notable absence of propeller induced vibration in the installation, this screw was adopted for other British warships. The characteristics were unusual, the individual blades being of very high aspect ratio but mounted in tandem.[30]

The iron-hulled Himalaya *of 1853 was probably the most adventurous shipbuilding decision since* The Great Britain. *The largest steamer in the world, she was ordered by P&O as a paddler but was converted to screw before launching. However, she did not see commercial service, being acquired by the Admiralty as a troopship for the Crimean War and retained thereafter – hence the White Ensign in this photograph.* (CMP)

Candia

The two blades on either side of the shaft obviously worked closely in cascade. The design of an efficient propeller of this type is difficult. Mangin produced a remarkable technological *tour de force* but of course the propeller would be difficult and expensive to make and of dubious longevity. Of considerable interest is the blade section diagram.

The Griffiths screw as fitted to The Great Britain.

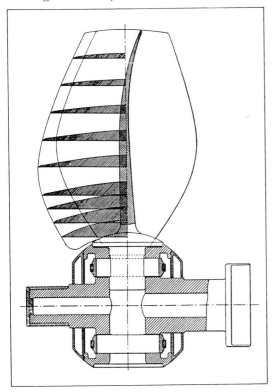

In 1860 Robert Griffiths took out a new patent which governed the outline shape of the blade from root to tip. The Archimedean screw propeller blade had its widest chord at the tip. This was inevitable, and produced two undesirable effects. First, it loaded up the blade tip, producing increased structural stresses at the root and, second, it encouraged spilling of flow over the tip of the blade which not only caused vibration but also reduced its efficiency. Griffiths stated that the greatest width of the propeller blade should be at about half the radius of the screw from the centre of the propeller shaft. He thereby unloaded the tip of the propeller. The practical result was undoubtedly an improvement of efficiency and a reduction of vibration.[31]

The two-bladed Griffiths propeller became virtually standard in ships such as *The Great Britain* in her later form, in the *Warrior* and so on, because it was both efficient and ideal for hoisting up into a stern trunk, out of the way when sailing.

Twin screws

Although the succesful twin-screw, direct drive iron steamship *Bangor II* had been built in the USA in 1844, it was only around 1855 that twin-screw propulsion began to arouse interest, partly because of the extra security it offered and also because it could improve the handling of the long narrow ships which were evolving. Captain

The Himalaya *was part of a large programme of expansion by P&O to meet the provisions of a new contract of 1852 to provide mail services not only between Britain and India, but on to China, to Singapore and from thence to Australia. More typical than the giant* Himalaya *was the* Candia *of 1982 tons, built by Mare at Blackwall on the Thames in 1854.* (CMP)

T E Symonds, RN was a leading protagonist, inspired by a Mr Christie of Rotterdam who built a remarkably sophisticated little vessel, the *Moerdyk*, in 1860 for the Antwerp Railway Com-

After hull lines of the twin-screw steamer Moerdyk.

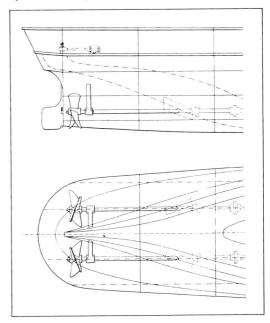

31. A Seaton, *op cit*, p131.

pany.[32] Only 90ft long by 12ft breadth, the little ship ran for years with complete success. Symonds was ingenious and in 1865 proposed several arrangements for accommodating twin screws, all of which later became standard practice. He also devised a method for 'lifting' twin screws.[33]

Contra vanes

A remarkable invention was patented in 1864 by Arthur Rigg of Chester. Rigg was an engineer, clearly with a fair understanding of the fundamental workings of the screw propeller. He proposed fitting a number of fixed radial twisted blades to the rudder post, aft of the screw. These were like the screw itself but twisted in the opposite direction. He stated that these radial arms constituted a stationary screw with a pitch about the same as the revolving screw, but of opposite hand.

> I place around and at the rear of the screw, a number of fixed curved blades or vanes so formed that the water as it passes from the screw is by them gradually deflected and caused to flow parallel with the axis of the screw. It is preferred that the commencement

of the curve of these vanes or blades should be the same as the angle of the effluent water.

The degree of sophistication shown in this device was remarkable.[34] The vanes were of cambered section and specifically stated to be placed so as to have a shock free entry for the water exiting the propeller. The latter has a rotary component, as indeed Rigg stated, and will impinge upon the blades at an angle of incidence producing a forward component of lift. This device, in little more sophisticated form, is used today in some vessels such as tankers optimised for propulsion and gaining 3–4 per cent extra efficiency as a result.

Ship development after *The Great Britain*

Development was now along fairly conservative lines, consolidating gains and eschewing the more avant garde and, certainly, any outré proposals.

The next large merchant ship built after *The Great Britain* was *Himalaya* in 1853 for P&O – their first large screw steamship. Of straightforward design, *Himalaya* was 340ft between

As the screw ship developed towards the point where it could challenge the paddler for speed, a less ambitious line of thought followed the Sarah Sands *in regarding the screw as an auxiliary to a large spread of sail. Because it was expensive to travel on the mail steamers, the sailing packets still controlled an extensive traffic with which vessels like the* Edinburgh *were intended to compete. Originally built for a Glasgow–New York service in 1855, the ship became part of the Inman fleet during 1859-1870, and after ten years as a cable ship returned to the North Atlantic in 1881 for Adamson & Ronaldson. (CMP)*

perpendiculars, 336ft 6in on the waterline, with an extreme breadth of 46ft 1in. Normal draught was more than that of *The Great Britain* at 21.5ft, displacement about 1000 tons greater at 4690 tons. The ship was driven by a two-bladed screw 18ft in diameter and of 28ft pitch; thus pitch/diameter ratio was very similar to that of *The Great Britain*.

32. Captain T Symonds, RN, 'On the Construction and Propulsion of Twin Screw Vessels', *Transactions of the Institution of Naval Architects* V (1864).

33. Captain T Symond, RN, 'On the Present and the Future of the Twin Screw System', *Transactions of the Institution of Naval Architects* VI (1865).

34. J Bourne, *op cit*, p162.

Power was supplied by rather extravagant twin-cylinder direct drive horizontal trunk engines of 2500ihp; and the trial speed attained was 13.78kts at a slip of 15 per cent. Coal prices rose sharply at the time *Himalaya* came into service, making the ship uneconomic. She was sold to the Government for a troopship for £133,000 – just about what she had cost. After forty years trooping she became a coal hulk and curiously still exists today – as a wreck – having been sunk in June 1940 at Portland by German bombers.

The *Great Eastern* was an extraordinary step in development. Completed in 1858, only fourteen years after *The Great Britain*, the ship was immense – at 32,000 tons, six times the displacement of any other afloat. With length overall of just under 700ft, breadth 83ft, the ship was too big to be propelled by the screw engines of the day. Power requirements approached 10,000ihp for the design speed of 15kts and it was simply not possible to manufacture a screw shaft large enough to transmit this power. Fur-

Bremen and New York, built by Caird at Greenock in 1858, were the first transatlantic steamers for the Norddeutscher Lloyd. The iron-built 2674-ton vessels were typical of their day in the absence of superstructure – more or less mandatory given the heavy barque rig. From A & R Murray, Ship-building and Steam Ships (Edinburgh 1861).

The immense and sophisticated stern arrangements of the Great Eastern. *(Brunel University)*

thermore, the engines themselves would be beyond the practice and capabilities of the day. Accordingly, both screw and paddle propulsion were fitted, of 4890ihp and 3676ihp, respectively.

The stern frame was ambitious, like all else in this ship, being the first ever of cast iron cellular construction and designed to spread loads into the stern structure. The pre-launch photograph shows the remarkable progress that had been made in a few years – both in the enormous size of the project and in the degree of hydrodynamic sophistication achieved. Some details such as the careful streamlining of the stern and rudder posts were in advance of much single screw practice of half a century later.

Another notable ship, *China* of 1862, was the first screw ship ordered for the Cunard company. Built as a pilot experiment, 326ft long by 40ft breadth, she was propelled by two oscillating cylinders driving an overhead crankshaft geared to the screw. This ship, even if very conservative, proved much superior to her Cunard paddle contemporaries and settled the fate of paddle propulsion for Cunard.

As a final example, Alfred Holt's cargo liners of 1862 to 1866 perhaps represented the most important step of all for steam/screw propulsion. Much the same length as *The Great Britain* and

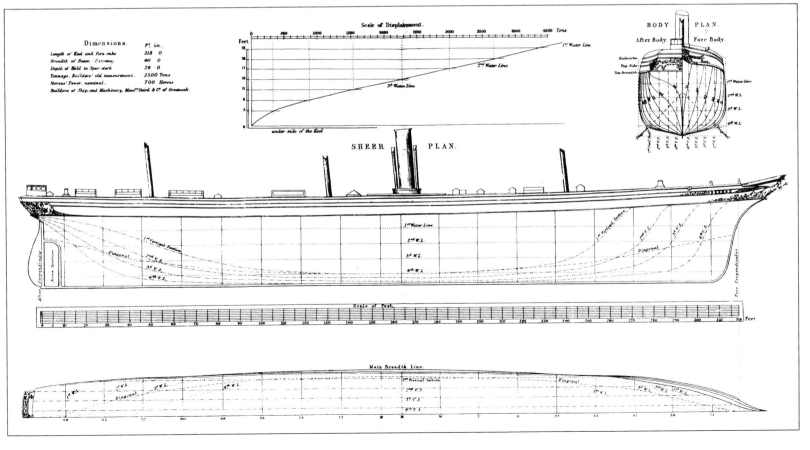

China (320ft), they were of 36ft breadth and could carry 3000 tons of cargo on 23ft draught at 12kts. With very compact compound expansion machinery, they achieved the excellent fuel rate of 2.2lb of coal per ihp hour at an output of 1350ihp.

First, placed on the Britain–China route, these ships opened up world trade to steam, fathering the thousands of tramp ships and cargo liners of the next three quarters of a century. Second, they established a type of machinery that was to be developed in Atlantic liners and led to the triple and quadruple expansion plants of latter years. They were true trend setters.

Practical considerations

Once *Archimedes* had demonstrated the fundamentals – namely the correct position for the screw in a single-screw vessel, the high level of efficiency of screw propulsion in all seagoing conditions, the excellent steering that resulted therefrom, the ability to use sail effectively in conjunction with a screw, the practicability of hauling a two-bladed screw out of the water into a stern well – it might have seemed that the way ahead was wide open. However, this was only the start of the process of producing what became the totally dominant type of propulsion for ships. There were other subsidiary but important problems which had to be solved, certainly for ocean-going ships.

---

35. Capt E Chappell, *op cit*, p15.

36. J Guthrie, *A History of Marine Engineering* (London 1971), p105.

Direct drive machinery had to be developed capable of producing power at the revolutions required by screw propellers: in round terms some three to four times that of paddle machinery. Furthermore, the fuel economy of marine engines sorely needed improvement. Both targets, higher revolutions and better economy, called for higher steam pressures.

Although with *Archimedes* and *The Great Britain* stern tubes had been developed that did allow the power to be transmitted to the screw without letting water into the hull, their bearings had a limited life. A new and more practicable stern tube arrangement was essential.

Then the thrust produced by the screw had to be absorbed in a practical and reliable form of thrust bearing. The type used in *The Great Britain* worked but was not suitable for long distance general use and at higher powers.

Except on coastal and transatlantic voyages, steamships of the period 1840–1865 could not carry enough coal for the very inefficient engines of the day. Hence on a long voyage, such as to Australia or in oceanic naval cruising, it was essential to use sail power as the prime mover. When sailing, the screw was a drag and cut down the performance of the vessel, and it was essential to develop a practical engineering method for avoiding this drag.

The basic structural design of screw propellers was unsatisfactory and needed radical improvement. Furthermore, theoretical understanding of the action of propellers was necessary which together with empirical data from trials etc could allow adequate design rather than design on a trial and error basis.

Direct drive engines

The practical originator of direct drive machinery may well have been Ericsson. From the very first he had built engines which could operate at propeller speed, the first being for the tow boat *R F Stockton*. Others were aware of this point, for example Chappell: 'a light iron boat is now in progress of construction to which will be applied one of Mr Galloway's patent rotary engines turning a screw propeller at a velocity of two hundred rpm.'[35]

One type of Ericsson's direct drive machinery was specifically intended to keep all machinery below the waterline for military reasons and was an ingenious and effective design. There were two steam cylinders placed end to end, each having its own running gear, piston, valve gear and so on. Each piston worked a separate crank which in turn drove a common crank shaft through a connecting rod. Air and circulating pumps were driven off separate arms on both lay shafts and it was impossible, with a two-cylinder engine, to stall the engine on centres.[36]

The development of direct drive engines proceeded initially using this layout of horizontal

Tasmanian was probably the most powerful screw ship afloat when completed in 1858. An ambitious design ordered by an ambitious company (European & Australia RM Co), the ship was constructed by the small but progressive shipyard of Lawrence Hill at Port Glasgow. The company collapsed before the ship could enter service and she was taken over by the Royal Mail Line and initially diverted to the Brazil mail run. She was not a success and after one voyage was transferred to West Indies service. (CMP)

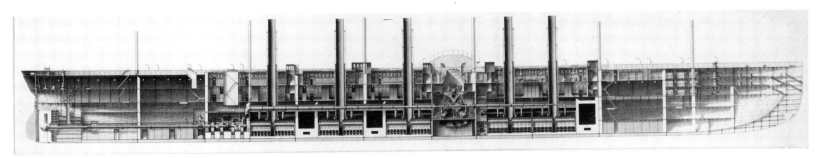

If Brunel's The Great Britain *was at the very edge of technological knowledge, then the* Great Eastern *was well beyond it. Twice the length of any ship so far built and over five times the displacement, the ship's dimensions were fixed by the requirement to steam from England to Ceylon, round the Cape, without taking on additional coal (bunkering was very expensive abroad). Because no known machinery could deliver enough power, the ship was designed with a unique combination of screw and paddle propulsion. The* Leviathan, *as she was most appropriately to have been named, bankrupted her builder and her owners and suffered a series of misfortunes in service. However, she represented one of the greatest engineering achievements of the century, and great pride in being associated with the ship is manifest in a collection of magnificent coloured lithographs presented by her builder, John Scott Russell, to the Science Museum. (ScM)*

cylinders. The 'Gorgon' type engine, named after the first ship to which it was fitted, was used in Britain although in its horizontal form it was never very popular, as it wore rapidly and was difficult to work on. When made vertical, inverted by Thompsons on the Clyde, it became the

37. D Griffiths, *Power of the Great Liners* (Wellingborough 1991), p28.

standard marine reciprocating engine for the best part of a century. It is familiar as the triple and quadruple expansion engines of later days such as were fitted in the great reciprocating-engined Atlantic liners – as well as thousands of liners and tramp steamers throughout the latter days of the nineteenth and the early twentieth centuries.

Horizontal oscillating engines were tried without much success and two other types of horizontal engines were developed in the 1850s giving direct drive specifically for screw propulsion – the trunk and the annular engines. The very first type of trunk engine was introduced by James Watt way back in 1784 but the engine builders William Penn & Co of Greenwich adapted it for marine propulsion. The principles of these types of machinery were similar but both had inherently high mechanical and heat losses. Fuel consumption was accordingly high, 4–4.5lb of coal per ihp hour – no better than that of *The Great Britain* although working at around 20psi rather than the 5psi of that ship.

Direct drive machinery as mentioned earlier was used by Ericsson from the start and the adaptation of the slow speed paddle type ma-

chinery such as in *The Great Britain* and *Archimedes* was merely a passing phase. As soon as the need for faster revolving direct drive engines was apparent a variety of types took over from the geared-up machinery. It is interesting, however, that the conservative Cunard company retained such gearing for its very first screw ship *China*, in 1860.[37]

This contrasts with *The Great Britain*'s successor, the *Great Eastern* of 1858, which was fitted with horizontally opposed direct engines running at 45rpm. These, built by James Watt, weighed 500 tons and consisted of four cylinders mounted as two horizontally opposed pairs driv-

Apart from the odd relief service during the Crimean War, Cunard first entrusted the mails to a screw steamer in 1860 when the Australasian *sailed from Liverpool to New York. This 2902-ton ship had been built of iron for the short-lived European & Australia RM Co by J & G Thomson, Clydebank, in 1857 and had particularly powerful machinery. However, the ship was not very successful on the North Atlantic – like her sister* Tasmanian *on the South Atlantic – and was eventually re-engined and renamed* Calabria *in 1870; in 1876 she was sold for employment as a cable-layer, in which guise she is seen in this photograph. (CMP)*

ing onto a central crankshaft. The cylinders were 7ft 4in bore with a short stroke of 4ft. At cruising rpm of 38.8 the screw machinery developed 4890ihp from a boiler pressure of 25psi.

The immense screw propeller was four-bladed, 24ft in diameter and of 44ft pitch, weighed 36 tons and was driven by a 2ft diameter propeller shaft.[38] On full power of the screw alone, the ship could make 9kts, at a fuel rate of 4.9lb per ihp hour. On screw and paddles together, the ship achieved 14.5kts – close to design speed. The paddle machinery was more economical than the screw, its fuel rate being 3.1lb per ihp hour.[39]

Another example of direct drive was HMS *Warrior*, completed in 1860. *Warrior* had two 'engines' or cylinders of trunk type, 104.625in effective diameter with a stroke of 48in. The two cylinders lay side by side driving athwartships, on to the crankshaft, rather like the much later 'steam hammer' type of reciprocating engine but laid on its side. The propeller was directly driven at a maximum of 56rpm and generally in service at 51–54. Indicated horsepower was rather greater than that of the screw machinery of

---

38. J Bourne, *op cit*, p326.

39. R Fuller, 'The *Great Eastern*', *Transactions of the Institution of Marine Engineers* (1961), p132ff.

40. H Dickinson, *A Short History of the Steam Engine* (Cambridge 1939), p156.

Great Eastern, 5269ihp at 20–22psi steam pressure. Like that ship, fuel consumption was high, over 4lb per ihp hour. The propeller was much the same size as that of the *Great Eastern* at 24ft 6in diameter but with a pitch of only 27ft 8⅜ins. It was two-bladed, 5ft 6in in length and could be adjusted for pitch between 25ft and 32ft by slackening off the securing bolts and twisting the blades.

Adequate revolutions for screw propulsion were attained by these engines, but only at the expense of high fuel consumption. Boiler pressures had risen from the 5psi, gauge, of *The Great Britain* to about the 20–25psi level, but the massive heat and mechanical losses of these monsters swallowed any resulting savings. What was needed was much higher pressures, better layout and expansion in more than one stage. If all the expansion took place in one cylinder, its walls were cooled and incoming steam suffered heavy heat loss. Compound engines, expansion in two stages, was not new in ships – the paddler *James Watt* in 1829 was only the first of several in the next two decades. The Pacific Steam Navigation Co's sisters *Valparaiso* and *Inca* of 1856 were compound expansion, working at 26psi and achieving the very creditable fuel rate of just over 2lb per ihp hour.

For real progress improvements were needed in condensers, seals and lubricants. The jet condenser dictated salt water feed which limited

boiler temperatures and pressures; tallow and similar lubricants caused heavy priming in the steam system – not to mention clogging of surface condenser tubes. Worse, they decomposed at high temperatures into fatty acids. Finally, improved seals were essential to prevent leakage of higher pressure steam.

All these developments were on the way. The specification of the *Warrior* of 1861 required all metal seals, while packed seals used with asbestos rather than hemp were found to stand alongside these. Mineral oil lubricants introduced in 1856 in the USA by Colonel E Drake were found to be temperature stable.[40] Indeed, Samuel Hall's surface condenser, used by *Sirius* as early as 1838 only became fully practicable after the introduction of these lubricants. By 1865 both surface tube condensers and cylindrical boilers which were suitable for high pressures were on the way to being adopted widely. Recognisably modern machinery had appeared.

Given its extensive long distance network, and the cost of storing coal at its bunkering stations, it is not surprising to find P&O an early convert to compounding. In the early 1860s they introduced a series of compound steamers, including the Mooltan, Carnatic, *and* Baroda *(seen here when new in 1864 at Southampton); most P&O ships were still built on the Thames and these vessels were fitted with Humphrys inverted tandem engines of about 2400ihp, consuming less than 2lbs of coal per ihp per hour.* (CMP)

The Bibby Line's Arabian *of 1862 was one of a number of cargo liners for the Mediterranean trade built at the famous Belfast shipyard of Harland & Wolff. In the late 1850s Harlands developed a hull form of exceptional length (ten times the beam in some cases, whereas eight was the norm) on the theory that for a given power output additional length could achieve much the same speed as a short one but with increased carrying capacity. Bibbys were an early believer in this view but experience proved that long hulls were not conducive to economy or capacity, but Harlands continued to apply it to fast ships, most notably to the White Star vessels of the 1870s. (CMP)*

In 1862 Alfred Holt introduced his single crank tandem compound engine for cargo liners. This plant marked a breakthrough for screw propulsion of cargo vessels and the start of the demise of sail, clinched by the triple expansion engine a few years later. The cylinders were mounted one over the other, high-pressure (HP) of 27in bore and low (LP) of 58in. Piston stroke was 5ft and the HP rod protruded up from the HP head, to carry a cross beam which in turn had two side rods, one at each end, coming down outside the HP cylinder, through glands and onto the LP piston. This was a simple and compact engine. At 60psi operating pressure, the fuel rate was 2.2lb per ihp hour, excellent for a low power engine and about half that of *The Great Britain*.[41] As a final example, also in 1862, P&O brought out *Carnatic*, 1800 tons grt, with cylinders 43in and 96in bore and 36in stroke. Boiler pressure was 26psi and a fuel rate of just over 2lb per ihp hour was achieved. The cylinder layout was tandem like the Alfred Holt ships.

The first problem, then, of developing direct drive machinery for screw propellers was solved, first by Ericsson in 1838 and in the next fifteen years by a number of engine builders, with increasing emphasis on economy and simplicity. By 1865 there was no longer any basic problem ahead, only a process of technological development.

Stern tubes and bearings

Still worrying, as power and steaming range increased, was the second problem – that of developing an adequate stern tube bearing design for the tailshaft. A standard practice for early screw ships had been derived but this was proving inadequate in service. In this, a brass stern tube was let into an aperture in the stern post. This pipe or tube had a stuffing box on its inner end and the brass itself formed the bearing for the shaft. Of poor fit, and with the metal to metal surfaces only water lubricated, this could not be expected to last very long. An additional external brass bearing was often fitted at the trailing edge of the stern post and sometimes one on the rudder post.[42] Essentially, this was the arrangement fitted to *The Great Britain* but no performance data is available from that ship. The shaft usually did not bear upon the brass stern tube throughout its length but only for a

certain distance at each end; however, in some cases, where the propeller did not lift, the whole of the stern tube was used as a bearing.

In their early screw engines Messrs Penn introduced a long bush fitted into the after end of the stern tube and lined with soft metal. This became the arrangement commonly in use up to and including the *Great Eastern* (her original stern bearing was 8ft long). There were four bearing surfaces 8ft long by 16in wide consisting of 8in thick wrought iron slabs mounted above, below and on either side of the shaft circumference. These slabs were lined with half an inch of white metal.

On the first transatlantic voyage in 1860 this bearing failed. It must be appreciated that in this ship there was an overhanging weight of 54 tons cantilevered on the stern tube. The result was a large downward force at the bottom of the after end of the stern tube bearing and a corresponding but lesser upward force at the top of the forward end of the stern tube. When the *Great Eastern* was put on the grid at Milford Haven it was found that the wear up at the forward end was 2in and a horrifying 4in down at the after end. Not only had the soft metal bearing liner worn through but the shaft had cut its way well into the supporting bush in the stern frame.

41. J Guthrie, *op cit*, p129.

42. J Bourne, *op cit*, p415.

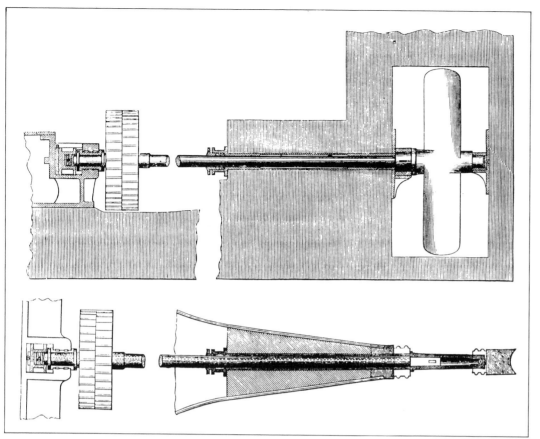

A standard tail shaft and stern tube arrangement of about 1850. Note the thrust discs, rudder post bearing and very small propeller blade tip clearances.

oped initially by William Penn & Co, responsible for so many of these essential practical steps. Collars were machined on the shaft and these fitted into grooves on a bearing or plummer block solidly attached to the structure of the ship. A cap, also grooved, was fitted on top of the plummer block and bolted to it. On top of that again was an oil box with oil drains to each of the grooves. The bearing faces of the grooves were lined with a soft bearing metal such as 'Babitt's'.[45]

The thrust block of the *Great Eastern* was of this type. Such collar bearings rapidly became standard until, much later, they in turn were superseded. Towards the end of the century thrusts had become so high that a much more sophisticated approach was needed. An Australian engineer, A G Michell, developed a hinged floating pad type of bearing where the soft metal faced pads automatically angled themselves to build up wedges of oil, capable of bearing pressures of 500psi or more. This type of thrust bearing is used to this day.[46]

Lifting screws

A reliable method for eliminating the drag of the screw when sailing was essential. *Archimedes* pioneered this with a primitive lifting system, much facilitated by using the final two-bladed screw. Other systems were tried – in some cases a sailing clutch, for example in the first conversion of *The Great Britain* for the Australian route. Here the propeller could be disconnected and allowed to windmill. With screws of the contemporary very high pitch ratio this gave an acceptable reduction in drag. However, the procedure was cumbersome and could be dangerous. Indeed, *The Great Britain* was nearly dismasted on one occasion when the propeller was engaged when the ship was sailing in a strong wind.[47]

An alternative was to feather the screw, but controllable pitch propeller technology was primitive and unreliable and no sane shipowner in those days would fit such a gadget, inaccessible as it was underwater, to an ocean-going ship.

The practicable method was to lift the propeller out of the water and this became popular,

Penn was on his mettle and proposed fitting a staved, water lubricated bearing of lignum vitae (an extremely hard wood), patented in 1854, as a replacement. This was a complete success and became standard in shipping for many years and is still used today. The ordinary brass bush had longitudinal dovetail grooves cut in it, filled with the staves of the hardwood lignum vitae. These strips of wood were 2½in wide with about ¾in between them and stood ¼in proud above the surface of the boss. The bearing was not in any way water-tight so water flowed between the strips along the shaft and was swept over them by the rotation of the shaft. The shaft itself was bushed so that the wooden staves ran on a brass surface rather than on steel. The forward end of the stern tube had the usual stuffing box and gland to prevent water leaking into the shafting space. In one brilliant stroke Penn had solved this really serious problem.[43]

Thrust bearings

As power increased rapidly so did the screw thrust and the development of adequate thrust bearings became crucial. In *The Great Britain* the thrust block was a circular steel plate 2ft in diameter supported from the engine beds, on to which bore a gunmetal plate of the same diameter attached to the end of the shaft itself. Water under pressure was fed to a cavity in the centre of the two plates, escaping radially. According to

contemporary accounts this lubricated them successfully.[44] However, even at the modest power of *The Great Britain* it was necessary to supply water at up to 200psi in order to float these two plates apart and lubricate them. It will be appreciated that the ability of such an arrangement to accept the much higher powers being installed was very limited, even more so as most vessels did not use high-pressure water between the plates but simply sprayed water onto them. This arrangement was only suitable for the relatively low levels of power and thrust available to the pioneers.

By the early 1850s the 'collar' type of thrust bearing had been introduced. This was devel-

The standard 'collar' type thrust bearing of the Great Eastern.

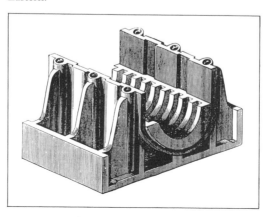

43. *Ibid*, p416.

44. T Guppy, 'Description of the *Great Britain* Iron Steamship', *Transactions of the Institution of Civil Engineers* 710 (1845), pp160, 161.

45. J Bourne, *op cit*, p412.

46. J Ewing, *The Steam Engine* (Cambridge 1926), p275.

47. E Corlett, *op cit*, p131.

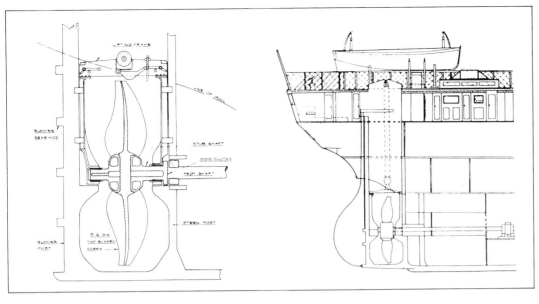

The 'banjo frame' lifting screw arrangement as fitted to *The Great Britain* in 1857.

being used for many ships until well after our period. One method was to carry the screw on a hinging tail shaft, aft of the stern tube, so it and the after bearing could be lifted, using an universal coupling, without disconnection. Scott Russell favoured this arrangement and it was even fitted to the Atlantic liner *Britannic* as late as 1874. Cumbersome and complicated, with awesome thrust absorption problems, it died a natural death.

In the widely adopted system, a two-bladed propeller on a stub shaft was set in a pair of bearings on a frame which slid on the stern frame rudder and stern posts in such a way that the whole thing could be lifted into a trunk in the counter by means of pulleys of screws. This arrangement can be seen on *Warrior* to this day, and the 1857 (lifting banjo) stern frame of *The Great Britain* is in the dock alongside the ship. It was taken out when the stern was returned to its original arrangement.

When the propeller was to be lifted the engine was first stopped and barred around until marks indicated that the propeller blades were in the vertical position. Locking gear on the frame mated with the blade tip to prevent rotation whilst the propeller was disengaged. An intermediate bobbin section in the propeller shafting was then removed, so the tail shaft could be drawn forward by an amount sufficient to clear its squared end out of a recess in the forward end of the shaft boss and which was carried by the bearings at the fore and aft sides of the banjo frame.

The whole frame plus the propeller could then be lifted up into the trunk out of the water, the tail shaft slid aft again and the bobbin shaft inserted. There was usually a ratchet arrangement to prevent any possibility of the banjo frame dropping. Sometimes, however, blocks and ratchets were dispensed with and a screw arrangement fitted. In the case of *The Great Britain* ratchet gear with stops on the two posts was used. Without such safety devices the propeller and frame could drop and take the sole piece off the bottom of the ship, causing heavy damage both to the propeller and to the ship. There is at least one recorded case of this happening.

This gear worked well. The bulk of the propellers used with it were of the Griffiths two-bladed type, as for instance was the screw of *The Great Britain* in service following 1857.

Screw blade strength

Early screw propellers were all flat plates twisted into a helix: the original Archimedean screws were simply strips of iron plate riveted helically round a tube. The type of screw that eventually became semi-standard after 1840, namely the two-bladed, one-sixth or thereabouts segment of an Archimedean screw, was simply a flat blade twisted but fixed to a solid wrought iron boss. This attachment could be by fire welding, as in the case of *The Great Britain*, or the entire propeller and blades could be cast iron, as was her second screw, and as became standard practice for very many years.

The Archimedean form of propeller with its very wide tip and flat-plate construction was inherently weak. Load was concentrated towards the tip, and the roots of the blades, where they joined the boss, had relatively small bending strength. At that time it was thought that the driving face of the propeller was all that mattered, so the obvious way to increase the strength was to add backing to the blade; thickening it up on the 'unimportant' side, particularly towards the roots. This meant, of course, that there would be flat faces at the leading and aft edges of the blade, producing undesirable drag.

Brunel mentioned the undesirability of this in his Screw Report.

Therefore, the backing thickness was sharpened up by chamfering it off forward and aft just as Brunel did in *The Great Britain*. What he did was too crude and eventually a type of section evolved with a flat driving face twisted into a helix and with 'round back' or 'ogival' sections backing it. This extra backing thickness would increase from very little at the tips, which were virtually flat plates, to quite thick sections near the blade roots.

In this way, for purely structural reasons, a reasonably efficient propeller section was developed which gave camber and much increased blade lift. The reason for the increase was that in a properly designed section perhaps two-thirds of the thrust is produced by the suction of the water as it accelerates round the longer back of the blade, in the process reducing its pressure. The essence of efficient hydrofoil design is to optimise the flow over the back, or suction side, to get the highest possible negative pressure without flow breakdown. Camber is inherent in any such section and this much increases the efficiency, as Mr Cowper found with his little air fan.

To show how little was known about section shape it is intriguing to note Seaton, even in 1909, saying:

> the shape of transverse sections of a screw blade should be 'shipshape' and designed to pass through the water with least resistance. For this purpose the maximum thickness or as it were the greatest beam should be nearer the leading edge than the following; that is, the 'forebody' is comparatively shorter than the afterbody and should be in the proportion of 3 to 6 if possible ... It remains to be seen if better results will not be got from true ship sections than by the present half elliptical sections necessary to get the flat acting surface.[48]

Here were sections beginning to approximate to aerofoils but totally unrelated to them in their origin.

At the same time the wide tip had the undesirable hydrodynamic and structural effects described earlier so propeller blades began to adopt a more modern shape, initiated by Griffiths. It can be shown nowadays, theoretically, that the maximum efficiency of a propeller blade is pro-

48. A Seaton, *op cit*, p177.

Like most of Cunard's early screw ships, the Aleppo *of 1865 was originally built for the company's Mediterranean service, although she spent the years before 1872 on the North Atlantic. Like her sisters,* Tripoli *and* Tarifa, *this 2057-ton vessel was built by J & G Thomson, Clydebank; principally freighters, they could also carry about fifty cabin and six hundred third class passengers. Cunard had yet to adopt compound engines and they were powered by two-cylinder inverted simple expansion machinery driving the ships at 11kts. (CMP)*

duced when its outline shape is an elongated ellipse not unlike that of Griffiths'.

With the type of boss pioneered by Roberts in 1851, the blade outline introduced by Griffiths, and the more hydrodynamically efficient cross sections introduced, perforce, by structural considerations, quite efficient propellers of reasonably modern type evolved. In the type of propeller fitted to *The Great Britain* in 1857, all these features can be seen, apart from the boss shape and also, incidentally, the socket for the squared end of the retractable tail shaft.

A bronze naval screw, of about 1909, some seventy years after these developments, shows features all of which were in being by 1865 – ogival sections (strength), blade outline (Griffiths), boss shape (Roberts). From 1865 to the end of the century, screw propeller development was really a matter of detail, coping structurally

with increased thrust, refining the mechanical, manufacturing and hydrodynamic details and developing quasi-empirical methods of design so as to be able to make reasonably accurate predictions. By then the power required by ships could be predicted fairly accurately from model scale following the work of William Froude. An understanding of flow breakdown, screw noise and cavitation only began around the end of the century.

Screw propeller theory

In the early days of screw propulsion it was thought that a screw propeller blade was in fact a skewed paddle; in other words, it drove water away from it by a wedging action, whereas with a normal paddle the wedge was at right angles to the water and simply pushed it. This was quite wrong as indeed Brunel pointed out in his Report to the Directors of the Great Western Steamship Company. Many of the more weird proposed screws were based on this fallacy.

This chapter has shown that by trial and error, accident and engineering insight it had been found that the screw propeller became more and more efficient as the length of the Archimedean thread was shortened. No one at the time really knew why, and by the end of our period it was

apparent that there was a real need for a sound theoretical basis of propeller design.

In 1865 Professor Macquorn Rankine formulated a simple theory of propeller action based on considering the actual motion of water through the propeller disc and the consequent changes in momentum, *ie* the product of mass and velocity. Thus the very first theory of propeller action came right at the end of the period under consideration – 1865. All the development of the screw propeller until then was totally empirical, intuitive and in some cases fortuitous. The Rankine theory was developed by the younger Froude and is now known as the Rankine/Froude Axial Momentum Theory. It was

A naval propeller of 1909 showing principal features, all of which had been developed by 1865.

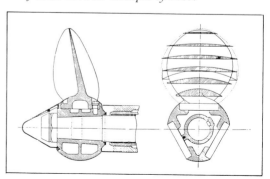

Alfred Holt's famous Agamemnon *of 1866, whose tandem compound engines were so economical that a long distance cargo steamer capable of competing with sailing ships became a possibility for the first time. She could carry 3500 tons of cargo but consumed little more than 20 tons of coal a day, which allowed her to steam the 8500 miles from Britain to Mauritius without coaling en route. (CMP)*

not concerned with the details of the propeller but with the general physical environment and did not help detailed design very much.

However, it did establish one or two very important points. The first was that the water forward of the propeller was accelerated into the screw and further accelerated aft of it. The velocity at the propeller disc was found to be the mean between the initial velocity some distance forward of the screw and the final velocity some distance behind it. This had a direct bearing upon desirable afterbody lines for a ship. The second important point was that even if one could conceive of a 'frictionless ideal screw', there was a limit to its efficiency, depending upon the area of the propeller disc and the speed of the advance of the propeller, in relation to the power developed. This is not the place to delve deeply into the further development of propeller theory but a sketch is helpful to understand and appreciate the remarkable achievements of the

early screw designers in the light of their theoretical ignorance.

In 1878 the elder Froude produced a theory considering various elements of the blade, *ie* circumferential strips at different radii from the boss, combining the axial intake and rotational velocities of the water entering each strip and deriving their effect. Summing for all the strips should give the effect of the propeller but it was found that the calculated result did not agree at all with practical ones.

This Blade Element Theory was refined but never gave satisfactory results until the effects of the vortices rotating round the propeller blade were investigated. It was found also that leakage of water over the tip from the high-pressure underside to the low-pressure back-side resulted in a twisting flow off the tip of the propeller forming a trailing vortex which modified the effect of the blade elements. Now one can see the origin of one of the defects of the tip loaded 'Smith' Archimedean screw.

To cut a long story short, the so-called Vortex Theory was developed in conjunction with the Blade Element Theory to a point that by the end of the Second World War screw propellers could be designed mathematically from scratch to give accurate predictable results. The process was laborious and impractical for detailed design

purposes until the advent of the digital computer; now it is normal practice.[49] But until then propeller design was based upon the results of model testing and a much developed version of the methods used in 1865.

The early propeller designers were considerably bothered by apparently anomalous results for 'slip'. Slip is the difference between the distance the propeller would advance if it was working as a screw in a solid (*ie* the pitch times the revolutions) and the actual distance travelled by the ship. This anomaly arose from the belief that the water entering the propeller was at rest, in other words that the propeller itself was advancing through the water entering it at the same speed as the ship through the water around it. For single-screw ships this is certainly not so and the less so, the bigger, fuller, and longer the ship. As a ship goes through the water the friction of its hull drags the water along with it, producing a wake which becomes thicker and slower the further aft one goes.

Just forward of the propeller, if the ship were being towed, the water may have a forward velocity of 0.3 or 0.4 times that of the velocity of the ship through the water. This is known as the

49. L Burrill, 'On Propeller Theory', *Transactions of the Institution of Engineers and Shipbuilders in Scotland* (1947).

'wake fraction' and the water velocity entering the screw will be only 0.7 or 0.6 times the speed of the ship. The blunter the ends of the ship the higher the 'wake friction' and similarly the rougher the hull.

There is another effect as the water forward of the screw is accelerated, *ie* sucked back with a considerable velocity into the screw. It has increased velocity and hence reduced pressure. This lowered pressure, acting on the surfaces of the run of the ship, tends to suck the ship back into the propeller and produces a reduction of thrust of the propeller. Typically for a full or heavy ship this may be around 0.2 of the thrust of the propeller. This is known as the 'thrust deduction'. It has a distinct bearing on the shape of the 'tuck' as the *Dauntless* experiments showed: too blunt and this 'thrust deduction' can be very high.

Suppose that a propeller has an efficiency of 70 per cent, in other words that it turns the power supplied to it into *useful* power at that efficiency, when rotated at its operating revolutions but clear of a ship. Suppose it goes through the water at the desired ship speed with a 'wake fraction' of 0.3 and a 'thrust deduction' of 0.2. The efficiency of the screw interaction with the hull is known as the 'hull efficiency' and is calculated as $(1-0.2)/(1-0.3)$, *ie* 1.143 in this case. The way in which shaft horsepower is transformed into useful power propelling the ship is the product of the two efficiencies $0.7 \times 1.143 = 0.8$. But it was not until long after 1865 that this was appreciated. It was only the work of William Froude in the later days of the nineteenth century that led to a thorough understanding of this effect.

So, if the water into which the screw was advancing was not travelling at the speed, V, of the ship but at say 0.7V then the slip of the propeller would be much affected and the apparently anomalous figures for slip, including negative ones, noted by some early experimenters explained.

Conclusion

By 1865 all the fundamental physical problems had been cleared from the path of screw propulsion and the basis for understanding the screw established. Complete domination of sea transport by the metal, screw propelled steamship was imminent and only needed the impetus of further improvements in the fuel economy of propulsion machinery. Even these were well on the way to being in place by 1865.

Undoubtedly this period 1840–65 was one of extraordinary technological progress. It saw the first screw propelled ships of any size and the first iron ones. Iron construction was essential to ensure the necessary rigidity for machinery seats and support for the long transmission shafts of screw propelled ships.

It saw screw steamships progress from *Archimedes* to the enormous *Great Eastern*, to the first Cunard screw propelled liner *Calabria* in 1860 and the first one specifically built for that company, the *China*. This ship was decisive by comparison with the previous paddlers and was followed by the larger *Russia*, in 1867, just outside our period, but the first screw propelled candidate for the Blue Riband and the final stamp on how to propel an Atlantic liner.

The Royal Navy had cast their die with the splendid *Warrior* and from that point in time it was screw propulsion all the way. The first practical steps to twin-screw propulsion had been taken – quite vital as power outstripped the capacity of single screws and the safety afforded by multiple screws became essential to large passenger ships.

The decade 1855–65 also saw the introduction, in significant ships, of compound engines where steam was expanded in two stages, much improving fuel economy, and sufficiently economical to allow long range steaming without depending upon sails, a theme developed in the following chapter.

To the modern engineer such progress without adequate theoretical and experimental understanding seems phenomenal. By 1865, as far as the propulsive side was concerned, there was little to be done with screw propulsion except to refine it, to produce adequate design theories and to deal with problems which only arose very much later from development to very high power, such as cavitation, extreme vibration and so on: 1840–65 was truly a golden age for the development of the modern ship and for screw propulsion in particular.

E C B Corlett

Although she was never an undisputed record-breaker, Cunard's Russia *of 1867 was the first screw liner which could compete with the crack paddlers for speed. By the mid 1860s the era of the ocean-going paddle steamer was drawing to a close and thereafter the paddle was confined to river and coastal applications where the requirements of shallow draught or manoeuvrability were paramount. (NMM)*

Typical Screw Propeller Ships 1840–1865

Name	Flag	Built	Completed	Hull	Dimensions (length pp × breadth × depth in hold; tonnage grt) Feet–Inches Metres	Machinery (Type, cyl diam × stroke in inches; power in ihp; max speed)	Remarks
ARCHIMEDES	British	H Wimshurst, Thames	1838	Wood	106–9 × 22–6 × 13–0; 237 tons bm 32.5 × 6.9 × 4.0	2cyl Rennie geared, 37 × 36; 80nhp; 8.5kts	Smith's demonstration ship
ROBERT F STOCKTON	British (later US)	Laird, Birkenhead	1838	Iron	70–0 × 10–0 × 6–9; 21.3 × 3.0 × 2.1	2cyl direct, 16 × 18; 50nhp; 10kts	Ericsson's demonstration ship
NOVELTY	British	H Wimshurst, Thames	1840	Wood	117–0 × 24–6 × 14–6; 300 tons 35.7 × 7.5 × 4.4	2cyl direct, 14.5 × 18; 25nhp; ?kts	Wimshurst's demonstration ship for his auxiliary steamer concept
THE GREAT BRITAIN	British	W Patterson, Bristol	1843	Iron	289–0 × 50–6 × 32–6; 3270 tons 88.1 x 15.4 x 9.9	4cyl geared diagonal, 88 × 72; 1500ihp; 10kts	Brunel's pioneer iron screw liner; largest ship of the day
SARAH SANDS	British	Hodgson & Co, Liverpool	1847	Iron	182–0 × 32–0 × 20–0; 1400 tons 55.5 × 9.8 × 6.1	2cyl oscillating, ? × ?; 200nhp; 9kts	Early screw steamer that sailed many oceanic routes
CITY OF GLASGOW	British	Tod & McGregor, Glasgow	1850	Iron	237–0 × 34–0 × 24–0; 1609 tons 72.2 × 10.4 × 7.3	2cyl geared overhead beam, 66 × 60; 350nhp; 10kts	Successful early Atlantic liner; became Inman's first liner
ANDES	British	Denny, Dumbarton	1852	Iron	234–0 × 34–0 × ?; 1440 tons 71.3 × 10.4 × ?	2cyl geared overhead beam, ? × ?; ?ihp; 9kts	First iron screw ship built for Cunard, though not for mail service
HIMALAYA	British	C J Mare & Co, Thames	1853	Iron	340–0 × 46–2 × 24–4; 3438 tons 103.6 × 14.1 × 7.4	2cyl Penn trunk, 84 × 42; 2500ihp; 13.9kts	Designed as P&O paddler but completed as screw and bought by Admiralty as troopship
BRANDON	British	Glasgow	1854	Iron	216–0 × 27–0 × ?; 764 tons 65.8 × 8.2 × ?	2cyl Randolph, Elder vertical compound, ? × ?; ?ihp; ?kts	Earliest compound engines in a seagoing ship
ROYAL CHARTER	British	Sandycroft, Chester	1855	Iron	320–0 × 41–6 × 26–6, 2719 tons 97.5 × 12.6 × 8.1	Penn ?; ? × ?; 200nhp; ?kts	An example of an auxiliary screw steamer
PERA	British	C J Mare & Co, Thames	1855	Iron	303–8 × 42–3 × 27–2; 2119 tons 92.6 × 12.9 × 8.3	2cyl geared vertical trunk, 70.2 × 48; 1500ihp; 12kts	Typical moderate size P&O steamer of 1850s
HAMMONIA	German	Caird & Co, Greenock	1855	Iron	280–0 × 38–0 × ?; 2026 tons 85.3 × 11.6 × ?	2cyl geared oscillating, ? × ?, ?ihp; 10kts	First mail steamer for HAPAG (Hamburg-America)
GREAT EASTERN	British	J S Russell, Thames	1858	Iron	680–0 × 82–9 × 48–2; 18,915 tons 207.3 × 25.2 × 14.7	Paddle: 4cyl oscillating, 74 × 168; 3410ihp; 7kts paddle alone. Screw: 4cyl horizontal direct, 84 x 48; 4890ihp; 9kts screw	Brunel's paddle-and-screw giant whose tonnage was not exceeded until 1901; could manage about 12kts with screw and paddles
BREMEN	German	Caird & Co, Greenock	1858	Iron	318–0 × 40–0 × 26–0; 2674 tons 96.9 × 12.2 × 7.9	2cyl inverted direct, 90 × 42; 1624ihp; 13.1kts	Norddeutscher Lloyds's first Atlantic steamer
CHINA	British	R Napier & Sons, Glasgow	1862	Iron	326–0 × 40–0 × 27–6; 2550 tons 99.4 × 12.2 × 8.4	2cyl geared oscillating, 80 × 66; 2200ihp; 12kts	Cunard's first purpose built screw mail steamer
CARNATIC	British	Samuda, Thames	1862	Iron	295–0 × 38–0 × 17–7; 2014 tons 89.9 × 11.6 × 5.4	Vertical tandem compound, 96/43 × 36; 2442; 13.9kts	One of the earliest P&O steamers with compound engines
ARABIAN	British	Harland & Wolff, Belfast	1862	Iron	335–0 × 34–2 × 24–1; 2066 tons 102.1 × 10.4 × 7.3	2cyl simple expansion, ? × ?; 225nhp; 10kts	Cargo steamer with the high length:beam ratio advocated by Harland
AGAMEMNON	British	Scott, Greenock	1865	Iron	309–0 × 38–6 × 29–6; 2347 tons 94.2 × 11.7 × 9.0	Vertical tandem compound, 62/30 × 52; 945ihp; 10kts	Prototype of Holt's economical compound steamers for Far East service
PERIERE	French	R Napier & Sons, Glasgow	1866	Iron	345–0 × 43–5 × 29–0; 3150 tons 105.2 × 13.2 × 8.8	4cyl compound, 84/45 × 48; 800nhp; 14.5kts	CGT (French Line) first screw mail steamer
CITY OF PARIS	British	Tod & McGregor, Glasgow	1866	Iron	346–0 × 40–6 × 26–2; 2651 tons 105.5 × 12.3 × 8.0	2cyl trunk, 82 × 42; 2600ihp; 13kts	First N Atlantic screw steamer to be able to compete for speed with paddlers

5

Triple Expansion and the First Shipping Revolution

THE application of compounding to the reciprocating steam engine improved operating efficiencies and encouraged eventual widespread adoption. Credit for the practical application of compounding to marine propulsion went to John Elder who also took out a patent for triple and quadruple expansion engines. Elder was well aware that satisfactory expansion in a number of stages could only be achieved if the initial steam pressure was high, or

In 1865-66 the Panama, New Zealand & Australian RM Co had three similar 1500-ton ships built with differing machinery in order to carry out comparative trials of their relative efficiency. Kaikoura *had simple expansion engines, the Randolph & Elder-built* Rakaia *that company's usual four-cylinder compounds, while the* Ruahine *was fitted with twin-screw annular engines. All three were acquired by the Royal Mail SP Co in 1871-72 when* Kaikoura *and* Ruahine *were re-engined with single-screw compounds. The latter then achieved an extra knot on speed trials, and with coal consumption reduced from 34 to 20 tons per day, could stow an extra 300 tons of cargo. In Royal mail service they were renamed* Tiber, Ebro *(shown here) and* Liffey *respectively.* (CMP)

as his patent stated 'for steam at very high original pressure'. What constituted high was not defined but it was certainly in excess of the 70psi (pounds per square inch) boiler pressure then normally achieved in marine practice of the 1850s. The reasoning behind compounding was to minimise temperature reduction during any stage and hence restrict the amount of condensation which could take place at the cylinder walls when steam next entered the cylinder. In order to achieve this the degree of expansion allowed during any stage had to be restricted and Elder readily appreciated that the same reasoning could be applied to more than two stages provided high initial steam pressures could be utilised.

As with most ideas practical application lagged some years behind simply because two stage expansion of steam (compounding) was all that was needed for the moderate pressures then available. During the 1850s, when Elder formulated his ideas, and even during the 1860s, when the first practical compound engines were entering service, boiler design and material limited

steam pressures. Wrought iron had limited strength and could not be employed for high-pressure work. Increasing plate thickness in order to withstand higher pressures was not a solution as impurities in the iron imposed limitations on strength. Steel was a much stronger material but it was only during the 1870s that supplies became available in any reasonable quantity and even then quality was so variable that no designer could rely on any two plates having the same strength. Boiler design during the 1850s still employed a number of flat surfaces which had to be stayed in order to provide sufficient strength to withstand internal pressure. The evolution of the oval, and subsequently cylindrical, boiler allowed higher pressures to be achieved without such extensive staying, circular surfaces being better able to support pressure than flat surfaces. Even with development of the cylindrical boiler, of the type subsequently known as the Scotch boiler, there were limitations due to the need to support the furnaces and improvements in design were needed to overcome such restrictions.

Ebro

The first Scotch-type boilers are thought to have been built by Randolph, Elder & Company, being installed in the steamer *McGregor Laird* (1862). These were actually double-ended boilers, there being two furnaces at each end with common combustion chambers for opposing furnaces. Although they only worked at the same moderate pressure then common at sea the design attracted interest and formed the basis of the standard Scotch-type boiler which was still being fitted in ships almost a century later. A similar claim to longevity can be made for the triple expansion engine except that the time period was somewhat less, extending from the 1870s to the 1950s. Over the years modifications were made to both items of plant in order to improve performance, and certainly better materials were utilised, but the same fundamental designs and concepts remained; in a rapidly changing technological world that says much for the ingenuity of the pioneers.

The early years: 1874–85

The first deep sea commercial steamer to be fitted with a triple triple expansion engine was *Propontis* (1874) owned by W H Dixon of Liverpool. Responsibility for engine design lay with Dr A C Kirk then employed by John Elder & Co, successor to Randolph, Elder & Co. Kirk

was an inventive engineer in the tradition of John Elder himself but to some extent that initial triple expansion installation was forced upon him as the owner had already decided to fit *Propontis* with high-pressure water-tube boilers of the form patented by Rowan & Horton. As far as Kirk was concerned he only had to decide upon the form of engine which would utilise the high-pressure steam advantageously.

Dixon was anxious to obtain improved fuel economy and to that end had decided to fit the Rowan & Horton boilers. A shipowner paid the bills and could have whatever plant he desired, but the more prudent owners relied upon the experience of the shipbuilder to guide him and it soon became evident that Dixon should have followed that course. Each boiler comprised a number of fairly large diameter vertical water-tubes surrounding the grate and combustion chamber, thus allowing heat transfer between combustion products and the water-tubes as the hot gases passed between the tubes on their way to the funnel. Unfortunately the boilers, which worked at a pressure of 150psi, gave trouble from the start and were removed after only a short period of service, being replaced in 1876 by Scotch boilers working at 90psi.

Kirk devised a three-crank triple expansion engine to make use of the high steam pressure available, cylinder diameters being high-pressure (HP) 23in, intermediate pressure (IP) 41in and low pressure (LP) 62in, all with a stroke of 42in. Apart from the fact that it possessed three cylinders instead of the normal two, Kirk's triple expansion engine differed little in constructional

Dr A C Kirk was the great proponent of triple expansion machinery and was responsible for the installation in the Propontis *while manager of John Elder & Co in 1874. However, after he became a partner in Robert Napier's shipbuilding business he was able to oversee the construction of the epoch-making* Aberdeen, *shown here, for George Thompson's Aberdeen Line. Built in 1881 this ship has been described as a masterpiece and established the efficiency of triple expansion engines in a quarter of a century's service on the Australian route. On her maiden voyage to Melbourne her cylindrical, double-ended steel boilers consumed coal at only 1¼lbs per ihp per hour, about 60 per cent of typical consumption for a similar steamer ten years earlier.* (CMP)

detail from compound engines produced by Elder & Co. The engine worked well and during the time the high-pressure boilers were in the ship it performed to the entire satisfaction of owner and builder. In later years further new boilers working at 150psi were installed and the machinery produced the results anticipated by Kirk.

Just before *Propontis* entered service the small steamer *Sexta* had been fitted with a triple expansion engine working with steam at a pressure of 120psi whilst in the years which followed a few further experimental installations were attempted including a two-crank arrangement for the yacht *Isa*. The 10in diameter HP and 16in diameter IP pistons were in tandem whilst the 28in diameter LP piston was connected to its own crank. It was not until 1881, however, that the real breakthrough came with the introduction of the *Aberdeen*. Kirk, and no doubt other marine engineers of similar mind, spent much energy trying to convince shipowners as to the advantages of the triple expansion engine but without any success until Messrs George Thompson & Co entrusted Robert Napier & Sons, for whom Kirk then worked, with the building of a steamer for the Australian trade. Such a service presented problems in terms of bunkering and Kirk probably convinced the prospective owner as to the economic advantages of expanding steam three times rather than twice. Lower fuel consumption not only saved money but it also meant that less coal would be consumed, resulting in fewer stokers and a reduction in bunker space.

Thompson's Aberdeen Line decided that a 40-day service to Australia could be profitable and the 3616grt *Aberdeen* was laid down. As with most ships of the period she had provision for a large area of sail but she was a steamship and was meant to operate under power at all times. Her three-crank triple expansion engine with cylinder dimensions 30in (HP), 45in (IP), 70in (LP) and 54in stroke could develop over 2600ihp (indicated horsepower) with steam at 125psi. The HP cylinder was not steam jacketed but in order to minimise the risk of condensation the IP cylinder had a jacket supplied with steam at 50psi whilst the LP jacket took steam at 15psi; in a paper presented to the Institution of Naval Architects Kirk stated the engines of *Aberdeen* and *Propontis* were essentially the same design and so it may be presumed that the machinery installed in *Propontis* was also steam jacketed in the same way.

During trials when developing 1800ihp coal consumption was only 1.28lb per ihp per hour allowing a sea consumption of 1.5lb per ihp per hour to be predicted. In a two-hour speed trial when running at 13.74kts coal consumption amounted to only 1.85 tons per hour indicating that for the service speed of 13kts the ship would burn less than 40 tons of coal per day. Service proved how good Kirk's machinery was and *Aberdeen* turned out to be a reliable and economical ship to operate, so much so that consorts to operate the service were constructed on almost identical lines.

Aberdeen's two steel boilers were of the double-ended Scotch type but the operating pressure of 125psi was considered high at that time. In order to withstand such pressure plate thickness

and all internal parts like the furnace and stays were more substantial than required by Lloyd's Register, allowing the test pressure of 250psi to be withstood without any problem. The tubular shaped furnaces of Scotch boilers were frequently weakened due to local overheating resulting from a poor fire and a number of boiler failures due to furnace collapse had been experienced in cylindrical and oval boilers. Increasing furnace plate thickness could improve strength and minimise, but not eliminate, the effects of overheating; however, thicker material reduced heat transfer and was not a real solution. Fortunately

such a solution was at hand in the form of the corrugated furnace and a number of individuals devised means by which corrugations might be provided in the furnace walls. One of the earliest in the field and probably the most successful was Samson Fox who, in 1877, devised a form of corrugation and the means by which it could be produced.

The Fox corrugated furnace became very popular and *Aberdeen's* two boilers were each fitted with six units of this type. During the outward journey to Australia whilst burning high calorific value British coal the effective

A Kirk-designed three-cylinder compound engine, built by Napier in 1880 for the Allan liner Parisian. *The HP cylinder was 60in in diameter, with two 80in LP cylinders and a stroke of 60in, developing 6000ihp, which gave the 5359-ton ship a service speed of 14kts. (Denis Griffiths)*

The Allan Line's Parisian *of 1881 had machinery designed by Kirk but although it had three cylinders it was only two-stage expansion (with two LP cylinders). In other ways the ship was very advanced, however, being one of the first mild steel ships, and the first North Atlantic mail steamer with bilge keels.* (CMP)

grate lengths were reduced to 5ft but for the return when using lower quality Australian coal the full 6ft length was employed. No trouble seems to have been experienced with the original boilers during their eleven-year life and the machinery installation as a whole proved to be a success which did much for the cause of triple expansion engines. Although Kirk and the owners of *Aberdeen* were instrumental in the triple expansion engine being accepted, others were also fighting for the cause.

The four years after *Aberdeen's* entry into service saw a number of installations which must at least have been at the planning stage before the success of her machinery was established. Engine builders on the Clyde, Tyne, Tees and Humber all produced triple expansion engines to their own designs, some of two-crank and others of three-crank formation but steam pressures gradually increased as did engine size and power indicating adoption for the larger and faster ships. During 1883 Napiers built two Kirk-designed engines for the steamers *Oaxaca* and *Tamaulipas*; these were the largest constructed during the period in question having cylinders 40in, 64in and 92in by 60in stroke and working off a steam pressure of 135psi.

By the end of 1885 some builders were employing steam pressures of 160psi but 150psi was the more usual. Although the three-crank arrangement tended to be the most popular some two-crank engines were also constructed, with William Denny & Co usually favouring the four-cylinder two-crank form. In 1884 the 9000-ton *Arawa* and *Tainui* were built for Shaw, Savill & Albion and at Dennys' suggestion two triple expansion engines were installed in each ship. The 37in diameter HP and 61in diameter IP pistons were each positioned above a 71in diameter LP piston producing a relatively short

engine for the power. At about the same time British India Steam Navigation Company took three ships with similar, but smaller, machinery installations. By dividing the low-pressure stage between two cylinders the maximum diameter of cylinder and piston required could be reduced, thereby restricting possible casting difficulties and minimising problems involved in balancing reciprocating masses.

Engine builders quickly adapted themselves to production of triple expansion engines and most developed their own particular forms which avoided patented ideas of competitors. Evidence suggests that builders were the driving force behind widespread adoption at sea, most shipowners accepting the advice of the shipbuilder as

to the type and power of machinery required for the ship ordered.

Steam generation for triple expansion

Although many different designs of boiler were developed during the final two decades of the nineteenth century, little interest was shown in any of them and most shipowners stipulated Scotch boilers for their tonnage. There were many good reasons for such a decision, including the relative simplicity of design, ease of maintenance and general reliability. Each builder had his own ideas regarding construction and modifications would be made to suit particular circumstances and the requirements of an indi-

Shaw, Savill & Albion's Tainui, *one of a pair of 9000-ton liners built for the company by Denny of Dumbarton in 1884. Denny were always in the forefront of technical developments and at their suggestion* Tainui *and her sister* Arawa *were fitted with a four-cylinder two-crank form of triple expansion machinery, where the HP and IP cylinders were mounted above two LP cylinders. Thus the third, low power, stage was effectively divided between two cylinders, producing a relatively short engine for the power.* (CMP)

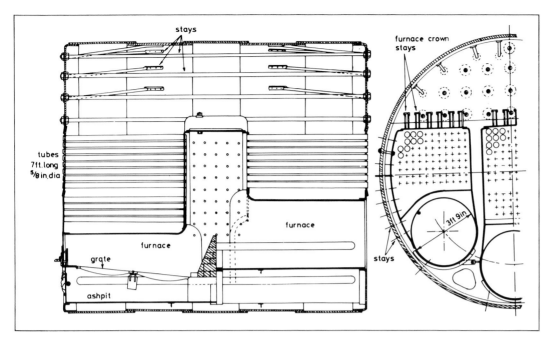

A typical Scotch boiler, built by Napier for the Allan liner Parisian *of 1881.* (Denis Griffiths)

the combustion chamber's sides and top required an extensive system of stays within the water and steam spaces. Simple stay bars connected combustion chamber sides to adjacent combustion chambers and to the boiler shell but the flat tops of these chambers had to be supported by means of bridge type girders. Long stay bars connected front and rear end plates in the steam space but a number of the fire-tubes were thicker than the rest in order to act as stay tubes and connect the front plate with the combustion chamber. A properly designed and operated boiler presents few problems, but, in the early days poor quality steel, defective construction or local overheating could result in weakened areas which consequently failed under pressure.

The Board of Trade, which controlled British shipping operations at that time, laid down strict rules with respect to boiler construction and op-

A typical fast passenger steamer of the period, the Royal Mail Line's Nile, *built by Day, Summers & Co at Norham, Southampton, in 1869-70, was 348ft pp and 2994 tons grt. Engined by the builders with two-cylinder direct acting simple expansion machinery of 450nhp, the ship was capable of 13kts.* (CMP)

vidual installation; but the design was still fundamentally the same. Size differed to suit steam requirements of the engine and space available. Boilers could be provided with anything between two and eight furnaces depending upon whether they were single- or double-ended. One change which did take place with double-ended boilers was the use of separate combustion chambers for each furnace rather than having opposing furnaces connect at a single combustion chamber. Such a move increased complexity but it did allow for more effective firing of the boiler and better control of steam generation.

In order to withstand the high pressures generated, all flat surfaces had to be effectively stayed. Flat front and rear ends together with

eration, these governing such aspects as plate thickness, rivet size and spacing, stay positioning, etc. Despite these safeguards, failures could still occur and although such explosions were fortunately rare the consequences would be severe, resulting in the death or serious scalding of anybody unfortunate enough to be in the boiler or engine room at the time. Dimensions of Scotch boilers varied depending upon the engine size but typically they might be 16ft diameter by 12ft to 20ft long depending upon whether single- or double-ended. Such a boiler would contain many tons of very hot water at a pressure of 150psi or more and if there was failure at any seam or plate the result was disastrous, all water escaping at once with explosive force. An important aspect of any boiler operation was to ensure that there was sufficient water present to cover any part of the combustion chamber or tubes through which hot gases flowed, as the water kept the metal cool and so preserved its strength. Board of Trade regulations governed the fitting of gauge glasses and their checking in order to ensure that the actual water level might always be known to the engineers in the boiler room.

Tubes, through which the hot gases flowed, connected at the combustion chamber and front plate and these connections had to be capable of withstanding the pressure without leakage. Usually tubes were expanded into holes in the tube plates; this essentially meaning that the tube was forced hard into contact with the side of the hole using a special tool known as an expander. Over a period of time due to vibration, corrosion or thermal movement these tube connections could weaken resulting in leakage. If not corrected this leakage caused a considerable wastage of water and resulted in damage at the sealing faces which could not easily be corrected. Re-expanding tubes whilst the boiler was still under steam be-

came common practice as to shut down the boiler and wait for pressure to fall caused loss of engine power and a waste of fuel. Re-expanding tubes at the end plates was a relatively simple and easy task but the tube plate connections in the combustion chamber presented major difficulties. Whilst the boiler was still under pressure the fire in that particular furnace would be raked out, firebars removed and wooden boards laid in the furnace. Engineers would then take turns to enter the combustion chamber through the furnace and expand leaking tubes a little bit at a time. Due to the roasting conditions, time spent in the combustion chamber was limited and the work could take many hours to accomplish but it was still quicker than allowing the boiler to cool down in order to make life easier for the engineers.

Superheating

Superheating of steam – the raising of its temperature above that at which it changed from water into steam – was known to be an advantage as it reduced initial losses due to condensation. Basic superheaters or steam dryers had been fitted to boilers supplying simple expansion and compound engines but their effectiveness was considered to be marginal when triple expansion engines were first introduced. Towards the end of the century it became obvious that even the small improvement which could be had from superheating was worth the effort and a few installations were so provided. The basic form consisted of a steam drum located in the flue uptake but after the turn of the century the tubular superheater became popular. This was essentially the same as the type used for steam locomotives and consisted of small U-tubes passing down the main fire tubes. Steam circulated through these U-tubes and was thereby raised in temperature. Application of super-

heating to triple expansion engines was a feature of early twentieth century development but the few applications of the 1890s indicated to designers a direction in which to take their work.

Forced draught

One aspect of boiler operation which did find application soon after general adoption of triple expansion was the employment of forced draught. Combustion of coal requires air and from the start of steam at sea an air draught through the boiler grate had been encouraged by the fitting of a tall funnel. Such an arrangement, known as natural draught, works admirably but there is a limit to the amount of air which can be drawn through a boiler grate even when a very tall funnel is provided. High-pressure steam and triple expansion engines reduced the mass of steam required per unit of power but the success of this combination in terms of efficiency promoted development of larger and faster passengers ships; this in turn encouraged owners to fit bigger engines which demanded an increased steam supply. The cost per unit of power may have fallen but the demand for power increased and in order to supply more steam it became necessary to fit more boilers. The problem became one of space as there was a limit to how many boilers could be fitted in the lower part of the ship and still leave sufficient room for engines and bunkers. Even for smaller ships any measure which could reduce the space taken by machinery would be advantageous in terms of increased cargo or bunker space.

A solution was to raise the rate of steam generation, but that could only be achieved if more coal was burned and that meant an increased air supply. The idea of forced draught was not new and a steamer had been fitted with a crude system as early as 1830, but it was not until James Howden began investigating the problem in the 1860s that any progress was made. Others also had ideas but Howden's system became the

The Pacific SN Co's Potosi *leaving Liverpool for the long run to Rio de Janeiro, Montevideo and round the Horn to Valparaiso (the Chilean courtesy flag is flying from the fore mast). A 4218-ton ship with a service speed of 13kts, built of iron by Elders in 1873, she was not much smaller or slower than the crack liners of the North Atlantic. Originally fitted with a barque rig, the square yards have been removed in this view, which was probably taken after the ship returned to the South American route in 1889 following a decade on the London–Capetown–Australia service. (CMP)*

most successful of the patented arrangements as it allowed the stokehold to be open to the atmosphere and also preheated combustion air, further improving efficiency.

An early arrangement of forced draught employed a closed stokehold which was kept at a pressure above atmospheric by means of fans driven by steam engines. This worked well in terms of increasing boiler air supply but stokers, engineers and anybody wishing to enter or leave the boiler rooms had to do so by means of double door air locks. Such a system did impede the work of coal trimmers as they moved coal from bunkers to boiler rooms and so it fell out of favour but did return with the introduction of oil firing during the twentieth century both for large liners and fighting ships. Perhaps the largest closed stokehold installations during the 1880s were those of the Inman liners *City of New York* (1888) and *City of Paris* (1889), but they did not last long in service, the boilers of *City of Paris* being converted to the Howden system in 1891.

The Howden forced draught system as fitted to Scotch boilers in the City of Paris *(1891). (Denis Griffiths)*

Howden first installed his forced draught and air heater system when a new boiler was fitted in the small 1724grt iron steamer *New York City* during 1884. This boiler was smaller than the original unit but it also consumed less coal for the same engine power. Howden had a fan supplying air to a trunking which in turn directed air to the boiler front; for larger installations two fans would be used for a single trunking which would direct air to the fronts of a row of boilers. Air for each boiler passed over tubes through which flowed hot exhaust gases from the boiler; thus the air was heated on its way to the furnace, a valuable aid to efficiency as the combustion gases in the furnace remained hotter and converted more water into steam. Hot air flowed to each furnace via a special arrangement of valves which prevented blowback of the furnace whenever the doors were opened to feed coal in.

Most large steamers, and many smaller vessels, constructed from 1885 to the end of the century had some form of forced draught, those which provided heating being preferred. There was a price to pay in terms of increased capital cost and extra maintenance but forced draught, like triple expansion itself, was a major breakthrough in marine power development.

Boiler corrosion

Using fresh water in boilers resulted in corrosion and the problem became more pronounced with the use of steel for boiler construction. During the early days little was known about the chemistry of corrosion but it became such a serious matter that in 1874 the Admiralty appointed a Committee to investigate the matter. Eventually a three-volume report was produced which resulted in the Admiralty publishing a manual for issue to the steam fleet. Commercial operators also took note and the Board of Trade iss-

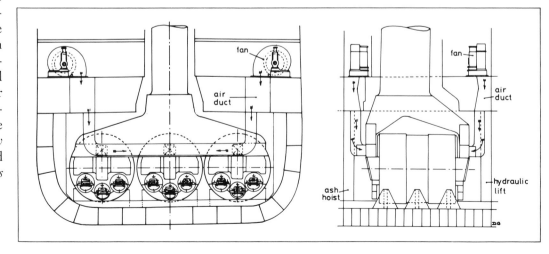

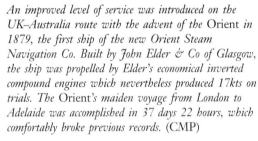

An improved level of service was introduced on the UK–Australia route with the advent of the Orient *in 1879, the first ship of the new Orient Steam Navigation Co. Built by John Elder & Co of Glasgow, the ship was propelled by Elder's economical inverted compound engines which nevertheless produced 17kts on trials. The* Orient's *maiden voyage from London to Adelaide was accomplished in 37 days 22 hours, which comfortably broke previous records. (CMP)*

ued advice regarding the operation and care of marine boilers.

Such matters concerned all boilers, not just those employed with triple expansion engines,

Cunard was somewhat eclipsed during the 1870s by its rivals the Inman Line and especially the new White Star. Compared with innovative vessels like the former's City of Berlin *or White Star's* Oceanic *and* Britannic, *the* Bothnia *of 1874 was neither fast nor particularly luxurious. However, she did follow the White star lead in moving the dining saloon amidships; it was also large enough to accommodate all three hundred first class passengers at one sitting. (CMP)*

but many aspects were linked with or related to the use of these engines. The higher pressures required for effective expansion in three stages required stronger boilers made from steel and steel corroded more readily than iron. Triple expansion engines required effective cylinder lubrication and oil or grease could be carried over from the condenser to the feed system and into the boiler. High pressures resulted in higher temperatures and under such conditions oils and greases would break down to form acidic compounds which caused corrosion. These conditions also promoted the formation of scale in the

boiler and scale impaired efficiency and could cause overheating.

Chemical treatments of boiler water were gradually developed from about 1870 onwards and most boilers would have employed some form of treatment as a means of limiting corrosion. In order to minimise the carry-over of oil and grease effective filtering systems had to be developed. The Edmiston pressure filter of 1891 fitted in the feed water line to the boiler but others of the gravity type were generally preferred as they allowed the condition of the water to be checked before it was pumped to the boiler. Corrosion due to air, or more correctly oxygen, had been recognised by the 1880s and de-aerators were developed to combat the problem. Most common were the combined de-aerator and feed heater introduced about 1887; these heated cold feed water by mixing it with steam and so liberated dissolved gases which would otherwise have been liberated in the boiler, any oxygen resulting in corrosion. In addition to this valuable effect the feed heater minimised the risk of boiler strains due to the effect of cold water on hot metal. Boiler efficiency was also increased because exhaust steam was used for heating the cold feed water.

The Union Line mail steamer Tartar. *As the advantages of triple expansion became clear, many shipowners were faced with the relative inefficiencies of new compound steamers they could not afford to replace. A cheaper alternative was to re-engine such ships. For example, the Union Line, in fierce competition with the Castle Line on the South Africa run, responded to the additional traffic occasioned by the gold rush of 1886 and a new mail contract in 1888, by fitting triple expansion machinery to the almost new* Athenian *(1882) and* Tartar *(1882) in 1887 and 1889 respectively. (CMP)*

Triple expansion: 1886–90

Shipowners quickly appreciated the advantages of triple expansion engines and orders for new deep sea steamers from 1885 almost always specified that form of machinery. Liner companies operating mail services saw the advantages in terms of higher speed and improved fuel economy whilst the cargo ship operator appreciated the reduction in coal consumption. Contracts for new tonnage would always stipulate triple expansion machinery unless the requirements of limited space or weight, as in river steamers, dictated otherwise but many compound engined ships were still relatively new and there was a better solution to that of scrap and build.

On the South Africa service the Union Line and Castle Line were in fierce competition and a slump in trade during the early 1880s affected both concerns. An improvement came about with discovery of gold on the Rand in 1886 whilst the new mail contract of 1888 required faster ships to meet the improved schedules. Construction of new tonnage was not considered economic as both fleets had many fairly new compound engined ships, nor was there sufficient time available to have new ships built. The immediate solution entailed re-engining of selected ships with triple expansion machinery, the most notable being Union Line's *Athenian* (1882) and *Tartar* (1883). In 1887 *Athenian* was given a triple expansion engine working at a boiler pressure of 160psi whilst the larger *Tartar* was converted in 1889.

Competition on the Atlantic was sharper than that to South Africa and owners always had an eye on improvements which could reduce costs whilst increasing performance. Inman Line, always to the fore in adopting new ideas, was quick to see the advantages of triple expansion machinery and in 1887 *City of Berlin* (1875) was

For a number of years the largest steamer on the North Atlantic, Inman's City of Berlin *(built in 1875), was also a short-lived holder of the Blue Riband in both directions. In 1879 she became the first British ship on the service to be fitted with electric light – although only six lamps – in the dining saloon and engine room. She was re-engined with triple expansion machinery in 1887 and is seen here after she became the American Line's* Berlin *in 1893. (CMP)*

provided with such an engine by Laird Brothers of Birkenhead. Comparisons between old and new machinery illustrate the advantages of re-engining.

	Cylinder diameter	Stroke	IHP	Boiler Pressure
Compound	72in + 120in	66in	5200	75psi
Triple Expansion	41in + 65in + 101in	66in	6025	150psi

Originally the ship had twelve cylindrical boilers but these were replaced by eight working on Howden forced draught and the space saved more than compensated for the additional room taken by the larger engine.

Happy with the outcome of re-engining, the Inman Line set about constructing two large and fast vessels in order to re-establish its pre-eminent position on the Atlantic. *City of New York* (1888) and *City of Paris* (1889) were the class liners of their day both in terms of accommodation and machinery. They were also twin-screw ships. Each main engine, which could develop in excess of 10,000ihp, occupied its own watertight compartment and could operate independently of the other. Three boiler rooms, each containing three Scotch-type boilers, supplied steam at a pressure of 150psi, the boiler rooms originally working on a closed stokehold system of forced draught. The engines were amongst the largest constructed to that time having dimensions: HP 45in, IP 71in, LP 113in and stroke 60in. In contrast to earlier marine machinery only the condenser air pumps were driven by the main engines, all other pumps having their own power units. This complicated the engine room system and increased cost but it did mean that almost all of the main engine power was available for propulsion, thus producing the high speed which was required for such ships.

On the relatively short Atlantic crossing space occupied by bunkers had never been as critical as it was for ships undertaking longer voyages but coal consumption always mattered because coal cost money which would otherwise have been profit. Triple expansion engines were more economical than compound and so increased the potential for profit. Cargo ship operators could also see the advantages and the economics of triple expansion put a further nail in the coffin of the sailing ship. The relatively low operating costs of sailing ships and their independence from coal supplies gave them an advantage in certain trades but application of the more efficient triple expansion engine reduced a steamer's operating costs and increased its range between bunker calls. Throughout the late 1880s the number of general cargo ships constructed increased and they were all fitted with triple expansion machinery. New operators entered the shipping trade but former sailing ship owners turned to the new method of propulsion in order to retain their place in the increasingly competitive industry.

Shipbuilders developed the three-island tramp steamer during this period, *Arbib Brothers* built by Swan Hunter in 1888 being a typical example. This 2653grt single-screw ship was propelled by a triple expansion engine (24in + 39in + 64in by 42in stroke) supplied with steam from six single-ended boilers working at 160psi. Many such tramps followed and British builders kept their world lead.

Construction and operation

In its basic form the triple expansion engine consisted of separate high-, intermediate- and low-pressure cylinders, each with a single piston driving its own crank on the common crankshaft. Pistons were double acting, which means that steam would be directed to the top of the piston, forcing it downwards whilst the underside of the piston was exhausting; when that stroke was completed the process would reverse with steam acting on the under face of the piston forcing it upwards, with the upper part of the

Early cargo steamers tended to be flush decked like the sailing ships they replaced but gradually they acquired a forecastle, poop and midships deckhouse, which helped to prevent the ship being swept from end to end by heavy seas. The forecastle offered protection to the anchor-handling gear and accommodation for the crew; the poop protected the steering gear (and the helmsman in early vessels); while the bridge house amidships raised the skylights and openings above the machinery out of the reach of all but the largest waves. These developments have been traced back to British Admiralty modifications to chartered colliers during the Crimean War, but in its developed form the classic 'three-island tramp' – typified here by the Crown of Aragon *– did not become common before the 1870s and 1880s. This 2293-ton vessel was built by Scotts of Greenock in 1883. (CMP)*

Above: One of the most forward-thinking of Atlantic passenger companies in the 1870s was the Guion Line. They built the first compound-engined steamers designed for the service in 1870, and in 1875 installed an early version of a watertube boiler in the Montana. *This is the company's* Alaska *of 1881, for a short while the Blue Riband holder in both directions. (CMP)*

Below: The steamers of the Royal Mail SP Co were always rather conservative in details: as can be seen from this view of the West Indies mailboat Orinoco *of 1886, for example, there is still a clipper bow and spike bowsprit and she could set a schooner rig. However, the style can be deceptive for the ship is steel-built and fully subdivided, with the latest inverted triple expansion machinery operating at 150psi. (CMP)*

cylinder undergoing exhaust. Steam exhausting from the HP stage passed as operating steam to the IP stage whilst exhaust from the IP stage was directed to the LP cylinder. From the LP stage steam entered the condenser where it was converted into water for pumping back into the boiler.

The unusual layout of the Allan Line's Buenos Ayrean *featured a long raised deck amidships. The ship was designed to serve in a variety of trades if necessary, including the transportation of live cattle. Built by Denny of Dumbarton, she was only the second seagoing steel ship, and the largest to date.* (CMP)

Careful design was essential with any multiple expansion engine to ensure that approximately the same amount of work was obtained from all stages as that produced an even turning action on the crankshaft and enabled a well balanced engine to be constructed. Each cylinder had its own valve for directing steam to and from the spaces above and below its piston, these valves being operated by means of eccentrics on the crankshaft. Separate eccentrics were normally used for ahead and astern operation, with a system of linkages being employed to reverse the engine and regulate the amount of steam being used. The most common valve system was the Stephenson gear but a number of other types were also used, all having the same purpose. By altering the position of the control lever the valve gear would change the amount of steam directed to the cylinders, thereby altering the power developed and the engine speed. The same control would also be employed for reversing the engine by directing steam to the cylinders for running in the opposite direction.

With a triple expansion engine it was essential that all valves were regulated together and that they allowed equal masses of steam to their particular cylinders in order to keep the engine balanced. If the HP stage exhausted a certain mass of steam but the IP stage valve gear did not allow an equal mass of steam to its cylinder then there would be a pressure build-up between the stages which would seriously impede performance in the HP stage. Careful design was required for the valves and linkages as well as the steam receivers or pipes connecting the stages. For large engines the power required to move the control linkage which altered cylinder valves was beyond human ability and in these cases a steam cylinder would be used for control purposes. The engineer would control steam to that cylinder and that in turn would regulate the engine.

A further problem with larger triple expansion engines involved racing when the propeller came out of the water during rough weather. Normal procedure was to shut off the steam supply to the engine when speed rose above a certain pre-set value, but with large triple expansion engines that only shut steam from the HP cylinder. However, steam still flowed from HP to IP and from IP to LP stages thus developing power af-

ter steam supply had been shut off. In such cases the engine could reach high speed with the propeller out of the water and damage might result. To minimise such problems engine builders developed governor systems which did not act on the main steam supply valve but acted to move the reversing gear to the neutral position so that steam was shut off from all cylinders. Matters such as this were important to the safe and economical operation of triple expansion engines.

With higher powered engines low-pressure pistons were massive affairs, those for *City of New York* and her sister being 113in diameter whilst the White Star duo *Teutonic* (1889) and *Majestic* (1890) had 100in diameter LP pistons. These were twin-screw ships and vibrations could result when such pistons operated in unison. During 1890 a representative from the journal *Engineering* carried out a simple experiment aboard *Majestic* to show that the periodic high vibration peaks occurred when the LP pistons of both engines were synchronised. There was little which could be done in such cases as two engines would always operate at slightly different speeds and there would always be times when the LP pistons were moving up and down together.

Better design, by means of the four-cylinder triple expansion engine, minimised problems of this type. Dividing the low-pressure stage between two equal but smaller cylinders resulted in lower mass LP pistons and by positioning their cranks 180 degrees apart they tended to balance each other. The four-cylinder design also enabled an overall balance to be achieved if the crank angles, distances between cranks and the masses on the cranks were taken into account. The balancing arrangement, known as the Yarrow-Schlick-Tweedy system, minimised problems of vibration and encouraged use of four-crank engines, particularly for passenger ships. For general cargo ships the normal three-cylinder form predominated, its design varying but little for the remainder of the nineteenth century and even into the twentieth century.

Steam jacketing had been applied to compound engines in order to minimise condensation losses in some cylinders and many triple expansion engines were also provided with such systems, particularly for IP and LP stages. The practice was not universal, however, as many builders considered it more suitable to expand that steam in the cylinders and provide effective lagging around them. Despite lengthy experimentation no evidence was ever produced that steam jacketing of triple expansion engines was economic and the practice generally died out early in the twentieth century.

Cylinders were supported on columns which also provided mounting points for the crosshead guide bars. The condenser was normally positioned as close to the engine as possible thus enabling a short lever from one of the crossheads to be employed for driving the condenser air extraction pump. Large engines with divided low-pressure stages would usually have separate condensers for each stage. Crankcases were open as that allowed access to bearings for lubrication and inspection; it was many years later after the introduction of forced lubrication that the totally enclosed crankcase became part of triple expansion engine design.

Whilst paddle steamers disappeared from the oceans before the triple expansion engine made its debut, there were numbers of paddle driven vessels constructed for river and short-sea duty with this form of machinery. Typical diagonal engines could be found in the Denny-built excursion steamers which Belle Line operated on the Thames between London and Clacton. *Walton Belle* (1897), *Yarmouth Belle* (1898) and *Southwold Belle* (1900) were almost identical paddle steamers of around 530grt with engine dimensions 20.5in + 30in + 43in by 60in stroke and steam at a pressure of 165psi. The boiler room, containing one single-ended Scotch-type boiler, operated on closed stokehold forced draught.

Paddle steamers with similar machinery arrangements were built during the late nineteenth

Liners continued to carry some sail area into the 1880s on the North Atlantic (and even longer on more distant routes). This was partly a holdover from the days of less reliable machinery but may have been reassuring to passengers and in some wind conditions could have been used to steady the ship against rolling. However, in 1889-90 the White Star Line abandoned sail altogether with their new Teutonic *and* Majestic. *The latter displays the new profile as she sails from Liverpool for New York on 10 July 1895. The engraving shows the middle level engine platform of the* Teutonic. *(CMP)*

lubricant. Lubricator pots would normally be provided for main and top end bearings, wicks being employed for conveying oil from the pot to the bearing area. Motion of the bottom end bearing generally prevented such an arrangement and it was left to the engine room staff to ensure that oil reached the bearing area by frequent applications of oil from a well directed oil can. Pots at the other bearings would be filled periodically as required.

Checks had to be kept that bearings did not overheat due to inadequate oil supply and the watchkeeping engineer would do this by feeling the metal in way of the bearing. Main and top end bearings were relatively simple to deal with even if care had to be taken, but bottom end bearings required extreme care and judgement if the hand was to remain undamaged. As the bottom end rotated towards the engineer he was required to swing his hand so that it contacted the bottom end and remained in contact long enough to detect overheating. A misjudged swing of the hand could have serious consequences for the engineer's career. Early engines would use rape oil (also known as colza oil), olive oil or castor oil depending upon trading pat-

and early twentieth centuries but what must be the last of the type was not constructed until 1948. For its Clyde river services the London & North Eastern Railway had *Waverley* built to replace a vessel of the same name lost at Dunkirk. A & J Inglis built the ship and Rankin & Blackmore constructed the machinery. The engine was similar to, but slightly smaller than, the one constructed two years earlier for *Bristol Queen* owned by P & A Campbell of Bristol. *Waverley's* engine developed an output of 2100shp (shaft horsepower) from cylinders 24in + 39in + 62in by 66in stroke. Fortunately *Waverley* survives, making regular trips from ports throughout Britain, and visitors are encouraged to view the engines.

Engine lubrication

For any reciprocating engine it is necessary to ensure adequate lubrication of all bearings and provide sufficient lubricant to the cylinder in order to reduce wear and maintain a seal between the piston rings and the liner. With the open crankcases of nineteenth-century triple expansion engines all bearings were accessible even if lubrication was not particularly easy. Bearings requiring attention were the top end (crosshead pin), bottom end (crankpin), main crankshaft bearing and the guide shoes at the crosshead. In all cases at the time manual lubrication applied and the engineers had to ensure that each bearing was supplied with an adequate quantity of

terns, the oil being obtained where most convenient. By the time the triple expansion engine became established the mineral oil industry had progressed and supplies of suitable lubricants of this type were available but some shipowners still used thickened vegetable oils. Mineral lubricating oils are produced by distillation of crude mineral oils obtained from wells in the ground. One reason for resistance to the use of mineral oils was the desire to carry a minimum number of different oils, and many tramp ships used colza oil for lighting, so the engine could make use of the same commodity. Although consideration had been given to the idea of forced lubrication systems for bearings and the Admiralty showed interest in such arrangements, they did not find favour with commercial

operators. Manual application of oil together with oil pots, wicks and siphon tubes remained very much the accepted method with nineteenth-century triple expansion engines.

Prior to the introduction of mineral oils for cylinder lubrication, tallow would have been used, usually applied intermittently via grease cups in the cylinder head. In order to enable the tallow to flow heating would have been essential, but once in the grease cup fitted in the cylinder head high local temperature would have maintained fluidity. As a lubricant tallow sufficed for the conditions existing in the early simple expansion and compound engines but a major problem resulted from its chemical decomposition in the presence of steam. Fatty acids produced by decomposition resulted in porosity of the cylinder and general wastage, whilst deposits would form which blocked steam passages.

The advent of high-pressure, and hence high-temperature, steam presented problems in terms of cylinder lubrication and many experiments were undertaken in order to find the best cylinder lubricants. Tallow was no longer suitable but

the mineral oils available during the early 1870s were also inferior to tallow as cylinder lubricants. Several compound lubricants were developed, these being mixtures of tallow or other animal fats and certain mineral oils. Within a triple expansion or compound expansion cylinder conditions differ depending upon the stage: at the LP, or even IP stage piston rings and cylinder walls are relatively wet and a good lubricant is required to combine with this moisture to provide a layer which clings to the wall. Sometimes water would be carried over from the boiler with steam, known as priming, and impurities in this water could react with the lubricant in an adverse way causing the formation of deposits. Oil viscosity is also important in order to ensure that it flows correctly and different viscosities were needed at each stage because of the temperatures involved.

It can be seen that ideal cylinder lubrication for triple expansion engines presented a problem as different cylinders required slightly different lubricant properties and owners were reluctant to carry a variety of lubricants. Throughout the

The Fairfield-built Tintagel Castle *of 1896 was a typical intermediate mail steamer (5531 tons, 12½kts), in this case for the South African service of Donald Currie's Castle Mail Packet Co (the forerunner of the Union Castle Line). She is shown at anchor in Southampton Water waiting to pick up the mails.* (CMP)

Before the widespread employment of refrigerated meat carriers there was a considerable transatlantic trade in live cattle, and White Star's first pure cargo steamers (Cufic and Runic of 1888-89) were reputedly the first vessels built specially for this trade. They also introduced triple expansion to White Star and were so successful that an improved twin-screw series was built in 1891-95, including the appropriately named Tauric of 5728 tons. Although they were nominally pure cargo carriers, very small numbers of passengers were carried on many occasions. (CMP)

final two decades of the nineteenth century considerable work was undertaken into the study of cylinder lubricants but no ideal single lubricant was developed which would satisfy all requirements. Compound oils had an advantage in that they reacted less with steam impurities than did mineral oils but they were more difficult to remove from exhaust steam and so could be carried over to the condenser and into the feed system. At higher temperatures many mineral oils would decompose and oxidise whilst others

could combine with water to form emulsified layers. Overall the mineral oil was best but it had to be selected carefully for the engine conditions and these also changed dramatically during that period. Engineers needed to exercise care in ensuring that cylinders received adequate lubricant if wear was to be minimised, but they relied very much upon the oil industry and its chemists to achieve that end. The same situation still exists in terms of reciprocating diesel engines as cylinder lubrication requires careful attention and the correct choice of lubricant.

Cunard's first twin-screw liner, the 12,950-ton Campania, *on trials in 1893. With five-cylinder triple expansion machinery developing 31,000ihp she achieved a maximum of 23.2kts; in service she and her sister* Lucania *averaged over 21kts, sufficient to win back the Blue Riband from Inman's* City of Paris *and* City of New York. *A new level of first class luxury was also introduced with the provision of suites – cabins with adjoining sitting rooms. The engraving shows the engines of these two ships.* (Photograph: Glasgow)

During the early twentieth century mechanical lubricators were developed for introducing measured quantities of oil into engine cylinders but throughout the nineteenth century grease cups and oil pots proved to be the favoured arrangement for applying lubricants. The method may not have been perfect, as it often resulted in over lubrication, but it did ensure that frequent attention was paid to the supply of lubricant to the cylinders.

The period 1891–1905

The final decade of the nineteenth century saw the triple expansion engine firmly established as many more shipowners turned from sail to steam. The economy of operation was obvious and machinery builders had further increased the efficiency of plant through use of forced draught and better engine design. The Institution of Mechanical Engineers played its part in sponsoring a series of marine engine trials during the late 1880s and early 1890s in order to determine the best systems to be incorporated in designs for the future. Ideas such as steam jacketing tended to fall from favour whilst the need for straight runs of steam pipes and large valve areas to ease the flow of steam was readily appreciated. The major gain was in the introduction of compounding, and other improvements would be less spectacular but no less important. In all fields of endeavour the early gains are usually the largest but later gains are harder won and in engineering this has always been the case;

engine designers worked progressively harder for each extra one per cent improvement in performance.

Understandably the large liners received most attention because of the size of engine plant installed but the small triple expansion engine fitted in the basic tramp steamer of the period had equal consideration from its designers and builders. Gains achieved in powering the ocean greyhound also went to help in designing machinery for the cargo ship; that one per cent reduction in coal consumption was as important to the operator of a 5000-ton tramp as it was to Cunard or any other liner company. It is, however, difficult not to consider the large ships simply because of the scale of the engineering task.

Cunard's *Campania* and *Lucania* of 1893 were provided with the largest triple expansion engines that that company ever installed in its ships and they were among the largest ever made for marine purposes. It had been decided that some 28,000ihp would be needed to push these 12,950grt ships at 21.5kts and the shipbuilders Fairfields (formerly Randolph & Elder) were entrusted with the work. Each of the two engines had five cylinders, tandem HP (37in) and LP (98in) cylinder pairs being positioned either side of the single IP (78in) cylinder; the stroke was 69in. With the large reciprocating masses involved both ships tended to suffer from vibration which was most severe at 75rpm, some 4rpm below maximum speed. Fairfields had strong views on engine design – they were one of the leading marine engineering companies in the world – and despite what had been found from trials employed steam jacketing on all cylinders and did not fit any forced draught for the

boilers. Such practices were normal for the successors to Randolph & Elder.

This decade saw other nations establish themselves on the Atlantic and in the marine industry in general. America returned to the scene during 1895 with two fine ships, *St Louis* and *St Paul*, and they illustrated the strength of American marine practice. The fact that there had been no significant liners built in America for many years did not mean that there was no industry. Ships had been constructed for coastal and worldwide trade but a devastating civil war robbed the country of more than the lives of its soldiers. Industry and enterprise had been shaken but the 1890s saw them re-emerge and these two ships were one result. Although not as large nor as fast as the Cunard pair they were innovative in an engineering sense in that they were the first large Atlantic liners to have quadruple expansion engines. Two HP and LP tandem pairs drove the forward two cranks whilst the first IP powered the third crank and the second IP the fourth crank. (Cylinder dimensions: 28.5in HP, 55in first IP, 77in second IP, and 77in LP; stroke 60in.) LP cylinders were steam jacketed whilst asbestos and felt hair lagging was applied to the others. The Scotch boilers supplied steam at 200psi, showing how adventurous the Ameri-

The French Line's La Touraine, *built at their own CGT shipyard at St Nazaire in 1891. By the 1890s both France and Germany did not need to go to British yards for their prestige ships but while Anglo-German political and commercial rivalry led German companies to attempt both the largest and fastest ships afloat, French ambitions were more restrained: the 9047-ton* La Touraine, *for example, was only the fifth largest vessel when built and her 18½kt service speed was nearly 2kts short of the current Atlantic record. (CMP)*

can designers were, 175psi being normal for the time.

Quadruple expansion was not a new idea and a number of vessels had been constructed during the 1880s with this form of machinery. In 1886 William Denny & Co built the 9500-ton *Jumna* for British India Line and this was fitted with a two-crank quadruple expansion engine, the cylinders being arranged in tandem. This system proved to be popular and Denny's constructed a number of cargo steamers with this form of engine. Although over the years a number of shipbuilders installed quadruple expansion engines in cargo steamers, they were more normally to be found propelling the larger and faster passenger vessels; for most cargo ships the triple expansion engine sufficed.

German shipbuilders and marine engineers were also beginning to take control of their own nation's requirements and expand into export markets. The 1880s saw a move towards self-reliance in shipping and by the 1890s most large subsidised liners were built at home as Kaiser Wilhelm II had decided that the German shipbuilding and marine engineering industries would become world leaders. Experience gained from British-built ships was put to good use and German marine engines of high quality resulted. Machinery designs differed little from those of the Tyne or Clyde except in areas where patented details were concerned. The turn of the century saw production of a series of express Atlantic liners equipped with probably the largest and finest steam reciprocating engines ever built. First of these was the 14,350grt *Kaiser Wilhelm der Grosse* (1897) which had two massive triple

expansion engines with cylinders arranged on four cranks in order to achieve balance. Steam at 175psi allowed each engine to develop 15,000ihp, the twelve double-ended and two single-ended boilers working on natural draught.

To compete with Norddeutscher Lloyd's (NGL) fast steamer, HAPAG (Hamburg Amerikanische Packetfahrt Aktien-Gesellschaft) built the slightly larger *Deutschland* (1900) fitted with two six-cylinder quadruple expansion engines. A boiler pressure of 220psi was used, all boilers working on Howden forced draught. Although it was a Blue Riband winner, *Deutschland* suffered from vibration which no amount of hull stiffening would cure; subsequently she was re-engined and converted into a cruise ship. NGL produced two other ships, *Kronprinz Wilhelm* (1901) and *Kaiser Wilhelm II* (1903), the former being similar to *Deutschland* but without forced draught. Comparison of engine dimensions provides an interesting illustration of developments:

The British India Line Jumna, *built by Denny of Dumbarton in 1886, was an early recipient of quadruple expansion machinery. Triple expansion was barely established as viable before four-stage expansion became a practical proposition; however, increasing experience tended to confine quadruple expansion engines to large fast steamers, since for more mundane vessels the theoretical economies of fuel consumption were more than offset by the greater capital costs, more complex maintenance and greater loss of earning space occasioned by the larger engine rooms required.* (CMP)

Kaiser Wilhelm II effectively had two separate four-cylinder three-crank engines driving each propeller, these engines being completely independent and in separate water-tight engine rooms. All NGL ships operated with open stokehold boiler rooms, forced draught not appearing to find favour. These ships proved to be record-breakers on the Atlantic and their engines were certainly fine examples of the marine engineer's skill. A final member of the group,

| | HP | Cylinder dimensions | | | Stroke | Boiler pressure (kN/sq m) | Power (kW) |
		IP (millimetres)	IP	LP			
KAISER WILHELM DER GROSSE	1320	2280		2450 (two)	1750	1207	11,190
DEUTSCHLAND	930 (two)	1870	2640	2700 (two)	1850	1518	12,310
KAISER WILHELM II	950 (two)	1250 (two)	1900 (two)	2850 (two)	1800	1552	14,920

Kronprinzessin Cecilie, appeared in 1907 but by then *Lusitania* and *Mauretania* had forcefully shown that the day of the reciprocating engined high speed liner had gone. That did not mean, however, that triple and quadruple expansion engines had overnight been displaced by the steam turbine; they still had a part to play in powering large passenger liners as well as cargo ships.

Cunard's identical *Caronia* and *Carmania* of

German companies became serious competition on the North Atlantic in the late 1890s with a series of large, fast – and very distinctive – ships. Norddeutscher Lloyd's Kronprinz Wilhelm *(14,907 tons, built by Vulkan, Stettin, in 1901) was a brief holder of the Blue Riband for a westbound passage with an average speed of 23kts. Four funnels in two groups was a feature of the Stettin-built express liners and was something of a Vulkan trademark. (CMP)*

1905 tested the merits of steam reciprocating engines and direct drive turbines over a number of years and the reciprocating engined *Caronia* proved to be more efficient. The company's engineering superintendent stated that for ships of that size and power requirement the steam reciprocating engine was still superior to the direct drive turbine. Only with the coming of turbine gearing was the triple and quadruple expansion engine ousted from the passenger liner, and it took many years more before the diesel engine finally displaced the triple expansion engine as a power source for the cargo ship.

Postscript and conclusion

Triple expansion engines revolutionised marine propulsion. They introduced the age of economic steam power for all trades and finally

displaced sail. There was no single design but a standard version eventually evolved which, with few variations from individual builders, lasted to the end of this form of steam propulsion. This type of engine was relatively compact, it was efficient and ideally suited to marine propulsion due to its relative simplicity, ease of operation and ability to perform well with only basic maintenance. It could also operate over a wide range of speeds, including down to such low speeds that it was almost stopped, and could be reversed for driving the ship astern. Although four-stage expansion did have benefits in certain specific cases, most propulsion duties called for no more than three stages of expansion even when higher steam pressures were available.

Flexibility made the triple expansion engine ideal for the nineteenth century and way into the twentieth century, especially for tramp ship op-

The advent of the turbine left the prestige liner companies with a dilemma since the new technology promised greatly increased speed but was unproven. Pressure was particularly severe on Cunard, which was keen to regain the Blue Riband that had been held by the Germans since the late 1890s. A technical committee recommended that two intermediate steamers then under construction should be given contrasting machinery, so the Carmania *was give turbines and the* Caronia, *shown here, quadruple expansion. On trials in 1905 the former made over 20kts, ¾kt faster than* Caronia, *but the latter's machinery proved more economical in the long run. (Adamson Collection)*

erators. Turbines cannot be directly reversed and require expensive gearing to produce a rotational speed low enough for efficient propulsion. The direct drive diesel engine stalls when operated below a certain speed, so it cannot drive a ship at very low speeds which might be required under certain conditions; this capability is re-quired of ships laying cables and into the 1950s some cablelayers were given triple expansion engines in order that they might operate at very low steady speeds.

From the 1920s onwards in the general cargo and tramp ship trade steam reciprocating triple expansion engines suffered increasing competition from the diesel engine, but many still championed its cause and steps were taken to improve its efficiency. The triple expansion engined ship could make use of coal in its boilers and so, unlike the diesel engined vessel, did not rely upon the availability of an oil supply. The use of superheated steam and then the reheating of steam as it passed between stages minimised the risk of condensation and improved overall performance whilst reducing fuel consumption. Fitting a turbine on the exhaust side allowed for more efficient expansion of the low pressure steam and hence improved overall performance.

Triple expansion engines did not exist in isolation: they required increased steam pressures for optimum performance and that in turn only came about through the availability of steel to withstand the pressure in boilers. Availability of methods to limit boiler corrosion and the ability to generate more steam from the same size of boiler through the introduction of forced draught

White Star's Oceanic *of 1899 was the first ship to exceed the length of the* Great Eastern, *although she was still of smaller gross tonnage. The ship marked a change in the company's policy away from sheer speed towards great comfort. The high power required for record-breaking produced excessive vibration, which was uncomfortable for passengers and encouraged machinery problems. The multiple expansion engine was reaching the height of its development at this time, and one of the benefits promised by the new turbine was increased power at reduced vibration. (Harry Weston Collection)*

The Allan Line's Corinthian (6227 tons, built by Workman, Clarke, in Belfast, 1900) preparing to sail from Liverpool for Quebec and Montreal. Although the express liners received most of the publicity and public attention, it was the more mundane ships like this that provided most of the communication links and carried the vast majority of the world's trade. Thanks to multiple expansion machinery, by 1900 the steamship had proved itself the most cost-effective carrier in all but a few low-value trades where sail could still compete. (CMP)

assisted in making the triple expansion engine an economical proposition for ship propulsion. Factors such as the use of steel for hull construction, thereby reducing hull deadweight and increasing cargo capacity, encouraged the building of powered ships and so promoted development of the triple expansion engine.

Many factors worked to bring about the change from sail to steam during the final two decades of the nineteenth century, but the intro-

duction of the triple expansion engine may be considered as the most influential. It should also be realised that these changes in the maritime world which the triple expansion engine encouraged also helped promote industry in general. World trade increased and Britain remained the world's leading ship and marine machinery builder, although increasingly challenged by Germany and the USA.

Denis Griffiths

The First Shipping Revolution: Typical Ships 1865–1905

Name	Flag	Built	Completed	Hull	Dimensions (length pp × breadth × depth in hold; tonnage grt) Feet-Inches Metres	Machinery (Type, cyl diam × stroke in inches; power; max speed)	Remarks
RUSSIA	British	J&G Thomson, Clydebank	1867	Iron	358–0 × 43–0 × ?; 2960 tons 109.1 × 13.1 × ?	2cyl inverted, ? × ?; 492nhp; 14kts	First record-breaking screw steamer on the N Atlantic
OCEANIC	British	Harland & Wolff, Belfast	1871	Iron	420–0 × 41–0 × 31–0; 3707 tons 128.0 × 12.5 × 9.4	Two vertical tandem compound, 41/72 × 60; 2000ihp; 14kts	First White Star liner; new standards of comfort on Atlantic
GLENARTNY	British	London & Glasgow, Glasgow	1873	Iron	331–2 × 35–5 × 24–8; 2143 tons 100.9 × 10.8 × 7.5	Two inverted tandem compound, 44/79 × 45; 320nhp; 10kts	Typical large cargo liner; one of the first in the tea trade through the Suez Canal
STRATHLEVEN	British	Blackwood & Gordon, Port Glasgow	1874	Iron	321–0 × 36–0 × 26; 2436 tons 97.8 × 11.0 × 7.9	Compound, 38/70 × 42; 1000ihp; 9.75kts	Pioneer purpose-built refrigerated steamer
ROTOMAHANA	British	Denny, Dumbarton	1879	Steel	285–0 × 35–0 × 25–0; 1727 tons 86.9 × 10.7 × 7.6	Compound, 47/82 × 60; 397ihp; 15kts	First large steamer of mild steel

Name	Flag	Built	Completed	Hull	Dimensions (length pp × breadth × depth in hold; tonnage grt) Feet-Inches Metres	Machinery (Type, cyl diam × stroke in inches; power; max speed)	Remarks
ORIENT	British	John Elder, Glasgow	1879	Iron	445–6 × 46–4 × 35–0; 5386 tons 135.8 × 14.1 × 10.7	Inverted compound 3cyl, 60/85/85 × 60; 5400ihp; 17kts	Pioneer Orient Line steamer; new standards on the Australia run
CITY OF ROME	British	Barrow Shipbuilding, Barrow	1881	Iron	560–0 × 52–2 × 37–0; 8415 tons 170.7 × 15.9 × 11.3	Three inverted tandem compound, 43/86 × 72; 11,890ihp; 18kts	Designed, but failed, to capture the Atlantic Blue Riband
SERVIA	British	J&G Thomson, Clydebank	1881	Steel	515–0 × 52–1 × 37–0; 7392 tons 157.0 × 15.9 × 11.3	Compound 3cyl, 72/100/100 × 78; 10,350ihp, 17kts	First steamer of Siemens steel and the first steel Cunarder
ABERDEEN	British	Robert Napier, Glasgow	1881	Iron	362–0 × 44–0 × 23–0; 3616 tons 110.3 × 13.4 × 9.8	Triple expansion, 30/45/70 × 54; 2600ihp; 13.5kts	Early successful application of triple expansion machinery
UMBRIA	British	John Elder, Glasgow	1884	Steel	501–0 × 57–0 × 40–0; 7718 tons 152.7 × 17.4 × 12.2	Compound 3cyl, 71/105/105 × 72; 14,321ihp; 19kts	Last compound express steamer for the North Atlantic
LA CHAMPAGNE	French	CGT (Penhoët), St Nazaire	1884	Steel	495–0 × 52–0 × 36–0; 7087 tons 150.9 × 15.8 × 11.0	Two tandem compound 3cyl, 39.6/78.8/78.8 × 70; 9800ihp; 17kts	French-built CGT liner; British engines
JUMNA	British	Denny, Dumbarton	1886	Steel	410–0 × 48–0 × 32–0; 5193 tons 125.0 × 14.6 × 9.8	Tandem quadruple expansion, 30/42/60/84 × 60, 3500ihp, 14.5kts	Early quad expansion steamer (for British India)
CITY OF NEW YORK	British	J&G Thomson, Clydebank	1888	Steel	527–0 × 63–0 × 42–0; 10,650 tons 160.6 × 19.2 × 12.8	Two triple expansion, 45/71/113 × 60; 20,117ihp, 2 screws; 21kts	First two-screw express liner; first to exceed 10,000 tons since the Great Eastern
ARBIB BROTHERS	British	Swan & Hunter, Wallsend	1888	Steel	320–0 × 40–0 × 27–0; 2653 tons 97.5 × 12.2 × 8.2	Triple expansion, 24/39/64 × 42; 230nhp; 9kts	Typical three-island tramp
TEUTONIC	British	Harland & Wolff, Belfast	1889	Steel	566–0 × 58–0 × 42–0; 9950 tons 172.5 × 17.7 × 12.8	Two triple expansion, 43/68/100 × 60; 17,000ihp; 2 screws; 20kts	First N Atlantic liner to Admiralty specification for war conversion to auxiliary cruiser
SCOT	British	Denny, Dumbarton	1891	Steel	477–0 × 54–10 × 25–11; 6844 tons 145.4 × 16.7 × 7.9	Two triple expansion, 34/57/92 × 60; 11,656ihp; 2 screws; 18kts	Union's record-breaking South African mail ship
CAMPANIA	British	Fairfield, Govan	1892	Steel	601–6 × 65–2 × 43–0; 12,950 tons 183.3 × 19.9 × 13.1	Two 5cyl triple exp, 37/37/79/98/98 × 69; 31,000ihp; 2 screws; 23kts	With sister Lucania shared Blue Riband for five years
INDIA	British	Caird, Greenock	1896	Steel	500–0 × 54–4 × 25–1; 7911 tons 152.4 × 16.6 × 7.7	Triple expansion 4cyl, 42.25/68/74.5/74.5 × 72; 10,000ihp; 18kts	P&O steamer for India–Australia service; to Admiralty standards
KAISER WILHELM DER GROSSE	German	AG 'Vulkan', Stettin	1897	Steel	627–0 × 66–0 × 43–0; 14,350 tons 191.1 × 20.1 × 13.1	Two triple expansion, 52/90/96.5/96.5; 30,000ihp; 2 screws; 23kts	First German Blue Riband holder
KAMAKURA MARU	Japanese	Workman, Clark & Co, Belfast	1897	Steel	445–0 × 49–9 × 30–5; 5846 tons 135.6 × 15.2 × 9.3	Two triple expansion, 20/33.5/56 × 48; 544nhp; 2 screws; 15kts	Typical British-built cargo steamer for export
OCEANIC	British	Harland & Wolff, Belfast	1899	Steel	685–8 × 68–5 × 49–0; 17,040 tons 209.0 × 20.9 × 14.9	Two triple expansion, 47.5/79/93/93 × 76; 28,000ihp; 2 screws; 20kts	First ship to exceed the length of the Great Eastern (1858)
KAISER WILHELM II	German	AG 'Vulkan', Stettin	1903	Steel	684–0 × 72–0 × 52–0; 19,350 tons 208.5 × 21.9 × 15.8	Four quad expansion, 37/49/75/112 × 70.8; 38,000ihp; 2 screws; 24kts	Two engines per shaft; Blue Riband holder 1904-7
CARONIA	British	John Brown, Clydebank	1904	Steel	650–0 × 72–0 × 52–0; 19,524 tons 198.1 × 21.9 × 15.8	Two quad expansion, 39/54.5/77/110 × 66; 22,000ihp; 2 screws; 19.6kts	Reciprocating machinery tested against the turbines in sister Carmania

6

The Industrial Background to the Development of the Steamship

FROM the perspective of the late twentieth century, two central features of the development of the steamship stand out as somewhat remarkable. In the first place, it seems extraordinary that an innovation which was to transform world trade and the character of sea warfare should have taken so long to mature. Experimentation in the steam propulsion of vessels, notably by William Symington in Scotland and Robert Fulton in America, began in the late eighteenth century. In 1807, Fulton successfully introduced a steam driven craft into service on the Hudson, while five years later Henry Bell emulated this feat on the Clyde, and in 1821 the *Aaron Manby*, in which steam power and a metal hull were conjoined for the first time, completed a voyage from the Thames to the Seine. Yet it was not until the 1850s and 1860s that the commercial and military potential of the iron steamer began to be realised, and not until the mid-1880s that steamships, now increasingly constructed of steel and equipped with triple or quadruple expansion engines, assumed a clear ascendancy throughout the shipping world. Secondly, it appears somewhat unlikely that so much of this seemingly protracted development, and so many of its ramifications, should have centred on Britain. Now that Britain is possessed of a small and shrinking mercantile marine, and has a relatively minor interest in shipbuilding, it is difficult to appreciate (despite the efforts of a burgeoning maritime heritage industry) that

Britons were responsible for the great majority of the multifarious innovations which under-pinned the maturation of the steamer, and that British shipbuilders adopted the new technology so comprehensively that over 80 per cent of the world's steam tonnage was launched from their yards by the early 1890s.

The reasons why steamship development was apparently tardy and certainly Anglo-centric – characteristics which were not unrelated, cynics might argue – lay in the process by which largely agrarian economies, like those in which Symington and Fulton conducted their experiments, evolved into the highly industrialised foci of a veritable world economy by the late nineteenth century. In essence, the steamship was a function of this process of industrialisation. While the vast growth in output, the ever-widening markets and the intensifying political rivalries associated with the industrial age called for improvement in the stock, size and calibre of ships, a further trait of industrialisation, technological change, effectively enhanced the quality of the materials required for steamship construction.

Once these factors of demand and supply harmonised, the steamer facilitated further diffusion of the industrial system: a function became a facet. This was by no means a smooth process, however, for industrialisation was marked by major regional, temporal and sectoral variations. With hindsight, the pace and pattern of steamship development may well appear odd. But in the context of the pace and pattern of industrialisation at large, as this chapter seeks to demonstrate, the advent and widespread adoption of steam at sea, and the consequences thereof, were perfectly logical.

Industrialisation and the world economy

The development of the steamship was determined to some degree by the requirements of trade and navies. Such demands were critically influenced by the intensification and spread of industrial capitalism, a productive system that passed through various stages during the long gestation period of the steamship. The first phase of sustained, as opposed to episodic, in-

The American Robert Fulton probably did more than any other individual to make steam navigation a commercial possibility, but for his earliest boats he was forced to go to England for the machinery. This drawing from Fulton's original American patents was submitted to the firm of Boulton & Watt, then the market leaders. Fulton visited the company's Soho works in Birmingham, the largest engine manufactory in the world, in July 1804 to discuss his requirements, but correspondence went on for some time afterwards. (Birmingham Public Libraries)

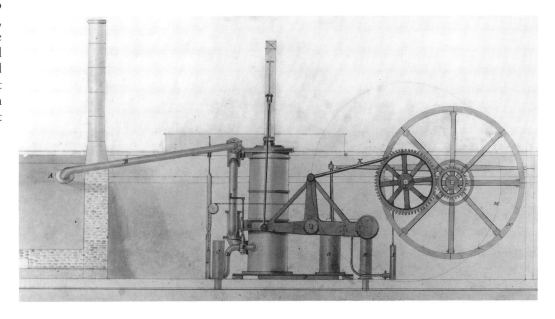

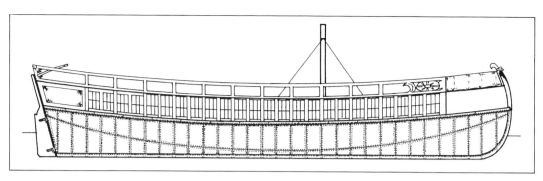

*Both canals and railways contributed to the industrial leadership of Britain. The latter are more obviously connected with the development of the ship and iron barges were being built from the late eighteenth century (*Trial, *the earliest documented vessel, was built of iron plates on a wood frame in 1787 and similar barges followed). The first all-iron vessel with any real claim to being a ship was the* Vulcan *of 1819, a passenger-carrying 'passage' boat for the Forth and Clyde Canal. (Reconstruction drawing by Fred M Walker).*

dustrial growth commenced in Britain during the third quarter of the eighteenth century. This fabled industrial revolution was rooted in technical and organisational change. The patenting by James Watt of the first true steam engine, and the introduction of puddling and rolling into the ironmaking process, were among the most notable of the innovations of this time, while the construction of a canal network was a further sign of a quickening of the economic pulse. However, it was in the cotton textile industry that the major developments occurred. Rapid increases in output and productivity were evident as innovations like Hargreaves' jenny, Arkwright's waterframe and Crompton's mule were applied to the spinning operation. Driven by water or, increasingly, by steam power, such machines and their derivatives facilitated a significant change in the organisation of work, from a domestic to a factory setting. Though limited essentially to cotton production, and therefore apparent in relatively few districts, the basic components of a decidedly industrial process – mechanisation, factory organisation, and mechanical power – were profitably deployed in Britain by 1800.

In the early nineteenth century this productive system spread to other facets of the textile industry, transforming the manufacture of woollens and worsteds, and bringing severe hardship to the legions of handloom weavers rendered redundant by the growing prevalence of the power loom. At the same time, partly stimulated by the textile industry's needs, rapid growth was apparent in Britain's iron output, while the engineering industry expanded dramatically and the production of coal multiplied as canals and waggonways opened up new fields and pumping engines permitted the exploitation of deeper reserves. These cornerstones of Britain's emergent industrial economy – textiles, iron, engineering and coal – featured strongly in the spread of industrialism to Europe and North America. The first continental region to experience sustained industrial growth was the area of Belgium and northern France centred on the Sambre and Meuse valleys. Adopting British techniques and equipment, much brought over by entrepreneu-

rial emigrants from Britain, cotton, wool, iron and engineering industries were quickly established in this coal-rich district. A similar pattern of imitation and import was evident as parts of Saxony, Alsace, the Ruhr, and the north-eastern states of America emerged as seats of industrial production in the first half of the nineteenth century. Thus, while industrialisation initiated in Britain it was also, in both a technical and a material sense, exported from Britain.[1]

This precedent was followed in that further phase of the industrialisation process associated with the development of railways. A British innovation, heralded by the opening of the Stockton–Darlington (1825) and Liverpool–Manchester (1830) lines, the new transport mode was rapidly introduced. Indeed, such vast quantities of private capital were invested in railway ventures, especially during the 'manias' of 1835–37 and 1845–47, that the basis of Britain's rail network was in place by 1850. Meanwhile, the innovation had spread, with pioneer lines opened in France, Belgium, Germany, Russia, Italy and the United States by the end of the 1830s, and in Switzerland and Spain during the next decade. If many of these lines lacked a follow-up, others, notably in Belgium and the American northeast, marked the beginnings of substantial regional systems, the main elements of which were completed during the 1850s. Again, British resources were instrumental in this process of diffusion. Capital was exported in ever-increasing quantities to fund the construction of lines in France, Germany, the Low Countries and, most significantly, the United States. Likewise, foreign railway concerns depended to a large degree on British equipment; for instance, approximately 60 per cent of the rails laid in the United States before 1860 originated in the foundries of South Wales, Staffordshire and other ironmaking districts.[2]

The ramifications of this surge of railway building were multifarious. It had a psychological impact, for it instilled the concepts of speed and 'progress' into the minds of the people it reached. Its social impact was immense, as it enhanced the mobility of a large proportion of the population.[3] In economic terms, the railway

effectively enlarged the market in a spatial sense, connecting manufacturing districts with areas of untapped demand and sources of raw materials, thereby facilitating regional specialisation. Moreover, other industries were stimulated by railway construction. Though coal, iron and engineering industries were well established – indeed, they were prerequisites – in the regions where early railway development took place, the new mode of transport entailed an increase in the demand for fuel, rails and rolling stock. Inevitably, this stimulus was felt most keenly in Britain, partly due to the rapid accretion of domestic railway mileage, but also because of the burgeoning export of railway finance, material and expertise. In essence, railway development and its knock-on effects, in repeating and reinforcing the pattern evident in earlier phases of industrialisation, consolidated and extended the process.

In spite of its dynamic expansion, industrial capitalism was by no means all-pervasive by the third quarter of the nineteenth century. Though its effects might be felt more widely, its incidence was limited to relatively few regions in northwest Europe and the United States. Within these industrial pockets, moreover, the productive range was narrow, extending only as far as textiles, coal, iron, engines and machines, and railway stock. Even in Britain, the leading industrial power by a long margin, over half of the population lived in rural areas in 1850, and over a fifth of the total labour force was engaged in agriculture. At this stage, the great majority of Britain's industrial workers were skilled craftsmen and labourers, while mechanisation had yet to be applied to many branches of industry and the factory system remained the exception rather than the rule.[4] By 1914, this profile – and those of the other early industrial nations, which were

1. S Pollard, *Peaceful Conquest: The Industrialization of Europe 1760-1970* (Oxford 1971), pp12-32.

2. R W Fogel, *Railroads and American Economic Growth* (Baltimore 1964), p135.

3. M J Freeman, 'Introduction', in M J Freeman & D H Aldcroft (eds), *Transport in Victorian Britain* (Manchester 1978), pp1-9.

4. A E Musson, *The Growth of British Industry* (London 1978), p149.

similar – as well as the face of the international economic order which it reflected, had changed out of all recognition. Indeed, in the light of its subsequent course, it was almost as if the industrialisation process had hardly begun to impact upon economic development by the mid nineteenth century.

Henceforth, especially from the mid 1860s, industrialism spread at an accelerating rate. In the economies where it had long since taken hold, industrial capitalism, with its ever-improving techniques and increasingly entrenched institutional structures, progressively permeated nearly every branch of production. On the outbreak of the Great War, to cite the British example once more, mechanisation, factory organisation and the decline of craft skills had become the hallmarks of the manufacturing sector, while agriculture now engaged just 8 per

cent of the workforce. The population had grown at a rapid rate and in 1911 stood at 40 million, as compared with 23 million in 1861.[5] It had also gravitated towards the cities and towns to such an extent that over 80 per cent of British people dwelt in urban areas in 1911. Moreover, far from enduring a Malthusian crisis, the bulk of the expanding population enjoyed a rising standard of living, especially from the 1870s, as a general, long-term fall in prices, particularly for foodstuffs, increased real incomes.[6]

This deflation was a central feature of the so-called 'Great Depression' which allegedly afflicted the British economy between 1873 and 1896.[7] A further aspect of this largely mythical recession was the marked erosion of Britain's industrial lead over other countries, a lead which had been substantial for almost a century. Though domestic output continued to expand in absolute terms, the rates of growth evident elsewhere, especially in the United States and Germany, were such that Britain inevitably experienced a relative decline. Accordingly, between 1870 and 1913, Britain's share of world

manufacturing production fell from nearly a third to just 14.0 per cent, while that of Germany rose to 15.7 per cent and the proportion accounted for by the United States increased substantially to over 35 per cent. Even in the export sector, for long the bedrock of her staple industries, Britain's lead was cut, though it was maintained until 1913 when almost 30 per cent of the world's manufactured exports emanated from Britain, as against 26.5 per cent from Germany and 12.6 per cent from America (see Table 6/1).

While it intensified in the early industrial economies, the process of industrialisation reached beyond the confines of the North Atlantic basin in the 50 years before the First World War. It commenced rather suddenly in Japan when the Meiji Restoration government started to reconstruct the economy along 'western' lines in

Suez, shortly after the opening of the canal. Because of the unsuitable wind conditions for sailing ships in the Red Sea, the canal was only of real benefit to steamers, encouraging their development for Far Eastern trade. (India Office Library)

5. *Census of the Population*, 1861, 1911.

6. Musson, *op cit*, pp150-1.

7. See S B Saul, *The Myth of the Great Depression 1873-1896* (London 1969).

Table 6/1: Percentage Distributions of World Manufacturing Production and Exports in Manufactured Goods

	World production %		World exports in manufactures %	
	1870	*1913*	*1880*	*1913*
UK	31.8	14.0	41.4	29.9
USA	23.3	35.8	2.8	12.6
Germany	13.2	15.7	19.3	26.5

Source: League of Nations, *Industrialization and Foreign Trade* (1945); A E Musson, *The Growth of British Industry* (1978), p155.

al system was rather different. Signalled in 1869 by the completion of the first transcontinental railroad across the United States, the virgin lands of the American west, the Argentinian pampas, the Russian steppes and the Australasian interiors, were penetrated by railways built with the capital, the products and sometimes the labour of Americans and Europeans. As a consequence, grain, meat, minerals and raw materials of all descriptions poured forth from these vast regions to feed the growing needs of the urban masses and the factories of the burgeoning industrial centres. By the early twentieth century, therefore, the somewhat limited industrial core of the 1850s had expanded greatly and now incorporated within its orbit a spatially immense, primary-producing periphery.[8]

The Aberdeen Line's Thermopylae *arriving at Sydney. The growing value of Australia to British trade promoted the development of economical shipping for this very long distance route. The answer was the triple expansion engine, convincingly proved by the Aberdeen Line in the early 1880s. (CMP)*

1868. Somewhat more typically, British, French and German capital, often an arm of the host state's policy, was instrumental in instigating the process in several parts of northern and eastern Europe, most notably in Russia during the 1890s. Further afield, the impact of the industri-

8. L Girard, 'Transport' in M M Postan & H J Habakkuk (eds), *The Cambridge Economic History of Europe* VI (1), pp249-70.

The limitations of early steam technology – particularly the combination of paddles and wooden hulls – ensured that steam navigation would be restricted in application and hence in numbers of vessels for decades. This E W Cooke engraving depicts the Gravesend steam packet Rapid surrounded by the traditional kinds of sailing vessels (the barge to the left and the colliers to the right) that still dominated the Thames in the 1840s. (CMP)

Industrialisation and the demand for shipping

From its early stirrings in the cotton spinning districts of Lancashire, the industrialisation process had fashioned a global economy within 150 years. During this span, transport provision generally reflected the needs of industrialism. In its early phases, industrial development was restricted to particular regions in northwest Europe and the American northeast. Demands upon the transport sector were accordingly limited. On land, canals and, more especially, railways developed rapidly to serve the burgeoning industrial sector, and in so doing intensified the spiral of growth. Nevertheless, such services and their ramifications were relatively confined in a spatial sense. On the seas, the volume of trade increased as the output of manufactures and capital goods expanded, but the pattern of exchange generally remained within the pre-existing framework, which was essentially limited to European and North Atlantic waters. In accordance, the change in shipping services was largely, though not entirely, one of degree rather than one of kind. However, as the industrialisation process entered a more expansive phase, from the mid 1860s, so it required much more in the way of transport provision. At this stage, the railways opened up the continental interiors of the Americas, Asia and Australasia, while the shipping industry, responding to the needs of the age of mass production and mass consumption, not only increased in scale but also experienced a major transformation in the character of its capital stock.

The central feature of this transformation was the introduction of the steamship into nearly all transoceanic trades. In many ways, this development was not a radical departure from the past, but rather a predictable extension of the shipping provision of the first half of the nineteenth century, an inexorable progression rooted in the very logic of the industrialisation process. Intrinsically competitive, industrial capitalism requires that producers of goods and providers of services should remorselessly seek to reduce costs in order that market shares be maintained or improved. Such an imperative naturally implies both productivity growth and technological change. Accordingly, as industrialisation gathers momentum, so the pace of these mutually stimulating factors increases in the service sector as well as in the industries at the core of the process. In line with this general pattern, marked productivity growth occurred in the shipping industry during the early phases of industrialism. For instance, in Britain, the most significant trading and shipping nation of the time, the volume of seaborne commerce entering the country expanded by 195 per cent between 1820–24 and 1845–49, while the tonnage of the British mercantile marine increased by just 40 per cent. Some of this extra work was undertaken by foreign vessels, chiefly flying the American flag, but a major part accrued from the greater frequency with which British merchantmen delivered cargoes to home ports.

Such productivity growth stemmed from two sources. In the first place, steam driven vessels, most propelled by paddles, were increasingly utilised in home and short-sea commerce. Though operating costs were high due to the heavy consumption of coal, and cargo capacity was limited by the size of engine compartments, these early steamers both penetrated and created a range of trades requiring the regular, relatively swift carriage of passengers and high value goods. As early as 1841, the work rate of these craft was such that they accounted for 22 and 18 per cent respectively of the tonnage entering and clearing British ports coastwise, even though they represented just 9 per cent of the coasters trading.[9] Secondly, substantial gains in efficiency were achieved in the operation of sailing vessels from the 1830s. A series of improvements in hull shape, the design of the bow, vessel size, rigging and the materials used in construction enabled the sailing ship to keep pace with the growing requirements of the industrial system, at least in the sphere of foreign commerce in the relatively restricted trading milieu of the mid-nineteenth

9. G Jackson, 'The Shipping Industry' in Freeman & Aldcroft, *op cit*, pp257-62.

century. Innovations like the Blackwall hull, the Aberdeen bow, and iron and composite hulls also meant that sail retained a competitive edge over steam in the majority of long distance trades down to the 1870s. However, this advantage did not defer the development of the viable, oceangoing steamship. Rather, by dint of its improving efficiency, the sailing ship demonstrated the potential of cheap transport links with markets and sources of raw materials beyond the North Atlantic, thereby participating in the spread of industrialism to the wider world. This diffusion, in turn, created its own massive demand for still cheaper, more efficient means of sea transport. Accordingly it was in the 1870s and 1880s that the steamship, now increasingly free of technical constraints, at last superseded the sailing craft in the inter-continental trades.

The pace of this transition reflected the competitive traits of industrialism in another way. Market forces operating within and across national boundaries inevitably generate political rivalry. This was evident in the efforts to enhance the quality of Britain's merchant fleet, which to some extent was a conscious response to the growing encroachment of American-built and -owned vessels in the transatlantic carrying trades in the years which spanned the peace of 1815 and the American Civil War. It was apparent more overtly in the second half of the nineteenth century as the intensive and extensive spread of the industrialisation process precipitated international tensions. As production and consumption levels heightened, so the industrial states turned increasingly to extra-economic means to secure outlets and raw materials for their manufacturing sectors. Protective tariffs, state subsidies and imperial adventures were symptomatic of this mounting friction. It also found expression in the growing, more positive interest with which navies viewed the use of steam, iron and steel in shipbuilding. Whereas, during the long peace between 1815 and 1854, naval administrations had generally adopted a passive, if not uninterested, approach to shipping technology,[10] the naval arms race which gained in intensity from the era of *La Gloire* and the *Warrior* added a military imperative to the commercial pressure which conditioned the quality of the shipping requirement in the late nineteenth century. Thus, by the Dreadnought age, the political ramifications of industrialism had underscored the economic to influence the pace of steamship development.[11]

A considerable part of this development occurred in Britain. Indeed, each of the major milestones which marked the route from the paddle steamer to the steel steamship, from the early 1800s to the late 1880s, was laid by British

engineers and shipbuilders. To some degree, this prominence reflected Britain's pre-eminence as a maritime power. In the context of the mercantilist world, which in a sense lasted until the abolition of the Navigation Laws in 1849, Britain had cornered a relatively large share of Europe's overseas trade, much of which was carried by a substantial home-owned fleet and protected by a navy which had controlled the seas, with minor interruptions, from the 1750s.[12] If this broadly-based maritime interest generated high levels of demand for the protected products of the domestic shipbuilding industry, it did not guarantee that the ships constructed would be of the highest quality or the best value. Accordingly, during the eighteenth century, it was widely believed that the French designed superior warships, while for some decades after Waterloo the cheapness and efficiency of American-built merchant vessels threatened Britain's supremacy in the shipping market. By this time, however, industrialisation had begun to alter the situation, affording clear advantages to Britain's shipbuilders, both with regard to the refinement of existing practices and to the development of new technology.

These advantages reflected national differentials in the pace and pattern of industrialism. As its fount, and the pioneer of many of its phases, Britain felt most acutely the general demands imparted by the industrialisation process on the shipping stock. This was exacerbated by the fact that a significant proportion of the nation's rapidly expanding industrial output was sold abroad, either to emergent industrial regions or in the vast markets opened up by the availability of cheap products. Imports likewise escalated as the demand for cotton, iron ore, timber and a host of other raw materials mounted. The particular importance of seaborne trade not only enhanced the demand for shipping, but also, in an increasingly competitive environment, intensified the pressure on the British shipping and shipbuilding industries to reduce the costs and improve the quality of their services. While such requirements underlay the productivity growth apparent in Britain's sailing fleet in the mid nineteenth century, the pattern of industrialisation gave Britain a clear lead in another facet of the shipping market. With coal, iron and engineering production at the heart of nineteenth-century industrial development, the capital goods which comprised the vital materials for steamship construction were manufactured in greater quantities in Britain than in any other nation. However, the quality of the most essential of these ingredients – iron and engines – imposed a constraint on the development of the ocean-going steamers for many decades. If demand for

the new shipping technology was slow to gather momentum, it was matched by the pace at which the supply of the requisite materials became available.

The supply of iron, steel and marine engines

As industrialisation proceeds, so the productive system it pervades inevitably assumes an ever more complex form. Accordingly, innovations in one industry or sector are increasingly likely to depend upon, and then to stimulate, developments in related areas of production. This dynamic characteristic is clearly apparent in the evolution of the steel steamship. While the widespread adoption of the steamer was essentially constrained by the cost and quality of metal and marine engines, the gradual lifting of such constraints not only transformed shipbuilding techniques and output, but also underlay major developments in the shipping and port industries and expedited the growth of world trade.

This particular cycle of technological change and industrial development, like so many others in the eighteenth and nineteenth centuries, centred on Britain. It was here, even at the time when Symington, Fulton and Bell were experimenting with steam powered vessels, that the most sophisticated and productive engineering and iron industries were located. 'Machine-making' and 'engine-making', the two main branches of the contemporary engineering industry, were largely geared to the needs of the textile manufacturing sector. As a consequence, the production of machines expanded during the first half of the nineteenth century, especially in the Manchester area where builders of jennies, waterframes, mules and power looms supplied the adjacent cotton industry. Diversification occurred in line with the gradual spread of mechanisation to other sectors. Moreover, machine-making naturally entailed the development of machine-tools (machines to make machines), and rapid growth was apparent in this area from the 1820s, with gauges and templates employed in shaping, planing and milling tools to produce standardised parts. Mechanisation, of course, was closely associated with the application of steam power. Accordingly, the output of steam engines proceeded apace during the early nine-

10. See A Lambert, *The Last Sailing Battlefleet: Maintaining Naval Mastery 1815-1850* (London 1991).

11. J T Sumida, *In Defence of Naval Supremacy: Finance, Technology and British Naval Policy 1889-1914* (London 1989), pp6-36.

12. See S R Palmer, *Politics, Shipping and the Repeal of the Navigation Laws* (Manchester 1990).

One of the most successful early manufacturers of marine engines was the firm of Penn & Sons at Greenwich. This mid century view of their works shows the kind of power driven machinery employed, the various belt drives being very prominent. This kind of machinery in turn spurred the need for a machine-tool industry to improve the quality of cutting, milling and planing equipment, itself encouraging more sophisticated engineering products. (By courtesy of Basil Greenhill)

teenth century, demand intensifying with the development of railways at home and abroad from the 1830s.[13]

The British iron industry also expanded rapidly after 1800. Building upon the innovations of the late eighteenth century, of which Cort's process was merely the most important of many, the output of pig iron almost doubled between 1815 and 1825, and then increased nearly four times during the next two decades (see Table 6/2). A basic intermediate product, pig iron was chiefly manufactured into cast and wrought iron during the early nineteenth century, though small quantities of blister and crucible steel were also produced. Demand for these metals came from all sectors of the economy. Iron formed the principal raw material for the burgeoning

engineering industry, being used in the construction of water-wheels, steam engines, boilers and all forms of industrial and agricultural machinery. In the building industry, iron pillars and beams were increasingly deployed to support large structures, while a miscellany of small manufactures – from nails to kettles to chains – was fashioned out of cast and wrought iron, and particularly hard or sharp goods like razors, clock springs, swords and cutlery were made from steel. However, from the 1830s the most important single consumer of iron was the railway industry. In the domestic market, sales to the railways, which chiefly comprised rails, accounted for up to a quarter of the iron produced in the 1840s and almost a half of that manufactured in the peak year of 1848. Though home railway demand declined thereafter, the export of rails expanded vigorously, rising from 578,000 tons in 1856 to over 1.3 million tons in 1870, by which time almost 30 per cent of Britain's pig iron was consumed by railways at home and abroad.[14]

The engineering and iron industries were thus of prime significance to Britain's industrial development, expanding rapidly in the first half of the nineteenth century to provide a growing volume and diversity of capital goods to an ever-widening market. It was within this context, rather than in the very different setting of the wooden shipbuilding industry, that the development of the steamship took place. However, a series of difficulties determined that the rate of progress in this sphere was almost pedestrian down to the 1850s, certainly compared with that

currently evident in the application of steam power to land transport. In economic terms, the increasingly efficient sailing vessel was a highly competent rival – much more so than the road vehicle was to the rail locomotive – in most facets of a shipping market which had yet to experience a significant spatial increase in demand. Technical problems explained the steamer's competitive disadvantages. Early marine engines were coal-hungry, bulky and equipped with poorly designed, wrought iron boilers in which only very low steam pressures were attainable. Metal hull construction was also hampered by considerations of quality and cost, for wrought iron was the only material suitable for plating and such plates were limited in size, variable in tensile strength and highly attractive to the animal and vegetable matter which caused fouling.[15] Nevertheless, by 1850 a core of accumulated expertise and productive capacity existed within the critical areas of British industry, engineering and ironmaking. From this substantial platform, the limitations of technique and supply which had afflicted early steamship development were successfully addressed, both directly and indirectly, during the third quarter of the nineteenth century.

A series of innovations improved the power and efficiency of marine engines during this period. The most notable developments were the compound expansion engine, patented in 1853 by the Clyde engineers John Elder and Charles Randolph, and the cylindrical 'Scotch' boiler, introduced by James Howden of Glasgow in 1862. As a result of these breakthroughs, and other, lesser improvements, the fuel consumption of the steamer had halved by 1875. Further economies ensued when the triple and quadruple expansion refinements of the compound engine were developed in the 1880s and 1890s. Of course, such equipment was best suited to large, rigid and durable hulls. From the 1850s, there-

Table 6/2: Pig Iron Output in Britain 1815-1875 (,000 tons)

Year	Pig iron output
1815	340
1825	580
1835	930
1845	2200
1855	3220
1865	4800
1875	6370

Source: P J Riden, 'The Iron Industry', in RA Church (ed), *The Dynamics of Victorian Business: Problems and Perspectives to the 1870s* (London 1980), p64.

13. A E Musson, 'The Engineering Industry', in R A Church (ed), *The Dynamics of Victorian Business: Problems and Perspectives to the 1870s* (London 1980), pp87-106.

14. P J Riden, 'The Iron Industry', in Church, *op cit*, pp81-4.

15. E C B Corlett, *The Iron Ship: The Story of Brunel's SS Great Britain* (2nd edn, London 1990), pp21-39.

Rotomahana, the first large steel ship, built by the 'high technology' firm of Denny of Dumbarton in 1879. She ran aground in 1880, with hardly any damage, but it was claimed that an iron vessel would have suffered a huge gash and would probably have sunk. Thus the technological superiority of steel could be demonstrated at the same time that industrial economics was making it more competitive in price. (NMM)

fore, iron quickly replaced wood in the construction of steamships, a trend accentuated by the growing numbers of iron and composite hulled sailing vessels built at this time. Eclipsing wood in terms of the tonnage launched from British yards in 1863,[16] iron was to retain its pre-eminence in British shipbuilding for over twenty years, even though the mass production of a superior material, mild steel, was rendered feasible by the converter patented by Henry Bessemer in 1856. Stronger, lighter and more durable than wrought iron, steel's potential for the construction of hulls and marine boilers was quickly recognised. Yet it was not until the mid 1870s that the chemical factors which embrittled mass-produced steel, and led to unevenness in its quality, were remedied by the innovation and refinement of the open-hearth process, a series of developments associated with Siemens, Martin and Gilchrist Thomas. Moreover, it was another decade before improvements and economies in steelmaking techniques significantly reduced the price differential between steel and iron plates. Once this had occurred, steel very rapidly became the dominant constructional material in the British shipbuilding industry (see Table 6/3).[17]

Almost seventy years had elapsed since the launch of the first metal hulled, steam powered vessel, the *Aaron Manby*. That the evolution of the steel steamship was such a seemingly lengthy affair reflects the context of nineteenth-century industrialism in which this developmental process was located. Thus, the technical difficulties which impeded the supply of the steamer's main components, steel hulls and marine engines, were overcome by virtue of a series of piecemeal, unco-ordinated innovations. This was the age of the inspired tinkerer, when even the most seminal of technological advances owed more to practical experience and rule of thumb than to scientific knowledge.[18] From Arkwright down to Percy Gilchrist Thomas, application generally preceded analysis so that screw propellers were built before the theory of screw propulsion was understood, and steel was used in structures before its chemical properties and weaknesses were appreciated.[19] Moreover, the would-be inventor generally worked in isolation, hindered by an archaic patenting system and the ignorance and prejudice of colleagues, insurers and government agencies. Most importantly, perhaps, it was not until the late nineteenth century that research and development was funded to any significant extent by the firms and state departments which stood to gain from the implementation of technological change. Instead, driven by the cost-cutting, profit-maximising imperatives of early industrial capitalism, potential beneficiaries like shipbuilders, shipowners and the Admiralty generally preferred to await, rather than to sponsor, developments, an approach which may have saved short-term expenditures on experimentation, but hardly expedited the introduction of new techniques and products.

In such an environment, the somewhat leisurely nature of the transition from wood to iron and then steel, and the associated shift from wind to steam power, was unremarkable. Nevertheless, the consequences of these cumulative developments were far-reaching. World trade, facilitated, expedited and extended by the increasingly efficient steamer, increased in volume by a factor of five between 1860 and the Great War. The maritime industries were likewise transformed, particularly in Britain. Here, the adoption of the steamship gave shipbuilders such an advantage that over 80 per cent of the world's

Table 6/3: Iron and Steel – Ship Plate Prices and Steamship Construction in the UK 1881-1891

	Ship plate prices (£)		Steamships built (,000 tons)	
	Iron	Steel	Iron	Steel
1881	7.75	11.0	361.5	46.3
1882	7.35	11.0	440.2	80.3
1883	6.5	8.75	508.6	111.8
1884	5.5	7.75	239.9	93.1
1885	5.1	8.1	87.8	108.3
1886	5.0	6.5	44.9	109.3
1887	5.5	7.5	18.9	205.9
1888	6.1	7.75	26.2	379.4
1889	8.75	9.75	35.4	518.1
1890	6.5	7.0	32.8	495.3
1891	6.0	6.5	16.0	462.1

Sources: Prices – J C Carr & W Taplin, *History of the British Steel Industry* (Oxford 1962), p110. Steamships – B R Mitchell, *Abstract of British Historical Statistics* (Cambridge 1971), p223.

16. A Slaven, 'The Shipbuilding Industry', in Church, *op cit*, pp110-4.

17. D N McCloskey, *Economic Maturity and Entrepreneurial Decline: British Iron and Steel 1870-1913* (Cambridge, Mass 1973), pp46-54.

18. D S Landes, 'Technological Change and Development in Western Europe 1750-1914', in Postan & Habakkuk, *op cit*, p486.

19. See Chapter 4, E C B Corlett's chapter; McCloskey, *op cit*, pp47-50.

tonnage was launched from British shipyards in the early 1890s. It also entailed a major shift in the location of shipbuilding activity. Whereas wooden sailing craft were built in virtually every maritime district, generally according to local demand, metal hulled, steam driven vessels were essentially produced by a branch – albeit a very important branch which in 1900 consumed nearly 50 per cent of the nation's steel output[20] – of the engineering and iron and steel industries. Accordingly, this 'modern' shipbuilding industry was concentrated in regions like the Northeast and West Scotland where endowments of raw materials, chiefly coal and iron ore, dictated that the capital goods industries should settle.[21] At the same time, the growing prevalence of the steamer underpinned Britain's maritime ascendancy in other spheres during the late nineteenth century. While it permitted the Royal Navy to maintain a technical and numerical supremacy, the steamship held major ramifications for the port industry as larger ships required bigger, deeper docks and more extensive cargo handling facilities.[22] The shipping industry, too, was transformed in character and in scale. Highly capitalised joint-stock companies, operating significant fleets from the principal ports, now dominated the business, which, in terms of tonnage owned, almost doubled between 1870 and 1900, with steamers comprising 90 per cent of the fleet.[23]

Thus, in line with the general pattern of nineteenth-century industrialism, the initial rewards of the new technology accrued to Britain, where it had largely evolved. The pace of steamship development was also typical of the early phases of the industrialisation process. While the global economic context which called for an efficient means of trans-oceanic transport emerged only gradually, the supply of the steamer's principal components was accomplished by virtue of a series of ad hoc innovations and improvements. In its protracted, Anglo-centric development, the steamship was therefore very much a product of the industrial age.

David J Starkey

20. McCloskey, *op cit*, p54.

21. See S Pollard & P Robertson, *The British Shipbuilding Industry 1870-1914* (Cambridge, Mass 1979).

22. G Jackson, 'The Ports', in Freeman & Aldcroft, *op cit*, pp234-50.

23. G Jackson, 'The Shipping Industry', in Freeman & Aldcroft, *op cit*, p277.

By the 1890s over 80 per cent of the world's new tonnage was being launched from British yards. The Clyde was the centre of British shipbuilding, which perforce made it the workshop of the maritime world. This 1898 view of Fairfield's fitting out basin shows the Roumanian steamer Regele Carol I *and a clutch of cruisers for the Royal Navy, a force that benefited from British industrial hegemony as clearly as it defended it.*

7

The Ship Propeller Company and the Promotion of Screw Propulsion, 1836–1852

THIS chapter concerns itself not with ships themselves, but with the finance and politics of nineteenth-century technological innovation. It will argue, in the form of a case study, that financial, political and official aspects determined which innovations were taken up, and which were left to fall by the wayside. The selection of the screw propeller as the basis for this chapter reflects the central importance of the subject, but similar lessons could be drawn from other technical developments in the history of the steamship.

One of the perennial, irritating features of so much comment on the supposed 'failure' of the Royal Navy and the mercantile community to adopt steam and the various improvements in power and propulsion at the proper time is the conceit that Ericsson, Pettit Smith and others were attempting to 'interest' their fellow men in the new technology. In truth the engineering community wanted to sell these new ideas, for significant financial reward. The subsequent disgust of Ericsson at the failure of his design in Britain should be viewed in purely commercial terms. It is simply not credible to argue that commercial success was not his prime motive.

Similarly Smith, and the backers of the Ship Propeller Company, were not interested in science and experiment, but in the royalties and financial success they anticipated from the patent of 1836. While the Admiralty demonstrated remarkable skill, or an incredible degree of luck, both in avoiding such entanglements and in securing proven technology for the country at a reasonable price, the mercantile community made relatively little use of the patented system. In truth the screw was of only limited value to the mercantile community before the development of compound engines. It should be recalled that any number of speculators and cranks

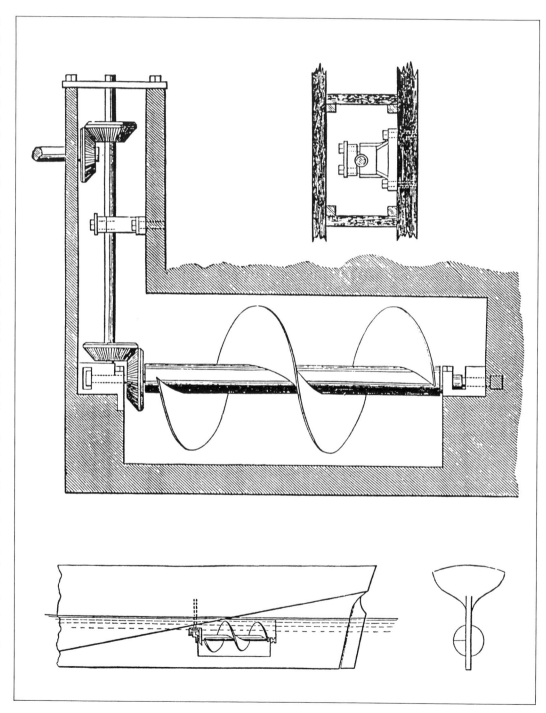

The original form of Smith's propeller and its position in the deadwood, from the first Patent drawings.

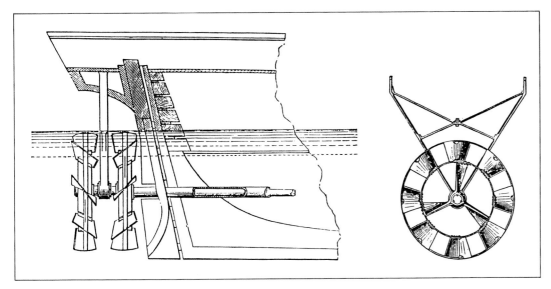

Ericssons's propellers from his first Patent.

were also trying to lighten both private owners and the Government of funds, making caution essential.

This chapter is a study of the Ship Propeller Company (SPC), as an example of the relationship between industry, commerce and government in the transitional era. While the SPC proved vital to the success of the screw in the period 1840–45, it failed utterly in its main object, to make money, and eventually split apart and collapsed.

The screw propeller: invention or application?

As the earlier chapters have demonstrated, the marine screw propeller was not 'invented' by Francis Pettit Smith and John Ericsson. Marine screw propellers had been used thirty years before these two men took out their patents. Furthermore Smith refined his original general patent of 31 May 1836, restricting his claim to the position of screw in the deadwood under the patent of 30 April 1839. Similarly, Ericsson's patent of 13 January 1837 was for 'An improved propeller applicable to steam navigation'.

There were at least five worthwhile 'inventions' of the screw propeller, for use with steam engines, before 1836. Those of Stevens, Owen and Ressel failed from the inadequacy of contemporary engine and boiler technology. Ressel's work, as might be expected in the hidebound Austria of Metternich, was brought to a premature end by the secret police.[1] Wil-

son's valuable work with hand cranked screws, which anticipated the correct position for the propeller, was never linked to an engine, while Marc Brunel did not realise the idea was sufficiently novel to be worth patenting.

Smith and Ericsson's deserved primacy in the field is a reflection of their ability to secure the funds required to develop and exploit the new technology, and not of any leap in design or technology. In Ericsson's case the funds were provided by a private individual, who anticipated sales to the American Government and profitable employment on his canal system. Smith's ideas were taken up on an altogether larger scale. The Ship Propeller Company was incorporated by an Act of Parliament on 29 July 1839. However, before examining the work of the company it is necessary to reconsider the origins of the patent that it was formed to exploit.

Francis Pettit Smith, although normally referred to as a 'sheep farmer', was an educated man. His father had been tutor to Lord Sligo, and he ended his days close to Sligo's seat as Postmaster at Hythe. In addition he had not neglected his son's education. Smith wrote lucid explanations for his ideas and developed rational, if not necessarily accurate arguments to support his work. It was no coincidence that he referred to the 'Archimedean' screw in his patent; this at once revealed his classical education, and placed his idea in a context with which all educated men of the age would be familiar.

Through his leading apologist, John Bourne, Smith initially claimed to have hit upon the concept of the screw placed in the deadwood in 1835. Following a particularly vicious pamphlet attack in the late 1850s, Bourne found it necessary to extend Smith's claims for the propeller back to 1834, and to add a lifetime of interest in marine propulsion in the second edition of his history of the screw propeller.[2]

James Nicol's pamphlet of 1858 accused Smith or his backers of stealing the work of three Scots innovators, and suggested that Smith was incapable of reaching the stage of development required for the patent of 1836 because he could point to no significant experiments before that date. Robert Wilson's pamphlet of 1860 merely raises doubt, suggesting that an experimental boat propeller of 1833, which had been tried by the Royal Navy at Woolwich and rejected but never returned, was used as a basis for the patent of 1836. Despite the close relationship between Pettit Smith and Bourne the second edition of Bourne's book is not a defence against these claims, and does nothing to dispel the possibility of conspiracy.[3] The two pamphlets suggest or imply that Smith was merely a front for improper conduct by named and unnamed individuals. It requires more specific rebuttal than Smith was ever willing or able to provide. However, the continued employment of Smith by the Admiralty, ever anxious to save money, after the collapse of the SPC, and his work with John Penn on stern gland bearings should be enough to dispel the 'front' element of the conspiracy theory. Whatever the source of the design Smith alone secured the vital element that his less fortunate predecessors were denied, financial support. From the spring of 1836, before the patent had been issued, the banker John Wright was acting as Smith's backer. This support was secured within a year of the first experiments. It allowed Smith to engage an engineer to assist with mechanical development, and to secure a patent, which was then an expensive business.

On the day the patent was proved the 6-ton boat *F P Smith* was tried on the Limehouse ca-

The amended forms of Smith's screw propellers: the single full thread (left), and the double half-thread.

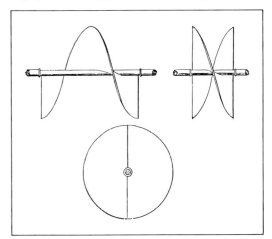

1. W M Petty, 'The Introduction of the Screw Propeller', Unpublished M A Thesis (London 1969).

2. J Bourne, *A Treatise on the Screw Propeller* (London 1853; 2nd edn 1867), pp188-9.

3. J Nicol, *Who invented the Screw Propeller?* (London 1858); R Wilson, *The Screw Propeller: Who invented It?* (Glasgow 1860).

THE ARCHIMEDES,
FITTED WITH MR F. SMITH'S PATENT SCREW PROPELLER.

STEAMER.
Built by MR H^Y Wimshurst of Limehouse, for the Ship Propeller Company

The famous demonstration ship of the Screw Propeller Co, the 200-ton Archimedes. *This lithograph was part of the promotional effort of the company.* (NMM)

nal. In February 1837 the full turn screw broke, creating a marked improvement in performance and suggesting an empirical approach to development. This is significant. Further trials at Dover in September 1837, in the presence of Wright, led to an approach to the Admiralty in March 1838. Smith and his backers, Wright and the Rennie brothers (then leading lights in the London engineering community and the earliest advocates of the screw), secured a favourable response from Sir John Barrow, the influential Second (permanent) Secretary to the Admiralty. In marked contrast to the dismissive treatment accorded to Ericsson, the Smith Consortium was advised that a 200-ton vessel would be required to demonstrate their system. This per

suaded the projectors that a quick response would prove financially beneficial, and in consequence they concentrated on the Royal Navy as the preferred customer. The support of the Rennies, in particular of Sir John Rennie, was of critical importance, for he had followed his father as the Admiralty's preferred consultant on all engineering matters.[4]

The 200-ton *Archimedes* was laid down in March 1838 by Henry Wimshurst and engined by George Rennie; both were consortium members, and both would have a major input into the prospectus of the SPC. The ship was launched a year later and completed just as the SPC was incorporated as a Joint Stock Company, its objects being to purchase Smith's patents and transfer the financial interest to the company. The business was begun on the largest possible scale, with a capital of £100,000 in 4000 £25 shares.

All existing sources suggest that Wright and the Rennies were the major backers, the Rennies to the tune of £1000 each, with a number of lesser speculators. Howe Peter Browne (1788-1845), the Second Lord Sligo, often named in this role, was a very useful front, being a leading Whig politician, a prominent yachtsman and a grandson of Earl Howe. He had also served as Governor of Jamaica between 1833 and 1836, where he came to appreciate the services of Commander George Evans, then in command of HMS *Rhadamanthus*, the first Royal Navy steamship to operate in the New World, between 1832 and 1835. Evans played a significant role in suppressing a native revolt. However, Sligo's will would suggest that he lacked the

---

4. Sir J Rennie, *Autobiography* (London 1882).

disposable capital to take a major financial stake in the company. Nonetheless, his friendship with Lord Holland, and close ties to other senior ministers, made him particularly useful.

The Company began with the widest parameters, including building, fitting or running screw ships, erecting workshops and selling licences. The prospectus emphasised the auxiliary role, placing the machinery abaft the main mast in merchant steamers, using Rennie's high-pressure machinery to save weight and space with the ultimate possibility of employing Earl Dundonald's rotary engine, to save three-quarters of the cost. However, the commercial sector was not the primary target. Only the Royal Navy could be expected to provide a major source of funds in the short term, the fifteen years in which the patent would remain in force.

The early trials of the *Archimedes* were attended by a large number of naval officers, both on active duty and on half pay. Earl Dundonald visited the ship while she lay at Portsmouth, while Admiral Sir Robert Otway, Commander-in-Chief at Sheerness, contended that she was the 'best steam vessel ever', being without paddle boxes and carrying her engines below the waterline, something which 'must lead to the introduction of the screw into Her Majesty's service'. He was also aware of the superior sailing properties of the screw steamer. Such testimony was particularly valuable when it could be reproduced, as Otway's was, in a sales brochure.[5] Otway's comments, and those of other officers, closely reflected the sales pitch being employed by the company. Of particular interest was the idea that a small steam engine, placed in the orlop, could provide a battleship with sufficient tactical mobility to manoeuvre in battle for a favourable firing position. The Seaward brothers had hit upon the same concept, but their effort was still linked to the paddle wheel, and as such was of limited interest, despite sea trials in two Indiamen in the late 1830s. The first report to a member of the Board of Admiralty, by George Evans, now a Captain, the first commissioned officer to command a Royal Navy steamship, as recently as 1828, was little more than a repetition of the company's claims. Evans was not a new convert to the system, having inspected the 6-ton *F P Smith* in London in May 1836, and suggested to Lord Sligo, who had taken him to view her, that it would be a good investment to build a larger version. In 1836 Evans was employed investigating the Post Office Packet Service.[6]

At this stage it should be emphasised that the politics of innovation had a major influence on the propeller. Sligo, Evans and Parker were all of the Whig/Liberal party. The most prominent public advocate of the system, Admiral Sir Edward Codrington, Commander-in-Chief at Portsmouth 1839–1842, was on the advanced, or radical wing of the party. Codrington's support was particularly useful, since he was the acknowledged master of naval tactics, the sphere in which the screw had most to offer.[7] This degree of success in their chosen market encouraged the SPC to pursue their preferred customer. Over the next six years the Company provided the Admiralty, or senior members of the Board, with details of all new ships fitted with the Smith screw – log entries, claims of speed and engineering improvements.[8] Not one of these approaches had the desired effect. The Admiralty took a long term view, and were well aware of the objects of the SPC. They waited for the company to complete the development of the screw, and built just one experimental screw warship, the *Rattler*, ordered in 1840.

Although only a secondary target, the mercantile community proved more receptive. By the end of her round-Britain promotional tour the *Archimedes* had garnered plaudits from every port visited. However, these did little to reward the backers of the project, and nothing to improve the cohesion of the company. Furthermore, many of the early screw steamers were designed with little or no understanding of the system, and were built in haste. The Londonderry-built *Great Northern*, which adopted the placement of the machinery in the after hold, as advocated by Henry Wimshurst in the SPC Prospectus, was the most ambitious, if not the best, of these projects. Few would serve in their intended role for long, while every one of the British commercial screw steam vessels completed by 1844 would be offered to the Admiralty by the end of the decade.[9] Smith was often called in after things had progressed so far as to restrict his role to damage limitation. The screw propeller and the related machinery, bearings and glands were insufficiently advanced before 1850 to be employed by cost-conscious shipowners. Only visionary men with access to other men's pockets could take the risk.

5. Otway to C A Caldwell 12 May 1839 in the SPC Prospectus of 1840.

6. Captain G Evans to Admiral Sir W Parker, Second Sea Lord 28 October 1839 in G H Guest, *A Record of the services of Admiral George Evans* (London 1876), pp11-14, 29-30; Surveyor to Seaward 9 October 1839, PRO ADM 91/9.

7. Codrington to Admiralty 28 May 1840, PRO ADM 12/375 A 502; Codrington to Sidney Herbert, First (or Political) Secretary to the Admiralty 6 October 1841 & 4 August 1843, NMM COD/172 & 20/2.

8. Caldwell to Lord Minto 3 June 1841, NLS *New Brighton*; SPC to Admiralty 11 June 1842, PRO ADM 87/14 geared crank; Barrow to Symonds 3 May 1842, PRO ADM 1/5522; Smith to Admiralty 31 December 1843, PRO ADM 83/26.

The contemporary Illustrated London News *engraving of the* Great Northern, *an auxiliary steamer that followed the scheme originally proposed in the SPC prospectus of fitting a small screw engine in the after hold.*

The Ship Propeller Company

The promoters of the SPC petitioned to bring in a Bill to form a limited company on 20 February 1839, eleven months after *Archimedes* had been laid down. The petition was referred to the Select Committee on Private Bills, and was in danger of being lost through the expiry of the time permitted. In a second petition of 31 May the projectors requested permission to proceed. Ten days later permission was granted, and two MPs were directed to prepare the Bill. The Bill was read for the first time on the following day. On 19 June a petition that the Bill be not passed into law was read and tabled. It was signed by Bennet Woodcroft and Robert Gardner. At the Second Reading a motion was raised that the Bill be delayed for three months, but this was defeated. Woodcroft's petition was read and referred to the Committee on the Bill, but when the Committee came to consider it no-one appeared to support it. One may suppose that Woodcroft and his backer did not have the capital to fight the SPC at this stage. The Bill was then read for the third time on 8 July. Amendments were added in the Lords, presumably by someone connected with the project, as their tenor was to widen the objects of the SPC. These were adopted by the Commons; the Bill received Royal Assent on 29 July.[10]

Formed on the grand scale, with a share capital of £100,000 the SPC had as its objects the purchase and exploitation of Smith's propeller patent. To this end it was empowered to build and operate ships and sell licences for the use of the patented location of the propeller, not the propeller itself. This approach was adopted by the other propeller patentees of the period. As a commercial venture the SPC proved to be an unmitigated disaster. The leading members, Wright, Currie, Lord Sligo, Caldwell, Smith, Wimshurst and the Rennie brothers, were unable to co-operate. Eventually the company became moribund, leaving Smith to sell his services direct to the Admiralty, and finally to surrender his patent and the right to royalties for a third share in the £20,000 once-and-for-all payment offered by the Admiralty.

Even as the company was formed, the seeds of disaster were evident. *Archimedes* (briefly the SS *Propeller*), its only major asset, had been built as a mobile test bed and demonstration model. She cost £10,500, a large sum for a 200-ton steamship, largely on account of her novel machinery and drive arrangement. Her design cruelly exposed the limited nature of previous experimental work. It soon became clear that the success of the *F P Smith* had been relative, for many details of the new ship were fatally flawed.

Early trials demonstrated that the final drive arrangement, which attempted to avoid using a shaft passing directly through the deadwood by having a shaft passing through two sets of bevels and emerging above the waterline just ahead of the screw, was unnecessarily complex, wasted power and space, and generated enough noise to render the ship unsuitable for naval service or passenger traffic. In addition the propeller aperture, intended for a screw with a full turn, was far longer than required, weakening the ship and wasting space in the hold. In essence the ship had been designed without conducting adequate experimental work. She was, therefore, too much of an experiment herself to do justice to the system she was supposed to promote.

To make matters worse George Rennie had, with the full concurrence of the Company, adopted his own experimental high-pressure boiler, breaking the cardinal rule of sound experimentation, that only one novelty should be tried at a time. Rennie's intention was sound, to employ the smallest powerplant for 'occasional use', the auxiliary role for which the SPC held out great hope. Unfortunately the boiler exploded before the first public trial, and, on the order of the Coroner's Court, was replaced by a conventional item designed by William Miller. This did not generate enough steam to work the 80hp engine up to the design speed. Until the screw was changed, and the boiler uprated, *Archimedes* would be capable of no more than 8kts, depriving her of even bare equality with paddle steamers of similar size. The SPC admitted the lack of speed in the prospectus, and stressed that the failure lay in the powerplant, and not the propeller. Fortunately the ship had been designed to sail as well as steam, with a good contemporary hull form. This combination of steam and sail was the real point of interest for the Admiralty.

It is important to note that *Archimedes* was demonstrated to the Admiralty before the mercantile community. In October 1839 the Master of the *William and Mary*, the yacht employed as the flagship at Woolwich, was ordered to take a log line on board *Archimedes* at London Bridge for the trial.[11]

Brunel, who inspected the ship after her trip to Holland, and the subsequent repairs to the broken crank, considered her an inefficient compromise. However, he had the vision to modify his new iron transatlantic steamer into a screw vessel. Alone of all those who first saw the ship he had recognised the fundamental advantages of the screw for full powered ships of the largest size, and was prepared to make a complete commitment to its success as the principal power for a massive oceangoing vessel.[12] After her round-Britain cruise, which was a critical rather than a

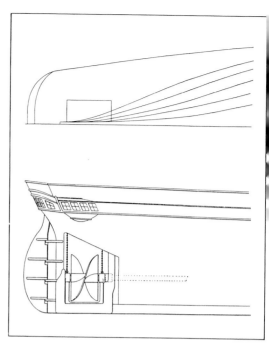

The after hull and screw of HMS *Rattler: the relatively fine lines allowed a good flow to the screw. From* Bourne's *Treatise on the Screw Propeller, a work which despite its apparent technical objectivity is also a powerful* apologia *for Smith and his efforts.*

commercial success, and her experimental work on the Dover-Calais run, *Archimedes* was offered for sale to the Admiralty.[13]

Although the SPC was only asking for £3500 the Board had no funds for such an unusual purchase, and more significantly had no use for the ship. Her role as a test bed had been effectively complete within a few months of first going to sea, and with *Rattler* approaching completion the Admiralty could afford to wait for a larger purpose-built warship to complete their study of the new system. In addition, *Archimedes* was of little value, being largely fir-built and lacking any stowage. Her last important task was to tow *Rattler* from Sheerness to the East India Dock to receive her machinery in April 1843. The

9. A Lambert, 'The Royal Navy and the Screw Propeller, 1837-1847' and B Greenhill 'The SS *Great Northern*', in S Fisher (Ed), *Innovation in Shipping and Trade* (Exeter 1989)

10. *Journals of the House of Commons*, vol 94: 1839.

11. Adm to Woolwich, 14 October 1839, PRO ADM 12/361.

12. I K Brunel, 'Report to the Directors of the Great Western Steamship Company on Screw Propellers' (1840), Wills Memorial Library, Bristol.

13. Caldwell to Laird 11 July 1840, Laird MSS 98; E Corlett, *The Iron Ship* (London 1990), pp59-66; I K Brunel, *The Life of I K Brunel* (London 1870), pp539-58; Pary to Claxton 12 July 1838, PRO ADM 92/4 thanking him for a copy of the published log of the first transatlantic passage of the *Great Western*, and 6 November 1840 asking for information on 'the large iron ship, including the *Screw*'; SPC to Admiralty 6 July 1842, PRO ADM 12/402 Pro S 480.

company offered to perform this service, for the promotional benefit of the occasion, and the parsimonious Board had no hesitation in saving the coal.[14]

By 1845 the ship was no longer on Lloyd's Register. She was re-registered in 1847, receiving the classification 3A1, and her machinery was removed at Sunderland some time before 1852. The continued use of so unsatisfactory a vessel, even with her engines out, can only be explained by the shipping shortage created by the Crimean War, and she disappeared from the Registry in 1856, after a voyage from London to California. It would appear that she was sold to local interests, and was last seen on the Valparaiso – Australia run, in 1856–57, presumably carrying Newcastle (New South Wales) coal to Chile.[15]

The builder of *Archimedes*, Henry Wimshurst, recognised her limitations. He designed a new ship to exploit the commercial potential of the system, in particular the opportunity to provide a small auxiliary powerplant with minimal impact on cargo capacity. The machinery was

Models of the stern of the Novelty, *the auxiliary screw ship built by Henry Wimshurst to demonstrate his ideas on the best layout for merchant ships. His model was presented to the Science Museum by Wimshurst himself, so may be regarded as authentic. A notable feature of his 'system' was the facility to lift the propeller and its bearings so it could be stowed on deck when the ship was under sail. (ScM)*

placed in the stern, in the fashion of a modern tanker. Wimshurst's ship, the *Novelty*, again employed Rennie's high-pressure boilers, until the engineers forced their removal, and used the iron mizzen mast as a funnel. This design had already been discussed, and was put forward as the best layout for merchant ships in the 1840 SPC prospectus. Although *Novelty* was a technical success – she made a return passage to Istanbul with cargo under charter – she was never used by the SPC, even in their attempts to promote the system. In 1842 Wimshurst offered *Novelty* to the Admiralty, proposing the anti-slavery patrol on the West African Station would offer a suitable area for her employment. The Board rejected her as 'entirely unsuitable', an opinion they repeated in 1843 and 1844, on further solicitations. On the last occasion the ship was surveyed for the Colonial Office.[16]

Wimshurst complained of his unjust treatment, and offered the Admiralty a series of new ideas, one of which required the loan of a small frigate. He also submitted plans for a 1000-ton ship with two 80hp engines and an 'unshipping' propeller.[17] All were declined as inapplicable or undesirable, although his high-pressure machinery was considered 'to show considerable ingenuity'. This, however, was not the royal road to commercial success, for the Navy and the naval engineering community at large had no intention of trying such a dangerous system.[18]

Wimshurst's motives for acting alone cannot

be established, but financial gain would be the most obvious. Clearly he had separated himself from the plans of the SPC at an early date, favouring a design more suitable for auxiliary than primary power. He was the one shipbuilder in the original consortium, so his defection, implicit in the failure of the company to publicise the voyage of *Novelty* in 1841, may have precluded any significant alterations to *Archimedes*. One possible explanation for his solo effort lies in a divergence of views concerning the future development of the screw steamship within the company.

The other syndicate members to make a significant contribution to the construction of *Archimedes*, the Rennie brothers, John and in particular George, the machinery designer, had a larger financial stake in the company. They ap-

14. SPC to Admiralty 20 April 1843 accepted 22 April, PRO ADM 12/417 Pro S 217.

15. Admiral Sir C Bridge, *Some Recollections* (London 1918), p14. I am indebted to Basil Greenhill for the suggestion regarding her cargo, in addition to much else of benefit to the development of this chapter.

16. Wimshurst to Admiralty 18 August; 15, 20, 21 September 1842, PRO ADM 12/402; 21, 24, 26 June 1843, PRO ADM 12/417; 18 January & 11 April 1844, PRO ADM 12/432.

17. Wimshurst to Admiralty 6 March 1844 & 23 March, 30 August, 23 September & 2 October 1848; PRO ADM 12/432 & 497.

18. Admiralty to Wimshurst 24 February 1843, PRO ADM 12/417.

pear to have moved in exactly the opposite direction to Wimshurst, and to have done so at an even earlier date. The explosion of George Rennie's boiler in 1839, as has been shown, prejudiced the success of *Archimedes*, and with her the whole company. This was recognised by the shareholders, who wisely accepted the judgement of the coroner that Rennie should not be allowed to repair the original boiler. Rennie was not dismayed by this setback, and his next set of engines, for *Novelty*, were even more remarkable, using a locomotive boiler working at 60psi and direct drive from engines of high crankshaft speed. Although the trial performance was satisfactory, an engineers' strike forced Wimshurst to fit a new boiler working at 15psi. His decision may well have been influenced by the need to operate at sea, where a locomotive boiler would be a liability. The low power of this plant reflected Wimshurst's views on the role of the screw, and there is no reason to doubt that the ship was built as a commercial venture.

The Rennies object in joining the Screw Propeller Company should be linked to their efforts to increase their share of the profitable marine

19. Rennie to Charles Babbage 27 November 1839, BL Add 37,191,f269.

20. Admiralty to Rennie 1 October 1841, PRO ADM 12/388.

21. Sir J Rennie, *op cit.*

22. Rennie to Admiralty 16 March 1842, Smith to report on the vessel. Admiralty to Rennie 8 June 1842, PRO ADM 12/402.

23. Admiralty to Admiral Collier at Woolwich 19 July 1843, to take over *Mermaid* from Rennie, PRO ADM 12/417; Rennie to Admiralty 21 & 22 August 1843, ADM 12/417; Comptroller of Steam to Admiralty 21 December 1844, ADM 12/432; Rennie to Admiralty 18 May 1846, ADM 12/465.

24. Goulburn to Lord Aberdeen 9 August BL Add 43,196 f214.

25. Parry minute of meeting sent to the Surveyor 28 September 1841, PRO ADM 92/4.

26. Smith to Admiralty 1 July 1841 and Brunel to Admiralty 1 August 1842, PRO ADM 12/388 & 402.

27. Board Minute 3 March 1843, PRO ADM 12/417.

engine market. The Thamesside works of Maudslay and Seaward were preferred by the navy, which used the largest engines, the former for quality, the latter from a perception of design superiority, a rather short-lived advantage in the event. George Rennie was committed to the marine engineering side of the family business, developing new paddle wheels, engines and boilers in an effort to secure naval orders.[19] In 1841 Rennie tendered for the engines of the first Royal Navy screw steamer, the *Rattler*, and his bid was initially accepted.[20] However, Brunel, with whom they were directed to liaise, had an almost hereditary predilection for Maudslays, and it was they who eventually provided the machinery.

In his search for a marketable design Rennie developed Galloway's high-pressure rotary engine, and ordered the iron-hulled trials vessel *Mermaid* from Ditchburn & Mare. However, before any trials had been run with his three-bladed conoidal propeller the ship was offered to the Admiralty. This sudden shift followed hard on the heels of the collapse of John Wright's bank, which had been funding the vessel.[21]

The hull of *Mermaid* was valued at £850, and the Admiralty directed Smith to report on her. Eventually the engine and a low pressure boiler were included in the sale price of £5350. Following a report by Ewart and Lloyd the Admiralty had no interest in the high-pressure system.[22] The vessel was purchased in June 1843. In the interval Rennie conducted his trials, handing her over with a Smith type two-bladed propeller. The Admiralty insisted that the conoidal type fitted at the time of the purchase be replaced. Although Rennie begged the Admiralty not to allow the SPC a sight of their design, the Board refused to involve itself in the difficult world of patent litigation. In fact the conoidal design proved successful enough for the Admiralty to continue Rennie's work, leaving Rennie with only the cost of casting a series of propellers. Rennie would have no part in the 1852 settlement of the propeller patentees.[23]

In fact the Admiralty had little need for a

trial platform, the only role in which *Mermaid*, renamed *Dwarf* for naval service, was of any value. When the Foreign Office and the Treasury were discussing the possibility of providing a gift for the Pasha of Egypt, a known admirer of the propeller, the Board offered *Mermaid*. In the event she was not used, but the discussions indicate a low level of regard.[24]

As the original members of the SPC moved away from the aims of the company, and other projectors appeared in the field, it became necessary for the SPC to defend its position. The economic well-being of the company depended on the strength of Smith's patent, covering the position of the screw, and his reputation as the leading authority in the field. In the latter respect Brunel was, in fact, far better equipped, and with *The Great Britain* and *Rattler* made important contributions to the widespread adoption and ultimate success of the propeller.

The Admiralty was far too cautious to enter into an open-ended financial arrangement with the company so obviously founded to exploit the Smith patent. In consequence Brunel was invited to oversee the application of the propeller to the first naval screw warship, on 27 April 1841, as an expert with no financial stake in the success of the patent.[25]

Smith was, understandably, far from pleased by this turn of events. A year later he was still arguing that Brunel had no right to interfere.[26] The Admiralty informed Smith that he could not be given the overall direction of a project, and that he must liaise with Brunel, who would be responsible for installing the machinery and propeller. He was to confine himself to the design, location and aperture of the screw.[27] The following year the Board made it clear that they would not confine their interest to Smith's patent, but would entertain any propeller designs. In consequence there was no interest in the offer of exclusive rights to the use of the patent. This

The lines of the screw propelled royal yacht Fairy *of 1845, from* Bourne's Treatise on the Screw Propeller.

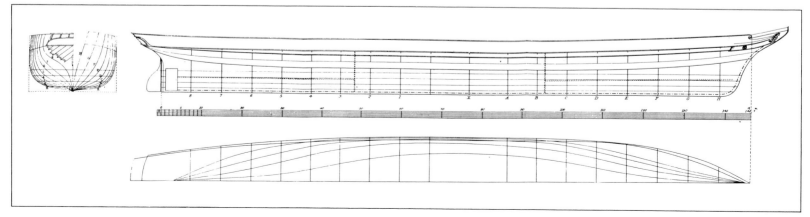

was hardly surprising when the Smith patent did not protect the propeller, only the location. However, the SPC found this a bitter pill, particularly when the most prominent designers were Woodcroft and Steinman, both of whom the company was threatening to prosecute. That the company was reduced to making the offer suggests that the commercial sector had been little more forthcoming than the Admiralty. The SPC was in financial trouble.[28] The Board considered that further trials would be necessary before reaching a decision. At this stage the trials were still running in the company's favour, with the Smith and Rennie forms proving superior to that of Steinman.[29] However, Brunel was still submitting valuable advice for the cost of his expenses. This only served to point out how much better qualified Brunel was than Smith.[30] The first trial of *The Great Britain* gave the SPC a welcome opportunity to recoup some credit from Brunel.[31]

However, the report of *The Times* indicated that the political world was still opposed to the SPC, and to Smith, making an inaccurate assault on Smith's propeller. This is significant for two reasons: clearly the leading London newspaper was ignorant of the Smith patent, and more significantly, was a sounding board for the opinions of the government. On 23 April 1845 *The Great Britain*, then at Blackwall, was visited by the Queen, Prince Albert and the Board of Admiralty, aboard *Dwarf*. Smith was on board, and presented the Queen with a gold model of the propeller of the new royal yacht *Fairy*, then fitting out at Ditchburn & Mare's yard. This, however, availed the SPC very little.[32]

Two months after this show of royal and political support the SPC received a significant rebuff. Their request for a royalty on the use of screws in the Arctic discovery vessels *Erebus* and *Terror* was ignored.[33] The screw used was of the Ericsson type, and the installation, designed by Master Shipwright Oliver Lang at Woolwich, appears to have been a deliberate attempt to evade the patent. If so, it was a qualified success, but the loss of both vessels and their crews, along with the change of ministry, ensured that nothing further was attempted along those lines.[34]

The letter of 11 June 1845 is the last reference to the Ship Propeller Company in the Admiralty files. It appears that the company simply disappeared. Unable to make any money from the patent, the collapse of Wright's bank in 1842 had been a major blow. The royalties paid on all screw steamers built down to 1845 would hardly have kept *Archimedes* in coal, which would explain why she had dropped out of class and, apparently, out of repair. The office at Fish Street Hill had been closed in 1844, leaving Smith to resuscitate the company at Beaufort Buildings on the Strand in 1847–48. Litigation both failed to establish the dominance of the company *vis a vis* other propeller projectors, and made inroads into the share capital. Other projectors, notably Woodcroft, were also selling licences.[35]

In consequence the SPC was essentially moribund after mid 1845, although it, or perhaps Smith acting alone under the company name, did contest the extension of Woodcroft's patent in 1846, without success. The SPC had failed to secure real financial reward from the Admiralty, and did little better with the shipowners. Only Brunel built a merchant ship that the SPC would look upon as an unqualified success, yet there was a marked reluctance to make too much of Brunel's work, for fear he might take further interest in the subject, at the company's expense. Before 1848 the commercial use of the screw propeller was dominated by Liverpool and Dublin. Even here *Great Northern* and the efforts of John Laird to sell iron screw steamers to the Admiralty were of only limited value. Liverpool steam tonnage had only reached 11,000 by 1851; the real growth came far too late to help the SPC. Only in the more favourable economic conditions of the mid 1850s did Liverpool move into iron screw steamships.[36] However, the General Screw Steam Shipping Company's success-

ful auxiliary voyages quickly reduced the insurance premium on screw ships from 4 per cent to 1¼. Until the mercantile community had brought this work to a successful conclusion the Admiralty was reluctant to act. The GSSC made the auxiliary work for short-sea service, and its experience influenced the design of the early screw sloops. For oceanic voyages, other than those on the subsidised mail services, steamships were simply uneconomical, be they paddle wheel or screw propeller. While the Royal Navy did not have to worry about economy in the same way, it was forced to rely on known coal supplies for service outside home waters. Few steamships were deployed further afield than the Mediterranean. The slow take-up of the auxiliary concept in the mercantile community, allied to the caution of the Admiralty, ensured that the SPC would always have problems securing the rewards that had been anticipated back in 1837–8. In this respect their failure to complete anything more than the most basic trials before launching the company, as indicated by the problems of *Archimedes*, proved critical. The product did not reach commercial maturity in the lifetime of the SPC. However, if the SPC failed it was not alone. The propeller attracted much interest, and it was largely to forestall other patentees that the SPC moved, and once it began to promote the screw the process could not be stopped.

Most accounts cite the loss to the projectors as approximately £50,000, half the share capital. Much of this went into building and running *Archimedes*; further sums were used to improve Smith's standard of living, when he moved from his Hendon sheep farm to a large house in central London.

Smith after the failure of the Company

After the effective collapse of the SPC Smith, who had no funds of his own, required some means of support. In mid 1846 he offered to superintend the installation of the screw for the Royal Navy. The Comptroller of Steam offered two guineas a day, with expenses. In addition the Surveyor of the Navy recommended that Smith be employed as the 'supervisor of screws'.[37] That this change in fortune for Smith was concurrent with the return of a Whig ministry may have been entirely coincidental, but that would appear unlikely.

The major problem for naval architects was the form of the stern run. Brunel had made it clear in February 1842 that a fine stern run was vital for the efficient use of the propeller.[38] However, this advice had either been forgotten or ignored in the Board's enthusiasm for auxilia-

28. Admiralty to Comptroller of Steam 23 October 1844; SPC to Admiralty, asserting sole rights to the screw 4 November 1844; SPC to Admiralty 17 December and Steinman to Admiralty 21 December 1844, PRO ADM 12/432.

29. Comptroller of Steam to Admiralty 21 December 1844, PRO ADM 12/432.

30. Admiralty to Comptroller of Steam 7 May 1844, PRO ADM 12/432.

31. Crispin and Lloyd to Admiralty 29 January 1845, PRO ADM 12/449.

32. E Corlett, *op cit*, p97.

33. Solicitor to Admiralty 11 June 1845, PRO ADM 12/449.

34. M J T Lewis, '*Erebus* and *Terror*', *Journal of The Railway and Canal Historical Society*, (October 1971), pp65-8; Lang was a favourite of the Tory Board, 1841-46, but on the change of ministry his star quickly faded. A D Lambert, *The Last Sailing Battlefleet: Maintaining Naval Mastery 1815-1850*, (London 1991), pp79-90.

35. J Hewish, *The Indefatigable Mr Woodcroft* (London 1980), p11.

36. Smith to Laird 22 January 1842, Laird MSS; P L Cottrell, 'The Steamship on the Mersey, 1815-80: investment and ownership, in Davis & Aldcroft *Shipping and Trade* pp137-163.

37. Comptroller of Steam to Smith 30 June, 20 & 30 July 1846, PRO ADM 12/465; Surveyor to Admiralty 10 July 1846, PRO ADM 12/465.

38. Brunel to Admiralty 10 February 1842, PRO ADM 83/25.

THE ARCHIMEDES,   STEAMER.

Another, less well known, lithograph of the Archimedes *produced at the behest of the Ship Propeller Co. This illustration is designed to emphasise the advantage of the screw in working with sail in situations where the paddle was at a distinct disadvantage – the paddler in the background is labouring under the usual difficulty, when the wind is anywhere but aft, of digging one wheel in deeply while the other barely contributes.* (NMM)

ry, low powered ships, and had to be re-learnt after much wasted effort with the first group of large screw steamships. Once again the shift in the balance of political power in naval design circles had a major impact on the resolution of this problem. The 'Tory' designers, those favoured by, and who supported the Tory ministry, had adopted very bluff stern lines for their screw ships.

During the period in which Lord Auckland served as First Lord of the Admiralty there was considerable pressure for economy, linked to, and largely created by, criticism of naval design, from concept through to execution. The Board baulked at the cost of Smith's services, but the Comptroller of Steam, Captain Alexander Ellice, was quick to defend the use of his expertise. The 'inconsiderable expense' contrasted sharply with the 'injury to the service' that might result from an early termination of his contract.[39] Ellice left office in February 1850, his post being amalgamated with that of Captain Sir Baldwin Walker, who became Surveyor of the Navy in 1848. Smith's patent had just been granted a five-year extension and this, with the opportune retirement of Ellice, prompted a sharpening of

the Board's methods.[40] Smith was informed that the Board would not continue his position, but would only call upon him as occasion required. The 'salary' was discontinued and a gratuity of £400 provided in final settlement.[41] This softened up Smith quite effectively, to judge from the haste with which John Wright wrote.[42]

The Board had exploited the opportunity created by the legion of screw projectors, and the

39. Ellice to Admiralty 22 January 1848 *On the Introduction of the Screw Propeller into HM Service* (London 1856), p24.

40. Solicitor to Admiralty 11 February 1850, PRO ADM 12/528.

41. Board Minute 8 March 1850; Comptroller of Steam 11 March reply 27 March 1850, PRO ADM 12/528.

42. Wright to Admiralty 2 April 1850, PRO ADM 12/528.

failure of the SPC to establish a dominant position in the field. From 1843 the Admiralty had studied the legal value of the various propeller patents, looking for an economical solution (in view of their limited requirements this was almost certainly the cheapest patent), holding off claims for payment for as long as practicable and ignoring the offer of 'exclusive rights'. In 1844 they requested all patentees to send in details of their charges for the use of their patent.[43]

By 1847 it was clear that the rights of Smith and the moribund SPC could be bought up for a reasonable sum; but still the Board waited.[44] The reason for the delay would appear to have been the timing of the patent. If the patent were to lapse, or could not be upheld against the numerous counter-claims and objectors, there would be no need to make any payment. In the event the patent was extended for five years on 11 February 1850. Negotiations for the purchase of all rights were opened immediately, by withdrawing Smith's 'salary'.[45] The Board concluded their manoeuvre by purchasing the patent rights of all patentees in 1851. They forced all interested parties to act together by the simple expedient of making a once and for all offer of £20,000. The patentees were represented by Henry Currie, MP for Guildford during 1847–52, a partner in Wright's bank and one of the original promoters of the SPC. Smith, Woodcroft and Lowe received one-third of the money each.[46]

Having carefully watched the development of the screw, with a degree of assistance in 1845, which was in itself more a product of international tension than technical commitment or

Smith later worked with William Penn, the famous Greenwich engine builders, to develop a water lubricated stern gland using staves of lignum vitae *wood. Another drawing from Bourne's* Treatise on the Screw Propeller.

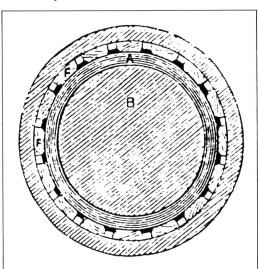

financial relaxation, the Admiralty finally moved to secure the patent rights in 1850. By this stage the twelve-year period of experiment was at an end. The private sector had funded the proving stage of screw propeller development, albeit unwillingly, having been outmanoeuvred all along the line by Admiralty Boards well aware of the financial savings.

Smith was awarded a Civil List pension of £200 on 21 January 1855. This was one of the first acts of the Palmerston government, coming into office in the middle of a major war. In addition he received £3000 from a national subscription among naval engineers and architects.[47] Subsequently Smith worked with John Penn on the critical issue of stern bearings, helping to develop the *lignum vitae* gland that was as important to the commercial success of the screw as the position of the propeller. His farm on Guernsey failed and in 1860 he was given a post in the Patent Office Museum, under Bennet Woodcroft, one of his rivals in the early days of the propeller. Knighted in 1871, he died at South Kensington in 1874.

Conclusion

The history of the SPC provides a sharp lesson in the dangers facing private capital when engaged in a commercial speculation with the government as one of the major potential customers. The problems were doubled by the fact that what was on offer was intellectual property, rather than a tangible product. In an age when both Brunels saw no point in patenting an idea, there was a marked resistance to the idea of paying for the use of intellectual property. This has implications far wider than the history of the Screw Propeller Company.

The Admiralty refused to be made use of in the manner the SPC had hoped, that is as a conduit to channel government funds into a commercial venture, the exploitation of Smith's patent. It is possible that the change of ministry in 1841 had a major influence on the situation, for the SPC had many supporters among the Whig elite, but found very few in Tory ranks. The Admiralty's handling of the screw propeller demonstrated the value of caution, and something approaching sharp practice. By holding back, experimenting and employing Brunel rather than Smith to install the screw in the *Rattler* the Admiralty paid very little for the use of the patent, and even then moved sufficiently slowly to deny the SPC any tangible reward in the time-frame anticipated at Fish Street Hill. By mid 1845, when the technical success of the screw could no longer be denied, the company had fallen apart, leaving Smith to act alone.

Without his backers Smith was forced to accept a modest daily rate for the benefit of his experience. When the patents were renewed, and well aware that the Navy would soon be shifting to an all-screw steam force, the Admiralty secured the undisputed right to all and any screw and placement for the sum of £20,000, only 40 per cent of the sum expended over the previous fifteen years by the SPC alone.

It would appear that the Admiralty, well aware of the value of Smith's patent, and of the intentions of the SPC, used their position as the target customer to break down the commercial value of the patent, and then to snap up the remains at a bargain price. That Smith received only one-third of the final settlement, the same share as Woodcroft and Lowe, is both revealing and startling. Smith and his backers built the *Archimedes*, which was the practical proof of the propeller. That they received no benefit for this supports the Victorian convention that they were merely attempting to interest the Admiralty in the invention for the benefit of the nation; for this was indeed all that they actually achieved. Having failed with their target market the SPC would draw little benefit from the few merchant vessels that used the patent. Failure in both markets reflected the lack of development of the system before taking out the patent, and the limited value of the *Archimedes* as a practical steamship. It is possible that the projectors acted in haste from a fear that other patentees might reap the anticipated benefits.

Without the SPC the screw would not have been adopted so quickly; similarly, without his backer, Robert Stockton, Ericsson would have abandoned his project, turning his fertile mind to other areas just as he had in the field of locomotives after the failure at Rainhill. Financial support was critical to the success of nineteenth century innovation and invention. Backers were vital to cover the cost of basic development and early trials; in return men like Wright and Stockton hoped to make money. Both were disappointed.

Dr Andrew Lambert

43. Solicitor 26 January 1843, re Ericsson & Blaxland; Rennie 21 August 1843, PRO ADM 12/417; Board Minute 5 September. Comptroller of Steam 23 & 24 October, SPC 4 November, SPC 17 & 21 December 1844, PRO ADM 12/432.

44. Lloyd Report for Solicitor 14 May 1847, PRO ADM 12/481; Law Officer on Patent Rights 23 August 1848, PRO ADM 12/497; Comptroller of Steam 30 November 1849, PRO ADM 12/512.

45. Solicitor 11 February 1850, PRO ADM 12/528.

46. Solicitor 13, 20 & 22 September 1851, PRO ADM 12/544; Currie to Admiralty, PRO ADM 1/5641.

47. Palmerston to Smith 21 January 1855, *On the Introduction ...* 1856.

8

Sail-Assist and the Steamship

GENERALLY speaking there were in the 1840s two distinct types of vessel using steam propulsion; the fully powered steamer, using steam as her principal means of propulsion but also equipped with some sail, and the auxiliary steamer, using the wind and her extensive sail plan as her principal means of propulsion and her steam power in restricted waters, in bad weather, in areas of the sea where the winds were unusually light or non-existent and, in the case of the warship, when going into action. The fully powered steamer was limited by the high fuel consumption of contemporary engines to a steaming range of twenty days or so. The auxiliary steamship had the almost unlimited range of operations of the sailing vessel, but her steaming capability was limited by the fuel she could carry and the opportunities for refuelling. Between refuelling, very generally speaking, her continuous steaming time was limited to three weeks.

The fact that it was necessary, or desirable commercially, for a fully powered steamer to carry masts, spars and sails at all was questioned at a very early date. Junius Smith, a financier whose inspiration and drive were largely responsible for the creation of the British and American Steam Navigation Company, the rival of the Great Western Steamship Company, wrote in September 1838:

Since I wrote to you respecting masts for steamships, I have, on more mature deliberation, satisfied myself that they are better without any masts at all. It may be expedient in the present stage of Atlantic steam navigation, to construct what may be called a deck mast, that can be thrown up on a hinge, or bolt axis, in case it should be wanted. I do not doubt that more power is lost by the resistance of masts and rigging in steamships, than is gained by the

use of sails. I am aware that it will be said that the sails relieved the engines; but upon the same principle, the resistance occasioned by the masts and rigging, distress the engines in proportion to the degree of resistance and the time of its continuance. The truth is, as I apprehended, the engines, if properly constructed, will perform their duty just as well without the aid of sails as with it. Everyone at all accustomed to the seas, must be aware that a steamship running off at a rate of ten knots an hour, would so far keep ahead of an ordinary breeze, that sails would have no effect in propelling, while the resistance of the masts and rigging would have a constant and considerable effect in retarding her. [This, of course, is incorrect. A vessel running at ten knots before a ten knot breeze would experience no wind resistance.]

In crossing the Atlantic one way and the other for twelve months, how few days out of the 365 would a ship have so strong a wind, and that a fair one, as to enable her to run ten knots an hour under canvas? And if the wind is not strong enough and fair enough to do that, sails can be of little or no use. If as contended, the use of sails does relieve the engines, all that can be meant by that is, that you can lessen your steam power and reduce the consumption of fuel. But I think that advantage will be more

than counterbalanced by the constant increased resistance arising from the use of masts and rigging.[1]

Smith went on in response to criticism to argue that a disabled steamer was in no worse position than a dismasted sailing vessel.

The wind resistance presented by masts, spars and sails concerned steamship operators from the very dawn of steamship propulsion. Early steam vessels tended to be relatively small and to be employed on short passages. From the start they were frequently equipped with the simplest of sail plans of schooner type. When, in September 1828, the steam paddle sloop HMS *African* was fitted out for a voyage to the Adriatic, the Comptroller of the Navy, Admiral Sir Thomas Byam Martin, wrote in his letter of instruction to her Commanding Officer, Lieutenant Grigg:

Your lower masts ought to be as snug and low as possible, with a lofty fore topmast, so that you may have least resistance when going head to wind, and the greatest speed of canvas when going free.[2]

1. Quoted in E L Pond, *Junius Smith* (New York 1927) p147/148.
2. Byam Martin MSS, BL Add 41,397 f146.

The Great Western *at anchor drying sails, showing the full spread of her four-masted schooner rig. Because of the publication of her deck and engine room logs, the sophisticated interaction of power and sail employed by this ship can be fully understood.* (Denis Griffiths)

The Cunard liner Etruria, *built at Glasgow in 1884, was photographed off the New England coast in 1896 with the breeze fairly fresh and a shade on her port quarter. Even at this late date a little canvas has been set – useful to dampen rolling – though as she was a single-screw ship the rig was essentially for emergencies.* (Basil Greenhill Collection)

In considering these instructions it must be borne in mind that the lofty fore topmast would be housed and the spars sent down when the wind was forward of the beam and the rig's windage much reduced and that when the wind was abaft the beam a large squaresail would be set from it, thus making maximum use of the favourable winds. Although, from the spacing of the masts, essentially a fully powered steamship's exiguous occasional sail-assist (to use the terminology of the last decade of the twentieth century), in the mid nineteenth century the *African* was probably usually described as schooner rigged.

From the very start of the commercial operation of steamships the merchant shipping industry showed remarkable enterprise in developing entirely new sail and rigging plans and in breaking free from the established traditional rigs which had developed in the long era of carpenter and blacksmith technology at sea. It may be asked why Junius Smith's suggestion was not widely put into practice, in view of the economies that could be effected by dispensing with sails altogether. But there were several good reasons why the retention of some kinds of sails was desirable. The first, perhaps, was a marketing factor. Sails were almost by definition what a ship had. A ship without masts was unthinkable and not acceptable to the passenger market; it was seen as far too risky a vehicle to travel in. Moreover, Junius Smith was, of course, not really justified in his assertion that a broken-down steamer was no more helpless than a dismasted sailing vessel. As countless cases had shown in the history of seafaring, the highly skilled seaman of the wooden sailing vessel could usually use spare material carried on board against the very contingency of dismasting to lash up a jury rig, as a small temporary arrangement of masts, spars and sails was called. Such a rig would enable the vessel to make some sort of a course towards safety. Given the relatively high possibility of some sort of engine trouble in early steam vessels, a sail plan that approximated at least to jury rig in area was an essential business precaution. Engine break-down was far more likely than dismasting. Such a rig was also a very useful 'flopper stopper', a role important before effective bilge keels were developed. It was helpful, too, if in adverse conditions the vessel was forced

to heave to. She had enough sail to lie to the wind like a sailing vessel, and not be dependent on slow-moving engines for survival in a very bad gale.

The problem was threefold. First, such a rig had to combine minimum windage when the vessel was steaming with the wind forward of the beam with a reasonable level of efficiency should it be needed in emergencies. Second, merchant steamships in the 1820s, '30s and '40s were a high-risk investment. With engineers and firemen they needed bigger crews to operate them than sailing vessels. Crew costs had to be reduced as far as possible, but engineers and firemen could not be reduced in numbers with safety, but reduction could be made in the number of seamen if labour-saving simplified rigs were developed. Moreover, reduction in the amount of rigging aloft meant reduction in windage. The necessity for large crews of highly skilled men could be reduced not only by simplifying the traditional rigging but also by eliminating as far as possible the necessity for working aloft when setting and taking in sail and on maintenance work. It was highly desirable that as far as possible sail should be set from the deck, and that there should be no topgallant masts to house in contrary winds and bad weather, but only topmasts, and that these should be so rigged that they could be housed from the decks with the minimum of manpower. Yards, with all their attendant rigging and the consequent windage, and the labour required to handle the halliards, buntlines and clewlines and the necessity to send perhaps two watches aloft to pass the gaskets and stow and make fast squaresails, had as far as possible to be eliminated. Moreover, the long, narrow, often relatively shallow draught hull forms of paddle steamers were not suited to much top-hamper – that is, the weight and windage presented by the traditional square rigs.[3] Yet it was the squaresails which were the most valuable at the only time when sail was of much use to a fully powered steamer in the course of normal operations as

opposed to emergencies, that is when she was steaming more than four points from the wind.

This last statement takes us straight to the third highly complex question in the rigging of early steamers. If the vessel had to have a rig for marketing purposes and against emergencies, could the power of the wind be used through the sails under some conditions at sea to provide driving force and thus reduce the load on the engines and, in consequence, reduce fuel consumption, with the consequent commercial benefit and advantage in increasing the steaming range for naval vessels? It must always be remembered in considering the operation of merchant ships that their sole *raison d'être* is to make money for those who own them and that their merits and demerits can be judged only against that standard. Early steamships were a high-risk investment, made often in the light of the judgement that although there might be a short term loss the long term gains might be considerable as the technology developed and those well established in the field had the advantage. Could advantage be derived from the unavoidable investment in masts, spars and rigging sails, and in the cost of their maintenance, by using them at times to reduce fuel costs on a passage at sea?

The deck and engine room logs of the first transatlantic round voyage of the *Great Western* in 1838 were printed together, day by day, and published in Bristol in the same year.[4] They give a complete and invaluable picture of the handling of the vessel. She was a full powered steamship and was operated as such, steaming all the time, following the shortest possible course from port to port and setting sails only when advantageous to progress.

When steaming in a fresh-to-strong head wind and sea, topmasts were housed, yards and gaffs

3. For a near contemporary discussion of these problems see E P Halstead, *The Screw Fleet of the Navy* (London 1850), especially p37.

4. Christopher Claxton, *The Logs of the First Voyage made with the Unceasing Aid of Steam between England and America by the Great Western of Bristol* (Bristol 1838).

sent down. If the head wind was not strong the sails were stowed and the yards braced up sharp. There was constant sail handling when the wind was more than four points off the bow – every effort was made to derive maximum advantage from it and so to reduce fuel consumption. The engineers took a constant interest in the sail set and recorded it in their log. Thus, on 11 April 1838, at one point the wind was light and variable, no sail was set, at 720 revolutions per hour the vessel was proceeding at 9 knots with the engine control cam set at 0 (dictating the cut-off of steam; see page 20). Later in the day with the same sea conditions but with a fine steady breeze on the quarter, the gaff lowers and the fore topgallant were set, the revolutions were still 720, the speed 10 knots and the cam setting the considerably lower 7. Thus power and coal consumption were reduced.

The entries for 21 April give a picture of an important use of canvas in a paddle steamer. The vessel, having consumed approximately 400 tons of coal, had a reduced draught. The wind was on the beam, Force 5, and the leeward paddle, more deeply immersed by the heel, had an increased turning effect. Efforts were made to reduce the heel, thus '... at 7, ship carrying weather helm, shifted the chain over to windward'. All the while the predominance of canvas set was forward of amidships to try to balance

the vessel and reduce the weather helm – the tendency of the vessel constantly to turn up into the wind. The vessel would have been very difficult to manage without her sail-assist.

From historical evidence it can be seen that the pioneer merchant steamship owners, builders and engineers showed quite remarkable skill, adaptability and enterprise in this matter of the rigging of their vessels. They were ready immediately to break away from the enormously strong influences of sailing ship technology. The requirements of sail-assist were logically met by the adaptation and development of the schooner rig. This may now seem obvious, but it must be remembered, once again, that in the 1830s, apart from a very few three-masted vessels, the schooner was by definition small and two-masted. The object was to reduce the deck crew to the minimum and there was no steam on deck.[5] So the gaffs were made standing, the sails brailing up to the throat (as in the *Great Western*) or to the weather, further reducing windage and lowering the centre of gravity aloft (as in *The Great Britain*). Topmasts could be housed from the deck, gaff topsails were set flying from the deck and not stowed aloft. From an early date there was liberal use of iron wire for shrouds, backstays, forestays, etc, which offered less windage, stretched only slightly and required far less attention in setting up with the deadeyes and

The Great Britain struck by a heavy sea on 24 January 1845 during her trials in the Bristol Channel. The lithograph is based on a painting by J Walter, who was on board at the time so presumably depicts accurately the canvas carried by the ship during the gale. (SS Great Britain Project)

lanyards which, because the rigging screw or turnbuckle was not yet on the market, were the only way of tensioning the rigging. It looks at the present state of research as if the four-masted schooner was 'invented' by whoever was responsible for the rigging of the *Great Western*. Certainly *The Great Britain* was the world's first six-masted schooner and certainly her spar and sail plan and her rigging were the most sophisticated and weatherly ever to have been fitted to a vessel, and far more sophisticated than the rigging of the four-, five-, and six-masted schooners built in the United States in the later

---

5. The date at which the first donkey engines appeared is uncertain. The low steam pressures used in the early merchant steamships precluded the use of deck machinery supplied from the main boilers. Units with their own boilers of perhaps locomotive type do not seem to have been thought of, even by Brunel in *The Great Britain*, perhaps because of the fear of boiler explosions as these engines worked at relatively high pressures. The four-, five-, and six-masted schooners built in the United States and Canada in the late nineteenth and early twentieth centuries with their hoisting gaff sails were entirely dependent on the steam or gasoline hoister and the use of lazy jacks.

years of the century and the early years of the twentieth. It seems quite likely that Thomas Guppy, a member of *The Great Britain*'s 'design team' who as early as 1824 had patented a bipod mast design may, working under Brunel, have been the main instigator of this revolutionary rig. This was an engineer's rig, which perhaps even took account of Brunel's experience as a builder of bridges, made possible by the use of low-stretch iron-wire rigging. It was the product of open minds approaching new problems rationally and using new materials, rather than remaining influenced by the enormously strong traditions of wood and hemp sailing technology, which had evolved in different situations for different purposes.[6]

The after four masts were stepped on deck, the heel retained by a large pin in a lug-type fitting, allowing the masts to have movement fore and aft with less stress on the hull, just like most modern yachts. (Virtually all seagoing vessels of the period had their masts stepped through the deck on the keelson). Hemp rigging which can stretch considerably could not be used to hold those tall masts up; iron wire was therefore essential for the shrouds and stays, *The Great Britain* being one of the first vessels to use this material. The stepping of the masts on deck and the use of iron wire must have astounded the seamen of the day, who would view such innovations with the utmost suspicion. Each mast, except for the topmast forestays, was independently stayed, so a forestay failure on one might not result in complete dismasting. This was much better than the system used in the much later multi-masted American schooners, in which the masts were joined together with a spring or jump stay at the lowermast cap. If this stay or the forestay parted, the vessel was dismasted, as happened to the first five-master, the *Gov. Ames*, on her maiden voyage. A wooden vessel will move considerably in a seaway, bending and twisting. As a vessel goes over a large wave and is only supported at the centre, the bow and stern will tend to bend downwards in a hogging action. One can see that this has the effect of applying great tension to the spring stays, which are trying to resist the motion and are then subjected to far greater strain than that induced at any time by the sails.

Several important features of the rig of *The Great Britain* are shown in the illustration (page

148). Unlike, for example, the spanker on a steel barque with a fixed length peak span, these gaffs could be topped up or lowered to pass from one side to the other under the topmast forestays when in the housed position (the topmasts were only sent up if a topsail was to be set). The sails were boomless and thus the clew could overlap the next mast aft, similar to the modern genoa, and we believe were sheeted in a similar manner using the two after-deck capstans. The ability to peak up the gaff for windward work and this overlap made the sails very efficient on this point of sailing. With a following wind the sails were less effective as she steamed all the time; a breeze of 20kts from right aft would only appear as 10kts if the vessel was travelling at that speed. Nevertheless, the lack of a boom on these gaff sails was no real disadvantage as the vessel had a beam on deck of 40ft, which was about the same distance between each mast, providing a very wide sheet base, and of course she was provided with a main course and topsail.

These gaff sails brailed into the mast, the head supported by hoops over the spar and controlled by a head inhaul and outhaul. It would be possible for two men to set the sail in moderate weather. First the gaff would be trimmed with the vangs to the desired angle athwartships and topped up as required, then the brails cast off and the clew heaved out with the capstan, the head inhaul let go then the outhaul heaved out, taking the head of the sail out along the gaff. The largest of these sails was close on 2000sq ft

and made of heavy flax. It would have been a long and arduous job to hoist a wet flax canvas sail of this size with the small deck crew it was good business to carry, in addition to the engineers and firemen.

The forestays, which were rigged from the hounds to the heel pivot pin of the next mast ahead (except the forestay leading down to the mainmast) appear to be in the way, when tacking. In practice no 'short tacking' would be necessary, as entering or leaving port would be under power, and, when on passage, whenever there was a change of course or wind shift which required the gaff sails to be got over to the other side, they would be temporarily brailed in and then re-set. *The Great Britain* followed fully powered steamer courses. She would not be diverted from such courses to increase the assistance derived from the sails.

The illustration is very interesting as it depicts a particular incident in the Bristol Channel when she was outward bound, and struck by a heavy sea which resulted in slight damage. Extracts from the log book at the time state that a fresh NW gale was blowing, and the tide on the ebb, causing a very rough sea. One headsail and two of the gaff sails are shown set, the vessel being under power, and one must assume accuracy in these details, as the artist, J Walter, was on

6. For a detailed examination and analysis of *The Great Britain*'s rig see B Greenhill and P Allington, 'The SS *Great Britain* as The World's First Six-Masted Schooner', *Maritime Wales* No 9 (Caernarvon 1985), pp84–109.

As late as 1874 the White Star liner Germanic *was rigged as a four-masted barque with a brailing gaff sail in place of the mizzen course. Although her twin compound engines gave her a speed of 16kts under power alone, her sail-assist was much used. In this deck view she has the wind on her starboard quarter. (CMP)*

board at the time. In the circumstances, the apparent wind must have been around 50kts and the strain on the gear tremendous, especially the load on the sheets. Why were these sails not reefed? A close examination reveals reef points on the sails. It is probable that these were drawn in by the artist, or perhaps added later by the engraver, along with the incorrect lead of the brails. In either case, the radical nature of the rig was not understood by the artists. Furthermore, no mention is made in the log book of reefing these gaff sails, only the two squaresails, for it would appear impossible if the gaff could not be lowered at the throat. There is mention however of bonnets being used with the gaff sails.

There can be no doubt that the sailors on board must have taken a dim view of carrying on in that weather, without reducing the sail area, so used were they to not only reefing sail, but spars as well – the gear must have been very strong indeed. This point emphasises the prime disadvantage with the standing gaff that is permanently carried aloft: one could only reef the sail in so far as the crew could reach upwards from the deck to tie the reef points. In the case of *The Great Britain*, and in many other large vessels built later that had several masts carrying standing gaff sails, so long as the gear was strong

Cunard's Catalonia *arriving at Boston during the late 1880s. The ship's exiguous barque rig has obviously been put to good use for the crew are on the yards stowing the square canvas in the bunt in the manner of the late nineteenth century.* (CMP)

they did not have to reef individual sails, only set those that balanced the vessel and gave some assistance to the engine.

The employment of sail-assist rigs

Given that the early merchant steamships and the smaller, fully powered, naval paddle vessels which had a restricted range of operation had to be equipped with a limited sail plan for use in emergencies and as a marketing factor, how were the sails actually used? Given that their investment cost was justified by the two purposes mentioned, could a bonus be derived from their use as 'sail-assist'? This is a highly complex subject and its proper resolution awaits detailed analysis from this aspect of the surviving log material of a number of vessels.

The question has a very modern ring. At times of crisis over the price of oil in the 1970s (between 1973 and 1980 marine diesel fuel increased nearly ninefold in cost) a great deal of scientific work was done on this very problem and a considerable body of theoretical knowledge built up, notably in the Hamburg Institut Für Schiffbau. Some of this material has been published in English – see Bibliography. There have been several conferences at which the nostalgia of sail sentimentalists for a world that never was (there is no conceivable way in which the working conditions normal on board merchant sailing vessels in the nineteenth and early twentieth centuries could be accepted in modern

Western Europe or North America, indeed they would be illegal) has mingled with the hard facts of engineering, aerodynamics, and the economics of merchant ship operation. The advantages of 'sail-assist', as the jargon of the period had it, were not at the time sufficiently certain to encourage even one order for a new vessel to be built, but in the early 1980s a number of practical experiments were carried out with existing tonnage. A small Japanese motorship, the *Shin Aitoku Maru*, launched in 1980, was equipped with two mechanically set and furled sails, designed to be used with the wind abaft the beam, and her operation during the next three years showed fuel costs savings significantly greater than the investment cost in the rig. The experiment with the *Shin Aitoku Maru* led to the equipping of the new 31,000-ton bulk carrier *Aqua City* with two computer-controlled rigid sail structures in 1984. A fuel cost saving of 10 per cent is reported to have followed. Danish and American experiments with mechanically controlled sails in existing vessels showed similar results.

Because world oil prices fell, there was no commercial incentive at the time to carry the matter of sail-assist for merchant vessels any further, except in one field of operations – the cruise business in limited areas of reasonably predictable weather. Here the search for a marketing edge in a highly competitive business led an Åland Finn, Karl Andren, a New York resident but heir to the traditions of Åland seafaring

as expressed in the big merchant sailing vessels that the community continued to operate until the middle years of the twentieth century,[7] to initiate the building of a sail-assisted diesel electric cruise vessel. She was designed specifically for a carefully researched slice of the cruise market and equipped with a four-masted staysail schooner rig fully computerised and entirely electronically and mechanically set, taken in, and matched to conditions of wind and sea (sail is automatically reduced if the heel of the vessel with the wind on or forward of the beam exceeds the 8 degrees which market research has shown to be the acceptable limit to the average passenger in the section of the market towards which the vessel is aimed). The vessel, named *Wind Star*, was successful, and there is now a small fleet of sail-assisted vessels operating in the Caribbean and the Mediterranean.

We have already seen some evidence as to the method of employing sail-assist from the log of the first Atlantic passage of the *Great Western*. It seems likely that *The Great Britain* was designed to operate principally with her topmasts housed (her topmasts and the gaff topsails which were set flying being used under conditions when studdingsails might be set: that is, with a strong wind abaft the beam), and that her lowers (or some of them) and squaresails were set to assist propulsion in any breeze more than four points off the bow that gave the vessel greater speed through the water than that at which her engine alone could drive her. There is a good deal of iconographic evidence, contemporary watercolours, paintings and lithographs, in other respects reasonably accurate, which show early schooner rigged merchant steam vessels steaming and sailing with sheets well in and foretopsail yards braced to take the wind forward of the beam. But, as everyone who has motor-sailed a yacht to windward knows, the greater the vessel's forward speed, the apparent (and, for sailing purposes, the effective) wind (as opposed to the true wind when the vessel is stationary) shifts finer on the bow.[8] This means that the vessel must be allowed to fall off a little and she does not point so well to windward as under sail alone, but, because of the power, she covers the ground more quickly and the resultant passage time, although she sails further, may be shorter than would be possible under sail alone. On the other hand the fore and aft sails may be sheeted home even harder while the vessel's heading is maintained to compensate for the apparent wind now being finer on the bow. The sails will now be less effective but nonetheless they will still assist the vessel to windward. In fact for all practical purposes she could not point higher than 4 points (45 degrees) from the true wind – and much

would depend on the state of the sea: if there was any sea running the vessel would have to be allowed to fall off.

Fully powered steamships like the *Great Western* and *The Great Britain* maintained steamship courses and used the wind when they could on these courses. A good illustration of this is provided by Cunningham.[9] He records:

In a conversation with Commander Tryon, of the *Warrior*, he related to me a circumstance of how, when once in that ship they were steaming against the strong head-wind and doing very little, she kept away sufficiently to allow the trysails to take; and he described it as being quite marvellous how instantly the ship was affected by it, how she sprang ahead directly she felt the canvas, at once increasing her speed several knots.

The use of sail in a low-powered vessel seeking to get to windward was to enable her to shorten her passage time by moving through the water more quickly, even though she could not make up so well on her course to windward. Conversely, the use of power in an under-canvassed vessel in similar circumstances to windward had the same effect. The two agencies worked together. These facts perhaps can help to explain the survival of the motor schooner in commercial use in parts of Europe until the middle of the twentieth century. In under-developed societies, deficient in capital and with low labour costs and low living standards, she remained economically viable.

Captain Søren Thirslund, a Master Mariner with great experience in the Greenland trade in the early years of this century when sailing vessels with steam or diesel engines were employed in the business, wrote of their handling,

I know a little about the difference it makes if you have a topsail schooner with and without an engine. I will describe a couple of examples: 1) You are running before a strong wind. You have power only for 3 to 4kts. With this fair wind, you may stop your engine and save fuel, and she will be running at almost the same speed. 2) The wind turns abeam on your course. Still good for sailing without a motor, but many would in this condition have the motor running, as it would on this course give a little extra speed. 3) Now comes the situation where the wind is directly from your destination. With a very low wind force, you may take in all sails and steam ahead with your 3 to 4kts, but with some wind force, say 3 to 4 Beaufort, you will stop completely. Then – up all sails and keep the motor running while you go 'Full

The Danish Greenland trader Svaerdfisken *in the 1930s demonstrating conditions under which it was advantageous to use both sail and power. Despite the sails on her fore mast she is technically a schooner because the mast is in only two parts.* (Captain Soren Thirslund)

and bye'. Now you would see the difference, if you stopped your motor. Her leeway will increase, and then your course in the water will be about 7 points from the wind. I am sure you would have six points in the water, if you kept the motor running. And another thing: When you are going to tack. Within normal wind forces, you will always get her on the other tack with the propeller jet on the rudder. No problem at all. Now let me describe the terrible situation, where you are in the gale force wind and on a lee shore. Without an auxiliary, you are stuck. With the engine running, you will be able to get the vessel through the wind and probably even get her moving away from the shore. Think of the enormous reduction in strandings after the introduction of auxiliary motors.[10]

7. For detailed accounts of the Åland community and its development through the use of sailing vessels into a prosperous centre of modern shipowning see B Greenhill and J Hackman, *The Grain Races* (London 1986) and *Herzogin Cecilie* (London 1991).

8. This is because the apparent wind experienced by a vessel under way is a resultant of the true wind speed and direction, and the vessel's speed and heading relative to it. The faster the vessel is moving the stronger the latter component will be and therefore the finer the resultant, or apparent, wind will be on the bow.

In simple terms, if a car is standing still with a wind of 20mph at right angles on its left side a flag on the bonnet placed to be free of local turbulence will blow out to the right at right angles to the fore and aft line of the car. If the driver accelerates to 20mph the flag will blow at 45 degrees to the right, thus indicating the apparent wind acting upon the car. As the speed is increased so the flag will move nearer to the fore and aft line of the car, but, even at 200mph, it will still (theoretically) never lie exactly on that line.

9. H Cunningham, 'On the Rig of Sails of Steamships of War', *Transactions of The Institution of Naval Architects* (March 1862), p105.

10. Communication to authors, 18 September 1991.

Sail assist and the navy

To steam and sail to windward with well designed and weatherly, if somewhat exiguous, schooner rig and relatively high power was one thing. To do the same thing in a square rigged vessel was quite another. A square rigged vessel's lack of weatherliness effectively meant that she could not motor-sail to windward, because the yards on a traditionally rigged vessel could not be braced far enough round to make use of the apparent wind which shifts further ahead as soon as she begins steaming. Her normal best performance of about 60 degrees to the true wind became 90 degrees at the best when steaming and sailing fast. This fact alone goes far to account for the merchant shipping industry's lack of interest in the auxiliary screw to which Andrew Lambert refers in Chapter 7 and for the fact that the steam auxiliary square rigged merchant ship remained a great rarity, confined to a very few special trades, such as that to Australia via the Cape of Good Hope and back around Cape Horn. In this trade the wind was usually abaft the beam, hence *The Great Britain*'s success as an auxiliary steamer in this business. Steam auxiliary square rigged vessels were also used in whaling and sealing, which involved work in the ice. And, of course, there were other powerful factors operating against the square rigged auxiliary merchant ship to which reference has already been made – investment cost, the loss of cargo space, the cost of additional skilled crew. None of these factors could be balanced in terms of earning power against any attributable financial gains. Moreover, if she could not steam-and-sail to windward she certainly could not get very far to windward under steam alone. The huge windage presented by the traditional square riggers precluded this, and any reduction meant sending down topgallants and even topmasts and yards. Although prime seamen of the mid nineteenth century found this no problem, it was a big job for the relatively small crew of a merchant vessel and could not be undertaken whenever she met a headwind.

For the navy the situation was quite different. The naval requirement, it will be remembered, was for worldwide sailing range. This meant, in the mid nineteenth century, the use of traditional square riggers. As we have also seen, increasingly in the late 1830s and '40s, the bigger paddle vessels were required to perform duties which took them further and further afield. In the mid 1840s the paddle sloop *Driver* became the first steam-assisted vessel to encircle the globe. She made her voyage mainly under sail and took several years over it in the course of a long commission. The next vessel to perform this feat was the paddle frigate *Inflexible*, which also took three years between August 1846 and September 1849 on her commission. She made most of her long passages under steam and sail.

The main problem for the navy was the drag presented by the square rigger when the course was to windward. For reasons explained above the vessels could not efficiently 'motor-sail', steam-and-sail, to windward. The navy however carried big crews based on the broadside gun crews for half the battery and therefore had plenty of manpower available for the complex task of sending down topgallants and even topmasts and yards. Murray reports the effects of reefing the top-hamper.[11]

All the vessels he refers to were paddle propelled.

Performance of steamers in the Royal Navy – with and without steam. In evidence before the Committee of the House of Commons, on the subject of arming the Mercantile Steam Marine, Capt Henderson, of the *Sidon*, declares his ship to be 'the best steam vessel he ever saw; she could take 700 tons of coals, which would last 20 days at full speed. She is rigged as a barque, and spreads as much canvas as a 32-gun frigate – more than any other steamer he ever saw. In cruising without steam, she kept company with the *Canopus* line-of-battle ship. Has never tried the *Sidon* with merchant steamers, but has had 12½ knots with 300 tons of coals. The *Odin* is about equal to the *Sidon*. Merchant steamers with their present masts and yards would be unable to keep up with a fleet without steaming. The masts of vessels in the navy prevent them steaming so well; but there is a great economy resulting from it, because they frequently sail for months without steaming at all. If a merchant steamer could perform 10 knots with sail alone, she would be able to accompany a fleet on ordinary occasions. Whilst commanding the *Gorgon*, found that in steaming head to wind, with all the masts and yards up, it might make two to three knots difference if they were struck. [In this paragraph Murray has made very clear the distinction between the merchant steamships' small 'sail-assist' rig and the naval vessels' full traditional square rig]...

A high speed in the Navy attainable only by an Extravagant Proportion of Horse Power to Tonnage. The three vessels last named (which we have already particularised) are probably the fastest war steamers, properly so called, in the Royal Navy; but it is apparent that their comparatively high speed has been obtained only by the use of an extravagant proportion of power to tonnage, such as is very rarely found in ocean steamers in the merchant service. The average speed of government steamers, when using their full power, not exceeding 8 to 8½ knots.

Comparisons between the Performance of Government and Merchant Steamers are generally imperfect. This comparatively low result has given rise to many unjust comparisons between the performances of government and merchant steamers; for when we consider the peculiar qualifications demanded by a vessel of war, it

11. R Murray, *A Rudimentary Treatise on Marine Engines and Steam Vessels* (London 1852), pp157-163.

The steam auxiliary square rigged merchant vessel was a rarity, for reasons explained in this chapter, and confined to such trades as that to Australia in which the wind was predominantly abaft the beam. The Durham *was built for this trade in 1874, but after only eight years was converted to a pure sailing vessel. (Basil Greenhill Collection)*

The steam auxiliary square rigged vessel was used in the sealing industry – which involved work in the ice pack – until the 1940s. This photograph shows part of the Newfoundland fleet at work during the 1930s. (Public Archives of Canada)

Time under one boiler	76¾ hours
Time under two boilers	4047 hours
Time under three boilers	3324¼ hours
Time under four boilers	844 hours
Total	8292 hours

Her fires have been lighted 483 days. Total consumption of coals while under steam, 8121 tons 12¾ cwt, coals expended in raising steam and banking the fires, 567 tons 16¾ cwt, average distance steamed per ton of coals, 7.938 knots. Consumption of coals per hour, 19.588 cwt, ditto per day, 23 tons, 10 cwt, 12½ lbs; average consumption of coals per nominal horse power per hour, 5.85lbs.

It is stated that the above-mentioned distances were obtained by the patent log, towed about 50 fathoms astern, out of the influence of the backwater from the wheels; the error arising from this cause, while throwing the common or hand-log, having been found on board the *Inflexible* to vary from one to four knots. It is recommended, therefore, that the patent log only should be used by a steam vessel, its results being verified by the bearings of the land, when the distances are known.

The expenditure of coal was taken by measuring every tenth bag in the ship, and every tenth bag as used by the fires, a mean being taken every four hours for the hourly expenditure.

Performance of the Inflexible. The distance accomplished by the *Inflexible* is stated to have been reckoned only from the time the patent log was thrown overboard, and when the final departure from the land was taken. It is further stated that she was employed for 15 months on the coast of New Zealand, during which time about 4000 tons of the Newcastle Australian coal were consumed, the best quality of which, delivered at the mines, is about ten per cent inferior to good English coal, but rendered fully 25 per cent inferior by being exposed on the open beach at New Zealand. A deduction should, therefore, be made for this circumstance in considering the expenditure of fuel.

On the outward voyage of the *Inflexible* to the Cape of Good Hope, in the months of August and September 1846, a run of 5502 nautical miles was accomplished on a single coaling, at a mean average speed of 7.31 knots per hour, and an average daily expenditure of

will be seen that the comparison cannot be made on equal terms. War steamers are built not only to steam but to sail well; and moreover they must be able to carry a great weight of armament on the upper deck without prejudice to their stability, and since the only effectual way of doing this is by giving them a greater relative breadth than merchant steamers are limited to, the consequence is that the hull opposes an increased resistance to the water, and the speed is diminished. Then the weight of hull and equipment of a war steamer is usually much greater than in the merchant service, causing a corresponding increase of displacement: the masts, yards and rigging, being of greater dimensions, oppose a greater resisting surface to the air: and owing to the weight of the large guns at the extremities of the vessel demanding support from the upward pressure of the water, the lines at the bow and stern cannot be made so fine as might otherwise be desirable. Hence it follows, that the speed of the contract mail steamers, for instance, averages from one to one and a half knots above that of vessels in the navy, with a similar proportion of power to tonnage; but if the proportion of horse power to displacement be taken, the comparison will generally become more favourable to the war steamer.

Economy of Steam Power the best Criterion of Efficiency in the Navy. In estimating the performance of a government steam vessel, therefore, we should look rather to the direct distance run by the combined action of steam and sails, at a moderate but uninterrupted speed, and with a low rate of consumption of steam and fuel, than to the attainment of a high velocity which is seldom wanted in war steamers. The best exposition we can offer of the practical working of this combined system of steaming and sailing in the navy, has been supplied by Capt Hoseason, in his account of the performance of the steam sloop *Inflexible*.

Performance of the Inflexible *in a Steam Voyage round the World.* This vessel, designed by Sir W Symonds, is of 1122 tons burthen, and 378 horses power. The engines are direct-action, by Fawcett, and the boilers are loaded to 8lbs on the square inch. The whole distance run (without counting going in and out of harbour) during the time she was in commission, from the 9th of August 1846, to the 28th of September 1849, was as follows:-

Steamed	64,477 nautical miles.
Sailed	4,392 nautical miles.
	68,869

Number of days under steam	345½
Number of days under sail alone	27¼
	372¾

Average daily steaming	186.62 knots
Average dailing sailing	161.18 knots
For the whole period	57.44 knots

12 tons, 19 cwt, 3 qrs, 14 lbs. This run was accomplished in 32 days.

On the voyage from the Cape of Good Hope to Port Jackson, Sydney, 5356 nautical miles were accomplished at one coaling, with an expenditure of 458 tons 10 cwt, being at the rate of 15 tons, 3 cwt 2 qrs per diem, and with a mean average speed of 7.87 knots per hour. Time taken, 30½ days. ...

After service on the coasts of India and China, the *Inflexible* returned to England by Cape Horn, thus making the circuit of the globe, and fulfilling her comprehensive mission in a manner most creditable to her able commander, Captain Hoseason.

Economy of a Moderate Proportion of Horse-power in combination with the Sails. These results show, in a most favourable light, the economy of a moderate proportion of horse-power in combination with the judicious use of the sails; and it is a question of much interest to the navy whether a better average result might not be expected and obtained from such a system, than from the present expensive fashion of loading the vessel with very large engines whose full power is but seldom wanted, and which monopolise so much weight and space that sufficient coals cannot be carried for the proper development of the steam power. It is true, that by the use of a high proportion of power to tonnage the vessel has the advantage of having always a high speed at her command, so long as the coals last; while, by expanding the steam in her large cylinders, she may burn the fuel, on ordinary occasions, most economically, still we must remember the increased first cost of the machinery, and the increase of displacement consequent upon the great extra weight to be constantly carried (whether it be used or not), by which the speed of the vessel is permanently diminished.

Here Murray draws attention to a factor which distinguishes the steam auxiliary from the vessel with a geared diesel. The steam engine was an altogether more flexible source of power. The actual power delivered could be varied while maintaining a constant number of revolutions per minute by manipulating the cut-off point and the expansion of the steam in the cylinders.

As to how windage was reduced in the navy, the accompanying diagrams, reproduced from a manual of 1838, show in detail the process when

This drawing from a naval manual of 1838 shows various stages in the process of altering the canvas set by a schooner rigged paddle steamer with the wind on different bearings.

steaming to windward in a schooner rigged paddle sloop with a great deal of square canvas on her foremast. At 5½ points from the wind the yards on the foremast are braced hard round, at 4 points from the wind all yards are sent down and topmasts housed and the gaff lowers and two headsails set, the jibboom being reeved in. Head to wind she sets no canvas. A square rigged vessel at 4 points to the wind would have sent down her topgallants, furled all square sails, braced the yards hard round to present minimum windage and proceeded under steam, staysails and headsails, taking these in as her course took her closer to the wind.

The illustration shows the screw frigate *Galatea* in this situation, though, because she is maintaining her windward course for only a short time (she is standing in to communicate with the shore), her top-hamper has not been sent down and the yards have not been braced round. Of great interest in this watercolour by Sir Oswald Brierly, whose care in the depiction of detail arose from his experience sailing in several naval screw steamers of the mid nineteenth century, is the fact that the *Galatea* carries three gaff sails set from her lower masts, which make her, in fact, a three-masted schooner inside a full rigged ship. At 4 points to the wind, as illustrat-

HER MAJESTY'S STEAM SHIP, PHŒNIX.

Plate

4 points from the Wind

5¼ points from the Wind

Head to the Wind

Before the Wind

The steam screw frigate Galatea *under fore and main spencers and spanker is effectively a three-masted steam schooner.* (The Medici Society)

ed, if on a prolonged course to windward her topgallant masts with their constituent royal poles and the yards would be sent down, the topsail yards and lower yards braced hard round, and she would proceed as a motor schooner under gaff sails and head sails. The presence of brails disposed in such a way as to indicate that the gaff sails on fore and main lower masts brail to the throat indicates that these are standing

gaffs. At this period these gaff sails would have been called 'spencers'. The gaff sail on the mizzen with its reef points is, of course, both the mizzen of the schooner and the spanker of the ship.

That this schooner-within-a-full-rigged-ship rig evidently developed very early in the history of the steam screw frigates is demonstrated by the lithograph of the first really successful one, the *Arrogant*, which clearly shows standing gaff sails brailed to the throat on each of her three lower masts. This lithograph is also important

for another reason. The *Arrogant* is steaming at about 5kts. Having altered course to enter Portsmouth, thus bringing the right wind finer on the bow, she is now taking in sail and steaming at about 5 points from the wind, but her square topsails, braced hard round, are full and drawing nicely, which suggests, perhaps, that they are stood off from the masts with some kind of crane as in a steel masted vessel,[12] rather than the hinged parral and truss batten, or even rope parral – it is to be remembered that at this period Dana defined a parral as 'the rope by which a yard is confined to a mast at its centre'. It could be, therefore, that just as the development of the multi-masted schooner seems to have been the product of the need for sail-assist for fully powered steamers, so the origin of the mast crane, which made the square rigged vessels of the later nineteenth century more weatherly than their predecessors, may have rested in the need to improve the windward performance under sail and power of the steam-assisted square rigged vessels of the navy.

Dr Basil Greenhill and Peter Allington

12. See, for instance, H Underhill, *Masting and Rigging*, (Glasgow 1946), p58 and 96.

The steam screw frigate HMS Arrogant *entering Portsmouth.* (Parker Gallery)

9

Alfred Holt and the Compound Engine

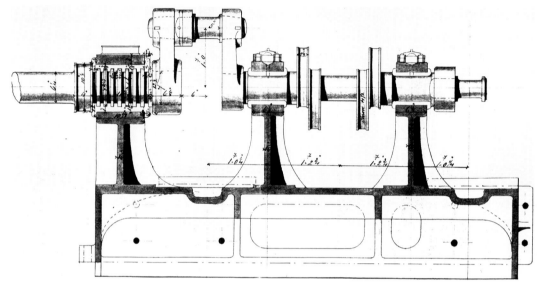

THE benefits in thermal efficiency arising from the use of higher pressure steam worked expansively had been well known since Richard Trevithick and his Cornish colleagues threw off the 'dead hand of Watt', and by 1845 the best Cornish pumping engines had achieved double the efficiency Watt had calculated as the theoretical maximum in a perfect machine. Jonathan Hornblower and Arthur Woolf had taken the further step of carrying out the expansion as a two-stage process in separate high- and low-pressure cylinders. The

Holt's own drawing for the boilers of Cleator. *Although Holt used the locomotive boiler as an argument for higher pressures at sea, he never actually employed it, although this design is obviously a close relative. Compared with locomotive boilers of the 1830s and '40s, which worked at similar pressures, the staying as shown is rather economical. (Merseyside Maritime Museum)*

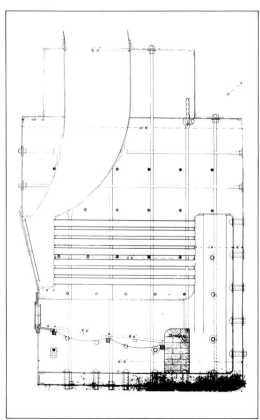

principle of the compound engine, and its practical application as an industrial prime mover, were well established by 1850.

At sea, the story was different, thanks largely to the inherently greater safety and maintenance requirements of marine boilers, and the resulting limitation of pressures to about 20psi meant that the benefits of compounding were long denied to the marine engineer. Few vessels of the mid 1850s could better a fuel consumption of 4lb per ihp (indicated horsepower) per hour. This miserable performance must have been intensely frustrating, for not only did it fail to bear comparison with what was happening ashore, but it was perpetuated by outside forces, namely the Board of Trade, at exactly the time when the new science of thermodynamics was reaching maturity. The presence of W J Macquorn Rankine[1] at the University of Glasgow, and the publication of his very widely used textbook *The Steam Engine and other Prime Movers* meant that marine engineers knew not only what they were missing, but could quantify it with some accuracy, and put a price on it.

In 1853, John Elder patented an arrangement of compound engine for use in conjunction with a screw propeller, but this was also something of a false start, for the only way to benefit from

Holt's drawing of the crankshaft, main bearings and bedplate for Cleator. *This was the contract drawing for Rothwell's of Bolton. Despite its slightly ornamental appearance and Holt's engineering training, the scale is often at variance with the marked dimensions. No contemporary explanation of the curious two-piece crankpin has been found: it does not appear to offer any advantage for maintenance purposes, but does provide an extra fastening which could work loose. (Merseyside Maritime Museum)*

compounding at low pressure was by the application of a considerable degree of superheat. That was exactly the expedient adopted in his *Carnatic* of 1863: although her boilers were pressed only to 26psi, this vessel succeeded in improving substantially on the fuel consumption of the best previous designs with a figure as low as 2lb per ihp hour.[2]

1. W J M Rankine (1820-72) trained and practised as a civil engineer, but became a prominent scientist, and claimed, probably rightly, to achieve a new harmony between theory and practice in a wide range of engineering fields. See D F Channell, 'The Harmony of Theory & Practice: The Engineering Science of W J M Rankine', *Technology & Culture* 23 (1982), pp39-52.

2. Elder was not the only pioneer: Rankine carried out experiments on an engine by Rowan & Co in 1858 which yielded the amazing figure of 1.018lb per ihp hour. F J Rowan, 'On the Introduction of the Compound Engine', *Transactions of the Institution of Engineers & Shipbuilders in Scotland* XXIII (1880), p59.

156

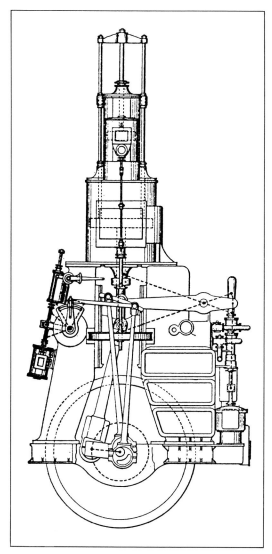

End elevation of the Holt-type tandem compound engine. Much of its layout, notably the large condenser (to the right) mounted both to the bedplate and to the frames, and the small reversing motor to the left are similar to that of side-by-side engines, as is the rocking lever for the condenser air pump (extreme right). This and the following drawings are from the 1881 volume of the Proceedings of the Institution of Marine Engineers.

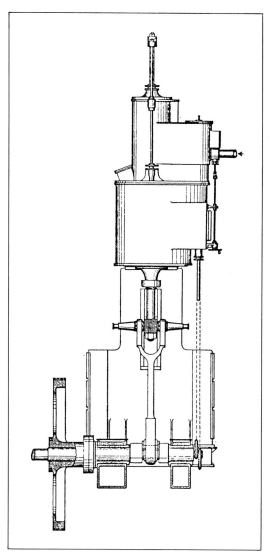

Side elevation of the Holt-type tandem compound engine. The piston rod extensions appear to make the engine taller, but allow a greater angular deflection of a relatively short connecting rod without putting excessive side forces on the pistons and rods, thus allowing the main framing to be both lower and lighter. The flywheel was thought necessary with a single crank layout, but was later discarded.

Soon after the end of his apprenticeship he had set up on his own as a consulting engineer, and within a couple of years was trying his hand at ship management. In this he succeeded well enough to enable him to raise capital for building the first of his own ships. By 1864, both he and his brother Philip had accumulated sufficient capital to be able to invest in fairly large ventures.

John Elder, and plenty of other engineers,

Valve-gear of the Holt tandem compound. A neat, compact arrangement with piston valve to the HP cylinder and slide valve to the LP. But on the early part of the upstroke, the HP is open to live steam at boiler pressure, while the LP is open to the condenser: with only a guidance bush rather than a gland between the two, this was a recipe for waste. Other designs foreswore the advantages of compactness and rigidity of this arrangement in favour of separate cylinder castings with glands between.

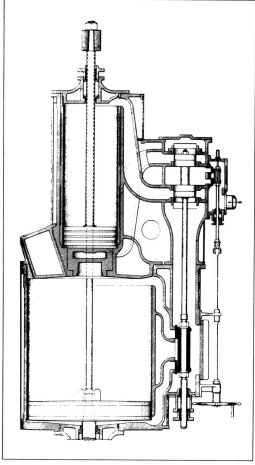

Every writer on the subject of the compound engine has remarked on the financial benefit to the long-haul steamship of the saving in bunker space brought about by these significant economies which freed capacity for paying cargo. Rather fewer have observed, as contemporaries did, that the benefits extended much further, for, other things being equal, shovelling half the quantity of coal required half the number of stokers, half the amount of supervision, half the stokers' accommodation and half their food and stores. These savings were obvious to companies with long-haul routes like Pacific Steam Navigation and P&O, each company building several compound steamers before 1865; but even the comparatively conservative Cunard Line had two compound steamers built in 1868.

By the time Alfred Holt began to experiment with a compound engine in *Cleator* in 1864, compounding was not only well known in principle, but had been successfully applied by two long-haul companies. Yet Holt was responsible for genuine innovation and may be claimed to be the man responsible for the rapid and widespread adoption of the ensemble of screw propeller, compound engine and iron hull of around eight beams' length, which was sometimes referred to as 'Holt Standard'.

Alfred Holt was the third son of George Holt, a substantial merchant with interests in cotton, banking and insurance. Young Alfred was, however, expected to make his own way in the world. He served an apprenticeship under Edward Woods, Chief Engineer of the Liverpool & Manchester Railway, in which he gained a thorough grounding in both civil and mechanical engineering, but to that practical and theoretical knowledge he was able to add considerable entrepreneurial and negotiating skills.

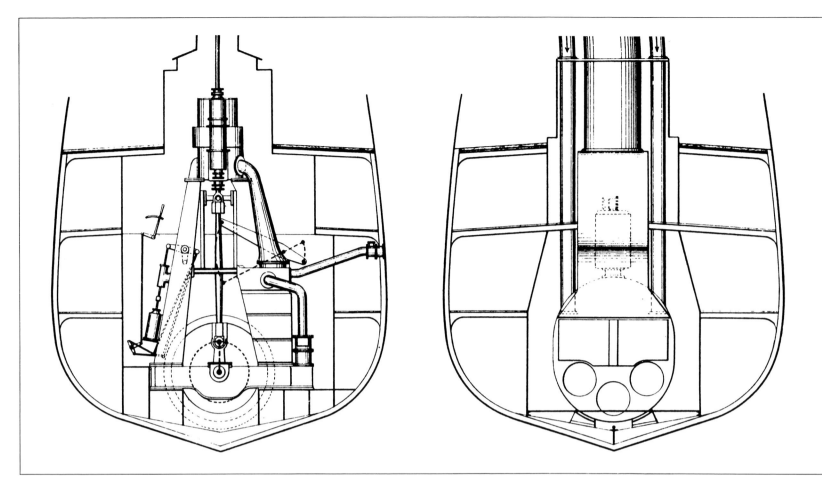

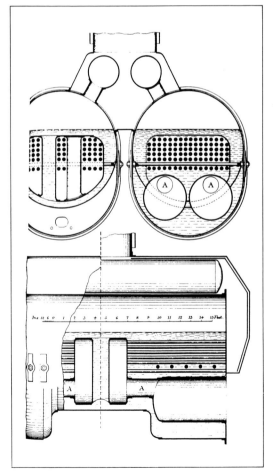

The later-type Holt boiler: it is basically two Cleator *boilers constructed back-to-back, resulting in a saving of space and weight.*

knew that the obstacle to the use of the compound engine at sea was legal rather than technical: under the Merchant Shipping Act 1854, steamships were subject to inspection by the Board of Trade. The Inspectors, and the rules under which they operated, erred on the side of caution, with the result that working pressures which were perfectly acceptable ashore were completely outlawed at sea. The future of

3. Charles Lamport, speaking in the discussion on J D'A Samuda, 'On the Influence of the Suez Canal on Ocean Navigation', *Transactions of the Institution of Naval Architects* XI (1870), pp1-11, at pp9-10. MacFarlane Gray was one of those stalwarts of the engineering institutions who almost invariably contributed in the discussions of papers. He was Chief Examiner of Engineers, Marine Department of the Board of Trade, and had a particular interest in the economy of steam at moderately, rather than very, high pressures. He was therefore an enthusiastic supporter of Holt's ideas.

4. Holt explains some of his views on hull structure in A Holt, 'Review of the Progress of Steam Shipping during the last Quarter of a Century', *Minutes of the Proceedings of the Institution of Civil Engineers* LI (1877-8), pp2-11. The discussion of this paper lasted four nights and extends to p135. See also F E Hyde, *Blue Funnel* (Liverpool 1956), pp165-70 and 172-5.

the compound engine depended on the arrival on the scene of someone who could convince the Board of Trade that pressures of over 25psi were safe at sea. Holt combined the engineering skills to devise a suitable boiler with the powers of persuasion needed to get it accepted, and *Cleator*, the ship he used as a floating test bed, worked at 60psi from the outset. This, of course, gave an immediate head start over anything Elder had built, and after Holt's *Agamemnon*, *Ajax* and *Achilles* entered service in 1866, it was said that: 'the Steamers showing the results (in fact, as Mr MacFarlane Gray stated, better than any he had in any case ever come across) are those of Mr Holt, engaged in the China Trade, by which the saving has been from 23 tons to 14 [per day]'.[3]

Nor had Holt's engineering talents been applied only to the engines and boilers: he had given a great deal of thought to the whole ship and had come up with a hull design which was strong in relation to its weight and cost as well as modest in its power requirements.[4]

Thus far, Holt's achievement places him alongside those engineers who have achieved fame through eclectic inventions whose novelty lay in the successful combination of other people's ideas. We might liken the iron compound screw steamer to the screwcutting lathe. What

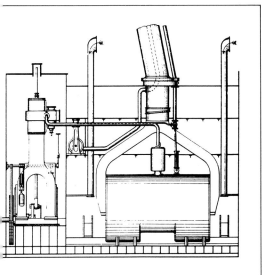

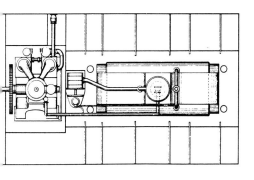

The 'Holt Ensemble'. Plan, longitudinal and transverse sections of a hull with Holt-type machinery. The great merit of it is its shortness, recalling Holt's famous remark that it was the 'part in the middle' (ie the cargo space) which made the money, so that the machinery areas should take up as little of it as possible. The engine is actually a simple single cylinder, which Holt was to advocate later, but the layout and spacing are the same as for the compound machinery.

'Holt Standard': Nestor of 1868, one of the early steamers of Holt's Ocean SS Co, combining an iron hull, screw propeller and compound engines to produce the first commercially viable long range steam cargo carrier. (CMP)

was novel in Maudslay's lathe was that he achieved a classic combination of features which had eluded others in a machine which marked a turning point: so it was with Holt.

There was, however, another significant factor. It is a commonplace to write of a failed engineer that he was ahead of his time: whether such a judgement (or excuse?) can ever be valid is open to question, but what is certain is that successful engineers are almost invariably men who appear at the right time. When some of Holt's contemporaries derided the idea that steamers could succeed in the China Trade, they were guilty of considering the compound steamer only as a machine. Alfred Holt had arrived on cue, for the decisive factor in his success was to be the opening of the Suez Canal in 1869. Towing sailing ships through the Canal was so difficult and expensive as virtually to exclude them. The captain foolish enough to persevere would emerge in the Red Sea, which was 'so unsuited to them that the owners of sailing ships must regard the Canal route as wholly unfit for their use'.[5]

This gave the steamship bound for the Far East a start of several thousand miles. Taken in conjunction with its already superior speed, the steamer's time advantage stretched to about three months on a return voyage. Hyde has questioned whether Holt foresaw such an immense competitive advantage when the decision was first taken to go into the China Trade, but that he later recognised its importance is quite clear: 'the Suez Canal opening the way to the East, "the hour and the man" seemed to have come together.'[6] It is for that reason that attempts to establish John Elder as the father of the compound engine (and Alfred Holt himself freely acknowledged his debt to Elder and others) seem misguided. Some detractors have also suggested that having arrived at a classic ship design, Holt failed to consider the need for continuing improvement, and certainly his very modest projections of future developments in thermal efficiency provided some support for that view. Yet Holt was the man who established the long distance steamer, and it was the complete design, not just the engine or the boiler, which enabled him to do that. Credit is certainly due to Elder, as also to Perkins, but they are forebears rather than fathers. The difference between a good engineer and a great one is often a matter of being there at the right time.

Adrian Jarvis

5. J D'A Samuda, *op cit*, p2.

6. A Holt, op cit, p6.

10

Marine Engineering Development in the Nineteenth Century

THE application of steam power to the propulsion of ships was a gradual matter and had its beginnings in the latter part of the eighteenth century. In America and Europe enthusiastic individuals perceived the advantages to be gained in freeing a ship from the vagaries of wind, but practicalities checked that enthusiasm and early ventures were limited to rivers and canals. Even there the benefits of steam for propulsion were evident, although some schemes were less successful than others.

John Fitch first operated a steamer on the river Delaware during the mid-1780s and several other larger vessels followed later in that decade,

One of the earliest experimental steamers that actually worked was John Fitch's boat that was tried on the river Delaware in 1786. The boat was unique in its propulsion by twelve individual paddles with a system of cranks and levers that allowed the machinery to imitate the action of human paddling motion. This was not as efficient as a conventional paddle wheel, but Fitch later built a larger boat that actually carried passengers at a speed of 5-6kts.

including one which carried passengers. In Britain Patrick Miller and William Symington were also aware of the advantages to be gained by the use of steam plant for propulsive purposes. Collaboration between the two resulted in a small paddle driven steamer which operated on Loch Dalswinton during 1788. Symington subsequently worked alone and in 1801 he fitted an engine in the *Charlotte Dundas* under the patronage of Lord Dundas, after whose daughter the vessel was named. Generally acknowledged as the first practical steamer, *Charlotte Dundas* was put to work towing barges on the Forth and Clyde Canal, her stern paddle wheel being driv-

It is almost impossible to credit any one individual with the 'invention' of the steam vessel, but William Symington's little towboat Charlotte Dundas *of 1801 is often described as the first practical steamboat. In March 1802 on the Forth and Clyde canal the vessel towed two loaded barges of 70 tons each, covering 19.5 miles in six hours. However, while this was a perfectly adequate performance, the canal authorities believed that wash from the paddle would damage the canal banks, negating any advantage from the use of a steam tug. The details of this craft are reasonably well documented and this model may be regarded as essentially accurate. (ScM)*

Robert Fulton had been operating regular services on the Hudson since 1807 but the first steamer to run commercially in Europe was Henry Bell's Comet, *built on the Clyde in 1811-12. The boat was underpowered with only a 4nhp engine and had difficulty stemming wind and tide, but sailed with success until wrecked in 1820. However, the engine was saved and is now on display in London's Science Museum.*

en by a single horizontal cylinder of 22in diameter with a stroke of 48in.[1]

In America and Europe other steam powered vessels were constructed during the early years of the nineteenth century and each provided valuable experience encouraging others to follow the lead. Fulton's *North River Steam Boat* (usually known as *Clermont*) proved to be a success when it commenced operations over long distances on the river Hudson during 1807. In 1812 Henry Bell introduced the steamer *Comet* which plied the waters of the Clyde between Glasgow, Greenock and Helensburgh until wrecked in 1820. *Comet* is recognised as operating the first successful regular passenger service in Europe, but she was rather underpowered and would often be reduced to a crawl even against light winds.

These early steamers were very much 'one-offs' and constructed to the owner's individual specification, but such is the way with all innovations. During the second and third decades of the nineteenth century the number of speculative ventures involving steam navigation increased both in Britain and in America. Enthusiasm for steam power on water was not confined to these two countries, but their extensive coastlines and large numbers of navigable rivers were ideal waters on which powered navigation could flourish. Britain also had the industrial revolution on which to call and it is not surprising that she took the lead in exploiting the power of steam for local, coastal and oceanic vessels. Steam engines for use in mines and factories, as well as on rails, were common features of the British industrial scene during the early 1800s, and the growth in engineering companies producing such machines had been rapid. Modification to suit marine applications had to be undertaken with care and skilful design work was required, but the industrial revolution had

spawned many such entrepreneurial engineers who were ready to answer the call.

Britain's reserves of coal and iron ore gave it the lead in the industrial revolution and that lead in land based engineering was transferred to the sea. Other nations were, naturally, keen to establish a presence on coastal and oceanic waters but the skill of its engineers kept Britain out in front for the whole of the nineteenth century. Ideas and innovation could be found in America, France and Germany but they had much to do in order to make inroads on the British lead, and for many years most European countries came to Britain for the construction of ships — only America tended to stay away, content to develop her own industry. In Europe, nations like France and Germany had little option but to make use of British shipbuilders and marine engineers if they were to take any part in oceanic commerce. However, they were not slow to realise that a nation with maritime aspirations needed its own shipbuilding and marine engineering industry, and whilst they reluctantly went abroad for powered ships they gladly accepted the knowledge that such ships provided.

Paddle wheel propulsion

Every new paddle driven steamer attracted interest, not least in terms of the type of engine installed. For land-based engines each engineering company had developed its own designs to avoid infringement of the many patents then existing, and it followed that variation on these machines would be used for ship propulsion. The firm of Boulton & Watt had an established reputation in the construction of rotative en-

gines as well as mine pumping engines and its products found favour with, amongst others, the Admiralty. In 1815 a scheme was proposed for the steam propulsion of a small wooden vessel to enable it to navigate the river Congo. It was proposed that a Boulton & Watt beam engine should be installed to drive the paddle wheels of the aptly named *Congo*, but the plan was abandoned before construction began.

The engine consisted of a cylinder whose piston connected with one end of an overhead beam, the other end of the beam driving a gear wheel which in turn drove the paddle shaft. Although used for some British river and harbour craft, the engine design was not favoured in the country of its birth but it did find extensive use in America. American practice saw the overhead beam directly connected to the paddle shaft and, because of the height of the engine, the beam could be seen protruding above the upper deck. From the early 1820s this type of engine quickly found favour with American steamer operators, many paddle driven vessels being constructed for duties on the extensive river system. Few paddle steamers were built by American owners for deep sea operations, the sailing packets still being very much in favour for that work. As part of a short lived American steam adventure on the Atlantic during the 1850s the Vanderbilt Line introduced a number of steamers all fitted with overhead, or walking, beam engines, and they must have been an impressive sight as their beams rocked rhythmically whilst paddle wheels thrashed water. Although they were admirably suited to operations in calm river waters, there must have been difficulties in such a drive system on the rough Atlantic; the opening for the beam connecting rods would surely have allowed water to enter the engine room. Services were short lived.

Other American Atlantic paddle steamers of

1. Units employed throughout this chapter are imperial in order to reflect those of the period under consideration. For those who wish to make modern comparisons the following conversions will be useful.

Mass 1lb = 0.4545kg:
Length 1in = 0.0254m = 25.4mm
Power 1hp = 0.764kW:
Pressure 1psi = 6.9kN/m^2 = 0.069bar
Consumption 1lb/hp.hr = 0.339kg/kW.hr
Gross tonnage: 1 gross ton = 100ft^3 = 2.83m^3

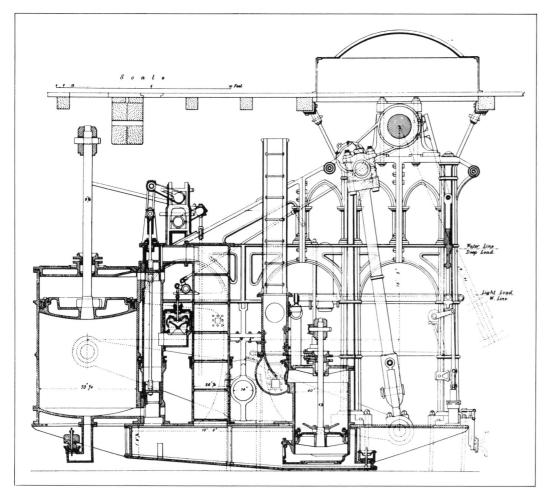

The most common design of machinery for early paddle
steamers was the side lever engine: this longitudinal
section shows the machinery of the pioneer Atlantic
steam packet Great Western. (Denis Griffiths)

these being set at 90 degrees to each other, thus producing an even turning moment for the paddle shaft. In order to ensure that the piston rods moved only in a vertical manner, clever systems of levers, known as parallel motion mechanisms, were employed. Each engine was self contained and included a condenser, air pump and hotwell, as well as the necessary linkages for operating the valve which directed steam to and from the cylinder.

For the early engines steam pressures were only about 5psi above atmospheric pressure and the major portion of work developed resulted from the fact that the opposite side of the piston was subjected to partial vacuum. Steam entering the space above the piston exerted a downwards force, but steam from the space below the piston was directed to the condenser by the slide valve. Condensation of the exhaust steam resulted in a dramatic reduction in pressure, thus the downwards force on the piston was much higher than it would have been had the cylinder exhausted to atmosphere – that is what happens with a railway locomotive, making such machines relatively inefficient. Atmospheric pressure is about 14psi and a steam pressure of 5psi is really 19psi (5+14) in absolute terms, but at most only some 5psi of that pressure can be used if the opposite side of the piston is maintained at a pressure equal to that of the atmosphere. In order to increase the amount of work a piston could devel-

the period adopted the more conventional side lever engine and that was the form into which the Watt beam engine evolved in British practice. Different engine builders applied refinements to the basic design but the essential side lever form remained the same from its introduction in the early 1820s until Cunard's *Scotia* of 1862. The 4570ihp plant installed could propel that 3850-ton ship at 14.5kts but at the cost of a coal consumption in the region of 350 tons per day. However, *Scotia* was the most powerful paddle driven liner ever built and the side lever engine proved itself to be the most suitable for that form of propulsion.

Each side lever engine – there were usually two fitted in a ship – consisted essentially of a double acting cylinder in which the piston worked vertically, the piston rod being attached to a crosshead from where connecting rods projected downwards to the side levers. These were fitted low down on each side of the engine and

rocked about a pivot located towards the engine's mid-length. The other ends of the side levers were connected together and drove a crank on the paddle shaft by means of a connecting rod. Each engine powered a different crank,

Unlike European practice, the Americans preferred overhead – 'walking' – beam engines for most applications. One exception was the Collins Line, whose transatlantic paddlers adopted side lever propulsion. This is a contemporary engraving of the machinery space of the Atlantic *of 1850. (Denis Griffiths)*

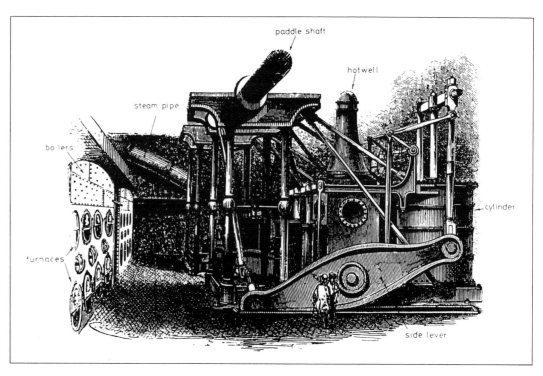

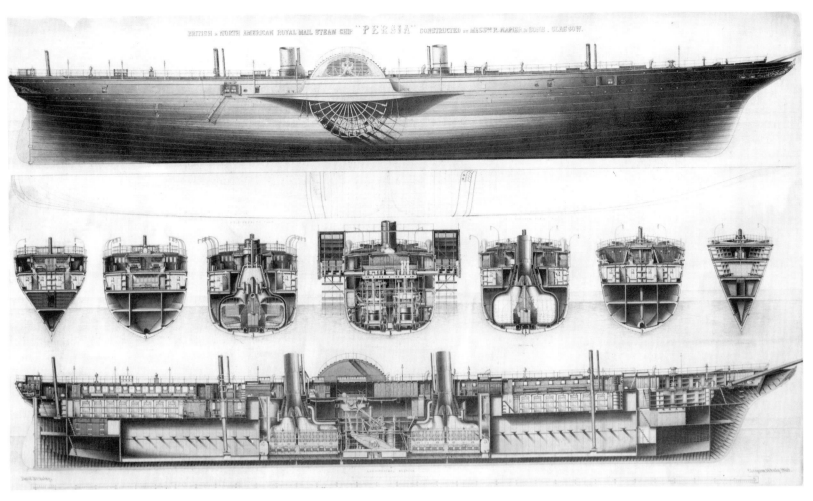

These magnificent lithographs of Cunard's iron paddler Persia, built by Robert Napier in 1856, give a clear view of the machinery layout and details of a crack steamer of the period. The work of Robert Napier's chief draughtsman was so highly regarded that the original drawings were exhibited at the Royal Society. (NMM)

op, and hence make the early steam engine an economical proposition, the opposite, or exhaust, side of the piston to which steam was applied had to be maintained at a very low pressure. By condensing the exhaust or used steam its pressure could be made to drop dramatically and a pressure on the exhaust of the piston side of about 4psi absolute could be achieved with early side lever engines. Most of the work was, therefore, really due to the low exhaust pressure rather than to any real steam pressure. Even in 1862 the steam pressure for *Scotia's* engines was only 25psi.

For almost all side lever engines condensation of steam was brought about by spraying cold seawater into the condenser. As the seawater was heated by the condensing steam dissolved gases were liberated and it was necessary to provide an air pump which removed those gases, together with the mixture of condensed steam and seawater, from the condenser in order to preserve

the partial vacuum. Air pump discharge passed to the hotwell from where the gases vented and warm water was taken for pumping into the boiler as feed. There were certain disadvantages to this arrangement, not least the fact that seawater was pumped into the boiler, resulting in the formation of salt scale. For these early marine steam engines tallow was employed as a lubricant for the cylinder and piston rod where it passed through the gland at the top of the cylinder, so some of that lubricant would flow through to the condenser with the steam. Inevitably some tallow would be pumped from the hotwell into the boiler, where it would break down to form corrosive products.

A solution to these problems lay in the surface condenser as developed by Samuel Hall, this device consisting of a seawater jacket surrounding a condensing bank of small diameter tubes through which exhausting steam flowed. Seawater never came into direct contact with the condensing steam, so the water produced (condensate) remained pure and did not introduce salt into the boiler. A defect of the system lay in the fact that considerable quantities of fresh water had to be kept on board to make up for losses due to leaks or escaping steam; for long voyages that could be difficult. More serious was the fact

that tallow entrapped by the steam solidified in the tubes, resulting in blockage. Two early Atlantic steamers, *Sirius* (1837), the former coastal vessel, and *British Queen* (1839), had side lever engines fitted with surface condensers but the problems outlined above militated against their successful performance.

Air pumps, bilge, boiler feed and assorted other pumps were driven by the engine side levers, thus making this type of engine very much self contained. Brunel's *Great Western* (1837) was provided with a pair of side lever engines constructed by Maudslay, Sons & Field and these had the latest arrangement devised to improve fuel economy. A system of cams allowed steam to be shut off from the cylinder at one of nine points during the piston stroke rather than have it enter the cylinder for the whole of the stroke. Such an arrangement allowed for expansive working of the steam and thus reduced coal consumption; this system probably more than any other made *Great Western* an economical proposition and encouraged the introduction of other steamers on the Atlantic.

Comparison of side lever engines in HMS *Dee* (1832), *Great Western* (1837) and *Scotia* (1862) illustrates the development in scale if not in form, as this type of engine remained very much the same from introduction until it ceased to drive paddle steamers.

	HMS Dee	Great Western	Scotia
Cylinder diameter (in)	54	73.5	100
Piston stroke (in)	60	84	144
Speed (rpm)	18	16	
Power (ihp)	272	750	4570
Steam pressure (psi)	3.5	5	25

Major disadvantages of the side lever engine were weight and length, particularly with respect to the propulsion of coastal and river craft. Heavy engines increased draught, so restricting the depth of water in which the ship could operate, whilst length of engine reduced the space available for cargo. Both were of concern to deep sea operators but the reliability and ruggedness of the side lever engines were more important factors in their continued use for larger deep sea steamers. For smaller vessels alternative forms of paddle drive found favour and many were developed, some being fitted in only one or two steamers before defects in form or operation came to light.

Directly connected engines had obvious advantages but there was a major disadvantage in the arrangement because of restricted hold depth in steamers of the day. Each cylinder was positioned below the paddle shaft but due to the limited space available the connecting rod between crosshead and crank had to be short, resulting in excessive sideways forces being exerted on the crosshead and uneven turning moment on the paddle shaft. In some cases this situation was tolerated as the reductions in weight and length were of paramount importance. A modification to the basic design by the Thames-based engine builders Seaward & Capel allowed the use of a long connecting rod through the elimination of the piston rod. This required an open topped piston which consequently could not be made double acting, thereby reducing the power potential.

A type of engine subsequently known as the steeple engine was first developed early in the nineteenth century and underwent many modifications over the years. Although there were a number of variants the essential form remained much the same, with cylinders being positioned below the paddle shaft with pistons acting upwards. The crosshead was located some distance above the paddle shaft, which it drove by means of a connecting rod returning downwards towards the cylinder. In order that it might clear the crank and connecting rod some designs had an open elliptical arrangement on the piston rod whilst others employed two separate piston rods, one each side of the crankshaft. The crosshead could slide in a slotted guide provided in a frame which extended upwards from the cylinder like a steeple, hence the engine's description.

A form of paddle engine which found popularity with many operators was the oscillating type as this was compact and did not require a connecting rod, the piston rod directly driving a paddle shaft crank. In order to allow for obliquity of the piston rod caused by the rotating crank it was necessary for the piston and cylinder to pivot or oscillate about an axis. That could be arranged quite simply, but the main problems with this type of engine related to the supply of steam to and directing of exhaust from the cylinder. The usual arrangement was for one of the trunnions or pivots to carry steam to the cylinder and the other to take the exhaust flow. Proposals for an oscillating engine had been made as early as 1785 and one of the first to be used afloat was put in the iron steamer *Aaron Manby* during 1822. Perhaps the most impressive oscillating engine was the 836-ton monster used to drive *Great Eastern's* paddle engines; this pair of 74in diameter and 168in stroke cylinders produced 3410ihp when working at 11rpm. The usual arrangement with oscillating engines was for all necessary pumps to be driven from cranks or eccentrics on the paddle shaft, although differences did exist depending upon the manufacturer.

As higher steam pressures became available, leakage at the trunnions became more of a problem, with the result that oscillating engines fell

from favour. The advantages of direct acting cylinders were too great to ignore but it was obvious that some penalty would have to be paid in terms of space occupied, and the inclined form of direct acting engine increased in popularity. This was no new idea, Marc Isambard Brunel having patented such a design in 1822, but shipowners were keen to keep engine rooms as small as possible and the inclined cylinders occupied more space than those positioned vertically below the crankshaft. Higher steam pressure did allow more power to be produced by cylinders of smaller size and so the space penalty paid through the use of inclined cylinders was not so great as it would have been when using lower pressure steam. The inclined direct acting engine became popular from the 1860s onwards and many were installed in cross channel steamers and those operating on large rivers such as the Thames and Clyde. With the introduction of compounding a number of compound inclined cylinder paddle engines were produced, and that form of engine remained popular until paddle steamers ceased to be constructed for commercial service.

Boilers presented problems from the beginnings of steam propulsion and to a great extent the limitations of steam generation imposed restrictions on power production. At almost any stage of engine evolution during the nineteenth century higher power would have been possible had improved steam conditions been available, particularly in terms of pressure. Material limitations and constructional difficulties seriously hampered boiler design, limiting pressure and output. Many early boilers were constructed from copper, which could not withstand pressures much above atmospheric. Even with the introduction of wrought iron there was little scope for much increase due to the basic design involved. The quality of iron, and even copper sheeting, was variable and could not be predicted with any degree of certainty during the first half of the century, so pressures had to be kept reasonable in order to minimise the risk of explosion. Even then some serious accidents did occur, which must have been a disincentive to adopt the new form of propulsion.

Boilers used for many early steamers were little different from land based 'kettle' type units with an external fire heating what was essentially a drum filled with water, that drum often being supported on brickwork. By the 1820s the flue-type boiler had evolved, this having internal furnaces and flues through which hot furnace gases passed on their way to the funnel. Flues were made to wind their way through the boiler shell, thus increasing the surface area available for heat transfer and hence the evaporative rate.

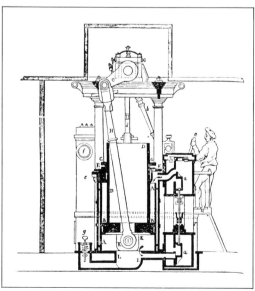

An alternative to the heavy and bulky side lever engine was the trunk engine. As shown in this Humphrys version, the trunk engine in vertical form could be made compact enough to fit under the paddle shaft, which it drove directly. (Denis Griffiths)

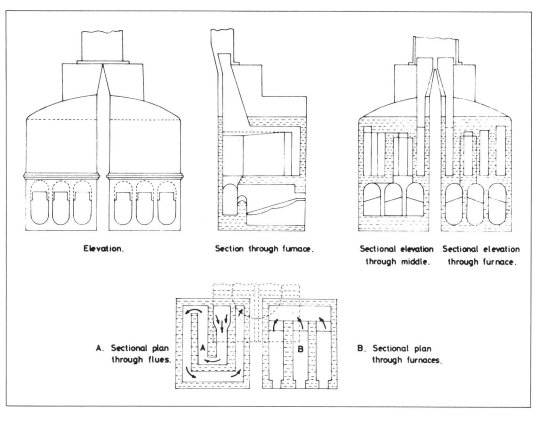

Elevation.

Section through furnace.

Sectional elevation through middle.

Sectional elevation through furnace.

A. Sectional plan through flues.

B. Sectional plan through furnaces.

The flue type boilers of the Great Western. (Denis Griffiths)

Such boilers could only be used for relatively low pressures (no more than about 12psi with safety), as the flat surfaces of the flues and the boiler shell could not withstand forces induced by any higher pressures. Each engine builder tended to produce his own flue boilers and a variety of different designs evolved, but all to the same general format; what differed was the way in which the flues were arranged.

Because of the difficulties presented by the use of surface condensers, most boilers up until the early 1850s employed seawater feed. That caused a layer of salt scale to form inside the boiler, which impeded heat transfer to some extent, but as this type of boiler was so inefficient it did not matter too much. The scale did have an advantage in that it helped prevent corrosion of the iron below the water level by providing a protective layer. Most iron boilers of the period actually tended to suffer from corrosion in the steam space. All seawater contains some dissolved oxygen and upon heating the oxygen is given off resulting in oxidation or 'rusting' in the steam portion of the boiler. High levels of salt in the boiler produced excessive scale which was undesirable and the usual practice was to blow down the boilers at frequent intervals in order to reduce the salt concentration. This blow-down represented a loss of heat and several devices were developed to recover some of that energy.

The return tube type boilers of the Cunarder Arabia *of 1853.* (Denis Griffiths)

The boilers fitted in *Great Western* (1837) were provided with heat exchanger units designed by Joshua Field of Maudslay, Sons & Field, builders of the ship's engines and boilers. The 'refrigerator', as the heat exchanger was known,

consisted of a cylindrical shell containing tubes, hot water being blown out of the boiler and circulated around the tubes, giving up some heat to the feed water which flowed through them.

Although it was more expensive, some flue boilers as late as the 1840s were still made from copper; this did not corrode so easily on the water side and it was also available in larger sized plates than iron, so furnaces could be constructed as single pieces without riveted seams above the grates. Leakage at riveted joints was a problem and a factor which restricted the pressures obtained. Copper did present problems, severe gas side corrosion often being found at the base of the flue uptake. Thus there was no ideal solution to problems of corrosion until more was known about its chemical action, and that did not come until later in the century.

The limitations of flues were recognised and from about 1835 the tubular boiler became popular. In this type the flues were replaced by a large number of tubes of about 3in diameter and that increased heat transfer surface area thereby allowing for increased evaporative rate from a boiler of smaller external dimensions. The resultant reduction in boiler size allowed for increased cargo space. Such tubular boilers were more efficient than flue boilers as the increased

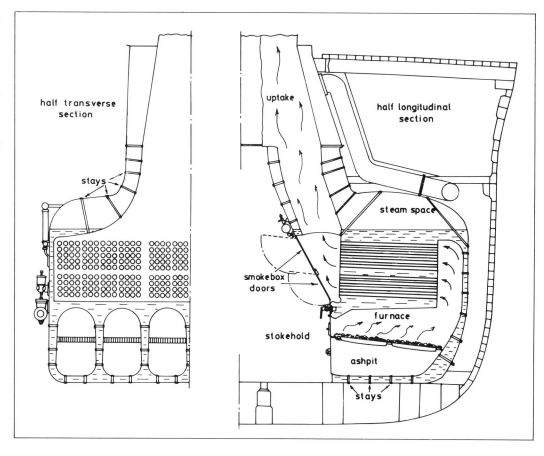

half transverse section

stays

uptake

half longitudinal section

steam space

smokebox doors

furnace

stokehold

ashpit

stays

heating surface could extract more heat energy from the hot combustion gases. However, careful design was essential, since if the funnel gases became too cold furnace draught would be reduced, resulting in poor combustion. The tubular boilers fitted in *Great Western* during 1844 suffered from this problem and several possible solutions were considered. Isambard Kingdom Brunel suggested the use of a steam blast like that employed for steam locomotives but the one adopted was to bypass some of the tubes, thereby reducing the effective heating surface and so allowing the uptake gases to remain hotter.

Even though tubes were used instead of flat-sided flues, the outer shell of the boiler was still box-shaped and so not very efficient for higher pressures. Flat surfaces had to be supported by means of stays, but even then pressures had to be kept reasonable as the iron plates and riveted joints were of variable quality. During the oceanic paddle steamer era, which ceased with Cunard's *Scotia* (1862), steam pressures only rose to about 25psi and that did to some extent limit the demands upon engine designers whilst also restricting operating efficiency. Better, and more consistent, quality iron plates, together with the use of fresh water feed through the reintroduction of surface condensers, allowed higher pressures to be achieved, but so did a change from box shape to oval and subsequently cylin-

drical boilers. There was no single factor which limited or brought about change in boilers of the period, many factors influencing design and operating pressure. Change was gradual but progressive, and on the way many novel ideas were tried. American designers were not slow to experiment and a form of cylindrical tubular boiler was built by the Novelty Iron Works of New York for the paddle steamer *Franklin* in 1850. The tubes were of relatively large diameter and could effectively be considered as tubular flues, but their use does not appear to have improved matters as the boiler pressure was a meagre 13psi.

Screw propulsion

Any form of propulsion means that a thrust must be transferred from the drive unit to the hull of the ship, and with paddle steamers that took place at the paddle shaft bearings. With the introduction of screw propulsion special regard had to be taken of such thrust transfer as the propeller shaft was axial and, unlike the paddle shaft, no support bearing was able to transmit the thrust. It became necessary, therefore, to provide special thrust bearings for screw steam-

ers and that fitted to Brunel's *The Great Britain* was probably the most basic possible, but it was nonetheless very effective. A 2ft diameter gun-metal plate was connected to the forward end of the screw shaft and this pressed against a steel plate of similar diameter connected rigidly to the hull structure. In order to reduce friction, and at the same time keep the thrust unit cool, water was forced under pressure through a hole in the centre of the fixed steel plate and escaped radially between the two plates. In later years thrust blocks were moved to a position just aft of the engine and these generally comprised a number of collars on the screw shaft with fixed bearing pads of horseshoe shape located between the collars. These pads had bearing surfaces on both faces as the thrust would be in opposite directions when the ship was moving ahead and astern.

It is often said that Cunard was unconscionably slow to adopt technical innovations like iron hulls and the screw, but while this may be true about their mail services (where government subsidies laid many of the ground rules), in general it is a gross simplification. The first iron screw steamers, Andes *(shown here) and* Alps *came into service in 1852-53, running a secondary service carrying a high proportion of second class passengers and 1000 tons of cargo, in a pattern just established by the* City of Glasgow. *Like the Inman liner,* Andes *was powered by geared beam engines. (Denis Griffiths)*

The key to the success of Inman's City of Glasgow *was the relatively economical machinery: a pair of geared beam engines.* (Denis Griffiths)

Effective screw performance required rotational speeds higher than that needed for paddle wheel drive, but during the 1840s and 1850s most engines were designed for paddle propulsion and hence operated at speeds not much in excess of 20rpm. Because builders had considerable experience in the construction of slow speed paddle engines it was understandable that modified versions of these were used for early screw steamers, but it became necessary to increase screw shaft speed. The engine originally installed in *The Great Britain* was a four-cylinder triangular unit, based upon the earlier patented paddle design of Marc Brunel with cylinders driving an overhead crankshaft. In order to bring the drive down to screw shaft level and at the same time produce a speed increase, a multiple chain arrangement was employed. The gear ratio of 2.95:1 produced a propeller drive speed of 53rpm when the engine turned at 18rpm. Although effective in achieving the design requirements, such chain arrangements were noisy and expensive to construct.

Gearing provided an alternative but at the time, the 1850s, gears were difficult to cut accurately for reasonable cost and were also noisy. An early solution which lasted until direct drive engines were introduced was the use of wooden gear teeth manufactured separately and individually fitted to iron gear wheels. Wood required minimal lubrication and teeth tended to bed themselves in as the engine worked. Inman Line's *City of Glasgow* (1850) had a pair of overhead beam engines located athwartships. Each vertical cylinder had a steeple guide arrangement for its crosshead, the connecting rod being attached to one end of the beam, whilst the opposite end of the beam rotated a gear wheel which in turn drove a pinion connected to the screw shaft. A 2:1 gear ratio was provided and cylinders were a modest 66in diameter with 60in stroke.

Cunard's *China* (1862) provided an alternative engine arrangement in that two oscillating cylinders, 80in bore by 66in stroke, rotated an overhead crankshaft attached to a large gear wheel with four rows of wooden teeth. This drove a pinion on the forward end of the screw shaft. There was nothing particularly remarkable about the engine, as oscillating cylinders had been frequently used for paddle steamers, but *China* did have a surface condenser which was successful and she emphasised the advantages of screw over paddles. Comparison with the contemporary paddle driven *Scotia* is instructive.

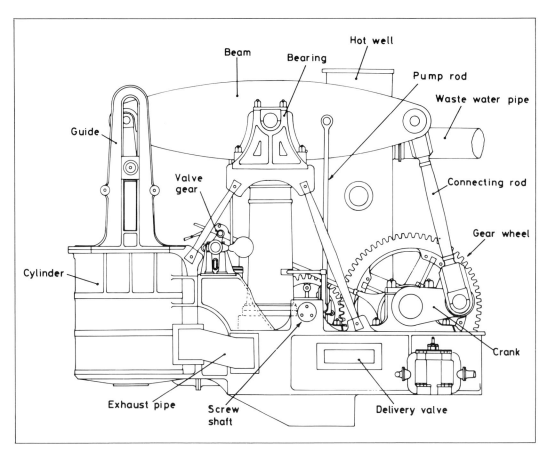

	Scotia	*China*
Tonnage (gross)	3850	2550
Speed (kts)	13.5	12.5
Power (ihp)	4200	2200
Steam pressure (psi)	25	22
Daily coal consumption (tons)	164	82
Cargo capacity (tons)	1050	1400
Bunker capacity (tons)	1800	1100
Passengers	275	930

Admittedly 770 of *China's* passengers were of the low paying steerage type whilst *Scotia* carried only first and second class passengers, but the advantage lay with the screw ship with its higher cargo capacity and lower fuel bill. Much of *Scotia's* greater tonnage was occupied by bunkers.

China was provided with surface condensers but jet condensers were also fitted for use in emergencies; obviously the engineers respon-

The geared oscillating engines of the China *of 1862, Cunard's first ever purpose-built screw mail steamer.* (Denis Griffiths)

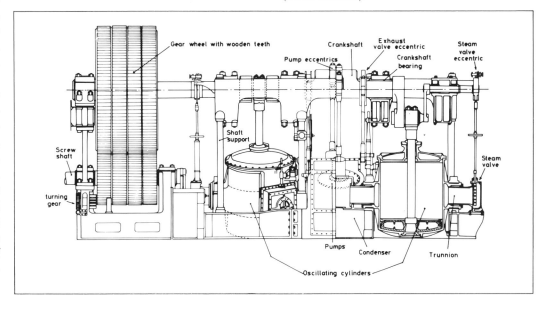

sible for her design were still not convinced as to the reliability of the surface type. Machinery provided by Napiers of Glasgow was similar in form to that constructed by John Penn for Brunel's screw steamer *The Great Britain* when she was re-engined in 1852. Penn's two-cylinder oscillating engine had a 3:1 gear ratio, the engine working at 24rpm. Based upon cylinders of 82.5in diameter and 72in stroke with a boiler pressure of 10psi, the power potential would have been about half that developed by *China's* machinery.

The lack of progress between Penn's engines of 1852 and those fitted in *China* a decade later is more apparent than real, for there were major developments in marine engineering at that time, even if new ideas took a long time to reach the engine rooms of large ships. Cunard and other Atlantic liner companies were slow to adopt innovations in those days as reliability was the prime concern on that highly competitive route. Many ideas had to be tested in coastal craft before venturing to deeper waters, and one of the major advances of the 1850s was the re-introduction of compounding. Unfortunately the advantages of compounding were not really evident with coastal and short sea operations but the message eventually got across to steamship operators and a revolution began.

Before considering the impact of compounding it is worth looking at some of the direct drive, simple expansion engines of the period. The Admiralty was quick to see the advantages of screw propulsion and development of a steam fleet brought much work to engine builders throughout Britain. A requirement that machinery must be located completely below the waterline produced an assortment of horizontal engine designs which have been considered else-where (see *Steam, Steel and Shellfire* in this series). Obviously these engines could also find use in commercial steamers and many did so, perhaps the best known being that fitted in Brunel's *Great Eastern* (1858) for driving the screw. There were four 84in diameter by 48in stroke cylinders driving two cranks set at right angles to each other. Each piston had two piston rods passing to the relevant crosshead which moved in guides. From each port engine crosshead there were two connecting rods which attached to their crankpin either side of the connecting rod from the opposing starboard engine. This enabled cylinders to be positioned exactly opposite and so preserved balance. Steam at 25 psi enabled the screw engine to develop 4890ihp which, under screw propulsion alone, drove the monster steamer at 9kts. Although interesting, the machinery of *Great Eastern* was something of a blind alley as far as commercial shipping was concerned and nothing of the size in that form was ever again constructed.

Horizontal engines of the trunk type were fitted in the Inman liner *City of Paris* (1866). Developing some 2800ihp from cylinders with dimensions similar to those of the *Great Eastern* and a boiler pressure of 30psi, the ship proved to be a record-breaker, but she burned over 100tons of coal per day. The lower height of horizontal engines might be considered ideal for passenger vessels in that it would allow for longer continuous accommodation spaces, but in fact there was little saving as machinery spaces had to be vented and illuminated, resulting in the need to carry the engine room casing to the top deck. If such space had to be provided then it was reasoned by some that it could be usefully occupied by engine cylinders positioned vertically. This arrangement of cylinders had advantages for commercial shipping as it freed space at the sides of the engine room for use as bunkers.

There is no date when such a vertical inverted form of engine can be said to have been introduced, as it is almost certain that some small steamers were fitted with machinery of that type soon after screw propulsion became popular. A number of large engines of the type were built for screw steamers in the 1850s and a typical example was that fitted to the liner *Australasian* (1857). Originally constructed for the European & Australian Royal Mail Company, she subsequently became *Calabria* of the Cunard Line and was re-engined in 1867. In both cases the machinery was of a two-cylinder vertical inverted form with cylinders originally of 90in diameter being reduced to 72in diameter when she was re-engined. In both cases the stroke was 42in but due to the reduction in bore power, and hence speed, ihp was lower after re-engining.

The above examples illustrate the diversity of engine styles which existed during the 1850s and 1860s, there being no preferred type or form. Gradually engine builders and shipowners settled upon the vertical inverted arrangement for direct drive screw propulsion, but even then there were many variations as different designers attempted to avoid infringing patents or the payment of royalties. The introduction of the compound principle served to improve efficiency but complicate the marine engine building industry as, once again, practically all builders developed their own variations.

Compounding has often been referred to as a system whereby steam may be used twice, thus increasing the amount of work derived from a

Inman's City of Paris *of 1866 in later life. This Atlantic record-breaker was powered by horizontal trunk engines.* (CMP)

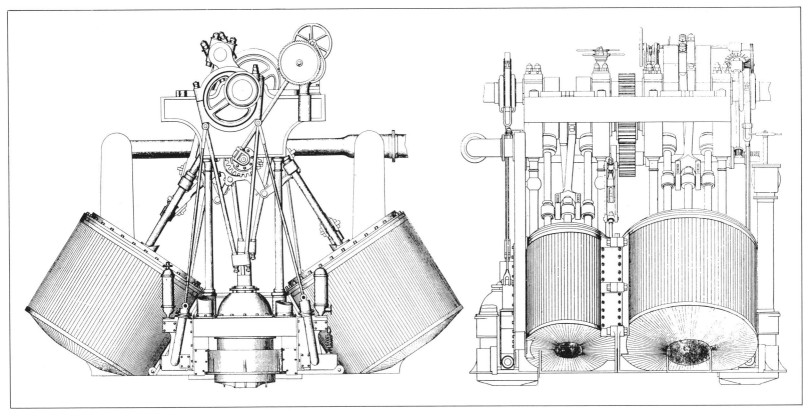

set amount of steam. Whilst the work obtained from a given mass is increased, the steam is not in fact used twice; it is simply expanded in stages. As steam expands in a cylinder the temperature within the cylinder and that of the cylinder wall reduces – the greater the amount of expansion the larger will be the difference between the inlet and outlet temperatures. If cylinder wall temperature falls too much some of the new steam entering for the next expansion will condense on the relatively cold surface and thus it will not be available to perform work on the piston. It follows, therefore, that there should be a restriction on the amount of expansion allowed in any cylinder in order that such condensation losses might be minimised.

For early engines operating with steam pressures up to about 25psi the amount of expansion was not too great, but as higher pressures became available cylinder losses due to condensation were significant. Using higher pressure steam was important as it allowed more useful energy to be stored per unit mass, and hence the engine output could be increased. Heat needed to turn water into steam, known as latent heat, can never be recovered; only the energy in the steam by virtue of its pressure (and, in later years, its degree of superheat) can be recovered, so the higher the pressure, the higher the energy output. As pressure increases the latent heat becomes a smaller portion of the total energy in the steam, so the overall plant efficiency is in-

creased. For this reason engine designers aimed at higher operating pressures even though boiler designers could not produce such pressures due to limitations imposed by the materials available.

Compounding allowed designers to expand steam by a limited amount in one cylinder and then pass that reduced pressure steam to another cylinder for expansion down to a lower pressure. In the first expansion stage there would be a reduction in temperature between inlet and exhaust but the cylinder walls would not cool so much that new steam would condense on the walls. The same situation existed in the second stage where, although the average cylinder temperature was lower than in the first stage, the temperature of the cylinder walls would not fall too low compared with the inlet temperature to cause condensation. In order to minimise the risk of condensation on cylinder walls some engine builders employed steam jackets around the cylinders. Steam from the boiler was circulated in a jacket surrounding the cylinder, thus keeping it relatively warm and reducing condensation. Theoretically the idea was useful but condensation of steam in the jacket resulted in a loss of steam energy and it was generally found that efficient lagging around the cylinder could be more beneficial.

A further advantage of compounding, or multiple stage expansion, lay in the fact that the length of piston stroke could be kept to a reasonable value, thus keeping engine height rela-

Pacific Steam Navigation was the first major shipping company to adopt compound engines when they were fitted to the new paddlers Inca *and* Valparaiso *in 1856. The experiment was so successful that the* Lima, Bogota *and* Callao *were sent home to be re-engined by Randolph & Elder. These drawings depict the four-cylinder compound fitted. From A & R Murray's* Shipbuilding and Steam Ships *(Edinburgh 1861).*

tively low. Expanding steam from a given inlet pressure to a set condenser pressure could, theoretically, be achieved in a compound engine with piston strokes half of that needed for single stage expansion. The reduced stroke not only allowed engine height to be limited but it also reduced crankshaft problems, as the longer the piston stroke the longer would be the crank throw.

The origins of compounding go back to the infancy of the steam engine itself. One of the earliest protagonists was Jonathan Hornblower in 1781, whilst the firm of Boulton & Watt had taken out patents prior to that. Arthur Woolf built a number of compound engines early in the nineteenth century for use in pumping out mines, and a number of small, but not very successful, engines were actually installed in ships during the 1830s and 1840s. Credit for introducing a practical compound engine to marine propulsion goes to John Elder who, in conjunction with Charles Randolph, founded the Govan shipbuilding and engine building firm of Randolph, Elder & Company. This subsequently became John Elder & Company, and then Fairfield Shipbuilding & Engineering Company.

Not unnaturally, the theoretical economy of compound machinery appealed most strongly to companies with long distance routes or operations far from sources of cheap coal. One of those with the greatest incentive to experiment was P&O who built a group of compound steamers in the early 1860s. One of the first was the Carnatic. (P&O)

Randolph and Elder took out a patent in 1853 for a compound engine and others followed in subsequent years as ideas for improvement occurred. Patents had to be scientific and minor changes meant a new patent to forestall other people making minor amendments and claiming it as a new design. This accounts for the plethora of engine types which litter the technical press of the period, most of which never actually saw production. In 1862 Elder even took out patents for triple and quadruple expansion engines, which shows how far ahead his thinking was. During 1854 Randolph and Elder fitted a compound engine in the small steamer *Brandon* and two years later its success encouraged the Pacific Steam Navigation Company (PSNC) to request the use of compound engines in its paddle steamers *Inca* and *Valparaiso*.

The cost of sending coal to the west coast of South America, where these ships operated, was high and that encouraged PSNC in its experiment. So advantageous did compounding prove that the company sent three other steamers home to be re-engined with compound machinery. Although steam pressure was only a moderate 30psi and some part of the success was claimed for the steam jacketing employed, there was no doubt that compounding reduced coal consumption.

The Peninsular & Oriental Steam Navigation Company (P&O) also saw advantages in the use of compound engines and commissioned construction of a number of vessels during the early 1860s. Humphrys, Tennant & Company supplied tandem compound engines for *Carnatic* (1862), *Poonah* (1863), *Golconda* (1863) and *Baroda* (1864). Each engine had four cylinders arranged in pairs with a high-pressure (HP) cylinder above each low-pressure (LP) cylinder and piston rods connected for a common stroke of 36in. Elder's screw compound engines were of the in-line form with LP and HP cylinders positioned alongside each other, an arrangement to which Elders adhered. The P&O ships returned very low coal consumption figures for the period, less than 2lb per ihp per hour on an engine power of 2440ihp, and others quickly became converts to the compound idea.

The shipowner Alfred Holt was also an engineer who appreciated the benefits of compounding, although he was not always convinced as to

its overwhelming advantages compared with simple expansion. Holt's Blue Funnel Line constructed three ships, *Agamemnon*, *Ajax* and *Achilles*, during 1866 and these were provided with vertical tandem engines design by Holt himself. A single HP cylinder was placed above the single LP, the common connecting rod driving the single crank on the crankshaft fitted with a heavy flywheel. Holt's engine was relatively simple, had fewer parts than those of Elder and Humphrys, and was short, thus occupying little space and allowing more to be devoted to cargo. Holt the engineer had devised a machine which satisfied the needs of Holt the shipowner.

Early users of compound engines operated on long-haul trades to places where adequate supplies of good quality coal were not available. Sending coal to bunker stations abroad was an expensive proposition and it is not surprising that shipowners looked for every means which would reduce overall costs. Compounding required less coal for a particular power and speed; reduced coal consumption meant that less had to

be transported, thereby cutting the overseas coal bill and hence the fuel costs for the voyage. In addition a lower coal consumption resulted in the need for fewer firemen and coal trimmers, which in turn reduced operating costs because fewer people had to be paid and fed on board ship. With lower coal consumption, bunker capacity could be reduced, whilst compound engines and boilers often required less space than simple machinery; these factors usually increased cargo capacity. It is little wonder that compounding found favour despite the slightly higher initial cost of the machinery. With the opening of the Suez Canal in 1869 coinciding with the general adoption of compound machinery, there was rapid growth in steam powered trade with Australia, India and the Far East.

On the Atlantic compounding took slightly longer to find favour; the relatively short distance and readily available coal supply at both ends meant that the advantages were less spectacular. The Anchor liner *India* introduced compounding to that waterway in 1869 but she

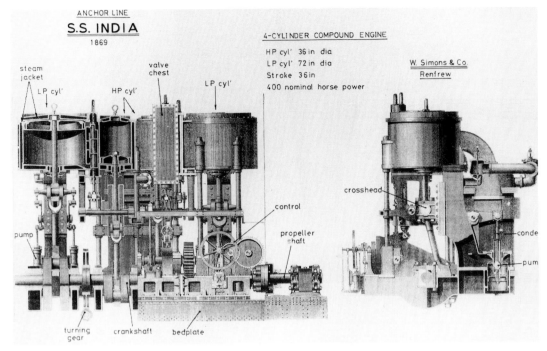

ANCHOR LINE

S.S. INDIA
1869

4-CYLINDER COMPOUND ENGINE

HP cyl' 36 in dia
LP cyl' 72 in dia
Stroke 36 in
400 nominal horse power

W. Simons & Co.
Renfrew

steam jacket
LP cyl'
HP cyl'
valve chest
LP cyl'
control
propeller shaft
pump
crosshead
conde
pum
turning gear
crankshaft
bedplate

The four-cylinder compound machinery of the Anchor Line's India of 1869. Compounding was not so crucial to commercial success on relatively short routes, and although India introduced two-stage expansion to the Atlantic it is significant that the ship was purchased while building and had not been designed for the service. (Denis Griffiths)

had not been laid down as an Atlantic liner. Guion Line's *Wyoming* and *Wisconsin* of 1870 were the first compound engined steamers actually built for Atlantic service and their machinery did not follow the standard in-line or tandem pattern of other ships. The 60in diameter HP cylinder was placed vertically and the trunk type 120in diameter LP cylinder horizontally, both pistons driving the same crank. This arrangement reduced engine height and length, thus keeping the engine room compact. Instead of the usual eccentric operated slide valves, steam was directed to the cylinders by means of Corliss drop valves, but they obviously performed well as the engines stayed in the ships until they were scrapped in 1893.

Encouraged by the success of these steamers Guion returned to the builders, Palmers of Jarrow, for two faster vessels, *Montana* and *Dakota*, to be delivered in 1875. Despite contrary advice from Palmers, the company entrusted design of the machinery to its engineering superintendent and neither the engines nor the boilers proved satisfactory. The engines were of similar hybrid form but there were two opposed horizontal LP cylinders (113in diameter) and a single 60in diameter HP cylinder, again all connected to the same crank. Although Corliss valves functioned satisfactorily on the earlier engines, problems were experienced with the later higher powered machinery.

The Guion Line's Wisconsin *of 1870 was the first Atlantic steamer designed from the outset for compound engines. These were rather unusual, with a vertical HP cylinder and horizontal LP, both driving the same crank. (CMP)*

The engineering superintendent was aware that improved performance could be obtained with higher steam pressure and decided upon an increase in pressure compared with the 70psi used for *Wyoming* and *Wisconsin*. At the time 75psi was considered to be the safe maximum for marine duties but the new engines were designed for steam at 100psi. No conventional boiler could achieve that and so a primitive form of water-tube boiler was designed, much against the advice of the shipbuilders. The experienced builders proved to be right and on *Montana's* delivery voyage from the Tyne to Liverpool many of the tubes failed, one failure causing injury to a fireman. Following repairs at Portsmouth the ship eventually made Liverpool, but the Board of Trade surveyor insisted upon a prolonged sea trial before he would issue a passenger certificate. Early in the trial more tubes failed and the ship returned to Liverpool. *Montana's* boilers were replaced by a more conventional form and *Dakota*, still under construction, had normal fire-tube boilers installed.

Replacing the boilers cost Guion Line £60,000 but the loss of reputation must have been greater. Both ships were lost before they were five years old and it is doubtful if the owners were too displeased in closing the book on an unsatisfactory experiment. The incident illustrates the problems involved for commercial companies in attempting to force the pace of technology with the limited experience then available; and even in the 1870s not everybody was convinced that compounding was a real advantage in terms of marine propulsion. In a paper delivered to the Institution of Civil Engineers during 1877 even Alfred Holt admitted '... it is a matter of reasonable speculation whether the compound may yet be abandoned and a return made to the single-cylinder engine modified in details to suit high pressure steam'. In terms of high pressure Holt would have been thinking only of about 70psi but the Guion Line experience and that gained from operating his own compound steamers must have made him cast doubt upon the advantages to be gained. At the time, however, many believed that pressures above 70psi were impractical and Holt, amongst others, realised that effective compounding required high pressure.

Fortunately, improved materials and design came to the rescue. Steel is a stronger material than wrought iron and the use of mild steel plate for boiler construction enabled higher pressures to be employed. It must be realised that the industrial steels of the 1870s were of very variable quality and certainly not as good as they are today, but they were, generally, an improvement on wrought iron. Progress in the use of steel for boiler construction was initially slow due to the

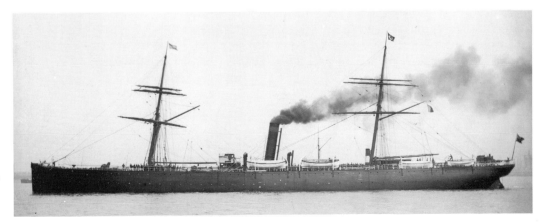

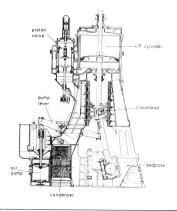

Guion's highly successful Arizona *of 1879, with a sectional drawing of her Elder-built three-cylinder in-line compound engine. (Photo CMP; drawing Denis Griffiths)*

variable quality, but when boilermakers were provided with reasonable consistency in terms of strength, confidence improved. During the three years to April 1881 some 560 boilers constructed wholly or partly from steel were installed in ships. Although its higher strength gave steel an advantage over iron, there was a price to pay in that corrosion tended to be greater. At that time the mechanisms of corrosion were only just beginning to be appreciated.

Advances in design also improved matters as the box-type tubular boiler gave way to the oval-shaped boiler and eventually to the cylindrical boiler, which subsequently became universally known as the 'Scotch' boiler. Effective staying of the flat surfaces allowed Scotch boiler pressures to be pushed to values not achieved with other types. The introduction of corrugated furnaces during the early 1880s saw pressures of up to 100psi become normal. These improvements did not simply happen; they were brought about by hard work and co-operation between many in British industry. Exchange of knowledge at meetings of the national and local learned societies enabled rapid progress to be made in British engineering, keeping it ahead of all other nations.

Despite the reservations of Holt and a few others the compound engine became firmly established during the 1870s and all important new tonnage was constructed with this type of prime mover. The actual form of engine adopted depended upon the builder and each attempted to produce an efficient unit with a high power-to-size ratio. There was also the problem of avoiding other designers' patented ideas.

Elders stayed with the basic in-line arrangement of cylinders and this Clydeside yard produced some of the best compound engines ever built. Guion's *Arizona* (1879) had a typical Elder three-crank compound engine, the single 62in bore HP cylinder being positioned on the centre crank and the two 90in bore LP cylinders on the outer cranks; the stroke was 66in. With steam supply at 90psi from one single-ended and six double-ended Scotch-type boilers the engine developed a remarkable 6357ihp, which could drive the 5147grt steamer at a speed of 17.3kts. In order to keep engine length reasonable, Elders placed the valves at the back of the engine rather than in line with the cylinders and this required the valve drive to be via levers rather than directly from the eccentrics. The air pumps, boiler feed pump and bilge pumps were also driven by levers from the main crankshaft. In order to minimise any possible problems each LP cylinder had its own surface condenser, these also being positioned at the back of the engine.

Other builders adopted different cylinder arrangements and the tandem form proved popular with Maudslay, Sons & Field as well as with the Barrow Shipbuilding Company. Maudslays provided compound engines for the first White Star liner *Oceanic* (1871) as the builders, Harland & Wolff, had no engine building facilities at the time. When the larger *Britannic* (1874) and *Germanic* (1875) were built Harlands returned to Maudslays for their engines. Propulsive units consisted of a pair of tandem cylinders with the HP above the LP, condensers and lever driven pumps being positioned at the back, resulting in a short engine for its power. The Barrow Shipbuilding Company adopted a similar tandem arrangement, although constructional details were different in order to avoid patent infringement. A six-cylinder, three-crank engine was constructed for *City of Rome* (1881), a similar engine being installed in the French liner *Normandie* two years later. Four other similar ships were constructed in France and these had the same type of engine built under licence from the Barrow company. The design allowed each

Although this painting of White Star's trend-setting Oceanic *of 1871 emphasises the ship's large sail area, the compound engines were an important contributor to her success. The sectional drawing shows the tandem arrangement of the engines (built by Maudslay, Sons & Field) with HP cylinder above LP. (Photo CMP; drawing Denis Griffiths)*

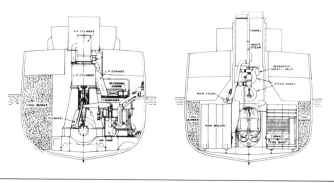

The elegant City of Rome, *built for the Inman Line in 1881 by Barrow Shipbuilding, employed six-cylinder three-crank tandem compound engines of 10,000ihp. The ship's performance in service was disappointing and despite various modifications to the engines the ship was never a record breaker.* (Photo CMP; drawing Denis Griffiths)

tandem pair to act as a separate unit in the event of failure of any other group, this being possible because each pair had its own condenser and necessary pumps. Separate steam driven pumps for boiler feed and bilges complemented the main engine driven units.

Smaller ships still generally had a single HP and single LP cylinder, as sufficient power could be developed from such an arrangement. The higher powers called for larger dimensions and although the HP cylinder diameter would not be excessive, large LP units were required to deal with the steam at lower pressure; in order to avoid problems with the crankshaft it was necessary to ensure that power supplied to all cranks was approximately the same. To minimise problems and avoid extremely large cylinders which would be difficult to manufacture, the LP was often divided into two cylinders of the same size.

Compounding improved efficiency but increasing availability of steel allowed designers to raise boiler pressures and construct engines capable of even greater efficiencies due to further stages of expansion. Compounding begat triple compounding or triple expansion.

Auxiliary machinery

For many years the only plant aboard any steamer was its propulsion engine and boiler, all necessary pumps being driven by the engine. All ships, whether powered by wind or steam, required a bilge pump and for sailing ships these

of necessity would be hand powered. Even when steam propulsion arrived hand powered pumps were still required in order to provide pumping capability when the engine was not working. Boilers required feed pumps to supply water, and in port when the engine was not working a hand pump would be needed to perform the duty. With the boiler under steam when preparing for sea, a small steam driven pump could be used, and during the late 1840s a number of such auxiliary engines were available for powering boiler feed pumps. The risk of fire was ever present aboard ship and more so in the case of steamers, so some form of fire pump would be an essential piece of equipment. During its first voyage from London to Bristol a fire broke out aboard Brunel's *Great Western* and, with the engines stopped, the ship's patented Merryweather fire engine enabled the conflagration to be extinguished.

In later years steam was applied to many items of auxiliary equipment and even for heating. Coal-fired stoves were often the only means of heating saloons and accommodation areas during cold Atlantic crossings, but very quickly it was realised that hot water circulated through pipes laid in the accommodation would be more effective and much safer. Brunel's screw steamer *The Great Britain* had such a heating system.

Steering gear

During heavy weather a number of men were required to steer even relatively small ships and as steamers became larger the difficulties of steering increased. Not only were there problems in arranging large numbers of men around the steering wheel, but even in good weather hand power took a considerable time to turn a large ship. The application of steam to the task was first patented by F E Sickells in 1862, but his installation attracted little attention and it was not until a steam steering gear was fitted in *Great Eastern* that any notice was taken. John

MacFarlane Gray was responsible for the machine which was installed in 1866, this consisting of two horizontal cylinders driving a crankshaft which turned the rudder shaft through a system of gears. The hand wheel on the bridge was connected with the steering engine by means of some 410ft of shafting, operating steam valves to rotate the steering engine in the direction required.

The success of MacFarlane Gray's engine resulted in trials of other forms of steering gear, including a number using hydraulic rams. These employed steam engines to produce hydraulic pressure which powered the tiller by means of rams. Not all systems were as effective as that fitted in *Great Eastern*, but by the 1870s all large steamers were fitted with powered steering gear. In all cases some form of mechanical back-up system was provided to enable the ship to be steered in the event of failure of the steering engine. This provision, which is still insisted upon today, was sometimes met by human power but more often than not it made use of other steam auxiliary plant aboard the ship. Rope connections between the tiller arm and a suitable winch would allow the rudder to be turned in an emergency.

Deck machinery

Manually operated capstans had been used in sailing ships long before the coming of steam, these being employed for lifting anchors and for similar hauling duties. With the introduction of steam they still served a useful purpose but by the 1860s it was realised that a small steam engine could be used to replace the efforts of several men. A steam engine, positioned immediately below the capstan drum or even on the deck below, required less space and could work faster than the usual human labour.

The windlass with its toothed drum for lifting anchor chains became a necessity when chains replaced rope for anchors. Winch drums on the

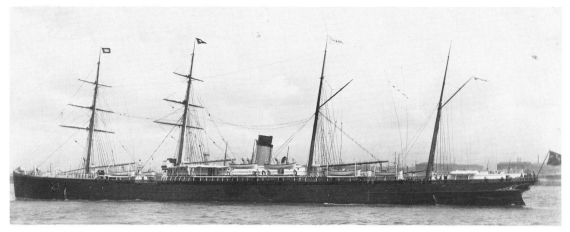

In a short-lived experiment the White Star line introduced gas lighting with the Adriatic *and* Celtic *of 1872, but the motion of the ship soon ruptured the rigid pipework and the idea was soon abandoned. The illustrations show the* Adriatic *with an engraving of the* Celtic's *gas oil generator. (Photo CMP; engraving Denis Griffiths)*

ends of the drive shaft and a means of engaging/disengaging the drums or cable lifter from the drive allow the windlass to be used for lifting the anchor and hauling ropes as required. *The Great Britain* was fitted with such a windlass and this is still in place on the ship as she undergoes restoration in Bristol. The drive for this windlass was through long handles which turned the shaft by means of ratchet mechanisms. With the development of small steam engines such units could be easily steam driven through suitable gearing and it did not take long for shipbuilders, and owners, to appreciate this fact. By the 1860s the basic form of steam windlass had evolved and there were then few changes in its form until electric drive became more usual towards the middle of the twentieth century.

The first volume (1856) of the journal *The Engineer* contains many illustrations and descriptions of steam driven winches and cranes designed for the loading and discharge of ships. Naturally not all of these succeeded but many ships of the period were fitted with such devices as a means to ease the task of handling cargo.

Shipowners of the period understood the advantages of steam propulsion in maintaining schedules, and the fitting of steam driven cargo handling equipment enabled human labour to be replaced, thereby minimising the period in port. This would have taken time to have its effect since, at first, few dock workers would have been familiar with steam winches, but as more ships were so fitted cargo handling times must have shortened. Competition between shipowners ensured that any new vessel had to be fitted with such equipment in order to maintain a share of the trade. Furthermore, steamers of the period still carried a fair amount of canvas and the use of steam winches would have eased the effort involved in handling sails.

The ancestor of the steam winch found aboard many cargo ships during the early and mid twentieth century may be seen in that devised by Taylor & Co of Birkenhead and illustrated in *The Engineer* of March 1856. The two separate single-cylinder reversible engines drove winch drums via gearing and clutch arrangements; when necessary both cylinders could be set to drive a single drum. Obviously such plant reduced the number of men involved in working cargo, whilst the application of other steam assisted equipment reduced the number of seamen a ship had to carry. It was, however, necessary to ensure an adequate supply of steam when using such plant and often a 'donkey' boiler would be

fitted rather than make use of the main propulsion boilers.

Electricity aboard ship

Illumination in all early steamers was by means of candles or oil lamps; in fact that form of lighting applied in the accommodation of some tramp ships built as late as the 1930s. The main problems with candle and oil lamps were that they needed frequent filling or replacement, they were dirty and posed a potential danger in terms of fire. Gas lighting found favour ashore and seemed to offer advantages afloat, so during 1872 White Star Line was persuaded to install gas lighting systems in two of its new steamers, *Adriatic* and *Celtic*. Gas was generated by heating oil, the vapour being subsequently cleaned and circulated around parts of the passenger spaces where it supplied between thirty and forty burners, each of which gave out light equivalent to twelve candles. Initially a success, the system soon failed for the simple reason that movement of the ship caused pipe joints to leak.

Servia of 1881, Cunard's first steel-hulled ship, attracted attention on account of her electric lighting. She was not the first with this feature, but had a more comprehensive installation than previous ships, including twenty lamps in the engine and boiler rooms as well as ten illuminating the shaft tunnel. (Photo CMP; drawing Denis Griffiths)

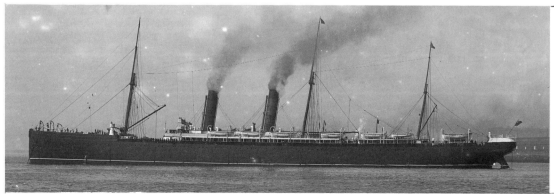
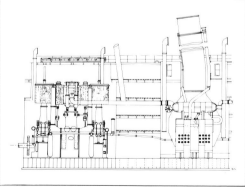

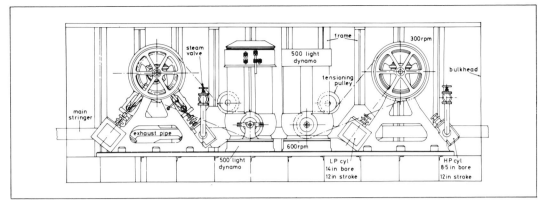

The lighting plant aboard the Oregon, *a typical late nineteenth-century steam powered generator set. (Denis Griffiths)*

The solution to shipboard lighting lay in the use of electricity. The Admiralty appreciated its benefits when applied to searchlights and a number of craft were fitted with generating equipment during 1876. One of the earliest applications to commercial craft was the saloon illumination system installed in the Inman liner *City of Berlin* during 1879. This trial proved to be a success and the owners specified a more extensive lighting arrangement for *City of Rome*, which entered service two years later. Fierce competition on the Atlantic prompted other owners to adopt electric lighting and from 1879 it was a brave owner who did not plan for electric lighting of the main public areas. Crew and working spaces normally received but scant regard from most owners, but boiler and engine rooms had always presented problems with regard to safe and efficient working due to the low levels of light generally available. *Servia* (1881), Cunard's first steel steamer, had an electrical system which supplied ninety-eight lamps in the accommodation spaces, fifty in the main saloon, together with a further twenty lamps in the engine and boiler rooms as well as ten in the propeller shaft tunnel, always a rather dark area.

So rapid was the development of electrical systems, and engine systems in general, that when *City of Berlin* was withdrawn from service in

1887 for re-engining she was provided with electric lighting throughout. *Umbria* (1884) and *Etruria* (1885) had four steam driven Siemens dynamos and an electrical installation which had the ship divided into six independent circuits, each capable of being connected to any of the dynamos. Simple single electric circuits had quickly given way to complex arrangements which allowed for areas to be isolated as necessary. Throughout the remaining years of the nineteenth century electric lighting was applied to more parts of the larger ships, particularly those carrying passengers. The interiors of such steamers became bright and remained clean, thus providing a pleasant environment for the passenger, but it was not just for illumination that electricity found a use.

Inman Line's *City of New York* (1888) made use of electric motors for powering ventilation fans, and her electrical system was so extensive that three electricians had to be carried for the specialist work involved. By contrast, Cunard's *Campania* and *Lucania* of 1893 carried eight electricians, these ships having two identical but separate generating rooms and a total power consumption of 42kW for lighting and electric motors. By the turn of the century the giant German liners like *Kaiser Wilhelm der Grosse* and *Deutschland* were using electricity for cook-

ing, cabin heating, water heating, cigar lighters and curling irons. Electric motors found considerable use in driving such items as engine room and accommodation ventilation fans, boiler forced draught fans and hoists for provisions and mail rooms.

Efficient electrical generation required a relatively high rotational speed and usually a belt drive from the reciprocating steam engine allowed for speed increase. However, *City of Berlin* was fitted with two turbines, directly connected to dynamos, and these proved popular with the engineers as they required little attention. It is likely that they were fitted during the 1887 re-engining of the ship.

Ventilation

As passenger ships became larger, problems involved in keeping the environment reasonably fresh and healthy attracted much attention. Natural ventilation had always been available but as ships became larger there were difficulties in ensuring an adequate supply of fresh air in the lower cabins. Fans were used from the 1870s but they required an extensive arrangement of ducting and several systems were devised to overcome this problem. Ports in the ship's sides allowed fresh air into the ship but these were only satisfactory in the upper tiers of accommodation, obviously the risk of flooding from an

The German express liners of the turn of the century adopted a number of advanced features, including quadruple expansion machinery and the widespread use of electricity for powering many shipboard services and auxiliaries. A good example is Hamburg-Amerika's Deutschland *of 1900. (Photo CMP; drawing Denis Griffiths)*

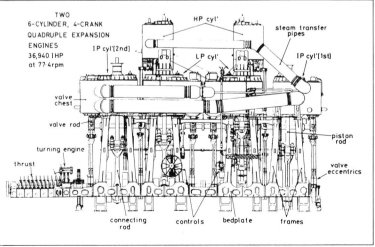

The New Zealand Shipping Co's Ruahine, *built by Denny of Dumbarton in 1891, was typical of the first class refrigerated ships of the day. With a speed of 14kts and substantial passenger accommodation, such vessels ran to liner schedules.* Ruahine *was originally rigged as a brig but the square yards have been removed from the main mast in this view.* (CMP)

open port being greater the lower in the ship the port was positioned. To enable a supply of fresh air to be drawn down to the lower cabins, *Umbria* and *Etruria* were provided with the Green's patent ventilation system. High velocity air was pumped through nozzles and this air induced a positive air flow in the surrounding atmosphere, thus drawing fresh air from above; stale air was expelled via the funnel casing which surrounded boiler uptakes, thus keeping the uptakes warm and maintaining boiler draught in cold weather.

The more conventional ventilation systems employed fans which for later ships were often driven by electric motors. *Deutschland*, for example, had seventy small fans for use in public rooms and larger cabins.

Refrigeration

Passengers required feeding during any sea journey and for larger ships on long passages this could present a problem. During the 1840s Atlantic liners were fitted with ice houses in which fresh provisions could be kept, but the limitation of such storage was availability of ice. In some American cities large warehouses would be filled with ice blocks during winter months and this could then be sold during spring and summer months for so long as it lasted. Development of

mechanical refrigeration systems made cold storage independent of ice availability and over the years a number of systems were introduced. Ammonia, carbon dioxide and even air were used for some early refrigeration plants with varying degrees of success.

At first refrigeration was applied to cold rooms for the storage of food and *Servia* had a Bell-Coleman cold air plant installed during construction. This was not, however, the first such system in a ship, for in 1876 a refrigeration plant had been fitted in the French steamer *Le Frigorifique* which traded between France and Argentina. Two years later the steamer *Paraguay* landed 5500 beef carcasses at Le Havre in excellent condition, the meat having been kept under refrigeration throughout the voyage. However, the French did not appear to be interested in this successful venture and further voyages were abandoned.

The businessman Andrew McIlwraith had inspected the *Paraguay*, which suggested the potential that refrigeration offered meat producers in Australia, and he arranged for his company to charter the 2436-ton British ship *Strathleven*. Outward from Britain the ship carried 575 immigrants, but for her return in November 1879

Built by Barclay, Curle & Co Ltd in 1900 for Elder Dempster's Canadian service, the 7392-ton Lake Champlain *made technical history in 1902 when she was fitted with the first permanent shipboard wireless telegraphy installation. Henceforth, ships were no longer out of touch when out of sight.* (CMP)

she carried a general cargo and a 40-ton refrigerated load of butter, beef, lamb and mutton, the ship having been fitted with a Bell-Coleman cold air system for that purpose. Success prompted others to involve themselves in the antipodean meat trade, and in 1880 the steamer *Protos* brought 4600 carcasses of mutton and lamb together with 100 tons of butter. A year later the Orient Line fitted three of its steamers with refrigerating plant and the trade in refrigerated cargo expanded.

Even on the Atlantic there was money to be made from the carriage of meat from America to Europe. Live cattle had been imported into Britain but the trade did not suit passenger ships because of the smell involved. Meat under refrigeration presented no such problems, and with express liners able to offer high speed crossings there was great potential in shipping frozen meat. White Star's *Teutonic* (1889) and *Majestic* (1890) were each provided with two meat holds of 40,000 cubic feet capacity. The ammonia plant cooled coils over which air was forced, this air then being circulated around the holds. So successful was this trade that the company withdrew two older ships, *Britannic* (1874) and *Germanic* (1875), for installation of refrigerating equipment. Because existing holds were converted it was decided to fit a circulating brine system, the brine being cooled by a carbon dioxide refrigerating plant.

The introduction of refrigeration provided better fare for passengers and opened up a trade which had not previously existed. Overseas areas were for the first time able to take advantage of European markets for many of their products.

Pumps

Any steam plant requires a number of pumps to ensure its operation and the early engines provided necessary power themselves by means of suitable levers. As engines grew in size this was no longer considered suitable in many cases due to the large water flows required. For high flows centrifugal rather than reciprocating pumps offered improved efficiency with small size, but these could not readily be driven by the engine. Condenser circulating pumps were very large for high powered engines and these had to be driven by small steam engines of their own. *Teutonic* and her sister required 4000 tons of seawater per hour to be circulated through the condensers and this was achieved using centrifugal pumps with impellers of 5ft diameter. Separate pumps for other duties became the norm for most large ships from the mid 1880s onwards and where large flows were required centrifugal types were used. In order to pump water into the boiler against high pressure the reciprocating type of pump still had advantages.

Conclusion

Over the years main engine and boiler designs changed to meet the requirements of paddle and screw propulsion but, because there was no single solution to any problem, engines (and to a lesser extent boilers) took many different forms. As particular problems arose builders found so-

Normannia

Crowds line the quayside at Le Havre to watch the departure of CGT's L'Aquitaine for New York in about 1900. The ship symbolised the nineteenth-century dominance of British marine engineering and shipbuilding: she was built and engined by Fairfields of Glasgow in 1890 as the Normannia *for Hamburg-Amerika, who required a first rate liner for a new express Atlantic service. However, by the time this photo was taken both Germany and France were capable of meeting their own shipbuilding requirements and neither country was ever again a regular customer of British shipyards for prestige ships. (CMP)*

The forgotten hero of the steam revolution, the fireman or stoker. Firing the furnaces required hours of arduous work of a monotony unknown to seaman in sail. Not surprisingly, in navy and merchant service, the 'black gang' remained a race apart. (By courtesy of Basil Greenhill)

lutions but they were always striving for greater efficiency and more compact designs, for that is what the shipowner required: machinery, although essential, took valuable cargo space and cost money to buy and operate.

Higher steam pressure posed problems but engineers found solutions in better design and the use of stronger materials. Marine machinery did not exist in isolation from other machinery and marine designers learned much from their railway and general engineering counterparts; by the same token they also contributed much to the knowledge of others through co-operation in learned societies. Boilers and many items of auxiliary machinery such as electrical generators, refrigeration plants and pumps were to be found ashore but the marine industry faced problems of space, vibration, corrosion and other conditions which were absent from shore installations. Large propulsion engines were not found ashore but steam engines were used in mines and factories; builders of such machines often gained from the experiences of the marine engineer. Everybody on board a ship relied upon the machinery for their safe return home and there was a pride amongst seagoing engineers which appears to have set them apart from their land based brothers.

This chapter has given only a brief view of the changing marine engineering scene during the nineteenth century but it does illustrate how rapid many of the changes were and how quickly new ships became dated by changes in design and materials available.

Denis Griffiths

The Earliest Steamboat Pioneers

Boat	Inventor	Place of trials	Date	Machinery (cyl diam × stroke in inches)	Dimensions (length × breadth × depth; tonnage) Feet–Inches Metres	Remarks
PYROSCAPHE	Marquis de Jouffroy D'Abbans	River Saone, France	1783	Horizontal double-acting cylinder, 25.6 × 77 stroke, ratchet drive to side paddles	148–6 × 14–7 × 3–3; 182 tons 45.3 × 4.5 × 1.0	On 15 July 1783 steamed against the current for 15 minutes
Un-named	John Fitch	R Delaware, USA	1786	Horizontal double-acting cylinder, 12 × 36 stroke, powering 12 vertical oars, 6 per side	34–0 × 8–0 × 3–6; 9 tons 10.4 × 2.4 × 1.1	Obtained 3mph on 27 July 1786; built other steamers in later years
Un-named	James Rumsey	R Potomac, USA	1787	Tandem cylinder 'atmospheric', 13 × 20, powering a water-jet pump	18–0 × 6–0 × 2–8; 3 tons 5.5 × 1.8 × 0.8	On 27 December 1787 moved against the current at 3mph carrying 2 tons
Un-named	Patrick Miller and William Symington	Dalswinton Loch, Scotland	1788	2cyl 'atmospheric', 4 × 18, chain drive to single paddle wheel between the hulls	Double hull: 25–0 × 7–0 × 2–2; 5 tons 7.6 × 2.1 × 0.7	Achieved 5mph on 14 October 1788
KENT AMBINAVIGATOR	Earl of Stanhope	R Thames, London	1792	2cyl high-pressure non-condensing, driving palmipede (duck-foot) paddles	111–0 × 21–0 × 10–0; 200 tons 33.8 × 6.4 × 3.0	The palmipede paddles were inefficient but drove the ship at about 3mph
POLACCA	Nicholas J Roosevelt	R Passaic, USA	1798	1cyl, 20 × 24, driving side wheels	c60–0 long; 25 tons c18.3	In October 1798 achieved 3mph; Roosevelt later built the first Mississippi steamer
CHARLOTTE DUNDAS	William Symington for Lord Dundas	Forth and Clyde Canal	1801	1cyl horizontal, 22 × 44, driving one central paddle in a recess aft	56–0 × 18–0 × 8–0 17.1 × 5.5 × 2.4	In March 1802 towed two 70-ton barges for c20 miles
Un-named	Robert Fulton	R Seine, France	1803	1cyl vertical, 17.7 × 31.5, bell crank side lever motion; side wheels	1st hull 66–6 × 10–7 × 3–3; 25 tons; 20.3 × 3.2 × 1.0 2nd 74–7 × 8–3 × 3–3 22.7 × 2.5 × 1.0	Fulton's first boat was destroyed before trials but the second managed c3mph against the current
LITTLE JULIANNA	Colonel John Stevens	Hoboken, New Jersey	1804	1cyl vertical, 4.5 × 9, overhead beam driving twin screw propellers	24–9 × 6–2 × 2–4; 5 tons 7.5 × 1.9 × 0.7	First practical screw driven boat; achieved 4mph in May 1804

Notes:
The table includes only those experimental boats that are known to have been moved significant distances by the power of steam. From H P Spratt, *The Birth of the Steamboat*, which has further details of the machinery and the experiments.

Bibliography

Edited by Robert Gardiner from information supplied by the contributors.

GENERAL

There is no entirely satisfactory general history of the introduction of steam navigation. The following titles are devoted to special aspects of the subject – particular routes, ship types or technical developments – that would not fit neatly into the listings for individual chapters below.

N R P BONSOR, *North Atlantic Seaway* (2nd ed, 5 vols, Jersey 1975–80).
A massive work chronicling every ship from *Savannah* that served the transatlantic routes from Europe to North America. Includes potted histories of the shipping companies, but little sense of context. A companion volume *South Atlantic Seaway* has been published since.

ADMIRAL P W BROCK and BASIL GREENHILL, *Steam and Sail* (Newton Abbot 1973).
Covers the period approximately 1840–1870 in both text and photographs, giving a good picture of developments of the time.

ROBIN CRAIG, *Steam Tramps and Cargo Liners* (London 1980).
In the National Maritime Museum's series 'The Ship', this excellent little book tackles the neglected subject of the ordinary cargo steamer and its development from about 1850.

JOHN KENNEDY, *The History of Steam Navigation* (Liverpool 1903).
Although old, this is still one of the better books dealing generally with this subject.

DAVID LYON, *The Denny List*, 4 parts (London 1975–76).
A comprehensive catalogue of plans and related documentation now held in the National Maritime Museum from this most go-ahead of shipbuilders. Most of the important developments of the century are reflected in Denny's ships, which are covered in detail (the first two parts deal with the period from 1844 to after 1900).

ENG VICE-ADM R W SKELTON, 'Progress in Marine Engineering', *Proceedings of the Institute of Mechanical Engineers* (1930).
A general survey by a distinguished naval engineer whose personal experience went back a long way.

PROF ANTHONY SLAVEN, 'Scottish Shipbuilders and Marine Engineers', in T C SMOUT (ed) *Scotland and the Sea* (Edinburgh 1991).
A thoroughly researched account of the biggest concentration of marine industrial capacity in the nineteenth century world.

H P SPRATT, *Handbook of the Collections illustrating Merchant Steamers and Motor-Ships*, Part II (London 1949).
Science Museum handbook of the collection (companion to an outline history) with a descriptive catalogue of the substantial holdings of models, prints, plans etc. The museum also published a selection under the title *Outline History of Transatlantic Steam Navigation* in 1950.

F M WALKER, *Song of the Clyde* (Cambridge 1984).
A well illustrated history of Clyde shipbuilding but of wider significance in giving an overview of nineteenth century technical developments in ship design and construction.

INTRODUCTION

S FISHER (ed), *Innovation in Shipping and Trade* (Exeter 1989).
Contains, *inter alia*, papers on the development of screw propulsion.

PROF F E HYDE, *Cunard and the North Atlantic, 1840–1873* (London 1975).
Solid, scholarly account of the early history of this great company.

SARAH PALMER, 'Experience, Experiment and Economics: Factors in the Construction of Early Steamships', in K MATTHEWS and G PANTING (eds), *Ships and Shipbuilding in the North Atlantic Region* (St Johns, Newfoundland 1978).
A useful paper on some of the less obvious factors influencing early steamship development.

R H DANA, Jr, *The Seaman's Manual* (London 1855).
An invaluable guide to what was expected of the nineteenth century seaman.

STEAM BEFORE THE SCREW

GEORGE DODD, *An Historical and Explanatory Dissertation on Steam Engines and Steam Packets* (London 1818).
A first-hand account of the first long open sea passage by a British steamer.

LT W GORDON, RN, *The Economy of the Marine Steam Engine* (London 1845).
Excellent contemporary work on the development and operation of the first generation of marine engines.

DENIS GRIFFITHS, *Brunel's Great Western* (Wellingborough 1985).
The best history of this vessel and her background, written by a marine engineer.

CAPT BASIL HALL, RN, *An Account of the Ferry across the Tay at Dundee* (Dundee 1825).
This little booklet has much to say about paddle steamer technology in the early 1820s.

ADMIRAL JAMES HOSKEN, *Autobiographical Sketch of the Public Career of Admiral James Hosken* (Penzance 1889).

——, *The Logs of the First Voyage made with the unceasing aid of Steam, between England and America by the Great Western of Bristol* (Bristol 1838).
Probably the most valuable single source on the operation of paddle steamers at sea.

GORDON JACKSON, 'Operational Problem of the Transfer to Steam: Perth & London Shipping Company *c*1820–1846', in T C SMOUT (ed), *Scotland and the Sea* (Edinburgh 1992).
An excellent case history with very useful documentation.

DIONYSIUS LARDNER, *Steam Communication with India* (Calcutta 1837).
Although a polemical presentation, it does contain useful contemporary information on steamers.

CAMPBELL McMURRAY, *Old Order, New Thing* (London 1972).
Probably the most instructive brief account ever written of the workings of the classic side lever paddle steamer.

DAPHNE POCHIN MOULD, *Captain Roberts of the Sirius* (Cork 1988).
A fairly heavily padded piece of local history which nevertheless contains useful material on the background to the pioneer crossing of the Atlantic.

ROBERT MURRAY, *Rudimentary Treatise on Marine Engines* (London 1854).
One of the best contemporary technical works on the early development of the marine steam engine.

CDR ROBERT OTWAY, *An Elementary Treatise on Steam* (London 1834).
Another valuable contemporary work, with good advice to the author's naval contemporaries.

LEROY E POND, *Junius Smith* (New York 1927).
Gives an excellent picture of the genesis, operation and disastrous end of the *Great Western's* rivals.

STEPHEN S ROBERTS, 'The French Transatlantic Steam Packet Programme', *The Mariner's Mirror* 73/3 (1987).
An account of a little known but important episode in early oceangoing paddle steamer history.

CDR R S ROBINSON, *The Nautical Steam Engine Explained ... for the use of Officers of the Navy, etc* (London 1839).
Another very valuable contemporary source; fulfils the claim of the title.

SAMUEL SEAWARD, 'Memoir on the Practicability of Shortening the Duration of Voyages by the Adoption of Auxiliary Steam Power to Sailing Vessels', *Transactions of the Institute of Civil Engineers* I (1842).
A revealing analysis of the limitations of the paddle steamer of the 1840s with the suggestions of a marine engine builder for a solution to the problem of the wider use of steam at sea.

SAMUEL SMILES, *Lives of Boulton and Watt* (London 1865).
The classic account of a partnership of fundamental importance in the history of the marine steam engine.

H PHILIP SPRATT, *The Birth of the Steamboat* (London 1958).
Excellent short 'biographies' of all the important early steam propelled vessels, including unsuccessful experiments.

——, *Transatlantic Paddle Steamers* (Glasgow 1951).
Similar work to the above but concentrating on those paddlers known to have crossed the Atlantic.

JAMES WALKER, *The First Trans-Atlantic Steamer* (London 1898).
Examines and rejects the claim that the Canadian *Royal William* was 'the first vessel to cross the Atlantic under steam'. Recent studies have shown that in the era when sail was an essential element in the operation of all steam vessels this kind of claim is quite unreal.

EARLY STEAMSHIPS IN EASTERN WATERS

For contemporary news of events consult also *The Illustrated London News* and eastern journals such as the *Bombay Times, Bengal Hurkaru, China Mail* and the *Straits Times*.

W D BERNARD, *Voyages and Services of the Nemesis, 1840–43* (London 1845).
Very readable accounts of the perilous outward voyage of first iron steamship to sail from Britain to the East (she nearly split in half off the east coast of Africa), and the important role she played in the Opium War.

H T BERNSTEIN, *Steamboats on the Ganges* (Bombay 1960).
Includes early steamships, with illustrations.

C B BUCKLEY, *An Anecdotal History of ... Singapore, 1819–67* (Singapore & Oxford 1984).
Includes frequent references to steamships.

E H CREE (M LEVIEN, ed), *The Cree Journals* (Exeter 1981).
Valuable and delightfully illustrated account by Surgeon Cree, RN, of his experiences (mostly in early steamships) in China, Borneo and elsewhere during 1837–56.

E J EITEL, *Europe in China: the History of Hong Kong* (Hong Kong & London 1895; reprinted Taipei, Taiwan 1968).
Includes the Anglo-Chinese wars.

C A GIBSON-HILL, 'The Steamers employed in Asian Waters, 1819–39', *Journal of the Malay Branch Royal Asiatic Soc* I (1954), pp120–62.
Deals especially with early steamships visiting Singapore.

G S GRAHAM, *The China Station, 1830–60* (Oxford 1978).
Includes the Anglo-Chinese wars.

C R LOW, *History of the Indian Navy* (London 1887).
Still regarded as a standard work on the 'I.N.' (created from the Bombay Marine in 1830 and disbanded in 1863).

SIR G R MUNDY, *Narrative of Events in Borneo ...* (London 1848).
Compiled from the journals of Captain Mundy and Rajah James Brooke; includes operations of HMS *Iris* for the suppression of piracy.

J OUCHTERLONY, *The China War* (London 1844).
A contemporary account of the naval operations in 1840–42.

G A PRINSEP, *An Account of Steam Vessels ... in British India* (Calcutta 1830).
An early work on the subject (note the date).

S RABSON & K O'DONOGHUE, *P and O: A Fleet History* (London 1980).
One of the most recent of several histories of the famous Peninsular and Oriental Steam Navigation Company.

A ROBINSON, *An Account of recent Improvements in the Navigation of the Ganges in iron Steam Vessels* (London 1848).
Includes the steamers and the accommodation boats towed by them.

W J ROFF, *The Romantic History of Early Steamships* (London forthcoming).
Covers the subject worldwide but, being subtitled '*Including Some Actions in Eastern Waters*', examines in detail a number of early steamers sent out from Britain and others that were built in the East; also deals with routes to India (including the early P&O) and roles played by early steamers west of India, in Burma, China and Borneo.

SIR S RUNCIMAN, *The White Rajahs* (Cambridge 1960).
The first part of this meticulous work of reference relates to Rajah James Brooke (the first white rajah) and includes descriptions of the several parts taken by early steamships in the suppression of native piracy.

JEAN SUTTON, *Lords of the East: The East India Company and its Ships* (London 1981).
This is a fine production covering the ships of the EICo from its foundation in the year 1600 to its winding up soon after the Indian Mutiny of 1857. Unfortunately (for the present purpose), the greater part of the work details matters relating to sailing vessels, and the lesser part dealing with steamers contains some errors.

R A WADIA, *The Bombay Dockyard* (Bombay 1957).
A useful record of ships built in the EICo's Dockyard. However, it does not readily differentiate between steamers *assembled* at Bombay (from parts prefabricated in Britain) and those built in their entirety at Bombay.

STEAM NAVIGATION AND THE UNITED STATES

This is a broad, and much-ploughed, field; the titles listed below are the more generally useful and avoid most of the monographs on particular lines or individual boats.

A C BROWN, *Steam Packets on the Chesapeake* (New York 1961).
Essentially an expanded history of the Old Bay Line, first published in 1940, to encompass others on the Baltimore-Norfolk service. The author also wrote a good history of the *Baltimore Steam Packet Company* (New York 1959).

ROBERT H BURGESS and H GRAHAM WOOD, *Steamboats out of Baltimore* (Cambridge, Maryland 1968).
A general history, based on modern sources, of the steamer services in Chesapeake Bay.

F E DAYTON, *Steamboat Days* (New York 1939; reprinted 1970).
A classic general survey of the whole field; well presented and very entertaining.

J T FLEXNER, *Steamboats Come True: American Inventors in Action* (New York 1944; reprinted as *Inventors in Action: The Story of the Steamboat* 1962).
Despite the original title, gives credit to the complex of contributions from France, Britain and America to the development of a workable steamboat.

HENRY HALL, *Report of the Ship-Building Industry of the United States* (Washington, DC 1882; reprinted New York 1970).
Originally part of the Tenth Census, this report is replete with information on the state of US shipbuilding in the third quarter of the century; contains much data and illustrations beyond the descriptive matter.

ERIK HEYL, *Early American Steamers*, 3 vols (Buffalo, NY 1953–56).
A good overall account of its subject; essentially illustrations of the ships with short histories.

L C HUNTER, *Steamboats on the Western Rivers* (Cambridge, mass 1949; reprinted 1970).
The best single work in the field, this 'Economic and Technological History', as it is subtitled, deals with both machinery developments and changing trade patterns.

RICHARD R LINGENFELTER, *Steamboats on the Colorado River, 1852–1916* (Tucson, Arizona 1978).
A modern study of steam navigation on this waterway.

W M LYTLE (F R HOLDCAMPER, *et al*, eds), *Merchant Steam Vessels of the United States, 1807–1868* (Staten Island, NY 1975).
A magnificent piece of research, the 'Lytle List' was originally published by the Steamship Historical Society of America in 1956. It gives basic data on ships built, lost and converted in the years before the official annual list of the *Merchant Vessels of the US* was produced.

J B MANSFIELD, *History of the Great Lakes*, 3 vols (Chicago 1899).
Although superseded in some respects, this comprehensive work still offers remarkable detail on the early steamers.

JOHN H MORRISON, *History of American Steam Navigation* (New York 1903; reprinted 1958).
A comprehensive and classic work in its field, but stronger on fact than analysis.

H A MUSHAM, 'Early Great Lakes Steamboats', *The American Neptune* III, V-VII, XVII, XVIII (1943, 1945–47, 1957–58).
An important series of articles based on a surviving contemporary manuscript by Capt James Van Cleve, a pioneer of Great Lakes steamboating.

C RIDGELY-NEVITT, *American Steamships on the Atlantic* (Newark, Delaware 1981).
A recent study of the oceanic arm of American shipping.

D C RINGWALD, *Hudson River Day Line* (Berkeley, Cal 1965).
A heavily illustrated history of one of the great steamboat companies of the East.

D B TYLER, *The American Clyde* (Newark, Delaware 1958).
A well researched history of shipbuilding on the Delaware from 1840 to the First World War.

THE SCREW PROPELLER AND MERCHANT SHIPPING

J BOURNE, *Treatise on the Screw Propeller* (London 1852).
A useful detailed contemporary account of the early years of screw development; the author was a strong supporter of Pettit Smith's claims.

? BYRNE, *On the Best Means of propelling Ships at Sea* (London & New York 1841).
A pamphlet contribution to the Anglo-American dispute about the relative merits of the different screw systems.

EWAN CORLETT, *The Iron Ship* (2nd ed, London 1990).
Essentially a study of *The Great Britain*, this important work tackles the whole context of the introduction of iron construction and screw propulsion, resulting in the best available single-volume study of mid-nineteenth-century ship development.

GEORGE S EMMERSON, *John Scott Russell* (London 1977).
Biography of one of the great Victorian engineers, written by an engineer; much of the middle section of the book is devoted to the *Great Eastern*, which Russell built and was financially ruined by. A good counterweight to the hagiographical writing about Brunel.

TRIPLE EXPANSION AND THE FIRST SHIPPING REVOLUTION

Many of the titles given in the General section are equally applicable; those listed below are confined to more technical titles relating to triple expansion machinery.

J F CLARKE and F STORR, *Strength of Marine Boilers and the Design of the Furnace* (Newcastle-upon-Tyne 1983).
One of a series of occasional papers dealing with the history of science & technology. Much useful and interesting information on the development of marine boilers.

A C KIRK, 'Triple Expansion Engines of SS *Aberdeen*', *Transactions of the Institution of Naval Architects* XXIII (1882).
Interesting paper which gives history of Kirk's involvement in development of the triple expansion engine. Describes *Aberdeen's* engines and those of *Propontis*.

F C MARSHALL, 'On Triple Expansion Engines', *Transaction of the North East Coast Society of Engineers & Shipbuilders* I (1884–5).
A useful if detailed paper which explains the advantages of triple expansion in thermodynamic terms.

G A NEWBY, *Behind the Fire Doors* (published by author 1979).
Small booklet describing the introduction and application of Fox corrugated furnaces. Useful and well worth reading.

A E SEATON, 'Further Experiences with Triple Compound Engines', *Transactions of the Institution of Naval Architects*, XXVI (1885).
Mention of different triple expansion installations which followed *Aberdeen*. Good discussion which includes further comments by Kirk.

R F THOMAS, 'Evolution of Lubricants for Marine Propulsion', *Transaction of the Institution of Marine Engineers* 101, 2 (1989).
An interest paper which describes development of marine lubricants from the early days of steam to diesel engines.

THE INDUSTRIAL BACKGROUND

Many thousands of works have been written on the process of industrialisation in general, and on British industrial development in particular. While the range of topics covered and approaches adopted is immense, relatively little attention has been devoted to the place of the maritime industries in the changing economic environment of the nineteenth century. A comprehensive maritime economic history may be lacking, but the following titles cover a good deal of the relevant ground, especially with regard to the context in which the steamship developed.

JC CARR and W TAPLIN, *History of the British Steel Industry* (Oxford 1962).
This detailed history of steelmaking in Britain since 1856 contains a short, but useful section on steel shipbuilding.

ROY CHURCH (ed), *The Dynamics of Victorian Business: Problems and Perspectives to the 1870s* (London 1980).
A collection of essays on the development of the main sectors of the British economy in the mid-nineteenth century. The articles by P J Riden on ironmaking and A E Musson on engineering sketch the principal features of the industrial background to steamship development, while A Slaven's piece on shipbuilding is particularly strong on the locational shift of the industry in the 1850s and 1860s.

ADAM W KIRKALDY, *British Shipping: Its History, Organisation and Importance* (London 1914; reprinted Newton Abbot 1970).
Despite its age this remains an important work on the British shipping industry down to the First World War.

DONALD N McCLOSKEY, *Economic Maturity and Entrepreneurial Decline: British Iron and Steel 1870–1913* (Cambridge, Mass 1973).
An analysis of British entrepreneurship which establishes why steel was not adopted in shipbuilding to any degree before the 1880s.

A E MUSSON, *The Growth of British Industry* (London 1978).
An overview of Britain's industrial development from 1500 to 1939, particularly useful on technological innovations.

SIDNEY POLLARD, *Peaceful Conquest: The Industrialization of Europe 1760–1970* (Oxford 1981).
A persuasive consideration of the diffusion of industrialism which emphasises the role of regions, rather than countries, in the process.

SIDNEY POLLARD and PAUL ROBERTSON, *The British Shipbuilding Industry 1870–1914* (Cambridge, Mass 1979).
The standard work on an important phase in British shipbuilding history, covering the evolution of the steel steamship, fluctuations in output, and the organisation of the industry as well as wages and labour relations.

M M POSTAN and H J HABAKKUK (eds) *The Cambridge Economic History of Europe, Vol VI: The Industrial Revolutions and After* (Cambridge 1965).
Amongst the various essays in this collection, the broad surveys of transport by L Girard, and of technological change by David Landes, are particularly relevant to the question of steamship development.

THE SHIP PROPELLER COMPANY

This chapter is largely based on primary sources quoted in the footnotes. There is little documentary evidence for the life of Pettit Smith (in contrast to the large archive left by his rival Ericsson) and no published works of direct relevance.

SAIL-ASSIST AND THE STEAMSHIP

Very little has been published on the subject of 'sail-assist' in the nineteenth century. The best primary sources are quoted in the footnotes to the chapter. In addition, there is a good discussion in Halstead, *The Screw Fleet of the Navy* (London 1850), especially p37. In relatively recent years successive scares in connection with oil prices have resulted in some scientific work being done on possible modern sail-assist. Some of the results are incorporated in, notably, Williams and Liljenberg, 'The Revival of the Flettner Rotor', *Proceedings of the Annual Meeting of the Society of Naval Architects and Marine Engineers* (New York, November 1983); Clayton and Nance, 'Wind Assisted Ship Propulsion', *Proceedings of the Conference of British Wind Energy Association* (1984); Molland and Hawksley, 'Propeller and machinery performance in wind-assisted ships', in *Windship Technology* (Amsterdam 1985); Bergeson, Greenweld and Harcourt, 'Wing Sails for Auxiliary Ship Propulsion', *Journal of the New England Section, Society of Naval Architects and Marine Engineers (New York 1984)*; *Novitski*, Wind Star: The Building of a Sailship, (New York 1987). See also *Windship News*, a journal published in June and November each year by Liverpool Polytechnic.

ALFRED HOLT AND THE COMPOUND ENGINE

Apart from a couple of standard company histories, the following lists important contemporary papers and biographical notices not referred to in the chapter footnotes but significant contributions to the debate about compounding.

ANON, 'Memoir and Minute on the Late Professor Rankine', *Transactions of the Institution of Engineers and Shipbuilders in Scotland* XVI (1872–73).

ANON, 'Obituary of Alfred Holt', *Minutes of the Proceedings of the Institution of Civil Engineers* CLXXXVII (1911–12).

F J BRAMWELL, 'On the Progress effected in Economy of Fuel in Steam Navigation', *Proceedings of the Institution of Mechanical Engineers* (1872).

M FALKUS, *The Blue Funnel Legend* (London 1990).
Good on company structure and management, but thin on engineering and its implication.

F E HYDE, *Blue Funnel* (Liverpool 1956).
Despite its age, this is still the best all-round account of Holt.

T S PRIDEAUX, 'On Economy and Fuel in Steam Ships', *Transactions of the Institution of Naval Architects* XIII (1872).

W J M RANKINE, 'Sketch of the Life of John Elder', *Transactions of the Institution of Engineers and Shipbuilders in Scotland* XV (1871–72).
A near-contemporary account of an important name in the history of marine compounding.

MARINE ENGINEERING DEVELOPMENT

Technical papers were often presented at meetings of learned societies such as the Institution of Mechanical Engineers, the Institution of Naval Architects and the Institute of Marine Engineers, and these provide much valuable detailed information concerning the period. Many large towns and cities had local engineering societies at which papers were presented and these give details of local industry. Technical journals such as *The Engineer, Engineering*, and *The Marine Engineer & Motorship Builder* provide detailed information on engineering equipment and on individual ships. The items listed below are typical, and the reader would benefit by consulting some of them.

DENIS GRIFFITHS, *Brunel's Great Western* (Wellingborough 1985).
Description of Brunel's first steamer with sections concerning construction and machinery. Explanations of side lever engine operation and boiler construction. Useful line diagrams of machinery and location in the ship.

——, *Power of the Great Liners*, (Wellingborough 1990).
A marine engineering history of Atlantic liners. Covers these liners from the 1840s until the 1960s, dealing with the nineteenth century in the first five chapters. Propulsion and auxiliary machinery is covered with line and photographic illustration supplementing the written descriptions. Very useful as no other book covers the topic in such detail.

A J MAGINNIS, *The Atlantic Ferry* (London 1893).
A good overall view of Atlantic liner operations with many interesting items concerning early machinery. Some useful diagrams and pictures.

E C SMITH, *A Short History of Naval and Marine Engineering* (Cambridge 1937).
Well illustrated but rather dated account of the subject, covering all aspects of propulsion and auxiliary plant from the introduction of steam power until the 1930s. Lacks a broader view of the context of technology.

H P SPRATT, *Handbook of the Collections illustrating Marine Engineering*, Part II (London 1953).
Extremely useful inventory of marine machinery in the Science Museum collection. Each entry gives details of the artifact, drawing, picture or model together with an explanation as to its operation. Very informative and invaluable as it covers all types of engines, boilers, steering gear, etc.

The Engineer (19 December 1890): Supplement about White Star steamer *Teutonic*.
Detailed and informative supplement with much useful detail regarding main and auxiliary plant together with details of ship construction. Good drawings of machinery and engine room.

The Engineer (13 October 1893): Supplement about Cunard steamship *Lucania*.
Similar to that for *Teutonic* with much detail and photographs as well as drawings.

The Engineer (Centenary Number 1956):
Marine Engineering section gives basic but informative detail of marine engineering developments during the century of the magazine's publication.

Marine Engineer & Motorship Builder (December 1932)
Excellent article on the work of Andrew Laing, showing the influence of one man on marine engineering during the latter part of the nineteenth century.

W PARKER, 'On the Progress of Marine Engineering', *Transactions of the Institution of Naval Architects* XXVII (1886).
One of a series of papers presented at regular intervals which review marine engineering developments. This covers the preceding decade and is useful as it shows how efficiency of plant was improved.

T BROWN, 'Marine Engineering Review – Past, Present and Future', *Transactions of the Royal Institution of Naval Architects* 102 (1960).
Good descriptive paper with plenty of detail covering the first 100 years of the Institution's existence.

HENRY DYER, 'Development of the Marine Engine', *Proceedings of the Philosophical Society of Glasgow* (1886).
Extremely interesting paper which covers engine developments from the start of marine propulsion. Readable and informative.

CC POUNDER, 'Some Notable Belfast Built Engines', *Transactions of the Belfast Association of Engineers* (1948).
Well illustrated paper covering the machinery installed in ships built by Harland & Wolff, including the famous White Star ships. Deals with engines, boilers and auxiliary plant.

Glossary of Terms and Abbreviations

Compiled by Robert Gardiner with the assistance of the contributors. This list assumes some knowledge of ships and does not include the most basic terminology. It also omits those words which are defined on the only occasions in which they occur in this book.

annular engine. A variation of the trunk engine (*qv*), but usually vertical, in which the cylinder was cast with a concentric central trunk; the piston was shaped like a ring doughnut to fill the space between trunk and cylinder casing. Two piston rods extended up to a crosshead, which rose and fell with the motion of the piston, driving a long connecting rod operating through the trunk of the cylinder to turn the crankshaft below.

apparent wind. The direction and speed of wind as experienced by a vessel under way, as opposed to the true wind felt when stationary. The apparent wind is influenced by the speed and relationship of the vessel to the direction of the true wind.

archimedian screw. A screw of continuous thread turning inside a cylinder to raise water for purposes of irrigation; its invention was attributed to Archimedes of Syracuse (*c*287-212 BC).

atmospheric engine. A simple form of steam engine in which the piston was driven by the pressure of the atmosphere, the condensation of steam being used to create a vacuum.

Babbit's metal. A soft alloy of tin, antimony and copper, particularly used in bearings to reduce friction; named after its American inventor (1799-1862).

banjo frame. In early screw steamers a device to enable a two-bladed propeller to be raised to prevent drag when under sail. The propeller was fitted inside the frame on a stub shaft; when disconnected from the main shaft, and with its two blades in the vertical position, the propeller in its frame was lifted in slides in the deadwood (*qv*) into an aperture in the stern.

barque. As understood in the nineteenth century, a vessel with three or more masts, square rigged on all but the mizzen, which set only fore and aft canvas. Any vessel, even steamers, carrying this arrangement were said to be barque rigged.

barquentine. A vessel with a full square rigged fore mast and fore and aft rigged main and mizzen; later vessels had four or more masts, with only the foremast square rigged.

beam engine. A steam engine with a vertical cylinder whose motion was transferred to the shaft by means of an overhead rocking beam (called a walking beam in the USA).

Beaufort. A conventionalised scale of numbers and related descriptions to categorise wind force (Force 9 is called 'Strong Gale', for example). Named after its devisor, Sir Francis Beaufort (1774-1857), the Admiralty Hydrographer from 1829 to 1855.

Bell-Coleman cold air plant. An early form of compressed air refrigeration system, in which the cooled air was circulated through the cold compartments or hold and returned in a closed cycle.

Bessemer steel. The first commercially viable process for manufacturing steel on an industrial scale, demonstrated for the first time in 1856 by the British engineer Sir Henry Bessemer (1813-1898). Early steel lacked ductility, malleability and uniformity and was difficult to work, but the perfection of so-called mild steel in the 1870s led to its rapid introduction as a warship building material.

bilge keel. Narrow wing-like extensions along the midships underwater hull at about the turn of the bilge designed to dampen rolling.

billethead. A simple form of abstract decoration to the top of the stem where more sophisticated vessels had a figurehead. It was often carved like the end of a violin, and was then specifically called a fiddlehead; if it turned outwards instead of inwards, it was called a scrollhead.

Bishop Arch. Nickname for the hogging truss (*qv*) of American steamers.

Blade Element Theory. Originally propounded by the naval architect William Froude in 1878 to account for the behaviour of propellers, it sought to give a theoretical basis to propeller design.

boards. The flat blades of a paddle wheel whose action provided the thrust; also called floats.

boot-topping. Originally the process of cleaning the area of the hull 'between wind and water' which could be achieved by heeling the vessel without docking; this band came to be known as the boot-topping and was eventually extended to the whole underwater hull if sheathed for purposes of antifouling.

bonnet. An addition to the foot of lower sails for fair weather; after the late seventeenth century they were replaced on all but small craft with deeper sails that were reefed (*qv*) in heavy weather.

bore. The internal diameter of a cylinder or gun barrel.

boss. The central hub of a propeller from which the blades radiate.

brails. Ropes from the leech or outer edge of a gaff or trysail to the mast or gaff which allow the sail to be furled up, or brailed, quickly.

brig. A two masted vessel with square canvas on both fore and main masts, but with a gaff-headed fore and aft main sail. Nineteenth century naval brigs usually set the main from an auxiliary spencer mast, so were technically snows; some also had a spencer on the fore mast and could set square canvas from the crossjack on the main.

bunker. The space devoted to the carriage of fuel, originally coal but later extended to the compartments for fuel oil; for reasons of weight and stability, usually along the sides or bottom of a vessel.

bunt. The 'bag' or curvature of a sail; when furled the centre gathering is called the bunt and in nineteenth century practice it was secured on top of the middle of the yard.

buntline. Rope from the foot of a square sail passing over the forward surface to the yard; used to spill the wind from a sail when necessary.

burthen. A measurement of capacity in tons calculated by formula from the dimensions of the ship. The formula varied over time and was different from country to country; it greatly underestimated the real displacement but may be regarded as a crude forerunner of gross tonnage (*ie* a measure of internal volume).

cam. A projection from a revolving piece of machinery, usually employed to actuate some irregular movement. On the *Great Western*, the 'cam setting' controlled the point at which steam was cut off in the cylinder, so called because a series of stepped cams on the crankshaft drove the valve gear.

camber. The athwartship curvature of a deck, designed to drain water into the scuppers; by extension the same sort of slight curvature in objects like propellers.

carronade. A design of short lightweight ship's gun developed by the Carron Iron-works in Scotland in the 1770s.

caulking. The operation to make planking seams water-tight, and by extension the material used for the operation, which was usually oakum (*qv*) or strands of rope junk rammed into the gap; it was then covered with hot pitch or a patent composition to form a seal.

CGT. Compagnie Generale Transatlantique, better known as the French Line. Formally established in 1861, the company was to become the leading French flag carrier on the North Atlantic, operating passenger services until the withdrawal of the *France* in 1974.

chord. The straight line joining the ends of an arc; hence a section through a propeller blade.

clew. Lower corner of square sail or after corner of a fore and aft sail; on square sails a tackle called a clewline (or clew garnets on the courses) hauled them up to the yards.

clinker. A form of construction in which planking is overlapped and fastened along the overlap (also called clench or lap construction), as opposed to edge-to-edge or carvel construction. It allows a hull shell to be built without prior framing, although internal strengthening is usually added later; mostly confined to small craft and boats.

collar. *See* thrust bearing.

combustion chamber. In a boiler, the area beyond the furnace in which the hot gases are concentrated before being applied to the task of steam generation. Provides space for complete combustion before being applied to the task of steam generation.

compound engine. Machinery in which steam was expanded in at least two stages, in a high pressure cylinder and then in a larger diameter low pressure one; eventually triple expansion (*qv*) became the norm, but quadruple expansion was also perfected. Generally compounding refers to two-stage expansion.

condenser. The power and efficiency of a steam engine depends on the difference in pressure of the steam between inlet and exhaust. By condensing the exhaust steam to water, the pressure is dropped to near vacuum, raising efficiency. It was convenient, and when pure feed water was introduced, essential to return the condensate to the feed tank by pump.

connecting rod. In a steam engine a bar transferring the thrust of the engine piston to the crank (*qv*) of the shaft. In a direct-acting engine this would be from the piston itself (or its crosshead), but indirect machinery had various forms of intermediate motion gear, such as a lever.

contra vanes. A form of fixed propeller set aft of the revolving screw but with blades of opposite twist designed to improve thrust; originally patented in 1864 by Arthur Rigg.

controllable pitch propeller. A screw in which the angles of the blade to the boss (*qv*) can be altered mechanically on command, when required to increase, decrease or even reverse thrust without changing the speed of the propeller shaft. It is of advantage with machinery like turbines, which cannot be reversed, or even those like diesels which operate most efficiently at particular speeds.

coppering. The process of sheathing the underwater hull of a ship with thin copper sheets (and later yellow metal alloy). This was originally intended to protect the hull from marine borers like *teredo navalis* but was found to have a very effective antifouling effect, the slow exfoliation of the metal preventing marine growths.

cord. A traditional measure of wood (usually a pile 8ft by 4ft by 4ft), but also applied to stone.

crank. Portion of an axle bent at right angles, used in an engine to convert reciprocating motion into rotary (or vice-versa). The axle incorporating the crank was known as the crankshaft.

crosshead. In a steam engine the bar at the end of the piston, sliding in straight guides to keep the motion of the piston true.

cutwater. The timber forming the foremost extension of the stem that in a ship under way actually divided the water.

cylinder jackets. Casing around the cylinders of steam engines through which steam passed in order to reduce power loss in the cylinders from cooling.

cylindrical boilers. The so-called 'Scotch' type, introduced from the late 1870s to withstand the greater steam pressures being demanded by triple expansion engines (*qv*).

deadrise. The angle of the floors in the midship section of a ship; one measure of the relative 'sharpness' of the hull lines, a vessel with a v-shaped section having much deadrise whereas one with a flat bottom had none.

deadwood. In a wooden ship the solid timbering fore and aft above the keel where the lines are too narrow to allow separate frames to be faired into the keel itself.

direct acting. Machinery with no intermediate motion gear between connecting rod (*qv*) and crank (*qv*).

direct drive turbine. One without reduction gearing, so the revolving speed of the propeller shaft was the same as that of the turbine.

dynamometer. An instrument for measuring energy output.

eccentric. In machinery a cog, wheel, etc whose axis is off centre, in order to produce an irregular motion; frequently used to convert rotary to reciprocating movement.

Edmiston pressure filter. Patent device fitted in the boiler feed water line to prevent the carry over of oil and grease from cylinder lubricants.

EIC. The English East India Company, known as the Honourable East India Company or colloquially as John Company, incorporated by royal charter in 1600. It maintained a monopoly of trade with the East until 1813, when India was opened to competition, but it retained its China monopoly until 1833. The Company was effectively the government of India from the mid eighteenth century until 1858.

Ericsson Wheel. A form of propeller patented by John Ericsson consisting of a 'wheel' with a large number of blades of helical segments around the circumference; originally the device consisted of two contra-rotating wheels, but Ericsson soon abandoned this as inefficient.

fantail. The overhanging part of a ship's stern; most common in the USA, 'on the fantail' has come to be almost synonymous with 'right aft'.

feathering paddle. A paddle wheel in which the angle of the boards (*qv*) to the waterline is altered by mechanical means to keep them vertical during their entrance, stroke and exit from the water, making the thrust more efficient. The term was borrowed from the action of an oar blade, which is turned, or 'feathered', between strokes to reduce resistance.

feed water system. An arrangement of pump, condenser and piping which supplied water to the boiler for conversion into steam.

fiddlehead. *See* billethead.

fire-tube boiler. *See* tubular boiler.

firebox. The furnace of a marine boiler.

floats. *See* boards.

'flopper stopper'. Steadying sail used to reduce rolling.

flue boiler. Early rectangular type in which hot furnace gases passed through the boiler water by means of a labyrinth of square section flues. Made from flat sheet, these flues were vulnerable to collapse and this limited boiler pressures to very low values.

forced draught. A method of increasing the rate of combustion in the furnaces, and hence the efficiency of the boiler as a steam generator, using fans to increase the amount of air supplied to the boiler under pressure. Naval practice favoured a closed stokehold whereas the merchant service preferred the relative simplicity of a closed ashpit only. The most common design in mercantile use was that of the British engineering firm of James Howden & Co.

fore and aft sails. Those carried on gaffs, sprits or stays that at rest hung in the fore and aft axis of the ship; the opposite of square sails which were set from transverse yards.

full and by. The point of sailing when a ship is as near the direction of the wind as possible ('by the wind') without the sails shivering (*ie* still drawing, or 'full').

gaff. A short spar to extend the head of a fore and aft sail; usually hoisted with the sail, for which purpose it was equipped with jaws that fitted around the mast. A larger permanent (standing) gaff was sometimes called a half-sprit.

gasket. Short rope or plaited tie, used to secure furled sail to its yard.

Griffiths propeller. A two-bladed screw patented by Robert Griffiths in 1860; notable for improving efficiency and reducing vibration, and widely used for more than a decade.

grt. Gross registered tons. A calculation of the total internal volume of a ship converted to weight by the formula 100 cubic feet equals 1 ton. Deducting the non-earning

spaces like machinery rooms, bunkers and accommodation gives net registered tonnage.

halyard. Rope or tackle used to hoist sail or yard; sometimes spelt haliard or halliard.

heel. [i] The angle a ship will lean away from the perpendicular, usually caused by the action of the wind. [ii] The after end of the keel, or the lower end of a mast.

HEIC. Honourable East India Company. *See* EIC.

helical. Of, or relating to, a helix (*qv*).

helix. A spiral or coil, usually in three dimensions like a corkscrew.

high aspect ratio screw. A propeller in which the blades are relatively long in relation to their chord (*qv*).

high-freight. Of high shipping cost, and by implication high gross profit margin (in the shipping business a 'freight' refers not to the cargo itself but to the amount paid to ship it).

hog chain. *See* hogging truss.

hogging. Because the usual hull form of a ship is finer forward and aft than amidships, there is less buoyancy at the ends of the hull than in the centre. At sea this tends to make the hull droop at the ends and the midships area arch upwards, distorting the structure and breaking the sheer, as it was described. This propensity to hog was greater in longer, shallower and more lightly constructed ships and was always a major problem. Structural improvements like diagonal bracing inspired by Sir Robert Seppings were introduced into warship building from the end of the Napoleonic Wars and made wooden-hulled steamers possible, even if the problem was never really conquered.

hogging truss. A mechanical means to counteract the effects of hogging (*qv*), especially in long shallow vessels, whereby cables, chain or girders are stretched from stem to stern over stanchions, rather like the string of a bow. The 'hog chains' of American river craft are the best known example, but the principle was applied to the seagoing craft of ancient Egypt.

Holt Standard. The combination of compound engine, screw propeller and an iron hull with a length:breadth ratio of about 8:1 used by Alfred Holt for his cargo liners in the late 1860s and established as something of a norm for this class of vessel.

horizontally opposed. Of machinery, having cylinders of horizontal bore on opposite sides of the crankshaft.

horsepower (hp). The early engineers described the power of their machinery in terms of the pulling power of horses, but seem to have chosen weak specimens to enhance the mechanical advantage of their engines. Eventually James Watt was instrumental in establishing a formula of 1hp = 550 foot pounds per second. Horsepower varies enormously according to how and particularly where it is measured; *see* ihp and nhp.

hot well. In a steam engine the reservoir which holds hot water from the condenser before it is fed to the boiler. *See also* feed water system.

hounds. The projecting section at the head of a mast to form a support for the trestle-trees or, in smaller masts, for the standing

rigging; on lower masts they are usually called cheeks.

Howden system. *See* forced draught.

HP cylinder. High pressure cylinder; in a compound steam engine (*qv*), steam first entered a relatively small HP cylinder before expanding into one or more larger LP (low pressure) cylinders. Steam in triple and quadruple expansion engines passed through three and four stages respectively.

ihp. Indicated horsepower, a measure of the pressure and volume of steam within a cylinder, gives the power available within the engine (1hp = 550 foot pounds per second). Once allowance has been made for power losses in friction, driving auxiliaries, etc, ihp may exceed real power output by as much as 25 per cent.

inhauler. The rope used for hauling in the clew (or corner) of a boom sail or the traveller of a jib; movement in the opposite direction is achieved by an outhauler.

IP. Intermediate pressure; in a triple expansion engine the middle stage, the steam having passed through the HP (*qv*) cylinder, it is expanded in the IP before passing to the LP (*qv*).

jet condenser. A primitive form of condenser (*qv*) in early steam machinery that operated by injecting a stream of sea water into the steam. *See also* surface condenser.

jibboom. The forward-projecting spar beyond the bowsprit; extends the foot of the outer jib, from which it takes its name. Originally known in the navy as the flying jibboom, this term was later transferred to the additional spar beyond the jibboom.

jury. Applied to rig or rudder, a temporary (usually emergency) contrivance to make a vessel manageable after damage; thought to be a contraction of 'injury'.

keelson or kelson. Internal keel fitted above the main keel and serving to secure the frames.

leeward. Downwind, or away from the direction of the wind; opposite of windward (*qv*).

lever beam engine. *See* side lever engine.

lifting banjo. *See* banjo frame.

Loper Wheel. An early four-bladed propeller patented by the American Richard Loper. Relatively inefficient but subject to little vibration and therefore popular in wooden-hulled steamers; also known as the Philadelphia Wheel.

LP cylinder. Low pressure cylinder. *See* HP cylinder.

lug. A rig characterised by a four-sided sail with a head about two-thirds the length of the foot; hoisted on an angled yard with about a quarter of its length ahead of the mast.

Martin boiler. An early form of water-tube boiler with brass tubes, of American origin and in service in the 1850s.

Merryweather fire engine. A patent fire pump built by the Merryweather company.

Moorsom's Rule tonnage. The basis of modern gross tonnage calculation (*see* grt) was worked out by a committee set up by the

British government under the chairmanship of Admiral Moorsom. It came into force in 1849 and for some time was known as Moorsom's Rule tonnage.

net tonnage. *See* grt.

nhp. Nominal horsepower, an early calculation of power based on the geometry of the engine. The formula was 7 × area of piston × equivalent piston speed, the sum being divided by 33,000. Piston speed for paddle steamers was taken to be 129.7 × (stroke) 1/3.35. Real power as expressed in ihp (*qv*) was usually greater than nhp and diverged more as engines improved, reaching ratios as high as 3–4 times nhp.

oakum. A material used for caulking (*qv*) made by unpicking the fibres of old rope which had out-lived its usefulness.

orlop. A deck, or system of platforms in the hold, used mainly for storage, but in the navy often containing warrant officers' cabins. The term is thought to derive from the Dutch *overloop*.

oscillating engine. Early form of steam engine in which the piston drove the crankshaft directly, obviating the need for a connecting rod (*qv*). In order to allow the rotary motion of the crank the cylinder was pivotted at or near its bottom end and swung to and fro with the stroke of the piston, steam usually being supplied through the trunnions (*qv*).

outhauler. *See* inhauler.

packet or pacquet. Fast mail-carrying craft; usually government sponsored like British Post Office packets.

parral or parrel. An assemblage of beads called trucks and wooden dividers called ribs strung on to a series of horizontal ropes. Forming a collar between the upper yards and their masts, and designed to allow the yards to be hoisted or lowered easily, it vaguely resembled a flexible abacus, although the beads were intended to revolve to reduce friction and the ribs stopped them moving from side to side. Later versions comprised hinged steel bands.

Philadelphia Wheel. *See* Loper Wheel.

piston. In a steam engine the sliding disc inside the cylinder on which the steam acts; its back and forth motion is transferred via a piston rod to running gear which eventually converts the reciprocating action to rotary in order to drive the propeller or paddle shaft.

pitch. One of the dimensions of a screw propeller, equating to the distance a ship would be moved forward in ideal conditions by one complete revolution of that propeller.

plumb bow. One with a vertical cutwater (*qv*) and not the cutaway of a clipper bow or the reverse curve of a ram bow.

points. Traditionally the circumference of the compass was divided into 32 points (each therefore being 11° 15'), which was probably the narrowest angle that could be determined by estimation with any certainty.

poppet valve. A valve which opens by being raised from its seating rather than by sliding or hinged movement (the original term was 'puppet' and the valve was named by association with the action of a marionette).

puddling. The process of turning and kneading iron in its molten state to get rid of carbon and make the iron more malleable and consistent; this was usually achieved in a reverbatory furnace.

quadruple expansion. The principle of four-stage utilisation of steam in an engine; a development of triple expansion (*qv*).

reciprocating engine. One in which the power was developed by a back-and-forth motion (such as a piston working in a cylinder) rather than a rotary motion like a turbine. The term usually implied a steam reciprocating engine.

rectangular boiler. Early form fabricated of flat plates and consequently less able to withstand higher pressure than the cylindrical (*qv*) or 'Scotch' type.

reef. The portion of a sail which could be shortened. A sail had one or more rows of reef points called reef bands which when hauled up and secured to the yard produced a fold in the reefed area of the sail, reducing the depth of canvas exposed to the wind. As the wind strengthened sail was progressively shortened to the first, second and third reef bands, when the ship was said to be single-, double- and triple-reefed, respectively.

reef points. Short lengths of cordage used to secure the sail when reefed.

return connecting rod engine. An ingenious solution to the problem of the short connecting rod imposed on horizontal engines for screw ships (where the cylinder had to lie on one side of the propeller shaft and so was limited by the breadth of the ship). Perfected by Maudslays, this type of engine had two piston rods passing above and below the shaft, power being brought back to the crank from the joint crosshead (*qv*) by a 'returning' connecting rod. Usually called a back-acting engine in the USA.

return flue boiler. One in which the flues carrying the furnace gases through the boiler double back on themselves to provide a greater hot area in contact with the water.

return tube boiler. A tubular boiler in which the tubes were U-shaped.

rotary engine. One which achieves its rotary motion directly from the action of steam, like a turbine, rather than a reciprocating engine which needs various systems of cranks and levers to transform back-and-forth action into rotation.

rotative engine. A steam engine in which reciprocating motion is converted to rotary motion by a system of cranks, levers or gears.

running gear. In a steam engine the ensemble of levers, cranks etc external to the cylinders which operated the valve gear and transferred the power from piston to crankshaft.

sagging. The opposite of hogging (*qv*), in which the hull distorts by drooping amidships rather than at the extremities.

sail-assist. Wind power adapted to operate in conjunction with mechanical power to increase the speed or, more usually, the economy of the engines.

scale. Incrustation formed in boilers (as on the elements of domestic kettles in hard-water areas).

schooner. A fore and aft rigged vessel with at least two masts (a fore and a main, unlike a ketch or yawl, which carried a main and a mizzen). Those setting square sails on topmasts were designated topsail schooners or fore topsail schooners if they had square canvas on the fore topmast only.

Scotch boiler. *See* cylindrical boiler.

screwlog. A patent device for measuring a ship's speed through the water, working on the principle of a screw revolved by the slipstream of the water and recording the number of revolutions in a given time. The principle was understood from at least the late seventeenth century but the first really practical Patent or Self-Recording Log was Massey's, introduced in 1802.

sheet. The rope confining the lower corners of square courses (and the after one of fore and aft sails), drawing them aft.

ship rig. In the sailing era the ship or full rig was defined as the principal driving sails on all three masts being square (later a few four and one five masted full rigger were built, but the vast majority carried three masts; two square rigged masts made the vessel a brig). The lower sail on the mizzen usually comprised fore and aft canvas but as long as square sail was carried above it the vessel was still rated as a ship.

side lever engine. Early form of paddle machinery, transferring motion from the piston (*qv*) to the paddle shaft via low rocking beams on each side of the engine, and associated connecting rods.

side-wheeler. Steamer with paddles on the broadside rather than at the stern.

single crank tandem compound engine. Two-cylinder compound (*qv*) arrangement with one cylinder above the other on a common axis; both pistons operated on the same rod so they drove only one crank. Popularised by Alfred Holt.

slip. In terms of propeller performance, the difference between the theoretical distance a ship should advance (if, for example, the screw was working in a solid) and the actual distance achieved.

snagboat. A river steamer fitted to remove obstacles, such as tree stumps, from the navigable channels.

spanker. Large gaff-and-boom sail; the main course of a brig and ultimately the replacement for the lateen mizzen on ships.

spar deck. Originally any light (often temporary) deck but later applied to the deck over the skid beams in the waist that effectively made the forecastle and quarter-deck into a single continuous deck; such vessels were termed spar-decked.

spencer. *See* trysails.

standing gaff. A spar that extended the head of a fore and aft sail and was more or less permanently in position. Possibly derived from the spritsail so sometimes called a half-sprit, it differed from the shorter hoisting gaff in that sail was taken in by brailing up the canvas to the mast and yard rather than by lowering the gaff.

stay bar. Rigid support or buttress used to add strength to metalwork like boilers subject to high pressures or stresses.

staysail schooner rig. A schooner (*qv*) whose principal canvas is carried on stays, not gaffs.

steam dryer. *See* superheater.

steam turbine. A form of rotary engine in which power is generated by the action of steam on a series of revolving rings of closely set blades. The perfection of the marine turbine is attributable to Sir Charles Parsons, his first practical success being dated to 1892.

steeple engine. A vertical paddle engine with cylinder(s) below the paddle shaft; long piston rods operated a high crosshead with a return connecting rod to the crankshaft below. The crosshead slide worked in a tall triangular framework which gave the engine its name.

Stephenson gear. Stephenson link motion was a patented system for operating the cylinder valves of a steam engine developed by the famous engineering firm of Robert Stephenson & Co in the 1840s.

sternpost. The vertical or near-upright extension of the keel and the principal structural member of the stern. Traditionally the rudder was hung from the sternpost, but with the introduction of the screw the rudder was fitted to an after post beyond the propeller aperture.

stern trunk. The water-tight vertical aperture into which a lifting screw and its frame could be hoisted.

stern tube. The gland in the sternpost through which the propeller shaft of a screw steamer passed.

stern-wheeler. A paddle steamer with a paddle wheel at the stern; initially this was one single wheel but eventually the wheel was divided in the middle, giving two independently driven halves; this allowed the stern-wheeler some of the manoeuvrability of the side-wheeler (*qv*).

Stockholm tar. A natural preservative and waterproofing agent for rope and canvas produced from the resin of pines and fir trees.

stokehold. The compartment at the furnace end of a boiler in which the stokers or firemen worked transferring coal from bunkers (*qv*) to firebox (*qv*).

stroke. In a reciprocating engine, a single complete movement of the piston or piston rod; also the measurement of the distance travelled by the piston or piston rod.

stuffing box. A compartment packed with water- or steam-tight material through which a piston or propeller shaft could operate without leakage.

superheater. A device for raising the temperature of steam above that at which water normally evaporates in order to make the steam do more work; also called a steam dryer.

surface condenser. An improvement over the jet condenser (*qv*) in which the cooling sea water was passed through the condenser in tubes, so that it did not come into contact with the steam. Initially the process was reversed, the condensing steam being passed through tubes surrounded by sea water, but the tubes proved vulnerable to blockages (the steam carried over some grease from the cylinder lubricants).

swivel gun. A small anti-personnel weapon mounted along the rails and in the tops of ships; it was fitted into a swivelling crutch thrust into a wooden stock.

tail shaft. The final section of a run of shafting, as for example the end of the propeller shaft that carried the screw.

three-island steamer. A steamship with a hull configuration of three raised sections above the upper deck – a forecastle, a superstructure amidships, and a poop aft.

throat. The part of a gaff (*qv*) nearest the mast.

thrust bearing. In a screw ship there needed to be some point at which the thrust of the propeller was transferred to the ship, and this required a bearing that could withstand considerable pressure. The first entirely satisfactory system was the 'collar' type invented by the marine engineers Penn & Co in the 1850s in which a series of raised rings or collars on the shaft fitted into complementary lubricated grooves in the bearing or plummer block. This was replaced in the late nineteenth century by the Michell hinged floating pad type in which the pads acted on wedges of oil.

thrust deduction. One of the elements reducing the theoretical efficiency of a screw propeller, it is caused by a suction effect on the hull immediately forward of the screw as the water is accelerated past it.

tophamper. General term for masts, spars and rigging.

tramp steamer. One not operating a regular scheduled service like a liner between prearranged ports but seeking out freights and going wherever the cargo requires; picking up and discharging freights from port to port gave the appearance of homeless wandering.

triple expansion engine. Machinery in which the steam is subject to three stages of expansion, driving in sequence a cylinder at high pressure, then a larger one at intermediate pressure, and finally the largest at the low remaining pressure. Since the same amount of steam was made to do more work, it was far more economical than simple expansion engines and resulted in significantly increased range.

true wind. *See* apparent wind.

trunk. In a general sense a pipe or tube; applied specifically at this period to the aperture into which a lifting propeller was housed when not in use.

trunk engine. A horizontal direct-acting engine for screw propulsion patented by John Penn & Co of Greenwich. The space restrictions on a horizontal engine – with a cylinder placed to one side of the propeller shaft, effectively only half the breadth of the ship – made it difficult to provide a long connecting rod. Penn's solution was to attach the connecting rod directly to the piston head inside a trunk of sufficient diameter to allow for the swing of the connecting rod. The trunk fitted through the piston head, moved with it, and was long enough to pass through the front and back cylinder covers. Because it was low and compact, and so could be fitted below the waterline, it was a particularly popular design for early naval screw steamers.

trunnions. Short cylindrical extensions at right angles to the barrel of a gun used to retain it on its carriage or mounting; the trunnions formed the axis on which the gun was elevated and depressed. Also used for the extensions that allowed similar motion in an oscillating cylinder (*see* oscillating engine) or walking beam (*see* beam engine).

truss batten. A chock attached to the after side of a yard recessed for the front of the mast; a hinged parrel (*qv*) secured the yard to

the mast. The batten held the yard off the mast to allow it to be braced up at a sharper angle to the vessel's centreline.

trysail. A gaff-and-boom sail set from an auxiliary (trysail) mast or rope horse; the trysails that replaced staysails were called spencers in nineteenth century navies. Trysail was also used of the reduced storm canvas employed by small craft in place of the regular main.

tubular boiler. One in which the boiler space was filled with tubes in order to increase the area of water exposed to heating. Initially the hot gases from the furnace passed through tubes in a body of water (the firetube pattern), but in the more efficient watertube type water passed through the tubes which were surrounded by the hot gases, allowing for more rapid and efficient steam generation.

valve gear. A mechanical arrangement to open and close the valves of the cylinders in a steam engine; usually derived via some patent arrangement of cranks, levers or eccentrics from the motion of the engine itself. The gear eventually became sophisticated enough to control the amount of steam supplied as well as the timing. *See also* Stephenson gear.

vane propeller. A propulsion system in which the propeller shaft was above water, so the large diameter propeller turned only partially in the water. It was invented in 1828 but was employed as late as the 1930s by Denny of Dumbarton for shallow draught river steamers.

vangs. Rigging to control the gaff (*qv*) yard; one led from the outer end to each side of the vessel.

vertical. Of machinery, referring to the orientation of the cylinders; initially the piston tended to operate in the upwards direction but the reverse, known as inverted engines, became common later.

wake friction. The restricting effect of the hull on the speed of water entering the propeller.

walking beam. *See* beam engine.

water ballast. Water taken on board an empty ship, usually in double-bottom tanks, to compensate for the weight of the missing cargo and to ensure adequate stability.

water-tube boiler. *See* tubular boiler.

weather helm. A well balanced sailing vessel will usually have a tendency to gripe or come up into the wind, which is considered far safer in emergencies because if control is lost the ship will end up head to wind and more or less stationary. However, under sail it is necessary to offset this tendency by use of the steering, holding the helm or tiller up to windward; for this reason a vessel with this most desirable characteristic is said to carry weather helm.

Welland Canal schooner. Traditional Great Lakes vessel designed to the maximum dimensions of the Welland Canal (between lakes Erie and Ontario), the main restriction being the width of the locks.

windmill type propeller. Those with distinctly separate blades as opposed to some early designs which were derived from the screw thread.

windward. Towards or on the side from which the wind blows; the weather side. The opposite of leeward (*qv*) or lee side.

Yarrow-Schlick-Tweedy system. A method of designing triple expansion engines with four cylinders (two equal sized IP cylinders) and four cranks that emphasised balance between the moving parts in order to keep vibration to a minimum.

yawing. Erratic movement either side of the straight line being steered.

Index